Logical Learning Theory

Logical Learning Theory

A Human Teleology

and Its Empirical Support

Joseph F. Rychlak

University of Nebraska Press

Lincoln and London

The paper in this book meets the minimum requirements
of American National Standard for Information Sciences—
Permanence of Paper for Printed Library Materials,
ANSI Z39.48-1984.

Library of Congress Cataloging-in-Publication Data
Rychlak, Joseph F.
Logical learning theory : a human teleology and
its empirical support / Joseph F. Rychlak.
p.   cm.
Includes bibliographical references and indexes.
ISBN 0-8032-3904-1 (CL: alk. paper)
1. Learning, Psychology of.
2. Predicate (Logic)
3. Psychology—Philosophy
I. Title.
BF318.R83   1994
153.1′5—dc20   93-49664
                      CIP

To the memory of Maude C. Clarke

Contents

Demonstration Experiments

Figures

Tables

Acknowledgments

I would like formally to recognize the assistance of several people in bringing this volume to completion. First and foremost I extend thanks to my wife, Lenora, for her editorial efforts and continuing encouragement over the years as we worked to this end. I would like to thank Loyola University of Chicago for selecting me to occupy the Maude C. Clarke Chair in Humanistic Psychology, a position that gave me the time and research support to complete this project. In particular, I would like to express my sincere appreciation to Larry Biondi, Raymond Baumhardt, Tom Bennett, Frank Catania, Matt Creighton, Jeanne Foley, Kathy McCourt, Dan O'Connell, Emil Posavac, Jill Reich, Ron Walker, and Jim Wiser for making this career development possible. Finally, I am grateful for the helpful support of the following individuals who worked on the demonstration experiments or helped materially during various stages of theoretical and manuscript development: Bill Ashton, Suzanne Barnard, Bill Chambers, Christine Feldmann, Harwood Fisher, Donna Hughes, Del Jenkins, Jim Lamiell, Larry Leitner, Nancy Norman, Tom Phelan, Ron Rychlak, Ann Sauer, Brent Slife, Joshua Soffer, Stephanie Stilson, Jonathan Thomas, Alec Ulasevich, Connie Vaughn, Mary Wandrei, Kevin Weinfurt, Rich Williams, and Neil Wollman.

The author is appreciative of the permission to reprint material from the following publications: Figure 18 is reprinted from M. S. Gazzaniga and J. E. LeDoux, *The Integrated Mind*, copyright © 1978 by Plenum Press. Portions of Chapter 8 and Figures 3, 4, 7, and 8 were originally published in my *Artificial Intelligence and Human Reason: A Teleological Critique*, copyright © 1991 by Columbia University Press, New York. Figures 9–15 were originally published in my *Introduction to Personality and Psychotherapy: A Theory-Construction Approach*, 2nd. ed., copyright © 1981 by Houghton Mifflin Company.

Preface

It has been over 35 years since I took my doctoral degree under Jules Rotter at The Ohio State University and set forth to "be a psychologist." I came out of Ohio State with a sheltered—or is it idealistic?—view of what psychology is all about. Rotter's social learning theory is a neo-Hullian formulation, with enough Alfred Adler tossed in to take the edge off its mechanistic tendencies. I also absorbed George Kelly's psychology of personal constructs, which drew from phenomenological rather than associationistic precedents of the Hullian variety. Both Rotter and Kelly taught me to value empirical validation of theoretical claims. I expected my career in psychology to be an easy extension of the open atmosphere of Ohio State, where any theory framed along the spectrum represented by Rotter and Kelly might be put to empirical test and thereby taken seriously by reasonably disinterested colleagues.

This expectation proved to be naive. Trained as a clinician, and having thereby come to view the clients with whom I worked as intentional organisms who advanced on life according to purposes, I began framing my empirical studies in terms of such descriptions. I soon found that it was difficult if not impossible to convey this image of humanity to colleagues—with or without research evidence in its support—because of their commitment to a Newtonian philosophy of science deriving from British empiricism. Equating their independent-dependent variable observations in the context of research with their stimulus-response constructs in the context of theory, my colleagues were confident that they were empirically proving that people were nothing but machinelike organisms being moved across time by a series of immutable physical laws. Any data that I presented in support of agential behavior had to rely on such independent-dependent variable (i.e., efficiently caused) regularities and could therefore be instantaneously translated into stimulus-response (i.e., efficiently causal) terminology. This meant that my constructs of intentionality (relying on final-cause meanings) slipped from view. The much vaunted role of empirical evidence that I had been taught to respect in graduate school seemed quite irrelevant at this point.

Research evidence alone could not solve my dilemma. The question of whether people are self-determining agents could not be properly framed because of two major stumbling blocks: (1) The philosophy of science on which psychology was situated was out of date. Psychology continued in a Newtonian vein, when other sciences like physics had moved on to the more dynamic views of people like Mach, Einstein, Heisenberg, and Bohr. (2) Thanks to this Newtonian commitment, psychology had never offered technical concepts that might conceivably describe a fundamental human agency, which then in turn might be put to experimental test. I found this paucity of technical terminology especially frustrating. After a few years in which I tried to compromise by hiding my teleological formulations under mechanistic-sounding terminology (like "reinforcement"), I realized that such half-measures would never succeed in changing anything. Only a completely different formulation of what it meant to behave, learn, cognize, and so forth, could rectify the situation. Some people believe that psychology has undergone a "cognitive revolution" and that now the errors of mid-20th century behaviorism have been corrected. I disagree. The input-output formulations of cognitive psychology, albeit made more sophisticated through additions like feedback, remain essentially the same as the previous mediational theorizing of behaviorism. Psychology remains imprisoned by its mechanistic, efficient-cause terminology.

Before I could frame a true alternative to this mechanical terminology, I was called on to do a lot of spade work, particularly in the philosophy of science. I had to point out the full ramifications of the Newtonian bias in psychology and show how there were significant changes taking place in the developments of modern science that brought this mechanistic world-view into question. Chapter 1 of this volume presents my basic efforts in this regard. Such material is not always easy reading, but I feel it must be confronted at the outset or many of the points to follow in the volume will be unappreciated or misunderstood. I have drawn up several figures to aid the reader in grasping the theory-construction issues of chapter 1—issues that will arise again and again in the subsequent chapters of this volume.

Chapter 2 takes the reader into an introductory overview of my recommended alternative to the traditional mediational theories of behaviorism and cognitive psychology: *logical learning theory*. The concepts of this theory flow naturally from the preparatory terminology of chapter 1. Even so, the reader will find the theoretical terminology moderately challenging—particularly if he or she is already steeped in the efficient-cause language of 20th-century psychology. Once again, I have designed several figures to aid in the presentation of logical learning theory. I think it is fair to say that chapters 1 and 2 are the most taxing portions of the book, but I trust that once these chapters have been traversed, the wide-ranging applications of their contents will prove instructive and satisfying enough to justify the reader's initial effort. For quick reference, there is a glossary of core concepts at the back of the book that can be used when the new terminology is employed under shifting topics.

Thus, over chapters 3 through 9 the terminology of logical learning theory is enlarged on as it is applied to the experimental literature in cognitive processing, human and animal learning, memory, emotion, motivation, perception, brain functioning, human development, language acquisition, and self-image. I have tried to confront alternative explanations of behavior, so the reader will find "mainstream" areas of psychological theorizing and research discussed in the proper context such as: prototype, attribution, script, dual process, artificial intelligence, depth of processing, encoding specificity, spreading network, classical and operant conditioning, metacognition, recall versus recognition, figure-ground, *Einstellung*, impression formation, mood induction, split-brain, and self-identity. Fourteen demonstration experiments, testing the basic concepts of logical learning theory, are presented sequentially throughout the volume. Chapter 10 summarizes the theoretical approach, demonstrates how it readily subsumes concepts employed in traditional outlooks like the Freudian, Jungian, Skinnerian, or existential, and then answers the most frequent objections voiced against it.

I cannot help but ask myself who I hope will have an interest in this book. I am hoping that there are enough colleagues who, like myself, consider themselves scientists and yet want to begin thinking about people as intentional, purposeful organisms instead of accepting the "business as usual" engineering strategy of turning people into machines. If we begin with a technical language that is intentional rather than mechanistic, we can end with a perfectly valid, experimentally proven view of human behavior. This was my initial assumption some 35 years ago. I took an agential view of the person and submitted it to empirical test with all the considerations of rigor that any experimental psychologist endorses. The findings as framed and rigorously tested by this agential perspective have generally fallen nicely into line. Though empirical facts are never the friends of one and only one theory, at least it can be said that they have not shunned my theory and indeed have welcomed its company along a vast array of psychological topics.

1

Explanation in Psychology

The word *explanation* derives from the Latin *ex* and *planare*, meaning "to make level or plain." When we explain something, we bring its description around to some common ground, a level basis on which everyone can agree that the description nicely clarifies things. We need go no further, because now everything makes sense. Unfortunately, psychologists have had a continuing dispute over the precise "common ground" on which to base our explanations (Rychlak, 1988). In particular, this conflict has focused on whether human beings may be said to possess agency. The tradition has been never to base a scientific explanation on agency. However, as the decades slip by, it is ever clearer that we require agential grounds to characterize human behavior accurately. Secord (1990) has called for such grounding, adding that "as long as the machine model remains implicit in our thinking as psychological scientists, we tend not to think of participants as whole persons acting in a relationship with the investigator" (p. 34).

The machine model Secord refers to is the bane of those psychologists, like myself, who have sought to explain behavior in agential terms. *Agency* is the organism's capacity to behave/believe in conformance with, in contradiction to, in addition to, or without regard for perceived environmental or biological determinants. In other words, an agent has something to say about what will happen to him- or herself as life unfolds. Because a machine is never capable of such self-determination (Rychlak, 1991), accepting the mechanical as the basic grounding for psychological explanations slams the door on agency. No matter how much research evidence a psychologist marshals in support of agency, the engineering-minded colleague sees beyond what is indicated in the empirical data to an unobserved mechanism that supposedly proves all this talk of intention, purpose, and choice to be illusory at best and spiritual at worst.

This rigidly mechanistic attitude has driven critics to overreact by denigrating the scientific method per se, which is erroneously blamed for mechanism's hegemony (e.g., Gergen, 1982; Rahman, 1987). The fault actually lies with the theoretical commitments of those who employ this empirical method. As a result, we now seem to have all manner of suggested revisions, such as narrative psychology (Sarbin, 1986), existential-phenomenological psychology (Valle & Halling, 1989), and qualitative psychology (Ashworth, Giorgi, & de Konig, 1986), all of which describe the person in agential terms. The revisionists invariably seek a change in the way that we conduct scientific psychological research rather than in the way that we explain the empirical findings of our experiments. It is, however, entirely possible that we can achieve a psychological science amenable to human agency without discarding the rigors of traditional scientific research.

I have proceeded on this latter assumption for over 30 years, and I have never found it necessary to dodge the empirical evidence issuing from all corners of psychological science. The problem facing the agency advocate is not empirical findings, because the facts are friendly enough; indeed, findings in support of agency are coming in at an increasing rate. The problem is getting psychologists to recognize the significance of these findings, which means that they must recognize a theoretical framework other than that of mechanism. I begin the present chapter with a consideration of certain issues preliminary to this broader task. The first issue to consider is whether, in our examination of behavior, we are out to model a process or a content of some process.

Theoretical Modeling: Process or Content?

Most psychologists today agree that they rely on a model of some sort to direct their understanding. We might define a *model* as a distinctive conceptual pattern used in the study of some topic as a standard to generate, organize, and communicate knowledge. Models enter into every empirical and nonempirical (qualitative, phenomenological, etc.) explanation that we carry out in psychology. The phenomenologists strive to avoid biasing their observations through fixed preconceptions like this, but even they recognize that they must "bracket" or set aside such presumptive influences on their work (Valle & Halling, 1989). Nonetheless, we might ask whether it is possible completely to set aside a modeling preconception. This is a touchy issue for the phenomenologists, but surely the answer here is no. This matter of a precedent in all human reasoning will play a fundamental role in the theory of this volume.

When we design and carry out a research experiment, it is easy to confuse the concrete empirical findings with the activity or process that supposedly brought these findings about or made them happen. The logic of experimentation gives rise to the following problem: for any observed fact pattern there are, in principle, infinitely many possible explanations. This follows from the necessity that, in conducting research, all scientists are constrained by the *"affirming the consequent"* fallacy (Rychlak, 1980). A simple demonstration of this fallacy begins with the factual statement "If a human being, then a mortal." The first term of this "if, then" sentence is called the *antecedent* (i.e., human being), and the second term is called the *consequent* (i.e., mortal). Having made this preliminary statement of fact, were we now to add "This is a human being appearing before us," we could conclude that "This is a mortal being" follows necessarily. We would have affirmed the antecedent term of an "if, then" line of thought (crystallized into a sentence). However, were we to say "This is a mortal being appearing before us," we could not conclude with certainty that "This is a human being." Other organisms, such as fish and insects, also are mortal, so maybe the mortal appearing before us is human, but maybe not. For "if, then" statements, the affirmation of the antecedent necessarily entails the affirmation of the consequent, but not vice versa.

Similar issues arise when we turn to the logic of a scientific experiment. When we say, "If our model is correct, then the experimental data will array as we predict," we are framing our experimental hypothesis as an "if, then" statement, and if we are fortunate enough to find that the data array as we predicted, we can draw encouragement from this finding. We have avoided falsifying our theory (Popper, 1959, pp. 40–42). We cannot, however, say that our theory is necessarily true. There will always be an alternative explanation possible for the observed fact pattern, just as in the earlier example there is always the possibility that some mortal besides a human being is standing before us. Instead of taking inspiration from this uncertainty in science— because it provides us with an opportunity to study the role that a human being's conceptualizations play in creating "empirical" knowledge—many psychologists have pessimistically concluded that this constraint on the scientific method means either that science cannot prove anything or that it can "prove" anything at all, but in a merely trivial way.

The proper reaction to this limit on scientific proof is to recognize that empirical data do not speak for themselves. We will always have (in principle, not necessarily in actuality) alternative explanations of sound empirical research findings. We should not expect logical certainty in science. Science has two sides. There is on the one hand a modeling of events, which involves *theory*, a schematic formulation relating the modeling pattern to expected or predicted events in the realm of interest. On the other hand there is *method*, which is a means or manner of determining whether the theoretical model is true (i.e., to be taken seriously as either the reflection of an independent reality, as some form of interpersonal but highly reliable construction, or even as illusion). Scientific method relies on *validating evidence*, which involves the control of relevant factors (variables) and the prediction to a predetermined criterion. Other forms of method (e.g., clinical, phenomenological) rely heavily or exclusively on *procedural evidence*, which draws on the plausibility, coherence, or internal consistency of a theoretical assertion (Rychlak, 1981, p. 75). Procedural evidence is sometimes referred to as "theoretical proof."

Validating and procedural evidence are both vital to the advance of science. For example, mathematics, the oft-cited "language of science," relies exclusively on procedural evidence. Scientists always take their theoretical assertions one step further, however. The scientist seeks empirical validation at least some of the time. Einstein did not personally conduct empirical tests, basing his convictions on his renowned thought experiments, but colleagues like Eddington did so in his place (Holton, 1973, pp. 33, 362). Einstein's procedurally tested ideas continue to receive validating evidence in subatomic experiments, as well as in space explorations, to this very day.

When theories yield contradictory interpretations of the empirical findings of an experiment, the discrepancy invariably concerns the nature of the process that produced the empirical findings, not the content of these findings per se. By a *process* I mean a discernible, repeatable course of action on the basis of which some item(s) under description is/are believed to be sequentially patterned. In physics and astronomy, for example, gravitation is a central process. Some presumed attraction "at a distance" holds the planets in sequentially patterned orbits as they fall through space within force fields. It is difficult to say precisely what gravitation is, of course. Newton frankly admitted that he did not know how the gravitational process came about, even though he could mathematically predict its effects in holding things in place (Wightman, 1951, pp. 101–102). Einstein was later to interpret gravity as curved space, and he and Whitehead had a famous disagreement over how best to construe the laws of gravitation (Palter, 1956).

But the nature of the planets, with their observed and predicted patterns of action, is not what is at issue here. These patterns of action were observed, tracked, and predicted long before physical scientists appeared on the historical scene. The planets are therefore to be construed as contents working within or issuing from the field forces of a gravitational process. It is in the precise nature of this process that we find our theoretical disagreements. Thus, a *content* is an ingredient that is produced, conveyed, or otherwise employed by a process. When we observe the empirical results of an experiment, we are limited to the content side of the ledger. We can "see" the content results, just as we can see the orbiting of the planets. The trick is to explain the process that produced these results.

For a more clearly psychological example of the process/content distinction, we can turn to contrasting characterizations of what an idea is, one advanced by Immanuel Kant (1724–1804) and the other proposed by John Locke (1632–1704). Is an idea a process or a content? Kant (1781/1952) considered the idea to be an aspect of the process known as "reason," which cannot be derived from environmental determinants or shapings but which innately helps to organize experience a priori (pp. 150, 193–194, 200, 238). We have, in contrast to this process conception of the idea, the notion proposed by Locke (1690/1952), who viewed ideas as just about anything that could be triggered by or recorded from sources external to the person's mental processes (pp. 127–128). Locke said that we have ideas of sight, sound, taste, and even feelings. Ideas are externally formed by an environmental process and placed thereby into the mind as if they were preshaped teacups placed into an "empty cabinet"—a metaphor he actually used in this regard (see Cranston, 1957, p. 266). Ideas are objects of the understanding, to be perceived and input as ordered environmentally instead of functioning innately from within to pattern external experience in the Kantian fashion. To claim such organizing capacities for the mind, said Locke, is to believe in innate ideas, by which he meant an innately fixed content rather than an innate capacity to process (pattern, order, organize, etc.) experience.

Learning theories have been the grand studies of process in psychology. Everyone knows that people can remember contents (words, facts, stories, etc.) of one sort or another with varying degrees of accuracy, but just how does this most basic of all human processes work? That is now and always has been the most basic challenge confronting psychology. It is frequently suggested today that learning theories are passé, at least the grand theories of yesteryear—Watsonian, Tolmanian, Hullian, Skinnerian. To avoid making global claims of universal validity, researchers in learning have supposedly moved to miniature theorizing, functionalistic studies with a circumscribed goal. Even more dramatic changes have supposedly occurred in the so-called cognitive revolution that swept through psychology in the 1970s. If the learning theories of old were studies of a process, then the cognitive theories of today are even more focused on something called processing.

It is my belief that learning theories are not passé, that they will always be with us, formally or informally, and that the cognitive revolution was no revolution at all—if we mean by a revolution what Kuhn (1970) means: a fundamental shift in the paradigmatic model guiding explanation and experimentation. I see no basic change in the fundamental theoretical paradigm of cognitive psychology compared to the modeling assumptions of traditional learning theory. We have old wine in new bottles. But I do believe there has been a modest revolution or "modification" in the experiments that we see being designed in the 1980s and 1990s compared to those of earlier years. There is today much more concern for so-called ecological considerations, for the study of learning and memory as they relate to what people actually do in their everyday lives. This shift in design has proven beneficial to those of us who would like to see a more humanistic emphasis in psychology. The image of the white-coated psychologist in a laboratory invariably fosters an engineering attitude and the mechanist model against which Secord cautioned. Even so, I want to show how we can stay in this lab—some of the time—and still retain our theoretical descriptions of people as they function in everyday circumstances.

Psychology as a Logical Enterprise

Psychology's problem with agency stems from the fact that the profession emerged as a science in the late 19th century, during the era of British empiricism (also called British associationism). This predates the rise of modern physical science, which brought about significant changes in the way that "reality" was to be described (Rychlak, 1991, chap. 2). British empiricism is Newtonian, but modern science is not. Newtonians presumed, as do all naive realists, that they were viewing reality without presumptive bias—we might say, without erroneously affirming the consequent—and hence could track what was there in experience for the tracking. Modern scientists recognize that they are participators in the pursuit of knowledge and that their precedent assumptions always influence and limit what they can know (Prigogine & Stengers, 1984, pp. 218, 224, 225; Zukav, 1979, p. 29). This brings the observer into the process of learning as one of the causes of what will be known. The participator's predicating assumptions are causes of the observed effects. The role that a psychologist can play here is to propose and empirically study a learning process that can explain this participatively creative influence of human reason. As I noted in the introduction, this is my aim in the present volume.

Referring to the observer as a cause brings up the issue of just what we mean by this concept. Psychologists have studied a research domain known as causal attribution (e.g., Jones & Davis, 1965; Kelley, 1973), but the kind of cause being attributed in these accounts is not necessarily clarified by those who conduct this research. That is, considered in historical terms, there is an ambiguity over which one of four types of causality is at play in a so-called causal attribution. These four meanings can be traced back to Aristotle (384–322 B.C.), but he built on the conceptions of others. Aristotle pulled together some explanatory assumptions of his predecessors, added an interpretation or two of his own, and offered what is in my opinion the most important classificatory theory ever proposed in the history of thought. To be clear on this question of causation, I must first summarize the Aristotelian formulation and then toss in a little history of science.

As a precautionary note, let it be clear that I am not committing myself to all of Aristotelian philosophy by beginning with his theory of causation. In fact, I will be departing slightly from Aristotle's broader uses of these types of causes—especially the material and formal causes, which have been interpreted somewhat differently by different Aristotelian scholars. I will not enter into such issues in this book, for they are irrelevant to my purpose. But I want it clearly understood that I am not representing Aristotelian philosophy per se; I am merely acknowledging a debt to his genius in a certain realm of his teaching. What I want to do now is to think of the causes as those grounding meanings that can "make plain" (clarify) the concepts we use in our theories. The causes are highly abstract, metatheoretical assumptions that frame literally any conception imaginable at a lower level of abstraction.

The word *cause* is a translation of the Greek word *aitiá*, which means "responsibility." So when we speak of the cause of anything, we are referring to what is responsible for a thing or event existing or taking place. Aristotle (1952b) elaborated on the meaning of a cause as "that out of which a thing comes to be and which persists" (p. 271), adding that we could dissect literally anything in nature as having four causes:

1. We can invoke a *material cause*, in which case we would be trying to account for something based on what kind of substance makes it up or constitutes it. For example, making a chair out of wood results in an item of furniture with different properties and a shorter life expectancy than one made of marble.

2. We can explain things in terms of an *efficient cause*, in which case we would try to capture the impetus, push, or thrust that instrumentally assembles things or otherwise influences events—as when one billiard ball strikes another and causes it to move.

3. We might also bring to bear the notion of a *formal cause*, thus explaining the thing or event based on its "essence," captured most often by its shape, pattern, or ordering of elements. Examples would include the patterning of a logical analysis (like our study of the affirming the consequent fallacy, above), the immediately recognizable outline of our friend's physiognomy (prominent nose, etc.), or the threatening funnel cloud in the distant sky that warns us of a possible tornado.

4. We might also rely on the notion of a *final cause*, or as Aristotle defined it, "that for the sake of which" an action takes place or anything now exists. Final causes subsume the meanings of reason, purpose, and intention. The

reason that someone has a yearly physical is for the sake of maintaining good personal health.

Final causes deal with ends, and as the Greek word for end is *telos*, we refer to explanations embracing final causes as teleologies. There are three forms of teleology possible: *deity, human,* and *natural*. When theologians contend that there is a divine plan reflected in world events, they are relying on a deity teleology. The plan per se is a formal cause, but the presumption that the deity has designed it and now creates a reality "for its sake" (based on it) brings in the final-cause meaning as well. Indeed, final causation *always* encompasses a formal causation. The "that" in the "that for the sake of which" definition of final causation is necessarily a formal cause (plan, design, strategy, etc.) of some type. A human teleology suggests that people behave for the sake of reasons, purposes, and intentions rather than solely in response to the impulsions of efficient causation.

In the latter case, we have a *mechanism* under description. Thus, we read in one philosophical dictionary that mechanism is the theory "of total explanation by efficient, as opposed to final, cause" (Runes, 1960, p. 194). In another we read that mechanical explanation is "any explanation which avoids teleology and final causation. . . . Mechanical explanations stress efficient causation and are reducible to laws covering instances of matter in motion" (Reese, 1980, p. 345). A natural teleology suggests that material events are moving to an inevitable and discernible end without a deity directing them, although humans may intentionally facilitate the process in some way. The communist thesis of an inevitable classless state exemplifies such a natural teleology.

Teleological explanation was common in science up to the 16th century, when a combination of events rendered it unfashionable. Newtonian science was soon to follow. The first destructive event was Galileo's (1564–1642) notorious clash with the churchmen of the Inquisition. The churchmen, relying on biblical accounts that asserted a deity teleology, held the solar system to be geocentric (as per the diety's supposed intention), whereas Galileo proposed a heliocentric organization of the solar system. His house arrest and recantation heralded the demise of such authoritarian final-cause description in natural science. There was, however, an even more telling reason for questioning telic description in science. Aristotle had favored using all four of the causal meanings in scientific description, believing that this would enrich the resultant account of anything. He therefore attributed purposivity to everything in nature, suggesting, for example, that leaves on trees existed for the sake of shading fruit on their branches. Aristotle (1952b) thus concluded that nature is a cause "that operates for a purpose" (p. 277).

It was Francis Bacon (1561–1626) who led the assault on such final-cause description in science (Farrington, 1949). Pointing his guns at Aristotle,

Bacon (1605/1952) said that it is bad scientific explanation to suggest that trees have leaves for the sake of shading fruit or that skeletal bones exist for the sake of holding up the body's fleshy parts (p. 45). Since we can fully explain trees, leaves, bones, and flesh using material and efficient causes, with the possible addition of occasional formal causes, it is unnecessary to mention final causes. Thus, the *Baconian Criticism* holds that telic description should not be used to explain physical events, for it adds nothing of merit to the account. Final-cause description is suitable to metaphysical explanation, paralleling but not to be mixed with physical description (p. 45). Scientists should describe the "how" of natural processes and refrain from guessing at the "why" (reason, purpose, intent)—which is a teleological analysis more suited to the metaphysician and theologian.

I should emphasize at this juncture that a theorist who accepts a human teleology is not thereby committed to a deity teleology. Nietzsche (1844–1900), for example, embraced human teleology even as he asserted that God is dead. I have found, over the years, that opponents of teleology are prone to assign a religious motivation to the psychologist who proposes a human teleology, no matter how often the independence between divine and human teleologies is pointed out. The present volume makes no claims of a theological nature; neither does it make claims in opposition to theology. In fact, it is possible to argue either for or against the validity of religious beliefs based on the tenets of this volume.

Bacon's criticism was well founded, but it addressed only one aspect of Aristotelian teleology, which can be shown to have two sides depending on how we look at things. That is, Aristotle drew no real distinction between the creative actions of nature—as in providing leaves to shade fruit—and the creative actions of a person like the architect who designs and then builds a home (i.e., who acts for the sake of this design) (Aristotle, 1952e, pp. 161, 162). There is, however, a vast difference in the perspective that our explanation takes when we shift from the silent workings of nature to the thinking of an architect designing a building. Nature functions impersonally, "over there," on its own (unless we assume a deity is directing things, of course). But the architect must be understood from within his or her point of view. What are the stylistic intentions being advanced as the architect designs the home? Are there any conflicts in the mind of the architect over precisely how to proceed? Have there been false starts in the design, changes that waver back and forth until a final decision is reached? These latter issues arise in telic descriptions of people even though they are—as Bacon suggests—unnecessary in the description of nature. Planets and clouds never waver at decision points. Trees do not choose to "grow up" in one style rather than in another.

Explanations of nature invite an *extraspective* theoretical perspective

(Rychlak, 1981, p. 27). The prefix *extra-* is from the Latin, meaning "on the outside," so an extraspective theory is always framed from the point of view of an observer on the outside of things. In other words, the extraspective theoretician not only takes the perspective of an observer situated "here" and frames explanations of what is taking place "over there" but also exclusively employs third-person terminology to explain things. Thus, in explaining human behavior, the extraspectionist selects terms like *he, her, they*, and so on, rather than *I* or *me*. Critics of extraspective theory in psychology sometimes claim that this style of explanation turns persons into impersonal objects.

In contrast, when we are attempting to explain a targeted item, even though we may be looking at it from the outside, it is still possible to frame our accounts from this target's perspective or point of view, resulting in an *introspective* theory rather than an extraspective one. The prefix *intro-* is from the Latin, meaning "on the inside," so in an introspective theoretical formulation, the account is always written from the point of view of the item (e.g., a person) under study. As introspective theorists we are "in the heads or hearts" of the item we are observing; we identify with the object of investigation. The targeted item being explained is situated "here" and not "there." Our theories therefore take on a first-person phrasing, involving "I" and "me" rather than "that" or "it." Obviously, the perspective taken by any theoretician depends on his or her interests, what is under study, and the instructiveness of the resultant account in light of such interests.

The reader can now appreciate that material and efficient causation require an extraspective perspective; the formal cause can take either perspective. The funnel cloud of a tornado can be explained in third-person fashion, but the often conflicting and inconsistent schemes and plans of a human being are fathomable only from the introspective point of view. Final causation seems best suited to the introspective perspective, but those theorists who rely on natural teleologies do end up proposing extraspective uses of final causation. I will return, in later sections of this volume, to this question of how best to conceptualize teleology. What is clear for now is that the Baconian Criticism *does not hold* when we describe the behavior of human beings from the introspective perspective (Rychlak, 1991, p. 41). From this internal point of view, the final-cause aspects of behavior do add something new or different to our theoretical account that is not covered by the notions of material and efficient causes. They inform us about meaningful purposes and intentions, aspects of a psychological process that do not exist—or are not required to function—in a physical-mechanical process. It is this lack of purpose in the mechanist account that its critics underscore when they suggest that extraspective theories of human behavior turn persons into (impersonal) objects.

But on what basis can we as scientists investigate such a nonphysical thing as an internal point of view, which cannot be observed directly? This question is frequently raised by psychologists who follow in the traditions of British empiricism, yet the truth is that science has always relied on the unobserved process known as mathematics—which, as I noted above, is frequently called the "language of science." Newton's problem about the nature of gravity reflects this reliance on an unobserved realm to frame an observed one. That is, Newton knew how gravity influenced events in a mathematical sense, even though he did not understand what this process was in the physical sense of an action at a distance. The physical things he could point to were of no help in explaining the basic nature of the gravitational process. The effects of gravity could be predicted mathematically—through the process of logic underwriting mathematics (Whitehead & Russell, 1963)—but gravity itself was not observable as a process. Thus, there is precedent for us to identify two processes at play in the explanations of natural science, one physical and the other logical.

I have argued that there are at least four complementary grounds on which psychologists have based their explanations (Rychlak, 1993). Each ground has its own distinctive process. The theorist postulates a process for the ground selected and then seeks to bring all explanation within this presumably clarifying "fundamental" context. The grounds I have in mind include the *Physikos, Bios, Logos,* and *Socius.* The processes of the *Physikos,* of course, are those like gravitation. The fact that the logic of mathematics tracks this process does not mean that gravitation is a concept of the *Logos.* The concept of gravitation has as its targeted meaning-referent something going on in the physical realm. As a virtual opposite to the *Physikos,* I suggest the *Socius*— a realm in which the process of socialization is said to function, shaping organisms into patterns of behavior according to rules that are not reducible to groundings of the *Physikos,* although they may coalesce with them.

The *Bios* and *Logos* are the classical grounds of explanation employed in psychology—usually contrasted respectively under the labels of "body" and "mind." What distinguishes *Bios* from *Physikos* is that the former is living whereas the latter is not. Even so, these two grounds have frequently been combined in psychology, as when Hull (1937) suggested that the same laws directing the actions of a raindrop direct the actions of a human being (p. 2). Animate and inanimate come together in such a view, enabling the reduction of psychological principles to physical principles. The *Bios* has taken the field in psychological theorizing, stemming as it did from the earlier medical/ anatomical model that was written into the physiological experiments of the budding German psychology departments of the late 19th century (Boring, 1950). The Baconian Criticism is honored here, carried over from Newtonian mechanistic explanations of the *Physikos* to the living mechanisms of the *Bios*. There is nonetheless a distinctive process postulated for the *Bios* in psychology, which I term "mediation" (I will discuss this in the following section).

The final grounding for psychological explanation, which contrasts markedly with the *Bios*, is the *Logos*. Given what we have already seen in Newton's thinking on gravity, as well as the fact that modern physicists consider themselves to be participators in the creation of their data, it seems quite plausible to consider patterned order per se to be grounds for an explanation. We see a recognition of the *Logos* realm in the thinking of early physical scientists like Heinrich R. Hertz (1857–1894) and Jules-Henri Poincaré (1854–1912), both of whom believed that theoretical constructs depend not only on what is observed but also on "the inner logic of the one making the [theoretical] assertion" (Cassirer, 1950, p. 110). Einstein (1934) referred to this as a "creative principle" (p. 18) residing in the logic of mathematics. If an inner logic influences the conceptions of the scientist, surely it can be said to influence the conceptions of anyone else, and who is better suited than a psychologist to investigate this introspectively conceived realm of interlacing patterns? As I will show in the section to follow, predication is the process of the *Logos*.

Before taking a closer look at the processes of the *Bios* and the *Logos*, I would like to mention another reason why the study of patterned order or logic is so important at this point in the history of psychology. This reason concerns a shift in the role that causation plays in the progress of scientific explanation (Rychlak, 1991, chap. 2). In Newtonian science, basic causation, to which all else is reduced, is efficient causation. At this underlying level of efficient causation, the bumping of atomic particles one into another supposedly "shapes" things—in bottom-up fashion—into their familiar overt structures, which can then be seen as molar entities. The moving atoms shape the tissues, bones, liquids, and so forth, which then constitute the pattern of a recognizable organism (e.g., frog, snake, human being). The shaping of behavior is a further manifestation of such efficient causation. Modern physics was to change this Newtonian scenario, because efficient causation breaks down completely at the subatomic level. Subatomic particles do not act like billiard balls bumping one another about; instead, they move about in ways that are explicable only in field or patterned terms, which means that they cannot be reduced to efficient causes but must be understood as formal causes (see Prigogine & Stengers, 1984, p. 173). The formal cause has emerged as the most basic sort of cause in science.

I believe it is incumbent on us in psychology to take up the challenge of a science resting on not efficient and material but formal causation. This recognition of a shift in the basic causation of science is fortuitous for the teleologist, because as I noted earlier, formal causation is a necessary aspect of final causation. If we begin to think of psychological reality's basic nature as *pattern* rather than *motion*, we have the basis on which to begin postulating how a "for the sake of" addition to the formal-cause pattern is possible. Pattern is fundamental to meaning, and to mean is to intend. But how are we to understand final causation working in this *Logos* realm of patterns, interlacing into other patterns?

Predication versus Mediation in Psychological Explanation

To mediate is to intervene or come between other active processes, thus bringing about some kind of action indirectly. The mediator is one who settles disputes between parties, each of whom has framed a grounding point of view that conflicts with the other's. The conflicting parties are the direct, or "immediate," cause of the dispute; they initiate and form its fundamental nature. Immediacy signifies instantaneous organization of experience, as when representatives of labor sit down with their counterparts in management. Each side has formed its stand in the dispute. Mediacy, on the other hand, signifies interdependent organization of experience, as when a mediator is brought in to resolve stalemates after labor-management negotiations have already begun. Whatever the mediator does depends on what the parties to the dispute have already done.

It is possible to think of mediation in this essentially teleological fashion, whereby a mediator's purpose is to bring together two sides with conflicting intentions. The resolution sought is some mutually satisfying end (telos). We require a final-cause understanding of the events in this case. But it is also possible to think of mediation as occurring in a nonintentional manner. Mediation can be strictly mechanical. A simple lever serves such a mediational capacity: A downward pressure applied at one end results in a force of lift at the other end. The mediational influence varies depending on the lever's placement on the fulcrum. Another form of mechanical mediation occurs when a thermostat in an automobile engine opens or closes depending on the temperature of the coolant in the radiator, allowing for greater or lesser circulation of the coolant through the engine while it is running.

The meaning of the term *mediation* changes dramatically when we move from the purposes of a negotiator to the mechanics of levers and thermostats. It is my contention that, by and large, the field of psychology employs the term in the latter sense. The realm of interest here is the *Bios*, the theoretical perspective is extraspective, and the causation is presumed to be exclusively material or efficient. In a *mediation process* of this mechanical type, something that is produced elsewhere and taken in or input comes to play a

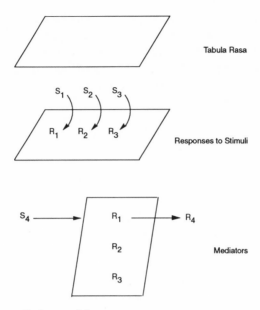

Figure 1   The mediation model

role in the process that was not initially a part of or intrinsic to it. Figure 1 has a schematization of the mediation process.

Reading downward in Figure 1, note that the mediation process is thought to begin as a tabula rasa (blank tablet). In time, certain externally formed stimuli impress themselves on this tabula rasa process, which records and stores them as input (engrams, encodings, etc.). There is nothing in the mediation process per se that influences the form of these incoming stimulations (S_1, S_2, S_3), referred to as "mediators" (R_1, R_2, R_3). However, at a later time the mediators can—singularly or in combination—influence the course taken by the mediation process when a new input (e.g., S_4) is engaged and worked over into an output (e.g., R_4). A perfect example of such mediational theorizing is the Hullian learning theory of Dollard and Miller (1950). The mediators in this case were termed "cue-producing responses," because their function was to produce a cue that would be part of the stimulus pattern leading to another response in the antecedent-consequent sequence of efficient causation (p. 98). This was conceptualized as occurring totally within the *Bios* realm; indeed, Dollard and Miller thought of logic as a content of the mediating learning process, as well as a learned drive to "be consistent" in the use of language (pp. 109, 288). I will have many occasions to comment on the mediation model of Figure 1.

Moving now to the predication process, it is important to appreciate that everything hinges on meaning. Meaning is patterned intention, as when we hear someone say "I am going home." There is a logical relation patterned between the identity ("I") expressing this intent and the end (telos) being intended (i.e., "being at home"). We know that in linguistic terms, "am going home" (verb + object) encompasses the complete predicate of this sentence, but it is not my intention to consider predication as based on syntax. Predication as used here is semantic in nature; it relates to meaning and not to grammatical rules. The primary focus of a mediation process is motion, the moving of events from an antecedent point in time to a consequent point in time. We could not have a mechanical mediation without time's passage, for it is the temporally antecedent that always impels, cues, or triggers the temporally consequent.

However, in predication the issue is not motion but patterned order. Rather than speaking of the antecedent-consequent over time, we now refer to the precedent-sequacious extension of meaning. A *precedent* occurs first in logical order, and the term *sequacious* refers to those extensions of meaning that occur second—that are, indeed, "slavishly compliant" (logically necessary) on what has gone before in logical order. Time's passage is irrelevant to a logical ordering of meaning. We eliminate time from the explanation when we rely on logic to explain cognitive events. A *predication process* therefore involves the logical act of affirming, denying, or qualifying precedently broader patterns of meaning in sequacious extension to narrower or targeted patterns of meaning. The target is the point, aim, or end (telos) of the meaning-extension.

The ancient Greek philosophers referred to this process as reasoning from universals to particulars or from the genus to the species, and they sought ultimate universal categories within which to subsume all of knowledge. The Greek word *katēgorein* means "to predicate," so in a true sense, when we seek categories (classifications, schemata, species, etc.), we are attempting to find a wider range of meaning that can frame and lend meaning to a targeted item of our interest. The predicational process can be modeled by the use of the circles introduced by the mathematician Leonhard Euler (1707–1783) (Reese, 1980, p. 160). The patterned relationship of these circles will serve as our model. Note that Figure 2 aligns smaller Euler circles within larger circles, signifying that the larger circle is the precedent extending its meaning to the smaller (darkened) circle. I am not symbolizing the actual placement of a smaller circle within a larger circle—like one of Locke's teacups placed into a cabinet. I am symbolizing that the smaller circle takes its very essence from the larger circle (in formal-cause fashion). Whatever the smaller circle means depends on the number and quality of larger circles that sequaciously extend their meaning to it.

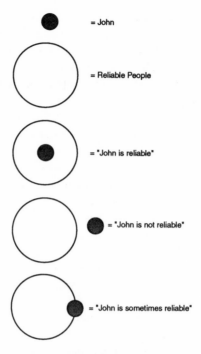

Figure 2   Euler circles as the model for predication

Thus, when we express the meaningful statement "John is reliable," we are affirming meaning that we take to have a wider range (reliable people) and extending it sequaciously to a narrower range of meaning (i.e., John). "Reliable people," or perhaps "reliability," is the larger circle acting as a logical predicate, and "John" is the narrower meaning targeted as a circle within this predicating meaning. Many people are reliable, but we are framing John for such meaning-extension at this point. We want to think of this background meaning-extension as a kind of "stretching forth" that literally creates some of the meaning of "John." There are many other predicating meanings we can extend to our friend John, such as that he is hard working, fears dogs, tends to be shy around strangers, and so on, but predication is not simply what goes on inside the broader Euler circle. Note that Figure 2 also has examples of the smaller circle lying outside or merely overlapping the larger circle. The former symbolizes "John is not reliable"; the latter, "John is sometimes reliable" or "John is sometimes unreliable." These are examples of what is defined above as the denying and qualifying aspects of predication. I will return later to this important tie of inside versus outside the larger, grounding circle.

Because it concerns broader-to-narrower ranges of meaning-extension, the predicational process always deals in *contexts*, as in the major premise of a syllogism that provides the broad context within which the minor premise and conclusion are reached, each in turn focusing the meaning of the major premise to an increasingly specific target (telos). Figure 3 demonstrates this "wider-to-narrower" funneling of meaning.

The major premise here might be the wide-ranging assertion that all humans are mortal, in which case "mortality" would already be framing "humans" as per the Euler circle arrangements in Figure 2. The minor premise is depicted as being more focused, since it states that this is one person among human beings. Our sequaciously flowing conclusion would then be even more delimited, taking meaning from the precedently wider context, in the form of "This *specific* person is mortal." Figure 3 should not be thought of as showing the major premise "driving" the minor premise, which in turn "drives" the conclusion—as if these were separate units under efficient causation in a computing network or some such system. Instead, the figure depicts a funneling of meaning; think of the increasing focus from major premise to conclusion as the vortex of a tornado, whirling meaning down from top to bottom. It is the overall patterning (formal cause) of this funnel cloud that I am depicting. The wide-ranging meaning at the top of the funnel gradually narrows and then zeros in on the targeted base of the funnel. Figure 4 symbolizes the direction of meaning-extension in the predicational process.

Figure 4 presents the major premise of a classical syllogism as a large circle, the minor premise as a medium-sized circle, and the conclusion as a tiny circle. At the top of Figure 4 we have these three circles positioned as if they were stacked one on top of another. I intend this schematization to

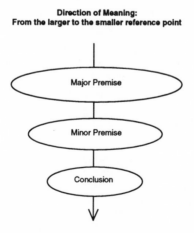

Figure 3   Funneling of meaning in the predicational process

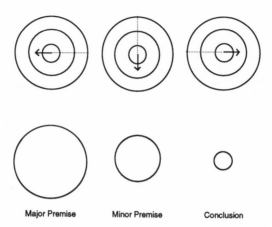

Major Premise   Minor Premise   Conclusion

Figure 4 Precedent-sequacious flow of meaning in the syllogism

say that the meaning of the widest circle "reaches" or "extends" to the other two, focusing on the conclusion in the manner of a vortex whirling to its target (see Figure 3). The arrows depicted in Figure 4 refer to the direction that meaning-extension takes in the syllogism. This is a sequacious flow of meaning resulting in logical necessity (e.g., "given this, that must follow").

Note the various orderings of the circles at the top of Figure 4. On the left, the meaning is depicted as extending (via arrow direction) from right to left, and on the right we see it extending from left to right. What these two arrangements have in common is that the arrows indicate a meaning-extension from the larger to the smaller circles. The arrangement in the middle of the upper portion of Figure 4 depicts the three circles as if they were directly centered, one on top of another. In this case, the arrow is extending forward, as if there had been a bull's-eye through the circles—but once again extending from the larger to the smaller of the three. The point I am making here is that the direction of the meaning flow is irrelevant, just as long as its course is from the broader or wider expanse of meaning to the narrower expanse.

This meaning-extension occurs instantaneously. As soon as the relevant meanings are aligned in the process, the extension from wider to narrower occurs. Time is irrelevant in this logical process. We can think of the broader circle as occurring "now" and the other two also as occurring "now," or the broader circle might be occurring "now" and the smaller circles might be thought of as taking place in either the past or the future. Nonetheless, time's passage does not influence, determine, or shape the predicational process. Order is the only factor that determines its course—from broader to narrower sequential extension in meaning expression.

There is an aspect of the predicational process for which the inside versus outside of the larger circle has immense significance. I refer here to *opposition-ality*. It would be easy to erroneously presume that predication is restricted to the inner portions of the largest Euler circle. All else, then, is nonessential or nonexistent. But the predication process takes place both within and without the encircling meaning of the major premise. Meaning is on both sides of the drawn line, which is why we have a clear meaning conveyed in the negation and qualification examples at the bottom of Figure 2, where the smaller circle alters its pattern in relation to the larger circle. Although the two circles are now more or less separate, there is still a meaningful pattern involving both. The peculiar function of oppositionality in this case is that it can have a directing influence on the course of thought. This can be clarified by beginning with Figure 5.

Figure 5 depicts the "reliable people" (larger) circle of Figure 2 surrounded now by other possible predications, such as "poor people, happy people, confident people," and so forth. The possibilities here are endless. Just because John is not to be predicated by "reliable people" does not suggest to us anything about his happiness, financial condition, or level of confidence. But there *is* an immediate implication being made once we remove John from the "reliable people" predication; namely, that he is unreliable. I will name this *delimiting oppositionality*, because it bounds a specific meaning that stands in relation to its bipolar counterpart—the meaning of "reliable" bounds "unreliable" (and vice versa). This would not have to be expressed in words. That is, to take one example from Figure 5, we could picture the

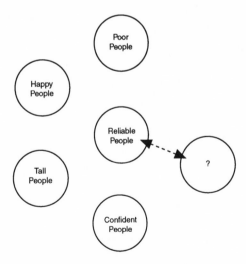

Figure 5   Possible predications of a target

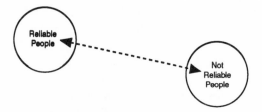

Figure 6   The directionality of meaning-extension
in delimiting oppositionality

encircled "happy people" as a collection of smiling faces, and this would in
turn delimit a group of "sad people" with unsmiling faces. For the sake of
ease in presentation, I will use descriptive words rather than such pictorial
examples. Figure 6 schematizes the directionality of meaning-extension in
delimiting oppositionality.

Sometimes oppositionality is limited to a negation of the encircled predication, moving the focus from inside to outside this encircled region without stipulating a direction for meaning-extension to take. I will name this
generic oppositionality, recognizing it as fundamental to the predicational process being modeled by the Euler circles. Every predicating Euler circle has an
inside and an outside; placement in either of these regions indicates whether
the target is to be included in the meaning under predication. Although we
have a delimitation here (inside delimiting outside and vice versa), it refers
strictly to the predicational process underway and not to the meanings (contents) under processing. This delimitation is at the metaconceptual level, so
to speak, targeting the process itself as a content in an abstract explanation
of how it takes place. Generic oppositionality does not specify anything beyond whether the target of the predication is to be included or excluded
(negated) in the process of meaning-extension taking place. It is impossible
to predicate (categorize, frame, schematize, etc.) without bringing generic
oppositionality into play. Predication and opposition are thus intrinsically
related. For example, if instead of "reliable" we were to predicate John by a
nationality, such as "German," we could not find this nationality's opposite
outside the predicating circle in the way that we found the opposite of the
adjective "reliable." Nouns are not necessarily linguistically oppositional, as
adjectives tend to be. So, if we were to say "John is German" and then negate
this predication ("John is not German"), we would be unable to say anything
about John's actual nationality in the same way that we drew an implication
to the opposite of reliability. We would know only what nationality John
is not (generic oppositionality) and have no idea of what nationality he is

(delimiting oppositionality). We would know that a disjunction existed concerning John and the Germanic nationality, but no more.

Once again: Delimiting oppositionality refers to the *contents* being processed, whereas generic oppositionality refers to the *process* per se. Generic oppositionality therefore underwrites both difference (falling outside the predicating circle) and the possibility for a further delimiting oppositionality. Implications that are drawn based on delimiting oppositionality may be wrong, of course. Saying that John is not reliable implies that he is unreliable, but this may be false. He may simply be moderately reliable, and so on. Considered more globally, *oppositionality* may be defined as a "double predication" in which one predicate of a duality intrinsically delimits its target as being a contrary, contradiction, contrast, or negation of the meaning under extension, and, pari passu, the target in question—serving now as a reverse predicate—returns the favor.

A *contrary* instance completely separates through difference: All is A. None is A. *Contradiction* encompasses a limited contrariety: All is A. At least one is not A. *Contrast* employs contrariety through a reversed direction of comparison: A leans in this direction. Non-A leans in the reverse direction. *Negation* involves rejecting or denying the initial assertion of contrariety: "All is A. A does not exist, is wrong, is irrelevant, etc." Contrariety appears to be the fundamental logical pattern in oppositionality, with the other three forms being variations on this basic theme.

Generic oppositionality is therefore at the root of "same/different" cognitive judgments. *Sameness* obtains when a target is subsumed by the meaning of a predicate, for it shares this meaning with other targets so subsumed. *Difference* obtains when this sameness is negated, thereby removing the target from the subsuming meaning without implying any further direction of meaning-extension. Generic oppositionality also makes judgments of "same/opposite" possible, however, for this is where delimiting oppositionality enters to extend certain predicating meanings beyond their focus to delimit what they are not saying—a direction for meaning-extension that can then be cognitively pursued and eventually expressed. In chapter 4 I will examine such directing implications empirically (see Demonstration Experiments 2, 3, and 4).

When we draw a Euler circle, it is natural for us to focus our attention inwardly. Early gestalt research demonstrated this clearly, as when Rubin (1921) proved that contour has a one-sided function, organizing the perceptual field from outside to inside, from ground to figure. Note that this is entirely consistent with predication We tend to forget about the ground as we focus attention on the figure. Indeed, we erroneously think of the ground as something totally separate from the figure. This either/or kind of thinking is what Aristotle (1952a) referred to as *demonstrative* reasoning, contrasting it with the more oppositionally oriented *dialectical* stance in human reason (p. 143).

Demonstrative reasoning follows the rule or law of noncontradiction, which states that A is not non-A (this is also sometimes referred to as the law of contradiction). Dialectical reasoning, on the other hand, views A and non-A as opposite sides of the same coin, captured in the principle of the "one and many" (see Rychlak, 1981, chap. 9). Framed in terms of our Euler circles, this means that we have to consider both the inside (A) and the outside (non-A) of the predicating (i.e., larger) circle lending meaning to the target (see Figures 2 and 6). Strictly speaking, this violates the law of noncontradiction. In other words, demonstrative reasoning is limited to the same/different (either/or, etc.) discriminations achieved through generic oppositionality, whereas dialectical reasoning moves forward from generic to delimiting oppositionality, drawing out a dimension in which one pole of meaning bounds and thereby helps to define its opposite (A delimits non-A). Aristotle said that all human beings reason both demonstratively and dialectically, and logical learning theory (LLT) concurs.

The demonstrative strategy of reasoning has always been important in science, for it focuses on what is seen or being considered and does not occupy itself with what is not under observation or consideration. In recent history demonstrative reasoning has achieved an even more important status due to the binary logic of computing machines. This logic of "artificial intelligence" is underwritten by Boolean algebra (Rychlak, 1991, p. 57). George Boole (1815–1864) proposed that everything under observation or consideration can be separated into either a "universe class" or a "null class," represented by the numbers 1 and 0, respectively (Boole, 1854/1958). The complement of each class is everything that is not that class, so that in the case of 1, this would be $1 - x$; and $1 - x = 0$. In effect, Boole took disjunction to mean "either/or, but not both," so that the total of events x and y would be $x + y$, excluding those cases that would be both x and y. This is an alternative phrasing of the law of noncontradiction (i.e., "A is not non-A" can be read as "either A or non-A but not both").

The word *disjunction* is from the Latin, meaning "to disjoin" or, we might say, "to separate into alternatives." Logicians draw a distinction between hard or strong disjunction and a soft or weak disjunction. Boolean algebra, on which modern cognitive models rely, uses hard disjunction (Aristotle would have considered this a reflection of demonstrative reasoning). To clarify how we might apply this to our "John is reliable" example, refer to Figures 5 and 6. The alternative predications of John presented as possibilities in Figure 5 (i.e., happy, poor, tall, confident) would be lumped with the oppositionally

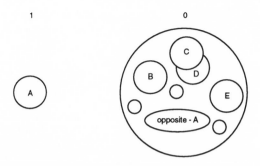

Figure 7 Boolean disjunction:
Opposition as among the members of the complement

derived predication of Figure 6 (i.e., not reliable) as the *complement* to "reliable people." The distinction between delimiting oppositionality (Figure 6) and generic oppositionality resulting in mere "difference" (Figure 5) would not be recognized in a Boolean formulation, where all that any one number is not forms the complement pool of other numbers in the series. At best, an opposite is an extreme difference. This state of affairs is schematized in Figure 7, which depicts Boolean disjunction. Note that we have A (1 in binary logic) situated on the left-hand side of Figure 7, and all that A is not (0 in binary logic) situated on the right-hand side.

If A in Figure 7 were the grounding meaning of "reliable people" (Figure 2), then "opposite-A" or "unreliable people" (Figure 6) would be tossed into the same complement heap as "poor, happy, tall, confident people" (Figure 5), not to mention myriad other potential predicate meanings that are simply different from A. Oppositionality is identical to difference on the Boolean view of disjunction. Oppositionality here lacks an intrinsic meaningful relationship like the double predication mentioned above (i.e., reliable people delimiting unreliable people and vice versa). Such delimiting oppositionality would be nonexistent. In fact, even generic oppositionality—which I argue is what makes judgments of difference possible in human reasoning—is not recognized in computer modeling. To speak of a delimiting oppositionality resulting in more than just difference, we require a soft disjunction, a non-Boolean disjunction as is depicted in Figure 8.

Figure 8 presents such a double predication on the right-hand side, in which A and non-A delimit each other. We do not find delimiting oppositionality within the complement, which lumps all differences together—that is, items that are merely different from A. Oppositionality in this case has a distinctively separate status in which it is possible to see how two seemingly different meanings are actually intrinsically related, with each delimiting and

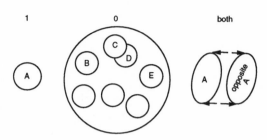

Figure 8   Non-Boolean disjunction:
Opposition as intrinsic to "both"

hence helping to fashion the definition of the other. In a non-Boolean disjunction, difference and oppositionality are not identical. Figure 8 therefore presents a soft disjunction, in which we can say "either *x* or *y* or both *x* and *y*" as we formulate our descriptions of John. That is, it might be possible to target John as both reliable and unreliable. This would be considered illogical in a demonstrative or Boolean formulation (hard disjunction), but in a dialectical, non-Boolean account (soft disjunction) it would be quite logical to frame such a statement.

In later chapters I will make considerable use of the soft disjunction that follows from the delimiting oppositionality of a non-Boolean formulation like the one depicted in Figure 8. Once again, I should stress that delimiting oppositionality refers to the content under processing, and the process itself depends on a generic oppositionality. When it comes to human reasoning, LLT holds that the Boolean hard disjunction is akin to a difference resulting from generic oppositionality and the non-Boolean soft disjunction is akin to the mutually defined alternatives resulting from delimiting oppositionality. Thus, oppositionality is fundamental throughout this theoretical elaboration of cognition.

One last observation on the hard disjunction of a computer model: It should not be thought that this "either/or, but not both" binary logic of Boolean disjunction occurs literally and solely at the level of a neuron. McCulloch and Pitts (1943) were the first to argue that the all-or-none firing properties of nerve cells could be construed in this binary fashion. An active or firing neuron is on and an inactive neuron is off. It is then possible to consider the on position as being "true" and the off position as being "false" when information is being moved along through a network. Indeed, McCulloch and Pitts introduced the neural network conception and tried to map the binary logic of the machine on the structure of the central nervous system. The Boolean logic that underwrote their efforts, however, is not limited to individual neurons, either firing or not firing (but never both). Even when we consider the whole system of supposedly firing neurons, as in a parallel distributed process or a connectionist model, the disjunctive logic being employed throughout—as a total mechanism—is Boolean (Ramsey, Stich, & Garon, 1993). Computing machines are exclusively demonstrative "reasoners"; they never "cognize" the opposite implications of what they are processing as they move information through their networks (see Rychlak, 1991).

Lockean versus Kantian Models of Explanation

I can now organize the various points of this chapter into two highly abstract models of explanation that have been influential in psychology (see Rychlak, 1988, chaps. 3 and 4). They are named for the two philosophers I discussed above concerning the interpretation of what an idea is: John Locke and Immanuel Kant. Although I am using their names to represent these contrasting models, the core difference in outlook can be seen occurring across the history of philosophy/ideas (ibid., chaps. 1 and 2). In using their names, therefore, I intend to capture not so much the details of their specific philosophies but rather two attitudes toward the nature of explanation. Note the significant role that oppositionality plays in drawing out these contrasting attitudes.

Figure 9 presents the Lockean model, which is a *constitutive*, or building-block, formulation. This model gives explanation a reductive turn because it construes explanation as an attempt to enumerate the elements making up the structure. The assumption is that meaning issues from below, and the

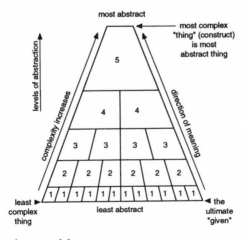

Figure 9   The Lockean model

patterning into complexity is unidirectionally upward, eventually forming into various mediational sequences. Note that we have a triangle of levels increasing from low to high, 1 through 5 (there could be any number). The triangular structure symbolizes the fact that as we ascend the levels of this model, the meaning units (concepts, constructs, etc.) are becoming increasingly abstract. *Abstraction* is a matter of leaving out details, as when we refer to a schoolhouse without detailing the constituting elements of this structure. The meaning of the word *schoolhouse* (e.g., at level 3) is thus more abstract than the meanings of the words it *subsumes* (*rooms, desks, blackboards*, etc, at levels 1 and 2). The latter words need not be mentioned, for we can leave out such details when we grasp that a schoolhouse is under consideration.

At the basic level of the Lockean model (Level 1) we have the "atomic" (i.e., uncuttable, singular, unipolar) building-block meanings that combine into increasingly complex meanings above (Levels 2, 3, 4, and 5). Note that all the numbers at any one level of abstraction are the same. This signifies a kind of stepladder effect; as we ascend from low to high levels of abstraction, the theoretical account becomes more involved (more elements of meaning get into the picture). The usual assumption is that this growing complexity occurs in a computational manner. Mathematical calculations track the interlacing of meanings issuing "from below," from the smaller building blocks to the more and more involved mediational formulations that are taking shape above.

The most complex meaning unit under theoretical description on the Lockean model is always at its top-most level, and the least complex meaning unit is always at the bottom level, where reality itself is confronted. Note that this model does not allow any influence to be made on reality, which stands independently at the lowest level of meaningful abstraction. It is here, at the base of the Lockean model, that we find the ultimate given, the source of knowledge that is fed into the mediational process winding its way upward. The Lockean model encourages the theorist to take an extraspective perspective, viewing things empirically and realistically in terms of material and efficient causation. Any formal-cause patterns at the higher levels presumably would be reducible to the underlying building blocks that constituted them.

Demonstrative or Boolean reasoning is also quite compatible with the Lockean model. That is, we see no oppositionality in the Lockean building blocks of Level 1, each of which is pictured as a unipolarity. It is impossible to reason dialectically on this model. Locke (1690/1952) called ideas at Level 1 *simple* and held that they are indivisible in meaning content (p. 128). This is actually a foretaste of Boole's binary assumption. Simple ideas lack what in Figure 8 I symbolize by the "both" designation. Oppositionality on

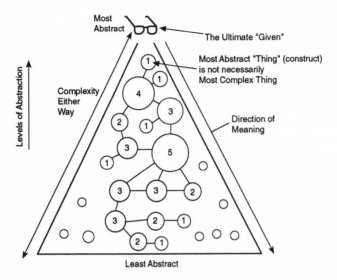

Figure 10   The Kantian model

the Lockean model occurs when two freestanding meanings like "good" and "bad" (Level 1) are united (connected, associated, hooked-up, etc.) at higher levels (2, 3, etc.). The Lockean attitude is surely compatible with explanations that are grounded in the *Physikos, Bios*, and even the *Socius* (although the last could be framed by the Kantian model).

Figure 10 presents the Kantian model, which is *conceptual* in nature. Note the pair of spectacles located at the very top of the triangular formulation, which acts as a framework of predicative meaning to be extended sequaciously below. As it did with the Lockean model, this pyramid shape symbolizes increasing levels of abstraction from bottom to top. The glasses are intended to represent not vision but rather the formative, active process of organizing a mental frame of reference and bringing it to bear on experience. As I noted in my consideration of the Kantian idea, this active process actually creates meaning by bringing itself to bear on sensory inputs from the external world. The ultimate given of meaning resides at the top of the model, issuing from the precedent formal-cause organization of the mental "glasses" in a top-down, sequaciously extended fashion. The reasoner's understanding resides on the wearer's side of the glasses (the phenomenal realm), whereas the source of all sensations resides on the external side of the glasses (the noumenal realm of "things in themselves"). The phenomenal realm is therefore what organizes the sensations that enter in an unpatterned fashion from the noumenal realm.

We cannot pass through our mental glasses—Kant referred to these as the *categories of the understanding*—to experience the noumenal realm directly. We may infer that the noumenal realm of things in themselves exists independently of our conceptualizing capacity, but we can never know noumenal reality except as we experience it through our glasses (categories), for they pattern (predicate) our sensory inputs, making them meaningful and hence knowable. The Kantian model is *pro forma* rather than *tabula rasa*, because the assumption is that the spectacles lend meaning to life from its inception. Thus, a meaning always begins and proceeds from the highest levels of abstraction to the targeted levels below. The ultimate given in meaning (where explanation is grounded) resides in the unique formal-cause organization of the conceptual spectacles, which from the outset provide a context framing the point of view.

The spectacles of the Kantian model stamp it as an active rather than a passive formulation of cognition. I have found that some people interpret the glasses as filters, which presumably refine the incoming information on the analogy of light rays passing through a pair of sunglasses. Others interpret the glasses as preshaped structures, inherited ideas that are contents of the Kantian process. Neither of these interpretations is correct. The glasses are to be understood as an aspect of the predicational cognitive process that lends meaning to ongoing experience in precedent-sequacious fashion. The proper metaphor here is one of sunglasses not filtering but rather coloring what will be known. People who look at the world through rose-colored glasses see a happier world than people who do not. It is this idealistic feature of cognition that I hope to capture in picturing the Kantian model as involving processing conceptual glasses that frame experience in positive, negative, or indifferent directions.

Increasing the levels of abstraction on the Kantian model (from low to high) does not necessarily mean that the theoretical account is becoming more complex. Complexity and abstractness are not uniform or parallel. To determine the complexity of a construct in Figure 10, we have to count the number of relations (symbolizing meaningful relations, not a "nodal network") that any one construct manifests with other constructs. This suggests that a 1-construct has only one meaning-creating relation, a 2-construct has two relations, and so forth. In the Kantian model, however, each of these relations would be under predication by the broadly framing, highly abstract glasses. At just what level of abstraction these meaningful relations take place is irrelevant to the question of construct complexity. The importance of this arrangement is that when we analyze a theory having a 5-construct complexity, it does not follow that the 3-construct or 2-construct meanings to which it is related will be any less abstract or more easily understood than the

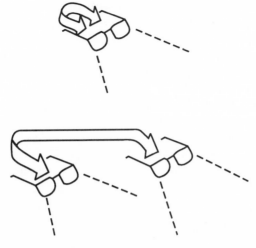

Figure 11   Kantian transcendence and reflexivity

5-construct itself. Meanings are not necessarily constituted of simpler meanings. Sometimes breaking an explanation down into more manageable pieces sends us up rather than down the ladder of abstraction. Figure 11 presents a further schematization of the Kantian model.

Figure 11 takes a closer look at the conceptual spectacles of the Kantian model. Note that at the top of Figure 11, we have a pair of glasses with a two-headed arrow looping on the phenomenal side of these conceptualizers. This arrow symbolizes the intrinsic oppositionality of conceptualization, for it suggests that this process can *transcend* itself—that is, that it can go beyond or ride above the meanings under affirmation to grasp their contraries, contradictions, negations, or contrasts. Kant (1781/1952) based this capacity to employ oppositionality on what he termed a *transcendental dialectic* (pp. 59, 109). Ideas can be formulated in this transcendent sphere, where they are not restricted by what is the case. They can literally rearrange reality, often to the detriment of the reasoner because of resultant distortions. Kant therefore framed a model of thought in which a generic oppositionality (process) is central, so that what is input through the sensations is not only ordered by ongoing cognition but potentially altered by it as well (this is akin to moving out of the larger Euler circle). Ideas can even transcend experience by concocting new possibilities (contents) through what I have termed delimiting oppositionality (see, e.g., ibid., p. 115). We might even describe Kantian cognition as a process of *taking a position* on what will be conceptualized. The organization into meaning that results from cognition is therefore never fixed into certainty by the externals of experience.

Thus, even though a person might ordinarily look through the conceptual spectacles, it is also possible not to look, not to take on their meaningful significance by transcending and affirming meanings that the glasses are not forming into cognizance. At the lower portion of Figure 11 I have symbolized this oppositional maneuver by showing two pairs of spectacles. The pair on the left might be thought of as A, and the pair to the right might be thought of as its opposite, non-A. The schematization here suggests that the dialectically reasoning organism can don an alternative pair of conceptual glasses *without further input*, simply by going from one end of the oppositionality (A) to the other (non-A) or by taking a stand at an intermediate point along this bipolar range of meaning (which is another way of understanding the shifting patterns of predicate and target in Figure 2). Once again, when we focus on the process by which this occurs, we are referring to generic oppositionality; when we focus instead on the specific contents (meaningful concepts, ideas, words, etc.) under processing, we are referring to delimiting oppositionality. The concept of dialectic includes both forms of oppositionality.

The oppositionality of dialectical reasoning makes transcendence possible as per the non-Boolean "both" of Figure 8. In addition, it makes *reflexivity* or *self-reflexivity* possible. These latter terms refer to a dialectically reasoning organism's capacity to turn back (via transcendence) on the line of thought being taken and to examine its assumptions, reaffirm its direction, or bring this direction into serious question — even negating it altogether. Such self-examination is not simply having thoughts about one's thoughts, as some would claim (see Bandura, 1979, p. 439). The latter can be simply examples of *reflectivity* (or *self-reflectivity*), which is a concept that is consistent with mediational, Lockean modeling. Locke actually spoke of reflection in thought, and because he held that complex ideas were formed from simple ideas, some psychologists today believe that his view of cognition is just as "active" as Kant's. If we look carefully at what Locke had to say we can dispel this erroneous belief.

Locke (1690/1952), who was out to counter the belief in "innate ideas," held that all ideas were initiated by the senses, which served to "convey into the mind" (p. 121) whatever was found there. Locke added, "This great source of most of the ideas we have, depending wholly upon our senses, and derived by them to the understanding, I call SENSATION" (ibid., p. 121; capitalization in original). A sensation traced the externally organized pattern of some item in experience — including its shape, color, texture, and so forth — and this sensed item would be recorded in the form received, in a way akin to the cabinet receiving preshaped teacups. It is this nonformulating, receptive nature of the mind in the Lockean explanation that gives it a passive quality. However, Locke also spoke of a second source of ideas: the operations of the mind such as perception, thinking, doubting, believing, reasoning, knowing, and even willing (ibid.). Man has ideas about such operations "wholly in himself" (ibid.) and does not learn about them through external objects. The ideas regarding mental operations arise through reflection. This notion causes some psychologists to question whether Locke's model is of passive cognition only, for reflection appears to be an active process.

Nevertheless, Locke makes it clear that his concept of reflection is not fundamentally different from his concept of sensation. Both are extraspective formulations lacking in the generic oppositionality of a predicational process. As such, Lockean reflectivity lacks a transcendent capacity to bring knowledge or belief into distortion or doubt in the way that Kant said a reflexively reasoning intelligence could. For Locke, to sense something is to passively receive preformed inputs; reflection, then, functions as a form of *"internal sense"* (ibid.). Sensation is external sense, and reflection is internal sense. *Reflection* is defined by Locke as "that notice which the mind takes of its own operations" (p. 122). The thinker looks outwardly to the world where his or her mental contents are formed and also looks in this third-person fashion at the operations of mind, as if they were "objects" (ibid.) to be sensed—that is, conveyed into cognizance. The treatment here is totally extraspective. The person is either looking at the world through the senses or looking at the operations of mind in the mediating sense of receiving what is there for reception. There is never any introspective cognizance of having to take a position, which is central to a transcendent process of reflexivity. It is this matter of taking a position that distinguishes the active from the passive mind. Internal sensation is just as passive as external sensation.

Although Kant (1781/1952) spoke of "reflection" (p. 99) in thought, I will adopt a distinction between reflectivity and reflexivity, suggesting that the former is Lockean and the latter is Kantian. By this I mean that Kantian reflexivity invites introspective explorations because in the Kantian model, there is always a fundamental implication, if not an actual awareness, that things could be other than they are. This is another way of construing human agency. Lockean reflection involves simply knowing what is the case, not what might otherwise be the case. Kant teaches us that thought involves taking a position and that a reflexive intelligence knows that positions can be arbitrary and subject to change. As human beings, we can go through life having self-reflections but never actually examine our fundamental assumptions in reflexive fashion. According to the Kantian model, because of the intrinsic human capacity for dialectical transcendence, there is always this potential for reflexion.

The Kantian glasses are formal-cause patterns "for the sake of which" we construe meaning "from above" or altogether rearrange its significance through dialectical transcendence and reflexivity. The pattern of the glasses finally affirmed will then predicate what can be known by way of precedent-sequacious extensions of meaning. Inputs from the external world never direct the Kantian process completely, not even at the organism's birth. There is little need for such theorizing in the *Physikos* or *Bios*. I think the *Socius* can be framed by the Kantian model, and most assuredly the *Logos* demands something of the sort. Of course, any one theory might be based on concepts drawn from *both* Lockean and Kantian assumptions; sometimes this is done well and sometimes not. It is not my intention to lump all theories into an either/or pile, but the pervasiveness of these contrasting outlooks in psychology is nothing short of amazing. I will make reference to Lockean and Kantian themes as we wind our way through the topics of this volume.

Concluding Comment

It should be clear that, as these outlooks have been framed in this chapter, it is not possible to reduce one ground to another, although it may be and often is possible to use complementing groundings in the description of things (Rychlak, 1993). The human being is obviously constructed of substances that exist in the inert physical realm. A theory based on the *Physikos* will therefore have relevance to the human as a natural product. We might say that the *Physikos* process makes it possible for a *Bios* process to function in nature. The *Bios* has even greater relevance for human description, for it enables a living organism to engage the *Logos* process. But to assume that the *Bios* process is a content of a *Physikos* process is a questionable and on my view untenable assumption.

The same holds for assuming that the *Logos* process is a content in either the *Bios* or *Socius* process. It is possible to frame such theories, but even if some of us in psychology take this alternative, it is also possible to ground explanation exclusively in the *Logos*. As a theorist grounding my explanations in the *Logos*, I can legitimately point out that no matter what the mediating *Bios* process turns out to be—a system of pulleys and gears, a telephone switchboard, a parallel processing computer, or a chemical reaction—the logical process of predication will not be affected one iota. It should therefore be studied in its own right.

When a word like *logic* is mentioned, the traditions established in philosophy predicate our understanding of this term. Classical logic is concerned with deriving rules for proper thought, as expressed in the following: "It is the concern of the science of logic, as contrasted with psychology, to criticize . . . [logical] assertions and inferences from the point of view of their validity or invalidity" (Johnson, 1922, p. 3). To be logical has traditionally meant to be rational, meaning that the reasoner was to avoid twisting things around through transcendent ideas of one sort or another. As I suggested earlier, Kant was critical of transcendent dialectical thinking, for it tends to distort reality. As a psychologist, however, I cannot limit myself to a logic of "correct" or "sound" thinking. People must be taken as we find them, and when we study them we find that they are not always logical in their reasoning. This is true even of modern physical scientists (Tweney, Doherty, & Mynatt, 1981, p. 7).

Thus, the word *logical* in the present volume has a much broader interpretation than is ordinarily given to it. *Logical* here means being concerned with meaningful patterns in cognition, as well as with the patterning of these meanings in ongoing experience, in what Heraclitus (ca. 540–480 B.C.) originally called the *rationale* or *logos* of existence. We are obviously dealing now with formal causes. The classical logician was to judge certain patterned alignments to be valid (logical) and others to be invalid (illogical) (see Mill, 1872/1974, p. 6). The former were embraced as logic proper, and the latter were dismissed—somewhat as the outside of the Euler circle is dismissed. But I will not dismiss this illogical (untrue, error-laden, etc.) side to human reason. Here is where a logic of oppositionality qua dialectical reasoning runs rampant, and its magnificent role in human cognition has been overlooked for too long. Probably the most prevalent mistake made in the study of patterned meaning—one that will arise again and again in the chapters to follow—is the confounding of the word-contents of the predicational process with the process per se. Predication is not carried by words. Words are contents in the predicational process. Any word can predicate any other word, whether they are opposites or not. For example, we can use the same words in a predicational process and, simply by reordering them, vastly alter the meaning under expression. Thus, the sentence "A person is like a tree" takes *tree* as the wider (predicating) range and situates *person* as the target within this range. The meaning being conveyed here might be that the person is rooted in tradition, has a hide as wrinkled and thick as bark, sheds hair like leaves in the autumn of life, and so forth.

If we reverse the sentence, however, and say "A tree is like a person," the meaning conveyed is immediately changed. This is not an example of "double predication," as in delimiting oppositionality, because the meaning of *person* does not intrinsically delimit the meaning of a tree or vice versa. There is nonetheless an immediate change in the meaning being patterned. To change is to evaluate the status of contents in a predicational process (e.g., same/ different, familiar/unfamiliar, positive/negative connotation, etc.). The reformulated sentence now conveys that the limbs of a tree reach out, that the tree bends under the weight of environmental pressure, or that it can lose its individuality when swallowed up by the crowding forest. Regardless of where we place the words tree or person, we immediately—*not* mediately—create a meaningful relationship, and hence the predication cannot be in the words but must be in the predicational process.

I suggest that psychologists gather empirical data on words (contents) in the mistaken belief that they are studying a process, or they simply assume that a mediational process is taking place when in fact their findings on the words studied are even more compatible with a predicational process. Given the limitations imposed by the affirming-the-consequent fallacy, one would think that the availability of an alternative process to ponder could only strengthen the future growth of psychology as a science. This is my hope, to introduce and empirically justify predication as an alternative cognitive process to mediation.

2

The Basic Concepts of
Logical Learning Theory

Now that I have established some of the sorts of issues that go into psychological explanation, I can move on to the basic concepts employed in logical learning theory (LLT). The word *logical* in LLT signifies that the grounds for explanation here are in the (formal-cause) patterns of the *Logos* rather than in the (efficient-cause) energies or (material-cause) structures of the *Bios*. In fact, when it comes to purely psychological events, LLT views elements in the latter sphere as instrumentalities of the former. There is a misunderstanding in psychology concerning nativistic explanation. Many assume that because a process in the *Logos* reflects the native equipment of the organism, this process must itself be reduced to the *Bios*. Since the organism is a biological structure manifesting logic, it seems to follow that the biology produces the logic.

This is not the case. In the same way that Newton's logico-mathematical formulations of gravity could not be found in (reduced to) the *Physikos*, so too logic cannot be reduced to biology. The *Bios* process may make it possible for the organism to participate in the *Logos*, in the sense that to function an organism must exist materially. There are certain biological requirements necessary for the organism to manifest the predication process. Nonetheless, this in no way means that logic per se is fashioned by the biological requirement, any more than dancing is fashioned by the legs. There is no need or evidence to suggest that the *Logos* process is a content of some *Bios* process. I will further test the soundness of this claim in chapter 8 when I look at the current trends in brain theory and research.

Thus, an assumption of LLT is that the *Logos* process of predication reflects the native endowment of human beings. This endowment is to be understood in the same way that we now claim that human beings "respond to" or "input" environmental stimulations. These latter concepts, which underwrite me-

diation processing, are efficiently causal in meaning. To devise a human teleology we require a concept based on final (which includes formal) causation.

Behavior as Telosponsive

As a Kantian formulation, LLT takes its stance introspectively, from the point
of view of the human organism whose behavior we want to explain. To be
a genuine human teleology, LLT must be able to show how it is possible for
the person to act for the sake of alternative meanings at any time, regardless
of the number of past stimulations or inputs that may be dictating one and
only one course of movement. We can achieve this if we take the Kantian
spectacles of Figures 10 and 11 (chapter 1) as representing the native (innate,
natural, etc.) logical process of cognition (mentation, reason, thought, etc.).
We require a technical concept to subsume this introspectively framed schematization. The technical concepts of stimulus-response or input-output are
of no help here, because they are extraspective formulations modeled solely
on efficient causation. If psychology must rely exclusively on such language,
it will never entertain a human teleology. My suggestion is, therefore, to
think of human behavior in formal- and final-cause terms as telosponsive
(Rychlak, 1987). *A telosponse* is the affirmation or taking of a position regarding a meaningful content (image[s], word[s], judgmental comparison[s], etc.)
relating to a referent acting as a purpose for the sake of which behavior is
then intended. Affirmation encompasses predication.

We must understand telosponsivity exclusively from an introspective perspective in which meaning extends as behavior unfolds. We are looking
through the "conceptual eyes" of the behaving person at this point. If there
is no meaning involved, then there is no telosponsivity involved. The position affirmed by a person in telosponding may be termed a *premise* when it
is the initiating precedent of a line of thought. Such affirmed meanings are
then extended sequaciously as thought progresses. *Affirmation* is therefore
the psychic equivalent of drawing a Euler circle within which a narrower
range of meaning is targeted for meaning-extension. A familiar example of
affirmation is "All human beings are mortal," but affirmations of meaning
are not limited to complete verbal expressions like this. An affirmation can
involve a single word, as when we target a certain word by its predicating
definition in a dictionary. Such meaning can also be assigned to a fragment
of a word or to any symbolically captured image. Images in motion can also
be affirmed meaningfully, as when we imagine ourselves doing something we
have never before attempted. Evaluations that contrast the relative merit of
one targeted item over another also reflect the affirmations of telosponsivity.

Meanings of all sorts are under creation in the predicational processing of telosponsivity. The *purpose* is the aim of the meaning of a concept, the point under meaningful expression, the very essence of what is being conveyed. Framed in causal terms, purpose takes its meaning from formal causation, as in the final-cause definition where it represents the "that" in the "that for the sake of which" phrasing (recall that the formal cause is a necessary but not sufficient ingredient of the final cause). Purpose may be thought of as the reason a certain intention is enacted. *Intention* refers to the remaining "for the sake of which" phrasing of the final-cause definition. Intentions enliven or create the "thats" (purposes) in words, images, assessments, and most important of all, actions. To mean is to intend. One intends the purpose of a pencil when one picks it up to jot down a telephone number. This is what one "means to do," and the act reflects what the pencil is meant to do (be used for, etc.). A pencil per se has no intention or purpose, of course. It is the person who picks up a pencil to record a telephone number who intends its purpose by acting intentionally. The reverse would also be true, in that *not* to pick up the pencil or *not* to record the telephone number would also be to act intentionally by negating a purpose, assuming that there was a change of mind about recording the number.

The telosponse is therefore a final-cause conception of cognition and its behavioral manifestations. In using this conception, I am saying that people behave for the sake of some reason or purpose framed precedently rather than respond to some unintentional antecedent impulsion. Both the precedent and the antecedent are "previous" or "earlier" occurrences. Recall from chapter 1 that the precedent is prior in logical order and that the antecedent is prior in time. If the logical development of a person's thought is traced over time, it may appear that the precedent logic—being correlated to time's passage—is being directed by the occurrence of past events per se. "Behavior is shaped by earlier experience" is a claim we often hear made in psychology. What is actually suggested in claims like this is that the formal/final-cause nature of logic can be reduced to past efficient-cause impulsions or shapings. Yet there is no evidence that logic can be "shaped," if we mean by this the process rather than its contents. Even psychotic people are logical in their thought (including demonstrative and dialectical strategies). They make the same number of logical errors that we all make, but it is in their premised meanings that we find their insanity. It is the content—what they think about—that stamps them as psychotic, not their thinking process per se. If we can grasp the meanings of their often neologistic premises, we can usually see the logic of their thoughts.

As for the specific claim that past events influence today's actions, there can be no dispute. Surely they do. The question remains, however: Are

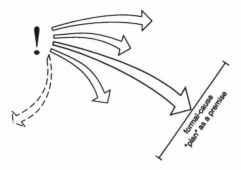

Figure 12   Affirmation in telosponsivity

these past events unpredicated? Logical learning theory's suggestion is that although behavior can usually be shown to be influenced by what has transpired earlier, this in no way contradicts the claim that these earlier events had their precedent influences as well, right down to the very first cognitions experienced by the human being. Thus, when we speak about earlier influences on later behaviors, we should be referring to content meanings and not to process. There surely are meanings framed earlier in life that continue to influence us today, for they can be used as predicating contents in the present. Unfortunately, the mediation modeler understands this claim of early influence solely as meaning that there are earlier inputs that serve a mediating role in today's behavior. In other words, the mediational theorist takes "previous experience" to mean recordings of contents in an efficient-cause process occurring over time (it is impossible to speak of efficient causation apart from time's passage; see Rychlak, 1988, pp. 44, 198, 275). In contrast, the LLT advocate suggests that "earlier" does not mean "unpredicated"; rather, it means the precedent contents framed in ongoing experience by a formal- and final-cause process. There is a challenge now for LLT to explain how it is that these very first contents of predication come about following birth.

Before I confront this challenge, however, I should clarify the telosponsive process itself. Figure 12 presents a schematization of the first step in the logic of the telosponsive process, referred to as *affirmation* or *taking a position*. The word *affirm* has Latin roots meaning "to make firm." Thus, when we take a position, we have a belief or assumption securely fixed, so that its meaning qua purpose focuses our attention and extends in the logical line of thought to follow (assuming it is not negated).

Note in Figure 12 that we have a series of arrows extending from a large exclamation mark. The latter represents the cognizer whom we presume is affirming or taking one of several possible positions. This could involve looking to the past in an effort to recall and understand some previous event, but

I will explain telosponsivity in terms of predicating the future. Let us take the introspective perspective now and see life through the cognizance of this individual, a person who rises in the morning and sets out on his or her daily routine. This may involve simply going to a job, picking up the laundry, and returning home for the evening meal, or there may be something different on tap today, such as shopping for a new automobile, interviewing for a job change, meeting a new, important person, and so forth. There are always several ways in which to "come at" or predicate these daily routines or changing circumstances. Delimiting oppositionality frames this range of specific possibilities in the sense of doing "this" or "that" to accomplish the targeted goals (contents) of the day. In Figure 12 the range of potential alternatives is symbolized as a series of arrows arrayed from top to bottom, with the lowest one, given in a broken line, standing for a possibility. There could be many such possibilities, of course.

Our person/telosponder has affirmed one of the alternatives regarding what to do today. This is schematized by the large extended arrow pointing to the line labeled "plan" (i.e., formal cause). The plan encompasses a premise of the following sort: "Today I'm doing only what I'm forced to do." Or it might be a more energetic: "Today I'm going to strike a good deal on the purchase of a new car." Predication is involved in such premises, of course, which means that generic oppositionality is active in the logical process as well. The projected image of seeing oneself approaching a salesperson to negotiate for the new automobile is the end (telos) or plan for today. Framing this situation now in the final-cause sense, we can also say this is the that for the sake of which behavior may—or may not—be intended. As I have noted previously, formal causation enters final causation as the (precedent) that for the sake of which meaning/behavior is sequaciously extended. This is why the line is labeled as a formal cause as well as a plan.

Once this plan has been affirmed, it acts as a precedent meaning, capturing the *understanding-intention* of the person for that day. Of course, I should point out that telosponsivity is not limited to such long-range intentions as automobile-purchasing negotiations to be made later in the day. We could have begun with the person's clothes selection for today. Here again, the particular outfit is selected from a number of possibilities (which always include combinations that have never been worn before, schematized by the broken arrow at the bottom). So descriptive concepts like "plan," "premise," or even "expectation" for today would all be subsumed by the precedent affirmation of the that (formal-cause) meaning for the sake of which events will begin to unfold today. Figure 13 takes this process one step further.

Notice in Figure 13 that now we have a further extension of the alternative selected. The initial extension is labeled "A," the plan or premise is labeled

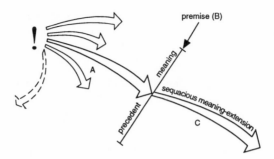

Figure 13   Precedent-sequacious meaning-extension in telosponsivity

"B," and the further extension is labeled "C." The A, B, C labeling captures *logical sequence*. It has nothing to do with time's passage. The A portion is affirmation, the B portion is the stipulation of the precedent meaning under affirmation in the premise, and the C portion is the sequacious extension of meaning in thought and then—unless negated—in overt action (behavior). So, if our person would now get out of bed, choose a wardrobe, get dressed, move out to work after a hasty breakfast, and then sometime later in the day actually meet with an automobile salesperson, we would witness his or her intention moving from understanding to overt action. An *action-intention*— which is the further development of an understanding-intention—pleases the teleologist because when people actually do what they "say" (plan, expect, promise, etc.) they intend doing, we have empirical evidence supporting the telic position. Unfortunately, people do not always enact what they tell us they intend to do. Many understanding-intentions never become action-intentions. This fact gives encouragement to the mechanistic theorist.

Nonetheless, if we believe in a human teleology, then we must hold not only that people can set their course of action initially (frame a predication, thereby involving generic oppositionality) but also that they can negate it in subsequent circumstances. They may even make projections that they do not really intend to keep. People can fool themselves. I have found that this is the most difficult fact for psychologists theorizing in the Lockean tradition to accept. Looking at people as unidirectionally influenced in the first place, mediational theorists cannot see how it is then possible to make a "free" choice—free of the past "mediators." To ask them also to believe that such choices can be arbitrarily projected or reversed is the straw that breaks the camel's back. But there is no need for an intention concept unless the person could also not intend the purpose being extended into overt action at any time at which the premise under affirmation is moving logically (sequaciously) from understanding to action. Here is where choice or decision enters the telosponsive process—thanks to oppositionality. This is another manifestation of human agency, a topic I will take up in detail at the end of this chapter.

Note that I am not vulnerable to the Baconian Criticism at this point, because I claim that people really do make a difference in selecting and carrying out the purposes that they intend. This is not a superfluous theoretical flourish on my part. If I simply tacked on final causation to an efficient-cause explanation that had already accounted for everything in need of explanation, then I *would* be in violation of the Baconian Criticism, but to understand human beings we need a genuine telic elaboration. Behavior is logically determined, but this determination extends sequaciously following the affirmation of the premise (encompassing the predication) to be enacted. Affirmation is like selecting one from among the many potential predicates of Figure 5 that could potentially frame John. Once we settle on "John is reliable," however, we have expressed a premise (understanding-intention) and thus necessarily extended this meaningful predication into our relations with John (action-intention), which involves giving him responsibility, counting on him to meet deadlines, and so on. In this case, the premise would be called not a plan but rather a belief or an attitude concerning John. There are dozens of such words to describe the contents of the telosponsive process.

Note that a succession of predications takes place in ongoing telosponsivity. For example, there is always an even more abstract predication framing the grounds for selecting "reliability" as the predication to be applied to John. Furthermore, the entire assertion "John is reliable"—which contains a predicational relation within it—acts as a predicating context for the sake of which we relate interpersonally with John. We treat him as if he were reliable because we have predicated him in this fashion from the outset. This complexity of meaning-extension demonstrates why it is essential to speak both of predication and oppositionality on the one hand and telosponsivity on the other. The former constructs are fundamental to telosponsivity, but they require a term that can subsume and enlarge on them in direct contrast to the efficient-cause concepts of psychology such as stimulus-response or input-output.

Predication is therefore a necessary but not sufficient ingredient of telosponsivity, which must be understood as involving a potentially arbitrary preaffirmation aspect. Arbitrary cognitions and actions are not without predication; they are based on shifting predications, drawing on the convenience of the moment to employ the generic oppositionality fundamental to this process. Nothing need impel these shifts; they can be based on whim. To capture the complete process of selection, affirmation, meaning-extension, transcendence, negation, and so forth, we speak of telosponsivity.

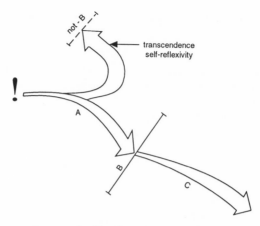

Figure 14 Transcendence and self-reflexivity in telosponsivity

An awareness of the transcendence made possible through the bipolarity of generic oppositionality helps us to grasp why understanding-intentions are not always carried out as action-intentions. Figure 14 presents the relevant schematization.

Figure 14 depicts *transcendence* and *self-reflexivity* in the now complete telosponsive process. Figure 14 is reminiscent of the elaboration of the Kantian model in Figure 11. That is, Figure 14 depicts the capacity that the individual has to reason from the affirmed meaning we have been calling the plan or premise (labeled "B") to its opposite (labeled "not-B") in a transcendent fashion, which then makes self-reflexivity possible. This schematization is also an alternative formulation of generic oppositionality, for in referring to the intrinsic tie of B and not-B in this process we are in effect talking about the framing Euler circle's inside and outside. Figure 14 demonstrates that when a person affirms or takes a position—brings to bear an assumption, and so forth—the negation of this meaning is necessarily implied in this general process. If we next recognize that delimiting oppositionality also occurs for specific contents being carried along by this process, we can appreciate how self-reflexive examinations are possible (see Figure 6). People can and do question what they believe, because the meanings of such affirmed belief-contents delimit—that is, directly imply—their contraries, contradictions, and contrasts (in addition to their negations).

This does not mean that the reasoning person always consciously entertains or overtly enacts the delimited opposite to what is being affirmed. Many of these alternatives are irrational ("crazy ideas," "impossible," "wrong," etc.). But even when they have potential, they must be dismissed or not enacted. The psychological state of being hung up between opposite poles of an affirmation is intolerable. The very point of human reasoning is to focus on targeted meanings that lead to desired ends, capture reality, speak to the truth, and so on. Still, the opposite meanings of such affirmations—undesired ends, unreality, falsehoods—are also available as potential grounds for a line of thought. Sometimes in life we are impaled on the horns of a dilemma when both the affirmed and the implied alternatives strike us as equally plausible or beneficial. We are likely to call this hang-up a conflict, especially if the stakes are high.

I do not mean for Figure 14 to suggest that every transcendent negation of an affirmation is an act of self-reflexivity. Nevertheless, I do mean to portray the capacity for self-examination, for rising above one's typical ways of looking at things to bring them into question. If our person who had planned to see an automobile salesperson does not actually do so, how would we understand this failure to carry out an action-intention? Simple explanations leap to mind at this point, like a heavy work load at the office, missing connections with the salesperson because of an incorrectly recorded appointment time, and so forth. Indeed, the real reason the appointment was missed requires an interpretation of the conceptualized facts of experience. The person concerned may not be in the best position to frame and evaluate this fact pattern, but the point LLT makes is that the person will (and indeed must) frame an understanding-intention to account for the missed appointment, even if this is a statement of negation such as "I don't know what happened, I just never got around to it."

The necessity for such reasons arises when, once again, a telosponse is to be framed on the morrow taking into consideration what has transpired today. As I noted above, in the comments regarding Figure 12, a telosponse can be focused on the past just as readily as on the future. We can conceptualize and reconceptualize the past (understanding-intentions) and seek thereby to change our recollections to meet our current activities (action-intentions). People regularly make up alibis and excuses as reasons for what they have already carried out on entirely different grounds.

Logical learning theory therefore holds that the person has the capacity to (transcendently) self-examine his or her day and come up with one or more reasons why the appointment was missed. In fact, one of the reasons could be that the person simply changed his or her mind about seeing the salesperson. This negation of the original intention is accepted as a genuine alternative—wound into the telosponsive process—for why an understanding-intention was not enacted. In other words, LLT does not dismiss the person qua reasoner as an influence on his or her behavior. The mediational modeler would want to find external circumstances bringing about this change of intention, but LLT holds that no additional input is required for a person to choose between alternatives on an issue under affirmation (of course, there may be such external factors present). As noted above, there is room in LLT for decisions based on arbitrary grounds, or even for behavior "just for the hell of it." Also, as I already suggested, people can think up, ex post facto, a more suitable understanding-intention, thus "rationalizing" the action-intention that they may have carried out impulsively.

Even if our person were to have found many factual occurrences blocking his or her intention to see a car salesperson today, this would not contradict telosponsivity. We do not require mediation to account for what has transpired in this case. Unexpected facts, like a heavier than normal work load, an error in the previous recording of an appointment with the automobile salesperson, and so forth, are never themselves free of predication. What a heavy work load is depends on the person's assumptive predications. And misrecording appointments is readily understood in terms of predicate expectations (wishes, fears, ambivalences, etc.) concerning what is to take place henceforth. Freudian psychology is fraught with accounts of unadmitted intentions to create "errors." To now say that circumstances external to the person's predications are determining her or his behavior is to speak from the vantage point of an extraspective observer, predicating theoretically what is taking place "over there" in mediational fashion rather than in predicational fashion. As I noted in chapter 1, the facts here do not speak for themselves.

Tautology in the Framing of Meaning and Its Extension

It is clear now that in telosponding, the person must have a framing predicate for the sake of which understanding and then action are carried forward. The predicate meaning is the content of the predicational process. In the Kantian sense, it is necessary for the person to have a ready frame of reference for knowledge to be underway—that is, formulated and elaborated. We must know in order to know. But how is the very first predicate (content) formed by the predicational process? Must not the LLT advocate postulate a series of beginning predicates, on the order of Kant's categories of the understanding, to explain how predication gets underway? I suggested in chapter 1 that Kant's conception of the idea was formulative, more a process than a content. However, just as he named certain beginning contents (e.g., quantity, quality, relation, modality) as his categories of the understanding, are we not called on to do the same?

I do not wish to follow Kant by naming a series of framing categories; these would undoubtedly be construed by my Lockean colleagues as inherited ideas. A preferred strategy here is to elaborate on the logical process of meaning-extension. I also want to theorize now more as a psychologist than as a logician—that is, with no preconceptions about sound reasoning or the drawing of correct conclusions. As a psychologist, I want merely to understand and explain how a predication extends to its target or a major premise unites with its minor premise, no matter how accurately the contents of such cognitive acts are framed and elaborated. Fortunately, I can at this point turn to the concept of tautology to assist me in explaining how the very first predicational contents are conceptualized. In its most general sense, a tautology is an identity in meaning that obtains between such logical items as a predicate and its target. Such identity can be complete or only partial. Oppositionality also plays a role in the tautology, as we shall see.

The dictionary definition of *tautology* stresses its meaning as redundancy or the needless repetition of words or explanations. Gertrude Stein's notorious "A rose is a rose is a rose" might be a case in point. Tautological statements are said to add no new information to an account, suggesting a pointless recasting of what is already known. In contrast to this view, I hold that tautology plays a profound psychological role stemming from its intrinsic tie to the framing and extension of meanings in ongoing thought. Meaning, as tautology, borrows from the formal-cause conception of an interlacing pattern. As I noted previously, meaning also refers to the relations between items (images, words, concepts, etc.) and their intended referents.

The introspective versus extraspective stance must be taken into consideration here. When we say that an item of interest, such as bread, means what it relates to—such referents as flour, oven, milk, butter, and so on—the relational ties can be framed entirely extraspectively, as when we write down a word like *bread* followed by its definition. But what if we were to relate the word *bread* solely to bread, as in the Steinian example given above? In this case, the relation would be tautological, reflecting 100% sameness: "Bread is bread." This redundancy is empty only when the question of existence is not at issue. Saying "that is bread" while looking at a referent is not empty expression when one is hungry and attempting to define the nearby edibles. In strictly psychological terms, the assertion "that is bread" is a variant of the tautology "bread is bread" or "that is that (which I seek)."

Note, however, that in this latter instance we are speaking of a tautology as it would be expressed from the introspective perspective. We are no longer speaking about the tie of that word to that definition "over there." We are now involved in the relation between the user of such items—ourselves, "right here"—and the item designated (the bread) to be consumed "right here." The tautological expression is made in a psychological fashion, as reflecting what meaningful intention the person brings to bear in predicating her or his experience. It is this presence and immediacy that I hope to capture in the exclamation marks of Figures 12, 13, and 14 above. The sequacious extension of meaning depicted in Figures 13 and 14 symbolizes the tautological extension of the meaning that has been framed precedently (at B). Tautology from the introspective perspective expresses how it is possible to take the meaning given as a precedent (B) and then sequaciously extend it into experience. As we have seen, LLT calls this *meaning-extension*.

Tautology of this introspective variety is also what induces the meaning-extension from predicate to target. Whereas traditional stimulus-response psychology relied on an efficient-cause thrust of force or energy to move events along over time (i.e., *local motion* or *locomotion*; see Aristotle, 1952b, p. 305), LLT postulates the "logical thrust" of tautology to explain why precedents necessarily (sequaciously) extend their meanings. Tautology is concerned with the similarity and differences to be noted in changing patterns (i.e., Aristotle's *qualitative motion*; ibid.). This conceptual understanding is necessitated once the patterned framework of meaning is there at point B. Thus, as soon as we put on "optimistic" Kantian spectacles, the future (or past) fills us with optimism. As soon as we affirm John as being reliable, we expect him to keep his promises. Here is the source of that immediacy that I have noted to be true of predication.

A psychological interpretation of the tautology is quite different from a strictly logical view. Classical logicians, who rarely take dialectical logic seriously because of its potential for use in sophistry, are prone to think of tautologies primarily in the extraspective sense. They are likely to say that a tautology is an analytically true statement, which means that it is true by definition. If we analyze the statement "All bachelors are unmarried males," we can determine that it really conveys the same notion as the statements "All bachelors are bachelors" or "All unmarried males are unmarried males," because the antecedent term is contained in the consequent term. This is comparable to word definitions—that is, we have here an extraspective relational identity between terms. If we are *psycho*logicians and take the introspective view of human cognition, would we see any difference in the processing of beliefs such as "All bachelors are unmarried males" and "All redheads are hotheads"? We have a difference in content, of course, but is the telosponsive process, with its tautological thrust, occurring the same way in both assertions? Surely the latter statement can be shown extraspectively to be nontautological. The definition of a redheaded person does not include hotheadedness, or vice versa. As psychologists, can we overlook the reasoning process of a person who may be tautologizing in the following limited sense: "Because both fire and hair are red, it follows that redheads are hotheads." To ask us to overlook such errant processing as if it were different from the more acceptable forms of tautologizing is like asking a physician to ignore the standard digestive process when a patient under treatment swallows a handful of sand, which is not the proper foodstuff to be moving through this biological system. Erroneous mental conceptions, like inappropriate foodstuffs in the digestive tract, do not alter or negate the uniform process by which such meanings are extended through understanding- to action-intentionality in overt behavior.

So it is the process I am out to capture in my telosponsive conception, and from the introspective perspective the sequacious extension of meaning is done tautologically. Whatever content is affirmed and then extended—as in the extended arrow of Figures 12, 13, and 14—is done as a tautology. The point at which the affirmation is rendered (labeled "B" in Figures 13 and 14) is referred to as the *protopoint*. The protopoint of a telosponse is where premise affirmation occurs. To delimit a telosponsive sequence, we must locate the protopoint, for this is where the framing meaning for that particular telosponse will be sequaciously extended. Whatever meaning is affirmed (at B) will be extended in the logical order to follow. The terms *precedent* and *sequacious* refer to the ordering of meaning-extension at any point in the sequence of intentional behavior. For example, if we study a person working through a puzzle, there will probably be a series of logical steps or stages through which the solution will be concocted. The initiating point for any such step or stage, however, where a certain strategy is affirmed, even one that may change what has been attempted to that point in the logical sequence, reflects a protopoint. In a sense, the protopoint is the first precedent for any discernible line of intentionality.

Of course, any protopoint affirmation—the content meaning involved— is itself under a predication of some sort. Here we have tautological extension deploying from even higher abstractions, as portrayed in the Kantian model (see Figure 10). At the highest levels of abstraction we would have what the ancient Greeks called the "universals"—meanings that could subsume literally everything in existence. Plato's realm of the Forms, which he termed "Being," is an example of such abstraction. Surely the four causes would fit this designation as well, since literally anything in existence can be subsumed by one or more of these predicates. But the Forms or the causes are contents of a predicational process, which means they too must be formed into existence by this process.

A process does not end at some higher level of abstraction. It functions up and down such levels. Of course, when we get to the higher levels of abstraction, we no doubt would begin to see a circularity in the contents being framed by the predicational process. For example, we could see how the causes would be predicated by some belief in things making up or bringing about other things. But then, any such things and other things could in turn be predicated by one or more of the four causes—and back again. Logical learning theory does not view such circularity as something to be dismissed due to its illogicality. Circularity is accepted as a normal outcome of the reasoning process.

We can now return to the challenge of explaining how the very first contents of telosponsivity arise. I have already suggested that it is not helpful to name some handful of inherited contents to explain how the telosponsive process gets underway at birth. For example, I would not want to say that everyone is born with a predicate-meaning like "things exist," so that as the infant looks out at the world, she or he has an initial content to use as a framework of meaning (B in Figures 13 and 14) to be tautologized as life unfolds—something on the order of, "I know 'things' exist." In LLT we believe that although one must know a precedent meaning in order to know (extend the framed meaning), this sequence refers to a process and not some content in this process. In other words, what the newborn has available at birth is a telosponsive process to create meaningful contents and not a prepackaged set of content meanings to be used as mediators.

How then does the initial protopoint, the very first pattern(s) to be used in cognition, arise? Here is the challenge that LLT must meet, and the answer is as follows: *The very first contents of the predicational process are items tautologized of themselves.* There is a process underway at birth in which contents must be created. The process is therefore order-creating. The first content is framed by tautologizing "it" with itself, in the Steinian sense, culminating in a known identity. The infant, in the first hours of life, conceptualizes "a nipple is a nipple," or some such notion. If we were to express this as a statement, "nipple" would be located in both the subject (target) and predicate location. Obviously, such a syntactic array does not make sense at this point, because the infant is cognizing in idiosyncratic images, feelings, sucking tensions, bodily sensations, tastes, and so forth. It is traditional to view such sensory tautologizing of an item with itself as perception (e.g., see English & English, 1958, p. 378). This view has it that a physical sensation is activated, which in turn is perceived. The process of such perception has traditionally been explained on a *Bios* ground, however. Logical Learning theory portrays the same action as being based on a *Logos* ground.

The initial tautologizing of a psychological content with itself might be called *recognition*. The infant comes to recognize the targeted item in question, for example, its mother's nipple. Now we have our first precedent taking shape, a recognized identity that is "known" so that further knowing is possible (doubtless several such initiating protopoints occur, as in the tautologizing of a bodily orifice like the ear with itself, etc.). What therefore follows in an infant's cognitive processing is *learning*. This occurs by predicationally extending the recognized or known meanings to other targets of knowledge in ongoing telosponsivity. Initially a target, the maternal nipple is now a predicating frame of reference as succeeding meaning-extensions take place to items presumed to be nipples or nipplelike. Recognition is therefore based on complete (100%) tautological identity between an item and itself. As learning proceeds, however, something less than 100% meaning-extension must occur, because everything is not like everything else in experience.

Partial tautologizing is now employed. For example, over the early months of life, the infant begins sucking any other items that, like the nipple, are capable of being sucked. Some of these items neither look, feel, nor taste like mother's nipple (difference). The concept of a partial tautology is actually an extension of what in chapter 1 I referred to as generic and delimiting oppositionality. Just as with our Euler circle model we necessarily find both an inside and an outside, so too when a tautology is extended from nipple(ness) to nipple(ness), the child cognizes an immediate sense of nonnippleness, thanks to the generic oppositionality of the predicational process. This allows the infant to learn that some things are like a nipple, but not exactly, which is what I mean by a partial tautology. As the child matures, delimiting oppositionality greatly enhances the experiential contents being processed cognitively through both imagery and language acquisition.

To the extent that such ongoing telosponsivity proves useful—for example, the baby learns to avoid sucking certain things because they are uncomfortably bitter, cold, or grainy—we can say that learning takes place. This example highlights the fact that learning can involve what to do or not to do, given certain circumstances. Thus, learning is an outcome of telosponsivity that is helpful in ordering experience so that it can be brought more or less under intentional control. We might even say that a person has learned or that learning occurs when he or she feels confident or convinced enough to employ a former target as a predicate. Predicates lend their meaning more or less to targets. Predicate knowing makes targeted knowledge possible. What is learned need not be true as assessed from another person's perspective, of course. People can and often do "learn error," because this erroneous grasp of experience provides them with reliable—albeit self-deluding or self-defeating—understanding. The paranoid always has his or her predicating reasons.

Incidentally, the theoretical device of tautologically relating a content to itself has a parallel in the literature on mechanistic association. To solve certain problems that arise in explaining associative processing, Jenkins and Cofer (1957) suggested that a word stimulus implicitly elicits itself 100% of the time. The stimulus "butter" always elicits the response "butter," as well as other less frequent responses like "bread" or "milk." Bousfield, Cohen, and

Whitmarsh (1958) subsequently referred to this implicit repetition as a "representational" response, for it identifies or represents the symbolic stimulus presented to the individual. The theory here is extraspectively framed, of course, and although the association of a word with itself is not said to represent a tautology, we surely can view it as such.

The partial tautology makes so-called analogical reasoning possible. As viewed from the introspective perspective, *analogies* are a special case of the tautology in which only part of the identity between what is predicated extends to what can then be known. In other words, we always have the tautological and the (opposite) nontautological or disanalogous aspects of meaning-extension to consider, which is just one more manifestation of generic oppositionality. Logical learning theory substitutes analogical meaning-extension for the mechanist's concept of stimulus or response generalization. Analogy qua partial tautology is the prototype for many other human capacities that will come into play in the meaning-extensions of telosponsivity, such as metaphor (a ship plows the sea), simile (a heart as big as a whale), synecdoche (typifying the whole person as a brain) or allegory (a lengthy metaphor in story form). All these examples reflect the human capacity to take what is known and use it in a less than literal manner, focusing on some feature shared by otherwise different items (e.g., a ship and a plow as both having a pointed tip, a person and a whale as living organisms of contrasting size, etc.) and expressing this meaning in a trenchant, knowledge-enhancing manner. The tie of predication to analogical conceptualization is clearly reflected in Lakoff and Johnson's (1980) definition of metaphor: *"The essence of metaphor is understanding and experiencing one thing in terms of another"* (p. 5; emphasis in original).

An even more important reflection of oppositionality in tautologizing occurs when we consider the myriad meanings like good/bad, reliable/unreliable, near/far, and tall/short that arise in human knowledge. It was Heraclitus, circa 500 B.C., who wisely noted that we could not grasp and name the meaning of justice if injustices did not occur. There is a profound insight to human reason here, one that has been known for centuries but overlooked completely in psychology by all but a few theorists, such as George A. Kelly (1955). The insight is that all such dimensionally framed meanings are fundamentally united through delimiting oppositionality. Even a linear ruler has oppositional features (beginning/end, more/less, low/high, etc.). In a strange way, the singularity of tautology coalesces with the generation of such cognitive alternatives. I believe that the "one and many" principle that so many dialecticians across history have emphasized gets at this unique tie of identity to multiplicity (see Rychlak, 1988, pp. 60, 65, 85). There is unity in thought even as there is variation. Meanings that are diametrically opposed to each other are also variations on a common, albeit wide-ranging, theme, so that they delimit and thereby enter into each other's meaning. Dialectical thinking is therefore dimensional in nature. By embracing such an insight, LLT takes the view of a soft, non-Boolean disjunction.

Thus, in the complete telosponsive process, we have sequacious extensions in the line of directed thought under affirmation and sequacious extensions to the opposite of this line of thought. In this context, it should be noted that before a cognizer makes the affirmation that will be carried forward from understanding- to action-intentions, he or she can mull over many such possibilities. The reason that certain affirmations are taken on and then rejected is because the inferences or implications they frame do not strike the reasoner as sound. A helpful understanding-intention is not framed. Thus, at this point, the entire dimension (the affirmation and its opposite) is negated or rejected and another alternative is tried. Note that such an evaluation process must itself depend on delimiting oppositionality (sound/unsound, helpful/unhelpful, like/dislike).

Further, people do not stay only at one or the other end of a bipolar dimension in affirming a meaning. There is obviously a range of meanings *between* such extremes that can be affirmed. When we call John reliable, we make it appear that he is "either/or" on a dimension that runs from reliable to unreliable. In fact, John could be placed anywhere on the intervening dimension and considered not perfectly reliable (one pole) but reliable enough (close to this pole of meaning or closer to it than to the pole of unreliability). Also, when we are engaged in a transcendent examination of our beliefs, we are necessarily dealing in higher-level abstractions, which in turn subsume (take as a target) the lower-level abstractions of our line of thought. I discussed this process in chapter 1, indicating there that in self-reflexive examination we target our most fundamental assumptions, which we now can recognize as the protopoint affirmations in any line of thought. Another way of expressing the meaning of reflexivity is to say that we can frame telosponses by other telosponses. Just as stimuli and responses can be ordered and combined into more complex combinations on the Lockean model, so too is it possible for telosponses to combine and transcend one another. Once again, the logical thrust for such transcendence, moving from the lower (concrete) to the higher (abstract) regions of thought, is tautology.

Before we move on in the next section to a consideration of the transcendent telosponse, I would like explicitly to frame a working assumption made in LLT, which I will call the *principle of meaning-extension:* All other considerations being equal, the patterning of meaning forming in a predication extends to the least understood or most poorly known target(s) having relevance to the predicating meaning in question. Thus, all things being equal,

a relevant content meaning in the predicational process that has two potential targets will enrich the less well understood target most directly and
immediately. Patterned meaning tautologically extends to the unpatterned.
The novice takes any scrap of information to fill missing gaps of knowledge
concerning the subject of interest. Given the strategy of a problem solution,
the person is more likely to try it out in an unfamiliar circumstance than to
use it as an alternative to a strategy that has already proven successful, albeit
moderately. Hearing a new word, the student of language is likely to apply it
to items for which he or she has no present word, even though it could be a
synonym for the already known words.

In line with my previous discussion, a prime rationale for the principle
of meaning-extension is the ancient Greek dictum that knowledge is organized in the *Logos* as a "one and many" in which bipolarities readily unite.
We might say that opposites attract, so that the most known reaches for the
least known in any tautological extension of telosponsivity. A target that
is reasonably understood by definition already has predications lending it
meaning; hence, when an additionally relevant predication is affirmed, it will
extend to the less well understood target as long as it is relevant. The person will sense that he or she already has some grasp of the relatively better
known target, hence meaning will extend as a first try to the least known
target quite automatically (or "assumptively"). Of course, LLT acknowledges
that this extension process itself could be negated.

Just as the meaning inside the Euler circle rests on the outside—and entirely different—meaning, so too does the best organized and hence best
understood knowledge reach for the least organized, most different, or most
poorly understood knowledge of experience. If the extension from the best
known to the unknown is not relevant, of course, it will be dismissed (negated) and a new predication taken on. Occasionally, however, even though
the person does not intend to bring a predication to bear on some poorly
understood or seemingly irrelevant target, it does extend to this target and
floods the understanding with a discovery or creation, which would be an
example of an understanding-intention that was not consciously sought but
was organized into existence nevertheless. Intentionality is not limited to
the consciously selected. A spontaneous development in thought of this sort
need not be "rational." Irrational thinking (dialectically generated) can lead
to serious adjustment problems for the individual, but as I noted above, LLT
is not oriented to studying rational or objective thought patterns per se. The
irrational and subjective thought patterns are of equal interest and equally in
need of explanation.

An interesting parallel to the principle of meaning-extension is what the gestaltists referred to as the *law of Pragnanz*. This law holds that "psychological organization will always be as 'good' as the prevailing conditions allow. In this definition the term 'good' is undefined. It embraces such properties as regularity, symmetry, simplicity and others" (Koffka, 1935, p. 110). There is a sense in which the law of Pragnanz reflects the fact that in organizing cognition, and in subsequent retention, the lowest common denominator is what is most tightly organized into a cognition. This tightly organized (i.e., symmetrical, closed, grouped, etc.) and simple cognition is found empirically to be highly resistant to memory loss. Although not identical to the law of Pragnanz, the principle of meaning-extension attempts to capture the fact that cognition readily processes to some such basic, fundamental, and simple organization.

The Ubiquitous Telosponse: Affective Assessment

To telospond is to cast about and select certain grounding meanings for the sake of which other meanings will be fashioned. An alternative term for this process is *cognition*. This process is a teleological progression, a final-cause action. The telosponder continually frames grounds for the sake of which behavior is then intended. Cognition on this view is fundamentally evaluative in nature. In answer to the Baconian Criticism, we can say that the person qua final-cause processor makes a real difference in what transpires. People not only can but *must* take positions in life. As Merleau-Ponty (1964) said, "It is never simply the outside which molds [the person] . . . it is he himself who takes a position in the face of external circumstances" (p. 108). The continuing necessity to take positions in life is what makes human behavior so varied and interesting.

A fundamental capacity that LLT assigns to all human beings is the ability to assess the contents of telosponsivity as either positive or negative in meaningfulness. As I suggested at the close of the last section, this evaluative rendering is made transcendentally, as a self-reflexive assessment of targeted contents from a more abstract level. Transcendence per se draws on generic oppositionality, and the focusing of such preferential judgment on the meaning of specific cognitive contents draws on delimiting oppositionality. Logical learning theory assumes that there is literally nothing in cognizance that escapes this idiographic judgment. The technical term describing such evaluations is *affective assessment*, defined as follows: a transcending telosponse in which the person predicates the meaningful contents of less abstract telosponses, targeting them according to their positive or negative significance. This is an idiographic evaluation completely unique to the individual making the judgment, although it is possible for people to predicate affectively in common (i.e., nomothetically).

Affective assessments are usually cognized as personal preferences — likes and dislikes. People do not always have well-defined grounds for why they may like or dislike items in their experience. Why do some people prefer the color green to brown or select apples over oranges as a favorite fruit? It is, of course, possible to seek grounds for these preferences in their early influences, but what of the newborn infant? Can the newborn infant express such affective preferences, or must we postulate innate preferences? If we choose the latter, we would once again confound a content (apples, green, brown, oranges, etc.) with a process (judgment of like or dislike). The LLT advocate assumes that human beings have, as an aspect of telosponsivity, the innate capacity to render affective assessments of all those meanings that they are coming to recognize and learn. This is assumed to be an ongoing evaluation based on delimiting oppositionality and rendered for all contents brought into the telosponsive process at any point in the line of logical development that we call thought. It is delimiting because in rendering a preference ("This is likable"), the assessing organism necessarily delimits the opposite direction ("This is unlikable") in the manner schematized by Figure 6.

Hence, although an innate generic oppositionality is fundamental to all telosponsivity, so that infants must be involved in this bipolarity if they are to predicate, infants also possess an innate form of delimiting oppositionality. As experience widens, as learning progresses, especially in the realm of language, the range of delimiting oppositionality increases. Thus, it should not be thought that generic oppositionality is a priori but that delimiting oppositionality is a posteriori. At least one form of a priori delimiting oppositionality functions in telosponsivity, and this is affective assessment.

Note that I use the concepts of idiographic and nomothetic in describing affective assessment. Windelband (1894/1904) coined these terms, and Gordon Allport (1962) subsequently popularized them in psychology. Lamiell (1992) has since criticized Allport's usage. In a nutshell, Lamiell points out that the nomothetic must not be thought of as an aggregate estimation. A nomothetic item of knowledge is a general law (*nomos* = law), one holding for all time regardless of historical changes or developments. Windelband analogized the nomothetic to Platonic Forms, suggesting thereby a universality to such lawfulness. Idiographic laws are drawn from particular or unique historical events that are not universally true in the sense that a natural law is. Gravity can be understood nomothetically, but languages evolve and change to meet historical circumstances — hence, they must be understood in light of their unique developmental course (i.e., idiographically). The same items of interest can serve simultaneously as targets for both a nomothetic and an idiographic investigation, the former concerning itself with the ever-enduring and the latter with the unique aspects of the targets under study. Sometimes a nomothetic item will occur just once, holding universally during a unit of time but not lasting beyond this period.

Because I have been influenced by Allport and have always referred to affective assessment as an idiographic (*idios* = one's own) measurement, I do not think it would be proper at this point to change usages. The interpretation I have followed is that an idiographic measurement is taken from a single person and hence is based on this person's life history. I follow common usage, as presented in a dictionary of psychology, where we read that the term *idiographic* characterizes "any system of psychology that searches for individual laws of behavior in order to explain individual cases" (Chaplin, 1985, p. 220). The likes and dislikes of person A need not mirror the likes and dislikes of person B, so there is no general law here about liking and disliking specific objects. On the other hand, when we study large groups of people and extrapolate measurements from them, we are prone to think of such findings as representing general laws (using *law* now in the sense of a reliable relationship obtaining between observed events). The dictionary defines nomothetic as "pertaining to the formulation of general laws and principles" (ibid, p. 305). Lamiell's criticism is that this usage confounds the concept of a general law with the concept of an aggregate estimate in measurement.

Because LLT holds that laws are actually affirmed predications leveled by an investigator who perceives a reliable relationship between independent- and dependent-variable observations, there is no serious confounding taking place. Since we are always framing our understanding of the investigator from an introspective perspective, it does not matter whether LLT refers to such observed relationships as idiographic or nomothetic. What is more important for our purposes is to clarify how we measure affective assessments. It is helpful to distinguish, following Allport, between individual (idiographic) and group-based (nomothetic) estimations of the targets in question, and that is what I will continue to do, even though I depart from Windelband's precise usage. I do not wish to reify the law concept. Lamiell's criticism has great import for various aspects of the measurement process, but so long as we are clear on the precise usage followed here, no difficulties should arise.

Another Kantian feature of affective assessments is that they devolve "from above." For example, assume that we are telosponding in some fashion regarding the meanings of symphonic music. The main line of meaning-extension here would involve an awareness of the specific piece that is being sent our way over the radio. Liking symphonic music in general, we may or may not appreciate the particular piece being broadcast. Logical learning theory would frame the telosponsive evaluation as follows: "I am listening to this symphonic music over the radio." Very shortly we could also add, if asked to evaluate the piece, "This is great, I like it" or "I find this kind of uninteresting [moderately disliked]." The precedent affective assessment sequaciously colors—via meaning-extension—our ongoing experience of listening to the musical score. We have a psychic determinism taking place here. It is not necessary to state these affective assessments to oneself, because the routine act of telosponding the musical score "connotes" intrinsically what we think of the piece. We often confound this connoted significance with an emotional reaction, but LLT distinguishes between emotions and telosponses like affective assessments.

Because LLT addresses the *Logos*, and emotions are rooted in the *Bios*, the theory maintains a clear distinction between these two grounds for explaining behavior (see Rychlak, 1993, in which I argue that psychology benefits from such complementary groundings of human behavior). This distinction between emotions and affections will be considered more definitively in chapter 7, where I will take up the role of these concepts in human motivation. For the present, the point should be made that *emotions* refer to patterns of feelings emanating from the physiological realm of experience and are predicated by the experiencer, usually in relation to certain lived circumstances (e.g., social contexts) that may—or seem to—provoke them. Insofar as they are physiological appraisals, emotions do not have the quality of affections. Various emotional moods may be brought about artificially through physiological stimulants (drugs, etc.) or through capturing the environmental situation that naturally provokes them. Even so, according to LLT, emotions must be predicated in the telosponsive process just as any other biological, physiological—or, indeed, physical—event must be lent meaning by the pro forma intelligence.

Logical learning theory therefore holds that even as an infant experiences the physical feeling (*Bios*) of pain, he or she frames this sensation telosponsively via tautological extensions ("Hurt is a hurt," "This hurt is like that earlier hurt"). In addition, a transcending telosponsiveness will also predicate the circumstance (assume that it is a matter of accidentally poking a rattle in the eye) to render it as disliked. Thus, the meaning of the emotional feeling known as "pain" for the child will be conceptualized by a certain pattern of sensation but also will be understood as something disliked. The meaning of an experience like poking the eye will then bear both predications in subsequent experience. Moreover, this meaning can be used analogically, so that any object in close proximity to the eye will immediately be framed by a (transcending) predication of "disliked." The important point here is that the negative evaluation of the eye poking was not efficiently caused by the poking per se. This negative evaluation is the "effect" of a final-cause evaluation rendered by the telosponding infant.

When I use an example of this type, it appears superfluous to add the judgmental process of affection. After all, a poke in the eye must necessarily be something negative to the person concerned. There are, however, many other examples in which the outcome is not so predictable. Thus, in time the maturing child is taken to church, to the grocery store, or on a visit to Aunt Agnes. Some children will find these activities reasonably pleasant, if not enjoyable. Others will find at least certain of them to be unpleasant. In distinguishing between these two evaluations of such events, is it necessary for us to chase after specific external determinants in these various environments that supposedly "shape"—which means in this context "make" or "decide"—these positive or negative evaluations? Is it not possible that the child has a cognitive capacity to render such judgments without situational impulsions bringing them about? Logical learning theory accepts the latter possibility. The child might even analogize (a partial tautology) from earlier experience by judging that a visit to Aunt Agnes is about as much fun as being poked in the eye. Both events share an (affective) identity even as they have their disanalogous—or merely different—aspects.

Another feature of the affection-emotion distinction is that although these processes (*Logos-Bios*) can be concordant, they can also be seen to bear an oppositional relationship to each other. An unpleasant circumstance, once meaningfully framed, often teaches us to do what is necessary to make it pleasant (thanks to the resultant delimiting oppositionality). The concept of emotion does not include such directional suggestions. For example, if an individual is "blue" or depressed in the biological sense of a literal feeling, he or she can reason to the opposite of the situation as follows: "Why not play my favorite recordings? The music will cheer me up." There is no need to have a fleeting emotion—a slight dash of "good feeling"—or a concrete recollection of how once in the past listening to music "took the blues away" before this individual can arrive at a projected action-intention of this nature. Innate delimiting oppositionality is quite enough.

Can the person be indifferent toward some item of experience and to that extent refrain from making an affective assessment of it altogether? The person may tell us, "I have no opinion about fishing one way or the other." Logical learning theory does not reject this possibility of negating the very process of affective assessment (which in itself reflects transcendence and reflexive dismissal of making a decision). However, as a practical matter, this failure to assess affectively seems to occur only rarely. What is probably meant by indifference concerning an activity like fishing is either that it is not conceptualized clearly in the person's mind or that it is affirmed as an understanding-intention but not an action-intention. In most cases, when something has no appeal one way or the other to the person involved, this very phrasing suggests a mildly negative assessment. The person with no opinion concerning fishing is probably slightly negative about the activity. I will review considerable research on such affective assessments in chapter 7.

Telosponsivity in Human Agency

There have been several attempts in psychology to explain agency or freedom of the will. Each of these efforts has advanced an interpretation of just what agency means. As might be expected, these interpretations vary considerably one from another. Agency was defined in chapter 1 as an organism's capacity to behave or believe in conformance with, in contradiction to, in addition to, or without regard for perceived environmental or biological determinants. It is now clear that if human beings telospond, they meet all these definitional requirements. Telosponders always contribute to the meaningful course of their behavioral acts (including the affective assessments of these acts). Understanding-intentions are always affirmed into cognizance. Nevertheless, the process of affirmation in telosponsivity is in principle arbitrary, in that the position taken could have gone "the other way" or "the opposite way." Of course, the conceptualized necessities of life usually override the arbitrariness.

This description of telosponsive affirmation as capable of arbitrariness meets the classical definition of *free will*, in which the agent is said to be capable of doing otherwise, *"all circumstances remaining the same"* (O'Connor, 1971, p. 82; emphasis in original). Telosponders are always in the position of potentially affirming one way (B in Figure 14) or the other (not-B in Figure 14). The final-cause usage in this description—stated now from the introspective perspective—would be "that, *as opposed to this,* for the sake of which" understanding is framed and actions are carried out (Rychlak, 1979, 1991). Oppositionality enables the affirmation to go this way or that, which is tantamount to the "free" in free will. Once the affirmation is made—in schematic terms, once the predicating Euler circle is drawn—we have accounted for the "will" half of the phrase under scrutiny. Following affirmation, meaning-extensions are 100% determined (final-cause or telic determinism; also sometimes called "psychic" determinism). The negational capacity made possible by oppositionality is therefore our key to agency, for an organism working in this manner is always capable of changing the course of events or refusing to change them when called on to do so.

I do not want to give the impression that there is conscious deliberation in all telosponsivity. Individuals sometimes take positions without "consciously" or "intentionally" opting to take them. The principle of meaning-extension suggests that, at times, a person can bring an understood or well-known predication to bear on an unknown target without an intention to do so. For example, the person may use some stereotypical image to predicate one ethnic group that he or she has consciously rejected concerning another ethnic group. The meaning-extension may "just happen" because of the circumstances—that is, a clear-cut ethnic stereotype combined with an unknown ethnic group. In considering agency, however, we must also appreciate that it is always possible for the individual to exert influence on the course of action-intentions. A stereotype "popping into mind" as an understanding-intention need not influence subsequent action-intentionality, for the person can affectively assess and thereby negate its intent if it is deemed to be an old and erroneous belief.

This is not to deny that there are unadmitted aspects of cognition. Sometimes the popping into mind phenomenon is such an unconscious intention. In this instance, no real choice of whether to hold the stereotype would take place. Logical learning theory does not view people as going through life choosing from moment to moment. Telosponding is what people do, and it is the transcendental telosponse of affective assessment that usually brings *choice* or *decision* into cognizance. These cognitive states are framed when taking a position involves alternatives of roughly the same affective quality and significance—as in having to select one of two highly desired foods or having to name which of two exhausting and equally despised exercises to perform. The LLT view is that the person makes this choice in final-cause fashion instead of his or her past shapings or reinforcement history making it in efficient-cause fashion.

Previous theoreticians have attempted to account for free will or agency using a variety of nonteleological characterizations. One popular interpretation is to view free will as statistical unpredictability (Boneau, 1974, p. 308). This reduces agency to the error variance in a distribution of measurements (e.g., test scores). Naturally, the psychologist advancing this view believes that if all factors could be measured reliably, and hence predictions of a person's behavior were perfect, there would be no such thing as agency. This explanation hinges on a confusion between a theory (of agency, etc.) and a method (of measurement, etc.). Free will is not unpredictability, since it refers to a willful effort to attain some end. The "freedom" aspect has to do with the psychological capacity to set the grounds for the sake of which (psychic) determinism will ensue. A highly predictable course of action may therefore reflect free will, as in certain religious practices that are formulated after considerable introspection (self-reflexivity) and decision making and then clung to rigidly (predictably) forever after.

Another explanation, this one advanced by mediational theorists, is that free will involves the number of mediating alternatives open to the organism. The more alternatives encompassed in such mediators, the freer the person is to behave. But is a dog who has been trained to perform five tricks freer than a dog trained to perform only three tricks? Obviously, such explanations focus on the contents of the process rather than on the process per se (see Bandura, 1986, p. 42). Theorists of this persuasion are also prone to confuse sociopolitical freedom with agency. For example, if a society affords many freedoms to its members, its members are thought to have "more agency" than citizens in a repressive society. This is like saying that if a person goes on a diet, thereby limiting his or her dining alternatives, agency reduces along with the weight loss.

Actually, from the strictly psychological point of view, it makes no difference whether people have many or few alternatives open to them in a society. Taking liberties away does not affect the psychological process underwriting agency. Even the prisoner has the same free will process as the free person. The challenge is to explain freedom in terms of this process rather than to conduct an inventory of the contents being carried along by some unknown or misunderstood (and probably mechanical) process. Psychologists who theorize in this vein also view agency as an illusion (Immergluck, 1964). Sometimes the illusion is even said to be useful because it strengthens the human's self-image as an influencer of events (see Lefcourt, 1973).

In fact, the emphasis on what freedom means may be entirely misplaced when we think of free will as the number of mediating alternatives open to the person. For example, when Skinner (1948, 1961) designed his cultural milieu, he thought he could build the illusion of free will into a society by increasing the number of preshaped alternatives open to people's behavior. This increased number of ways in which to behave ensured that people would feel freer to behave. What is overlooked here is that the real source of freedom may lie not in the affirmative capacity to choose from among alternatives but in the capacity to negate what is there for the choosing, no matter how many alternatives are involved. Negation can be expressed even when there is only one alternative open to the person. Could this be the ultimate basis of personal freedom? The LLT answer here is yes, indeed.

An interesting variation on the mediational model is the claim by some psychologists that free will refers to when on the passing time dimension that mediating influences really determine behavior. For example, suppose a person as a youth has learned to goof off on the job and then later in life is under pressure from fellow workers to get a job done; if this goofing off continues despite such interpersonal pressure, then this resistance reflects the goof-off's free will (see Hebb, 1974, p. 75). There is obviously an appreciation here that agency is frequently manifested in situations where pressure is ignored or countered (negated). In this treatment it is not that the person can intrinsically reason to the opposite of such pressure, as LLT contends in its telosponse concept, but that early inputs are "negating" later inputs without intention, as a kind of mechanical primacy effect. Logical learning theory holds that the person could counter the early training to goof off as well as the later pressure to work.

Probably the most common treatment of free will in a mediational model is the suggestion that, as the sequence of cause-mediation-effect is being carried out across time (see Figure 1), it is possible to delay this process at some point and thereby throw one's weight "this way" or "that way" in the succession of efficiently caused events. This hanging-fire or suspended action explanation was first advanced by John Locke (1690/1952, p. 190). It has been expressed in psychology as the capacity to delay the flow of stimulus to response (see May, 1977, p. 7). Although we are now considering process rather than content, neither Locke nor those psychologists who follow his lead today have explained on what basis the mediating process can hesitate or suspend action in the first place. Actually, it cannot do so based strictly on the Lockean model, because, as I noted in chapter 1, Lockean reflectivity is not a true reflexivity, in which there is an intrinsic capacity to ponder and affirm alternatives in contradiction to what sensory input is conveying.

Because Lockean formulations of cognition lack notions of a transcending self-reflexivity, it is difficult if not impossible to explain agency using them. A self-reflexive mind can redirect the course of action through an intrinsic examination of the meanings under formulation or halt things completely by negating what is taking place. The Lockean, mediating mind is limited to what it can receive through the senses or reflectively observe taking place in the mental operations "over there." It cannot turn the "is" into the "is not," or vice versa, but must wait on sensations and reflections to accomplish this reversal. Any agential decision would therefore be the "effect" of an externally initiated "cause." Usually, such mediational theorizing on agency involves suggesting that older mediators—previously input and now stored as potential sources of influence—efficiently cause a hesitation sans intention. In more extreme cases, a homunculus is sneaked into the account to place a check on events and choose the direction that thought will take.

On the Kantian formulation, we do have the possibility of a delay occurring. In telosponsivity the person is always taking a position on upcoming life, and quite often this logical process may be undecided as a vacillation occurs between what I schematized in Figure 14 as meanings B and not-B. This vacillation can be clocked by an independent measure of time's passage, but this does not mean that a unilinear, efficient-cause process is being tracked as it unfolds mechanically. Logical affirmation, the taking of a position, may and often does "hang fire" in this sense.

With the advent of cybernetics and the computer model, we have new proposals being advanced to explain free will. These formulations are rapidly finding their way into the psychological literature. In a classic paper, Rosenblueth, Wiener, and Bigelow (1943) tied free will to negative feedback. Feedback is a much abused conception today. Psychologists use it to refer to any kind of interpersonal request (e.g., "Give me your feedback on this, will you?"), but in Wiener's original cybernetic formulation, feedback is of two types. There is a *positive feedback*, which is a fraction of the machine's output returning as input (ibid., p. 19). *Output* is any change produced in the surroundings by a machine; *input* is any event external to the machine that modifies its actions. Feedback can therefore be *negative* when the machine is directed by the margin of error obtaining between its actions and a specific goal (ibid.).

For example, if a missile is aimed at a certain target, it will continually monitor its position relative to this target, from which it can bounce off signals. If the missile strays off course, this negative feedback will be duly recorded and adjustments made in its rocket firings to correct its course. As it does so, positive feedback can also be used to signal that these adjustments are being made in flight. It is on this negative feedback, oriented as it is to a goal (telos) that Rosenblueth et al. base their claims of accounting for agency: "Teleological behavior thus becomes synonymous with behavior controlled by negative feedback, and gains therefore in precision by a sufficiently restricted connotation" (ibid., p. 24).

It is clear that this account is open to the Baconian Criticism, for there is nothing teleological here that makes a difference or adds to our understanding of what is taking place. The missile does not affirm or choose its goal. It does not "know" its purpose to begin with, and it cannot negate its course to the goal either before or after launching. Indeed, if there were no actual goal present against which to bounce signals, there would be no basis on which to claim that the missile is directing its course. But human beings frame and then behave for the sake of goals that do not even exist. We have here an instrumental account of action rather than an intentional one.

There has been a kind of reprise in computer modeling of the free-will explanation that I discussed above as the error variance in predicting human behavior. In this case, however, the suggestion is of a *Physikos* qua *Bios* mechanism of built-in randomness that will ensure behavior's unpredictability. Thus, Dennett (1984) tells us, "Not only can we greatly improve the existential predicament of the robot by installing a radium randomizer or other quantum-effect amplifier, but we can pin our own hopes for free will on the discovery of similar organically based hardware in our brains" (p. 119). This kind of formulation not only mangles several grounds for explanation (Rychlak, 1993), but it completely misses the fact noted above that freely willing organisms can be exceedingly predictable. Kant, for example, was so routine in taking his daily walk that people were said to have set their watches when they saw him leave home each day (Russell, 1959, p. 238). Why could not this routine be intentional, affirmed as a way of life by a freely willing organism? Presumably, according to Dennett, we could speak of Kant's free will only if he were, one day, to leave home ten minutes later than usual.

The final effort to account for free will by way of artificial intelligence (AI) or computer modeling is the most interesting of all, for it tries to capture transcendence and self-reflexivity in the machine process. This explanation draws on *recursivity*, which has to do with various levels of machine processing and also with the repetition of functions within a system's programming. Thus, an algorithmic rule of some sort can be repeatedly used in a program at both greater and lesser levels of complexity. This process of breaking a problem down into subprocesses, solving each part (or "chunk") in turn according to the algorithmic rule, permits the AI theorist to draw a parallel with the human reasoner, who intentionally breaks down a complex problem into more manageable units, solving the less complex aspect before returning to a solution of the whole (see Minsky, 1986, p. 161).

Hofstadter (1980) has probably done more with recursion in his explanation of behavior than any other AI theorist. He begins by drawing our attention to a *strange loop*, which takes place in a hierarchical system so that, in moving upward or downward through the levels of this system, "we unexpectedly find ourselves right back where we started" (p. 10). He also calls this a *tangled hierarchy* and offers the feedback conception as a "simple tangle" (p. 691). Hofstadter's next move is to tie recursion to *nesting*, including such things as stories inside stories, musical passages inside musical passages, and even parenthetical comments inside parenthetical comments (ibid., p. 127).

The strategy is now complete. Machine programs can loop across hierarchical levels of a system, and some of these more complex (strange) loopings or tangled hierarchies can nest certain contents at one level and then return to them at a later time. Indeed, we might say that, looked at from lower to higher levels, a machine process can loop above itself and reach a higher level outside of itself—reaching not outside the entire system but to a larger subsystem. This would be like reversing the direction of recursion. Something in the system jumps out and acts on the system, as if it were outside the system (ibid., p. 691). Would this not be akin to the Kantian transcendence on which LLT bases telosponsivity? Could we not then say that agency is based on the self-reflexivity achieved through recursivity and strange loops, whereby a course of behavior is under intentional direction through transcendent influence or choice? Hofstadter tries to adopt this stance by turning to Gödel's famous proofs. He must do so, actually, because as Lucas (1961) and others have pointed out, there are important implications for the looping phenomenon in the arguments of Gödel.

There are two primary theorems of *Gödel's proof*. The first establishes that any consistent system powerful enough to produce simple arithmetic yields formulas that cannot be proved in the system but that a human intelligence can see to be true. In effect, this theorem states that it is impossible to achieve an axiomatic method in which all true formulas about some area of inquiry will be generated (Nagel & Newman, 1958, p. 6). Gödel's second theorem, which is a corollary of the first, establishes that it is impossible to prove in some consistent systems that the system *is* consistent. The uniqueness of this proof is that it calls for a self-reflexivity in the system. As Lucas (1961) has observed, "The essence of the Gödelian formula is that it is self-referring. It says that 'This formula is unprovable-in-this-system.' When carried over to a machine, the formula is specified in terms which depend on the particular machine in question. The machine is being asked a question about its own processes. We are asking it to be self-conscious, and say what things it can and cannot do" (p. 124).

Right here we have the key to all these mechanistic efforts to account for human agency. They are exclusively extraspective formulations, calling on efficient causation to do a job that only an introspectively framed final causation can accomplish. Machines do not function by way of either generic or delimiting oppositionality; they are *never* dialectical "reasoners." In typical mediational fashion, Hofstadter (1980) ties strange loops to the continuing flow of past inputs, which in this case are language terms: "Where language does create strange loops is when it talks about itself, whether directly or indirectly. Here, something *in* the system jumps out and acts *on* the system, as if it were *outside* the system" (p. 691; emphasis in original). According to Gödel's proof, this transcendent capacity of rising above (outside) the system is not an "as if" phenomenon—it actually takes place. Recursion cannot account for the fact that human cognition can rise above and beyond itself (jump out of the Euler circle) to spot an inconsistency in the systematic processing going on below (inside the circle). A generic oppositionality in the reasoning process is required to do this. Recursion is *always* within the system, which is why Hofstadter needs the "as if" phrasing in the above quote. In fact, even if this jumping outside of the system occurred, it would be like the Lockean reflection, an extraspective looking at the system rather than a transcendent, self-reflexive examination of the premises under affirmation in the system.

A Gödelian perspective from outside or above the system is not a more complex version of this system, as is true of recursion. The Gödelian perspective is a different system, with broader meanings going beyond those of the less complex system. This is reminiscent of the analogy, for although the broader realm has its identities in meaning with the system targeted for assessment, there are also meanings extending beyond such partial tautologies. There are other assumptions that must be framed to assess the truth value of the assumptions grouped within a specific systematic presentation. Indeed, to explain anything is to target it within a context of wider meanings.

In his final summation, Hofstadter suggests that "what we call free will is a result of the interaction between the self-symbol (or subsystem), and the other symbols in the brain" (p. 710). The self-symbol is a higher level symbol—an emergent—that influences from above the mechanical substrate processes of the systems below, in some combination of jumping out as well as recursion. The self monitors not only the growing knowledge of the system but also what is not known. Hence, "from this balance between self-knowledge and self-ignorance comes the feeling of free will" (p. 713). This strikes me as the old homunculus emerging in the bottom-up process and jumping about to monitor inputs as they stack up over time. There is no encouragement here for the teleologist, because Hofstadter's argument, like all the others above, denies the possibility of a truly introspective cognition.

Concluding Comment

We have now covered the essential language of LLT, and I am fully aware that it requires effort on the reader's part to begin thinking in terms of precedent affirmations, sequacious meaning-extensions, tautologized opposites, and transcending self-reflexivities. Experimentally oriented colleagues have been highly critical of placing such demands on them, often suggesting that they can accomplish the same objectives as mine without noticeably altering the professional lexicon in this manner. When I then ask them to frame a final-cause conception using available theoretical terminology, what transpires is invariably along the lines of the previously discussed extraspective attempts to explain free will. The teleology I am after is lost to the mechanism of a mediating efficient causality.

The plain truth is that we cannot capture intentionality through efficient causation. Telosponsivity draws on an introspective teleology, and not one of the suggestions made by countless critics in over 30 years has been so framed. My colleagues want me to rephrase what they already know, a characteristic of human reasoning that I am only too familiar with and rely on in my theorizing. I can appreciate such predicational processing even as I resist this effort to draw me into using bankrupt concepts — bankrupt, that is, as far as teleology is concerned.

The next proper step is to take on the telosponsive process as an assumption, just as traditional psychological explanation incorporates the mechanistic/mediational process. Then, by keeping empirical evidence and theoretical explanation clear and distinct (recall the affirming-the-consequent issue in chapter 1), we can judge how reasonable it is to think of people as telosponders rather than as responders or outputters. How well does the concept of telosponsivity frame (i.e., predicate) the huge body of empirical evidence on human beings in which traditional mediational explanations have been used? In the succeeding chapters of this volume I assess this experimental evidence in light of LLT, expanding on the latter's tenets as we move along. I will review considerable research and sample theoretical positions that present the received (Lockean) views in psychology. Fourteen demonstration experiments will be presented in reasonable detail, providing the reader at crucial points of the exposition with concrete examples of how LLT is tested, as well as how it empirically confronts alternative theoretical views of cognition and behavior.

3

Predication as Context Meaning

The Rise of Formal Causation in the Cognitive Revolution

Logical learning theory began to develop during a period of psychology's history in which a "cognitive revolution" was taking place. Gardner (1985) has pinpointed the onset of this revolution to the summer of 1956, when an institute on computer technology was sponsored by the Rockefeller Foundation at Dartmouth College. One of the leading participants in this gathering was Herbert A. Simon, who has since been given credit for seeing the immense possibilities that the field soon to be called artificial intelligence had for psychology (Dreyfus, 1979, p. 82). The pioneering work of Newell, Shaw, and Simon (1958) on list processing set the stage for psychological theorizing in the information-processing mode, and Simon's student Quillian (1967) drafted the prototypical network model of semantic memory, which encompassed several principles of explanation that are still important working assumptions of such theoretical efforts (e.g., concept representation in nodes, network connections, class storage, and negation as a default marking).

The distinctive feature of the computer is that it encompasses both a program (software) and electrical circuitry (hardware). This permits the psychologist to draw an analogy to the mind-body distinction that has so dominated and even plagued the descriptions of human beings. That is, experimental psychology had, by the mid-20th century, been nurturing a hard-won tradition of disregarding "inside the organism" speculations in favor of "observed behavior." Underwritten by naive realism, positivist empiricism was being practiced to a fault in the psychological laboratories of this period. The leading behaviorist of the time, B. F. Skinner (1950), actually suggested that psychology could do without theories of learning altogether by simply sticking to the observable facts of behavior. Trace what can be seen occurring overtly and do not speculate on the unseen processes supposedly going on inside the black-box organism.

Today, with the rise of cognitive science, a broadly conceived extension of computer theory (information processing, artificial intelligence, etc.) to such fields as psychology, linguistics, anthropology, organic evolution, and sociology, we see descriptions of precisely those unseen processes against which Skinner had railed. This changing description is made necessary by the fact that the initiating source of the computer or information process is the *program*—and a program works from the inside. The engineering process derived from the work of Shannon (1938) and Wiener (1954). Shannon drew a clear distinction between information per se and the machine process that conveys information; one need not have any relation to the other (Shannon & Weaver, 1962, pp. 3, 99). Engineering processing deals in *bits*, or the halving of an informational signal. There is a reduction of uncertainty here, a halving of the possible routes that a signal might take in a network. Following a Boolean logic of either/or, each bit tells us the amount of information needed to select one electrical signal from two that are equally probable. To speak of bits of information in this sense has to do with the control of information flow and not with any intended meanings under elaboration in that flow (Dreyfus, 1979, p. 165).

Wiener (1954) coined the term *cybernetics*, which is based on a Greek root meaning "steersman," for he wanted to convey the fact that a machine with input, output, and especially feedback capacities could direct or control its behavior (recall the discussion in chap. 2 of negative feedback as free will). This control could be accomplished through linguistic communication, as well as through other forms of control (ibid., p. 16). Language in turn demands that we consider both syntax and semantics. The concept of information processing now rises to a new level of complexity and frequently confusion, because linguistic information does involve meaning, and nowhere is meaning more important than in the program under processing. The circuitry remains constant, following out its hard disjunctions of "either/or, but not both" at the network's electrical gates, but the program's patterning conveys distinctively different meanings across this uniform Boolean pathway. How do we understand such differences in the meaning under processing?

Many psychologists believe that this issue of differences in meaningful expression has been sidestepped because of the current stress on the information process per se rather than on the specific meanings being conveyed by such information flow. The rise of information-processing models has paralleled the decline of learning theory, which is where we might find considerations of how it is that human beings come to express different meanings in their ongoing behavior. In a strangely indirect fashion, there has been a dramatic shift in the type of causation on which psychologists rest their explanatory cases, from the earlier efficient-cause basis of stimulus-response psychology to the current formal-cause basis of cognitive science.

When the founder of behaviorism, John Watson (1924), asked his psy-

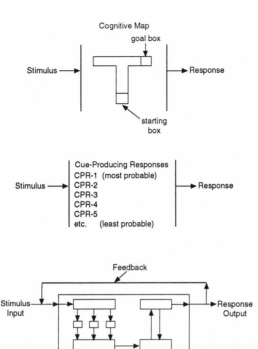

Figure 15 Typical mediation models

chologist-colleagues to "*try to think of man as an assembled organic machine ready to run*" (p. 216; emphasis in the original), he was focusing on the efficient-cause aspects of shaping this machine's potentials. The machine concept encompasses material causation in its substances (pulleys, gears, etc.), but we focus on the unique feature of efficient-cause manipulation in getting it to run and directing it. There is no possibility here for a final-cause directionality (with its formal-cause "that" acting as patterned purpose). This is why we occasionally find the behaviorist sneaking a homunculus in to steer the organic machine. When Tolman (1932/1967) later introduced the formal-cause notion of the cognitive map, he continued the efficient-cause emphasis by suggesting that this map worked as an intervening variable (pp. 2, 414). The intervening variable is an efficiently caused past response that is currently slotted between a presently occurring stimulus and its response. Hull (1937) expanded and perfected such mediational modeling. Figure 15 presents a schematization of three such mediation models.

Tolman's model is at the top of Figure 15, where a T-maze is depicted as the intervening variable (i.e., a cognitive map that had been previously input by

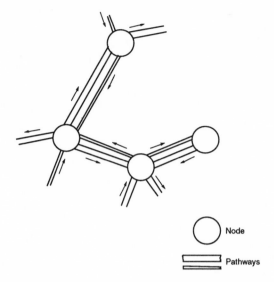

Figure 16   Network model

the rat's response to the external realm). Below it comes a Hullian model as adapted by Dollard & Miller (1950); here, the intervening variables are cue-producing responses, which are previous responses acting later as cues. These cues might be words previously learned as responses ("eat, food, thirsty," etc.) and subsequently used to mediate ongoing stimulus-response cognition and behavior. At the bottom of Figure 15 we have a computer model, which has the essential layout of mediation from input through various processors and memory storage units to output, but also there is the addition of the feed-back mechanism that I discussed in chapter 2. Figure 16 presents a different form of schematization in computer modeling—that is, a network model.

Network models vary, but in Figure 16 we have a fairly common variety in which various *nodes* are connected by *pathways* (after Wyer & Carlston, 1979). The pathway is in all essentials identical to what stimulus-response psychology called associated connections or bonds. The model depicted in Figure 16 has two pathways between each node. The thicker pathway signi-fies that the connection going in one direction (note the arrows) is stronger than the other, which is termed an asymmetrical associative pathway (Rosch, 1973a). For example, we know that in a sample of college-student subjects, the word *hand* is more likely to suggest the word *foot* in a word-association test than *foot* is to suggest *hand* (Palermo & Jenkins, 1964, pp. 119, 136). If this connection were represented in Figure 16, the disparity in association strength would be depicted as the pathway leading from the "hand" node to the "foot" node being thicker than the pathway leading in the opposite direction. In typical nodal network models the *activation* of the network is thought of as occurring in quasi-electrical fashion. Meanings are united not through a logical arrangement like predication but through the energization of some kind of mechanico-electrical signal analogous to the current running through a computer's hardware. A node is said to be active when the amount of electrical signals arriving at its location is above some threshold value. The pathways in network models are frequently named for some functional relationship between nodes; for example, a pathway might signify "has" so that it can connect the nodes "bird" and "wings" to convey "A bird has wings." I will return to nodal networking when I take up the nature of cognitive processing in chapter 4.

The formal cause qua *intervening variable* is always an effect, that is, a pattern that has been shaped into existence and then input via past efficient causation in the organism's life history. Thus, traditional behavioral explanations of learning did not rest on the formal-cause pattern that a mediator took on. The mediator (cognitive map or cue-producing response) was merely an instrumentality in the ongoing process, shaped—in the bottom-up fashion of the Lockean model—by earlier efficient causation into the form it came later to have. If we were to carry this style of explanation over to the computer process, we would say that the program as a quasi-cognitive map (formal cause) is itself shaped by an even earlier process (of efficient causation). In short, the intervening variable is a content in a process, and it is up to psychology to describe the presumably underlying quasi-engineering process. To stop with the program as an explanation of the process would not satisfy traditional learning explanations, yet this is what many critics of cognitive science believe has taken place. That is, what we witness in the so-called cognitive revolution of psychology is a willingness on the part of most theoreticians to rest their explanatory case with what are clearly formal-cause conceptions. If this is true, it favors LLT, because the *Logos* is readily seen as a ground for such program formulation.

The framing program that guides computing qua information processing has been recast theoretically into a plethora of conceptions, including the following: *plan* (Miller, Galanter, & Pribram, 1960), *schema* (Ruble & Stangor, 1986), *causal attribution* (Kelley, 1973), *concept feature* (Smith, Shoben, & Rips, 1974), *script* (Schank & Abelson, 1977), *category/prototype* (Rosch, 1978), *mental model* (Gentner & Stevens, 1983), *frame* (Minsky, 1986), *strategy* (Cantor, 1990), *heuristic* (Gigerenzer, 1991), and so forth. When a theoretician did consider how it is that such formal-cause patterns are brought into the computing process, the explanation drew predominantly on the frequency-repetition-contiguity rationales of traditional learning theories (e.g., Rumelhart & Norman, 1981; Johnston & Dark, 1986, p. 47). Another important influence here was Hebb's (1949) *cell-assembly theory*, a Lockean (*Bios*) formulation that attempted to show, by way of these traditional rationales, how cerebral neurons are grouped into stable patterns.

It is therefore possible to question just how revolutionary the cognitive revolution is compared to the theorizing envisioned by Tolman and Hull. It is probably fair to say that modern cognitive theorizing has placed formal causation closer to the role of a basic explanation than Tolman, and especially Hull, had suggested. This development concurs with the point in chapter 1 concerning the shift in natural science from the efficient to the formal cause as basic to all physical explanation. I find it interesting that Bartlett's (1932) notion of the *schema* is often cited in cognitive textbooks as a precursor of the conceptions listed above (see, e.g., Anderson, 1985, pp. 181, 182; Eysenck & Keane, 1990, p. 275). Bartlett was interested in demonstrating the role that cultural expectations play in memory when people hear a story beyond the purview of their culturally influenced predications. People distorted the story content to conform to their culturally biased understanding.

Lippmann (1946) used the word *stereotype* in modern times to describe other forms of cultural distortion. Analogizing from the newspaper printer's page layout, which is often blocked out using routine stories or advertisements, so that it has a certain prearranged form even before the major story of the day is slipped in, Lippmann observed that people carry about in their mind's eye various stereotypes that frame their attitudes toward public issues or toward other people. It is easier to shuffle such stereotypes about mentally than to think through the nuances and accomodate for the multiplicities of social issues and public policies.

Initially, therefore, schemas and stereotypes were thought of as conceptual expectations that lead to some level of error in people's thought—a distorted, poorly understood, flatly incorrect, or simplistic formulation of what is perceived and remembered. Attitude research has probably focused on this more negative side of things. Thus, today we are likely to read that a stereotype refers to "those interpersonal beliefs and expectancies that are both widely shared and generally invalid" (Miller & Turnbull, 1986, p. 233). The array of concepts referred to above, however, does not merely point to invalid beliefs or inappropriate cultural expectancies. Rather, it underscores the fact that pattern plays a central role in human cognition. We really cannot explain human behavior unless we recognize this fact. From the view of LLT, the rise of cognitive science in recent times signifies the emergence of formal-cause explanation as paramount in psychology, unlike the earlier days when efficient causation held sway.

What does this say about the cognitive process under study? Are these formal-cause concepts produced by this process, or are they merely various contents shaped externally and then entered into the entirely separate cognitive process? We are now, of course, at the very heart of the predication/ mediation distinction in theoretical modeling. Logical learning theory has some things to say about such issues, and I next turn to a discussion of psychology's growing string of formal-cause conceptions.

Is Context Essentially a Process or a Content?

The formal-cause concepts reviewed in the previous section are all concerned with what is usually termed cognitive *representation* in computer/network models. Medin (1989) has opined that "concept representation remains as a cornerstone issue in all aspects of cognitive science" (p. 1469). This has resulted in a vigorous study by psychologists of how people employ their cognitive representations—now referred to collectively as *classes* or *categories* (Hunt, 1989, p. 620). The LLT position is that all such representations result from a predicational process (recall that *katēgorein* is from the Greek, meaning "to predicate"). It would be instructive to examine a few of these areas of investigation from the perspective of LLT.

The first point to draw an LLT advocate's interest concerns a frequently overlooked process/content issue in research on categories. Whereas in LLT *all* such patterned conceptions in cognition are to be viewed as predicates, framed by the process of predication and now standing as contents with different names (scripts, plans, etc.), the typical researcher today studies the category as a content and devotes little time assessing the implications of this evidence for the process, which is presumed to be mediational. Even though the evidence seems to point to predicational processing, the major preoccupation of these investigators involves a detailed examination of content differences. Schneider (1991) has actually noted the fact that in modern cognitive theories the "process is general and fundamental . . . [and] is detached from any particular content" (p. 531). This assumption is what sustains mediational theorizing, for the goal now becomes to study the structural differences of categories rather than the process that forms them. The possibility that accruing evidence is relevant to categorization (process) and not strictly to the categories (contents) is rarely entertained. When it is, the typical maneuver is to speak of a multiple number of mediating processes rather than to challenge the Lockean efficient causation on which everything hinges.

In LLT, on the other hand, there is a recognition that the word *predicate* has relevant meaning as both a verb and a noun; the former meaning is "to affirm or deny" (process), and the latter meaning is "that which is affirmed or denied" (content). Hence, when we study a patterned concept like a "script," we are studying both the scripting (verb or process) and the resultant script (noun or content). Evidence for one necessarily involves evidence for the other. Indeed, as far as LLT is concerned, the predicate meaning used to frame a target in the process of predication always frames a context meaning. The predicate meaning is the wider context lending its significance to the target. Thus, in the "John is reliable" sentence analyzed in Figure 2, we have the predicate "reliable" (reliability, reliable people, etc.) establishing a context within which we then target "John." This context can be pristine or compounded, depending on the particular meanings under affirmation in the telosponsive process. Several predicates (qua contents) can be used to frame (qua process) the same target. The patterned concepts of the previous section (schemes, prototypes, plans, etc.) are different predicate-contents of this sort rather than different predicating processes. This is clear from how the theorists concerned make use of them.

For example, Schank and Abelson's (1977, p. 42) "restaurant script" stipulates a routine series of actions that will be carried out as the person enacts it, but the script is never described as a framing process per se. The script is gradually shaped into existence by external influences that are continually being input and cognitively processed. In contrast to this mediational view, LLT suggests that the script, like all such predicates (noun usage), has been gradually ordered into existence by the process of predication (verb usage) that I have named telosponsivity. The process in this case creates the script. This process has not simply input these meanings already patterned by frequent (efficiently caused) encounters with restaurants in the past (ibid., p. 37). The past experience occurred, of course, but it was framed into experiential relevance by the telosponder at the time. There would be no script in the present without the creating, formal/final-cause process of telosponsivity functioning in the past. Indeed, according to LLT, the past is also continually under predication (and repredication). Humans frame their experience both forward and backward in time. *Time* is itself a formal-cause conception taken on and behaved "for the sake of," because it lends order to ongoing events (Slife, 1993).

There are intimations of a dawning awareness that evidence accruing in the study of categories may have relevance for process as well as content. The empirical work on prototype theory is a good example of this possibility. It was Eleanor Rosch who more than anyone gave this area of study its major impetus. A *prototype* refers to certain members of a category that best represent—are "best examples" of—the meaning conveyed by the category in question: "Prototype members are usually those which share the most common elements with other members of a category, and the least with members of other categories" (Erickson & Jones, 1978, p. 79). For example, when subjects rated the extent to which certain members of a category like "bird" actually represented this meaning, Rosch (1973a & b) found that robin, sparrow, bluebird, and canary were rated high in the category evaluations and chicken, turkey, ostrich, and penguin were rated low. Note that we are considering meaning now. Engineering is not involved. Although there is a common meaning shared by members (contents) of the category "bird," only some of these members capture this meaning.

It is not easy to identify the precise meaning of a category (or its prototype). Experimental subjects not only disagree with one another concerning category membership but also contradict themselves when asked about membership on different occasions (Bellezza, 1984; McCloskey & Glucksberg, 1978). Because of this unreliability, parallels have been drawn between prototypes and Wittgenstein's concept of a *family resemblance*. Wittgenstein (1968) first pointed out that, for example, various games (board games, card games, ball games, etc.) have similarities but also significant differences. There is a "fuzziness" in the meaning of words like *game* which is not limited to language. There are also undefined (fuzzy) aspects of certain mathematical concepts (sets, etc.; see Schmucker, 1984). According to LLT, there is always some lack of precision or completeness in a predicating meaning because of the wider range of this meaning that the predicate assumes, including the opposite implications of what is being affirmed. The family resemblance phenomenon is entirely in line with this predicational process. We cannot hope to understand this interesting capacity of human beings to conceptualize their experience broadly by limiting our study to the structural differences among categories qua contents.

Fortunately, we can sort experiments into those that are strictly tied to content differences and those that reflect the previously mentioned dawning intuition that something more fundamental may be called for in the description of the process. For example, Armstrong, Gleitman, and Gleitman (1983) demonstrated that people could produce reliable prototypical ratings for objects in classes that did not admit of degrees of membership, such as odd numbers (which follow a hard disjunction in that they are either odd or even). This is obviously a study involving the content of the category, no matter how it is processed into existence (via input and mediation or via predication). Although LLT does not distinguish between a category and a context—viewing these as simply different aspects of the meaning encompassed in predication—Roth and Shoben (1983) have conducted studies on this assumption. Expressing their findings in line with Rosch's work on the category "bird," Roth and Shoben demonstrated that if we were to take the lowly rated "chicken" exemplar and place it in a barnyard context, the degree to which it is taken as typifying "bird" would rise dramatically.

The LLT explanation here is that the meaning under predication (context) is different when we compare birds to birds than when we compare our feathered friends to other animals in a barnyard. This is not a question of context versus no context. There is no need to distinguish between the category and the context, because the one is always tied to the other in telosponsive meaning-extension ("bird vs. other birds" or "birds vs. other animals"). As a telosponder, the human being always targets certain meanings in terms of grounding contexts — that is, broader predicating meanings. The trick is to understand this grounding meaning as framed introspectively by the person concerned.

Of those whose work has implications for the process itself, Barsalou (1983) first distinguished between natural categories like "fruit" and ad hoc categories like "ways to make friends." Both forms of categorization were found to have prototypical or "best" examples. Barsalou argued that people frame such ad hoc categories to achieve a goal. I take this as evidence in support of a process — that of framing meanings that serve a purpose — rather than of just a "structural" difference in the resultant categories (the typicality of their contents, etc.). Murphy and Medin (1985) have taken a similar path to suggest that the relation between a concept and an example is comparable to the relation between theory and data. Categories or concepts are organized by a theory of what experience is supposed to be like. For example, Medin and Shoben (1988) found that the phrases *white hair* and *gray hair* were judged to be more similar than *gray hair* and *black hair*, but the phrases *white clouds* and *gray clouds* were judged as less similar than *gray clouds* and *black clouds*. The interpretation here is that white and gray hair are developmentally linked by a theory of aging, whereas white and gray clouds are related by a theory of weather forecasting. This explanation is highly compatible with LLT, where no line is drawn between theorizing and thinking. Both cognitive activities involve telosponsivity — that is, the taking on of precedent assumptions (theories) for the sake of which a purpose or an end (goal, etc.) is intended.

In fact, one could now readily enter into an analysis of language representation, for, as Lakoff (1987) has noted, "Every time we see something it is as a *kind* of thing, for example, a tree, we are categorizing. Whenever we reason about *kinds* of things — chairs, nations, illnesses, emotions, any kind of thing at all — we are employing categories. . . . And any time we either produce or understand any utterance of any reasonable length, we are employing dozens if not hundreds of categories" (pp. 5, 6). Note the winding of both content and process into this rich observation. Lakoff points to another area of study I will look at below when he says that people "attribute" real existence to their categories of experience (p. 9). Lakoff also astutely observes that "prototype effects, in themselves, do not provide any specific alternative theory of mental representation" (p. 42). Indeed, he quotes Rosch as saying the same thing—that "prototypes themselves do not constitute any particular model of processes, representations, or learning" (p. 44). This leaves the door open for LLT, which is an account of how something like a category or prototype might come about in human learning.

Incidentally, I have noticed a trend in descriptions of how categories arise: theorists like Lakoff use—sometimes quite informally—the term *construction* to explain how categories are framed as theoretical assumptions made in the act of cognition (this is reminiscent of Barsalou, 1983, and Medin & Shoben, 1988). Unfortunately, construction as a theoretical concept readily confounds Lockean with Kantian modeling. I will look carefully at this concept in chapter 4, so for the present I will simply call attention to this trend of speaking about categories or classes as being constructed (see Lakoff, 1987, p. 45).

Are Attributions Mediating Inputs or Predicating Premises?

In an important series of experiments, Jones and Nisbett (1971) found that actors in situations tend to list the factors in the circumstances facing them as the causes of their actions. However, observers are likely to assign the cause of the actions to the actors' stable personality traits or habitual dispositions to act in a certain way, regardless of situational circumstances. Kelley (1972) then underwrote this work by introducing the theoretical concept of causal schemata, which he said subjects use to organize the formal relations among causes and effects in perceived experience. This line of investigation was also influenced to some extent by the then current debate in personality theory, initiated by Mischel (1968), over the comparative roles of "situation variables" (circumstances) and "person variables" (traits) in the prediction of behavior. The fascinating thing about Jones and Nisbett's findings was that what they called the *causal attributions* of actors and observers could be reversed by having an observer look at things on videotape from the viewpoint of the actor, and vice versa (see also Arkin & Duval, 1975; Storms, 1973). The area of study emerging from this early work was called *attribution theory*, and I would like to discuss it as another example of how context and categorization are involved in human cognition. Also, I want to point out how consistent the findings in this realm are with the tenets of LLT. Of course, attribution theorists have not budged from mediation modeling.

According to LLT, to understand the disparity between actor and observer, we must capture the meaning being predicated by these independent contributors to what we might now term the "categorization" of ongoing events. We must understand the perspective from which these contributors are theorizing (categorizing) about what is taking place. Continuing the analysis of the previous section, we can frame this as a question of the context from which observers and actors extend meaning. The actor is in the situation, looking at the fact pattern of the circumstances and behaving for the sake of what is under premising. There is a sense of personal identity in this premised outlook—what I have to do given that certain factors in the situation confront me. This is an introspective theoretical perspective. The observer, on the other hand, viewing things extraspectively, finds it reasonable to premise the actor's behavior in third-person terms. The person qua actor "over there" is not telosponding but responding to past habitual shapings or perhaps from inherited traits.

Buss (1978) was to call the actor's formulation a "reason" and the observer's formulation a "causal" description, but this distinction merely adds to the confusion of terminology in psychology. As I noted in chapter 1, a reason is clearly a formal-final cause. It is ironic that we have an entire area of research on causal attribution but almost no appreciation for the fact that such things as attributions must necessarily draw on telic meanings, which translate into formal-final causation. The word *attribution* takes its Latin roots from "to bestow," and hence it seems to be highly compatible with the concept of telosponsivity. Meaning that follows from premises is clearly bestowed. In LLT we call this bestowal meaning-extension.

Although the subjects in the Jones and Nisbett experiments framed different causal explanations of the events taking place, the LLT position is that these divergent views were contrasting contents framed by the *same* "bestowing" process (i.e., telosponsivity) going on in the separate cognitions of the actors and the observers. This process is intrinsically capable of generating differences in its contents. Indeed, it can turn content meanings into their opposites or reject them altogether. We might frame the issue now under consideration in terms of the following question: Where does attribution predominantly occur, in the process of attributing causal influence to experience or in the specific content meanings (attributes) so assigned? As I already suggested in the previous section, LLT stresses the role of the process over the content because the former always produces the latter. Traditional attribution theorists put their emphasis on the contents, for it is here that their differences are thought to arise. The mediating process does not create these differences; it simply employs them, combines them mathematically, and follows what they indicate programmatically.

In a widely cited paper on attribution theory, Kelley (1973) relied on information-processing theory to make the following claim: "It must be emphasized . . . that attribution theory deals only with the processes by which attributions are derived from informational input" (p. 126). If an attribution takes its organization from informational input, we do not have a bestowing but a receiving taking place. In telosponsivity, the person is always bestowing meaning because a position is continually being taken, a premise is under affirmation, and meaning is extending thereby to enrich ongoing experience. Attribution theorists, on the other hand, are prepared to say that the person is not *always* attributing in the cognitive process (Jones, 1972, p. xii). It all depends on the mediating cues that have been previously input in the information-processing system. If these cues are of a certain type, then attributions will be forthcoming; if not, then no attributions take place.

A routine finding in the attribution literature having special significance for LLT is that subjects are more likely to offer causal attributions for unanticipated occurrences than for anticipated ones (Lau & Russell, 1980; Pyszczynski & Greenberg, 1981; Wong & Weiner, 1981). If we can draw a parallel between the unexpected and the less well known, then there is the suggestion here that the principle of meaning-extension may be involved. The attribution/predication more readily extends to what *is not* well known than what *is* well known in the relevant circumstances.

Many causal attributions are clearly teleological in nature—intentions, purposes, and the like—yet attribution theorists categorize all such formulations as information concerning plans and goals that is input and stored in long-term memory (see Black & Bower, 1980; Graesser, Robertson, Lovelace, & Swinehart, 1980). Causal reasoning is said to be elicited rather than premised (Hastie, 1984, p. 44). Indeed, a caution has been voiced in this literature concerning the *fundamental attribution error,* which is the tendency to overestimate the contribution made by the actor (where agency might reside) and underestimate significant situational determinants (Ross, 1978). Situational control is, in LLT terms, control that is initiated externally and subsequently input to move the person along in mediated fashion. Critics have questioned whether there actually is such an error in attribution, relying on a sophisticated analysis of the predications affirmed by subjects (via experimental instructions) in these attribution experiments (Hamilton, 1980; Harvey, Town, & Yarkin, 1981; Funder, 1982). This is the line of criticism that LLT takes, since what is or is not an attribution error depends on the experimenter, who ultimately sorts such determinants into situational or actor variables.

Demonstration Experiment 1 : The "Predication Effect"

A challenge for LLT is to demonstrate empirically that something like a predication effect actually takes place. This is not easily managed through an experimental (independent-variable) manipulation, because it can never be a question of "predication versus no predication" when telosponsivity is under study. The person continually extends some kind of meaning in the experimental context. The Wurzburgers formalized this meaning affirmation as an *Einstellung*, or *set*, that was based on the *Aufgabe*, or experimental (task) instructions (Boring, 1950, p. 404). It is impossible to avoid some kind of predication taking place in a research context, where the subject must make sense of the proceedings based on what the experimenter says (*Aufgabe*) plus the subject's own surmisals. I decided that the "taking a position" aspect of telosponsivity in framing the *Einstellung* might provide a means for demonstrating a predication effect.

A simple sentence reflects both a content (words) and a process (resulting in a syntactical alignment). In chapter 2 I used the example of "A tree is like a person" or "A person is like a tree" to make this point. In both instances, the right-lying noun provides the predicating (context) meaning for the left-lying noun. Admittedly, the symbolic system known as English permits other syntactical alignments, but for my present purposes I can use this pattern to design an experiment. Clearly, the syntactical arrangement does not create the predication. Which arrangement is the correct or best one? Obviously, no such decision is possible, for it is up to the thinker, the user of words like *tree* and *person*, to make this selection depending on what he or she intends to convey—the purpose, reason, or end (telos) being sought in the position taken and expressed linguistically.

It may be possible to show how such position taking (*Einstellung*) influences independent ratings of the words used in the sentence. For example, assume that we administer the words *satisfaction* and *understanding* to a person. These words are to be dealt with on two separate tasks. The subjects will assess the relative significance these word meanings hold for them and rate them on a scale. Which word is more significant? Because, as Lakoff has taught us, words represent categorizations, we are also asking the person which category is more significant. The other task confronting the person involves placing these two words in an incomplete sentence, as follows:

_____ is stronger than _____ .

In an evaluative sentence of this type, we must consider the verb and adjective relating the subject word to what I will term the object word. The basic meaning that the verb relates in the preceding sentence requires that the more significant of the two words will be placed in the target (subject word) location, lying to the left. The less significant meaning must establish a predicating context that is weaker than the meaning represented by the more significant word. I assume, with some empirical justification from work like that of Osgood (1952), that a word judged to be significant will be considered stronger in meaningfulness than its counterpart. Now consider what would happen if we frame the incomplete sentence as follows:

_____ is weaker than _____ .

In this case, we would expect the person to place the more significant word meaning into the sentence's object slot. Here, the verb and adjective relation requires that the predicate context of strength be established, calling for the use of the more significant word. The subject word still represents the point of the sentence, but the meaning being expressed concerning this target is a detraction. The meaning of the sentence has flip-flopped because of the oppositionality of the verb and adjective employed.

The following question arises: Is the significance of word meanings like this carried entirely "within" the words (as a marker of some sort), or can the task of having to take a position during the completion of an evaluative sentence actually create or significantly influence the comparative word evaluations? Because the relational estimate is a cognitive process, and LLT places its emphasis on the conceptualizing (bestowing, attributing, categorizing) power of this process, we should expect to find a clearer difference between word estimations if they follow sentence completion than if they precede it. Since a position must definitively be taken in completing a sentence, this cognitive action should have an effect on the relative estimations of the words that would not be found if the words were judged for comparative significance *before* a sentence is completed. The basic strategy in this experiment was therefore to have people make ratings of the significance of two words either before or after taking a position in sentence completions of the type just presented.

Hypotheses

1. When college students complete sentences with two nouns, they will place the noun they judged as more significant in the *subject* location of a sentence in which the verb frames a positive relative evaluation between the words and in the *object* location of a sentence in which the verb frames a negative relative evaluation between the words.

2. The differences predicted by hypothesis 1 will be larger when the students take a position by completing the sentences *before* they make their judgments of the two nouns' relative significance than it will be when they do not.

Rationale

There have already been intimations of a predication effect in the research literature. Probably the most prevalent suggestion along this line is the finding that subjects judge similes more positively and remember them better if they have an alignment of the sort "A pliers is like a crab" rather than the less meaningful "A bumper is like a statue" (Katz, 1982; McCabe, 1982; Stein, 1977). The pincerlike quality of a crab's claw can be tautologized to the pliers in a fuzzy yet meaningful way, but what meaning is there to extend from a predicating bumper to a statue? We can probably squeeze something out here—statues can absorb a bump. Indeed, sometimes there are highly subjective formulations of this erratic sort that make sense to the person framing the simile. For example, an artist might stand a bumper on end and call it a statue. Nonetheless, it is easy to see why the statue-bumper relation is not meaningful (well-patterned) and hence is readily forgotten (see chap. 5 for an extensive review of such considerations in learning and memory).

The experiment closest to the demonstration study under presentation was conducted by Rosch (1975). She presented sentences for completion of the following type: _____ is essentially _____ .

The relation here is termed a "hedge," which modifies the predicate location according to what Lakoff (1972) considered was the "metaphorical distance" between items that we might place in the blanks. Other hedges used were *basically, roughly, almost,* and *sort of.* What Rosch was studying here was the symmetry or asymmetry of comparisons between members of a category. Her expectation was that if two members of a category, neither of which was a prototype ("best example"), were presented, the subjects would show no preference regarding their placement in the sentence blanks. The placement would be symmetrical (i.e., likely to go in either order). For example, for numbers within the decimal system, multiples of 10 have been shown to be better reference points for the category "number" (i.e., they are prototypical numbers) than other numbers. So, if people are asked to put 862 and 866 in the above blanks, it will not really matter which number goes into which blank. The placement is expected to be symmetrical.

On the other hand, if we have people place the numbers 996 and 1000 in the above blanks, the placement is expected to be asymmetrical—which means that the number that is a multiple of 10 will appear in the right-hand blank (termed the "reference slot"). This is what Rosch predicted, and it is what she found. This asymmetry of blank placement held even if a person was placing two colors in the blanks, one of which was more prototypical of red than the other. The best example of red was most often placed in the right-hand blank.

Exactly why the asymmetry should align in this manner is not made clear, except that the meaning of the sentence follows here what Rosch (1975) called the "logic of natural language" (p. 533), as discussed by Lakoff (1972). From the point of view of LLT, however, the placement is readily understood. The right-hand blank is the predicational location in English syntax, which therefore means it acts as the that for the sake of which the target is understood (framed, bestowed meaning, etc.). If there is a best example of colors or numbers, then we would expect this meaning to be situated in the predicate location when the hedge directs the meaning from something less than ideal to something that is an ideal of the category in question. I therefore consider this earlier study by Rosch to be a precedent for the present demonstration experiment.

Experimental Sample

One hundred and sixty college students, evenly divided by sex, were recruited as subjects. They received course credit for their participation.

Procedure

Two paper-and-pencil instruments were assembled for this research, the *Sentence Completion Scale* (scs) and the *Word Significance Scale* (wss). Each of these scales was constructed around 12 nouns, combined into the following six pairs: confidence-knowledge, suspicion-insincerity, satisfaction-understanding, anxiety-pain, respect-honesty, and forgetfulness-disinterest. These words were selected from a pretest group of 50 words that were submitted to roughly 100 college students, who circled words that they believed held significant meaning for them. Note that three of the pairs are positive in meaning and three are negative. All the words used were circled by at least one-third of the pretest group.

On the wss, students were presented pairs of nouns and asked to circle the noun that they considered to be the more significant of the two meanings. Order of the nouns on the wss was varied so that position bias could not influence the ratings. On the scs, students were presented six incomplete sentences in which the verb stipulated either a positive relative evaluation or a negative relative evaluation, as follows:

Positive Relative Evaluation

_____ can hasten _____ .
_____ rises above _____ .
_____ can go beyond _____ .
_____ is stronger than _____ .
_____ is better than _____ .
_____ can add to _____ .

Negative Relative Evaluation

   _____ can delay _____ .
   _____ sinks below _____ .
   _____ falls short of _____ .
   _____ is weaker than _____ .
   _____ is worse than _____ .
   _____ can subtract from _____ .

Note the oppositionality of the various verb relations in the incomplete sentences. The six word pairs of the wss were presented in random order to the students when they took the scs (to counter position bias), and the task here was simply to place the words in what they took to be the appropriate blanks. The students were tested in groups of 10. Half the students ($n = 80$) were given the wss first, and half ($n = 80$) were given the scs first. Within each of these ordering conditions, half the students were administered the positive verb relation and half were administered the negative verb relation. Also, half the subjects in each of these sample divisions were males and half were females.

Results

The dependent variable of this experiment was termed a *match score*, which could theoretically vary between the value of 0 and 6. This score reflects the number of times that a student circled a word on the wss and also placed this word in the subject location of the sentence on the scs. Hence, higher scores mean that significant words are being placed in the subject location of the sentences; lower scores mean that significant words are being placed in the object location of the sentences. The match scores actually varied their full range in the data collection, from a low of 0 (all object completions) to a high of 6 (all subject completions).

The match scores were entered into a factorial analysis of variance having the characteristics of a 2 (Sex) × 2 (wss First vs. scs First) × 2 (Positive vs. Negative Verb Relation). All these variables are between subjects. No sex differences emerged in the analysis. Hypothesis 1 can be tested in the main effect for verb relation, which was as follows: verb framing a positive relative evaluation, Mean (M) = 3.95, Standard Deviation (SD) = 0.99; verb framing a negative relative evaluation, $M = 2.38$, $SD = .91$ ($F = 107.38$, $df = 1, 157$, $p < .001$). Students were thus more likely to place their significant words in the subject location when the sentences included a positive verb relation, and vice versa for a negative verb relation.

Hypothesis 2 predicts that this difference will be greater when the scs is administered before the wss than it will be if the opposite order of administration is followed. The latter prediction can be tested in the interaction

Table 1 Mean and standard deviation of match score

	Match score	
Order of administration	Mean	Standard deviation
Sentences first (SCS)		
Positive verb relation	4.10	0.87
Negative verb relation	2.15	0.96
Significance first (WSS)		
Positive verb relation	3.80	1.11
Negative verb relation	2.63	0.87

Note: Interaction between order of administration and positive/negative verb relation significance, $p < .001$.

between order of wss/scs administration and the positive/negative verb relation. Table 1 presents the means and standard deviations of the match scores, broken down by order of wss/scs administration and positive/negative verb relations.

Note in Table 1 that the differences between positive and negative verb relations is greater when the scs is administered first ($M = 4.10$ vs. $M = 2.15$) than when the wss is administered first ($M = 3.80$ vs. $M = 2.63$). This interaction proved to be significant ($F = 6.92$, $df = 1, 156$, $p < .001$). Percentages of the sample selecting various words as "most significant" in the pairings of the wss were as follows (percentage of students in parentheses): confidence (37%) vs. knowledge (63%); suspicion (36%) vs. insincerity (64%); satisfaction (36%) vs. understanding (64%); anxiety (54%) vs. pain (46%); respect (39%) vs. honesty (61%); and forgetfulness (43%) vs. disinterest (57%). An examination of these selection patterns in terms of the Thorndike-Lorge (1944) word count failed to suggest that mere frequency of contact with these words could account for their selection as significant meanings.

Conclusion and Discussion

The experimental hypotheses have been supported. The observed differences in match scores are small but highly significant. Also, it should be noted that the findings on the positive verb relations validated an earlier study in which the identical procedure was followed (Rychlak & Rychlak, 1991).

A critic might suggest that our findings reflect not predication but memory. The claim would be that it is easier to use two nouns in a sentence and remember their relative significance later than to judge their relative significance first and then use these nouns in a sentence. There appear to be two problems with this suggestion. First, the students were not asked to remember anything—neither the words nor their judgments of the words. Although memory doubtless enters into any behavior that people carry out through experimental instructions, there are no grounds on which to claim that writing the sentence primed memory to rate the nouns consistently whereas the reverse ordering of tasks did not. We have these findings, of course, but to use them to make this claim is an unwarranted circularity.

Second, even if we rely on memory in our explanation of the findings, we must say why priming worked better in one order (scs, wss) than the other (wss, scs). The LLT explanation hinges on predication, which is operationalized in the syntax of the sentences. The present experiment was designed on the assumption that the relationship that combined words into sentences would establish a (positive or negative) predicating context within which the relative standing of two words would be affirmed—for this experimental hour. In the next hour of a student's life this standing might be reversed as different meaningful patterns are framed within changing circumstances.

Of course, when a student taking the wss before the scs contemplates the relative significance of the two words, he or she must be doing something similar to the process that will be followed later in completing the sentences of the scs. That is, some kind of relational assessment must be rendered, probably calling for comparable verb meanings. We do gain some influence over the wss ratings by having the students take a clear position in completing the scs first, but we cannot be certain precisely how they predicated the two words in their wss judgments when it lacked this precedent influence. There are, no doubt, eccentric, poorly organized comparisons occasionally being drawn. It is the slight advantage gained by providing the students with a requirement to take a clear, well-organized position in the sentence completion that influenced our findings.

The Influence of Predication on Reality

As I noted in chapter 1, the inevitability of affirming the consequent in scientific method requires that the results of any experiment that may be conducted be subject to more than just the theory (if any) postulated by the experimenter who gathered the data (this holds true for LLT as well). In this closing section of the chapter, I will survey a number of studies that demonstrate how predications influence the "reality" of the people who frame them. These studies did not refer to a "predication effect" as the topic of their investigation, but we now have the background enabling us to see how this cognitive process is involved. What matters are not the ready-formed inputs that lend quality to behavior but the conceptualizations placed on the forming of experience. Logical learning theory is itself predicated by a Kantian critical realism rather than a Lockean naive realism. Logical learning theory might also be characterized as a form of *objective idealism*.

Naming (categorizing) events lays down the grounds for the sake of which we experience them and overtly behave in relation to them. Experiments have shown that a predicating judgment as to whether an event is physically pleasant or unpleasant can exert a greater influence on behavior than the actual physical properties of the event in question (Dulany, 1968). Adults will assault a coparticipant more than twice as aggressively when the behavior is called a game than when it is called hostility or aggression (Diener, Dineen, Endresen, Beaman, & Fraser, 1975). Values play a role here. Subjects do not like to be typified as behaving in a hostile manner. There is evidence that people can intentionally negate an impulse to behave negatively in relation to others (see, e.g., Bond, 1972).

Once a predication has been framed it may require justification. Why did the person frame things in this or that way? There is evidence that the grounds may well shift at this point. What people select as grounds for a categorization need not be the grounds that they subsequently employ to justify their decision (Landau, 1982). Having to evaluate and justify one's grounds for predication necessarily involves an even more abstract framing predication—as in the case just mentioned, where an abstract value system may be brought to bear. The initial context meaning must become the target of yet another, more abstract context meaning. We must think of this in terms of the Kantian model, as ever-broader meanings being framed "from above." At the highest levels of abstraction, we can speak of *universals*. People are not always cognizant of these more abstract contexts in their thought, such as the well-known "halo effect" that can arise when we view others as behaving in either a warm or a cold manner (Nisbett & Wilson, 1977a). This abstract affective predication of the other person can influence our acceptance or rejection of his or her viewpoints (see chap. 7).

The evidence thus suggests that, as the level of abstraction increases, there will come a point at which the person's predications devolving from above are no longer directly or actively involved in the specific predication under affirmation in overt telosponsivity. The knowledge required in such overt telosponses is limited to that which focuses on the relevant target of the moment. The person need not elaborate more abstruse predicating assumptions in order to act. I will develop this theme more fully over the next two chapters, for it has relevance for cognitive processing, learning, and remembering.

Once people hit on a predication that works in life, that solves a problem for them (Schwartz, 1982), or that solidifies an opinion (Hovland, Janis, & Kelley, 1953), they are not likely to change the meaning so patterned. People become committed to those predicate meanings (contents) that have worked or paid off in the past. This is what William James (1907/1943) was driving at when he referred to the practical consequences, or "cash value," of ideas (pp. 42, 162). In fact, people have trouble relinquishing the meaning they affirmed initially even when their hypotheses begin to fail (Wason, 1960). Mitroff (1974) found that NASA scientists considered themselves strongly committed advocates of particular theoretical assumptions about their subject matter rather than impartial seekers after truth. This commitment to a certain theory was often maintained in the face of contradictory empirical evidence. Bazerman (1985) found that physicists read only those research articles that can be subsumed by their mental representations (i.e., their predications). There is an amusing incident along this line in the life of Einstein. A student-colleague once asked him what his reaction would have been if the famous experiment conducted by Eddington on the island of Principe during a solar eclipse had not turned out in favor of relativity theory. Einstein's reply was "Then I would have been sorry for the dear Lord [Eddington]—the theory *is* correct" (Holton, 1972, p. 361).

The point is this: Human beings always frame (theoretical) assumptions acting as prototypes in ongoing thought. These are called attitudes, opinions, points of view, personal beliefs, and the like. In time, a person may forget the initiating (protopoint) events that prompted him or her to affirm a prototypical assumption. As I have noted previously, from the LLT perspective, thinking is theorizing and vice versa. Such theoretical assumptions endow life with its meaning, and the more comprehensive and reliable they become in ongoing experience—as assessed introspectively, by the person concerned—the more difficult they are to dismiss. Rather than being readily dropped in favor of conflicting evidence, these assumptions are likely to redefine—put a new "twist" on—the evidence in question. The same dynamic is to be seen in paranoid behaviors, although in this case the coherence attained may be highly subjective and therefore difficult for others to assess. Eventually, however, the scientist, like all normally functioning human beings, comes to adapt his or her theory to the evidence of experience. One cannot negate sound evidence forever.

Prompted initially by the work of Rosenthal and Jacobson (1968), there has been considerable research on the influence of self-fulfilling prophecies in bringing about concrete changes in human behavior. In Rosenthal's initial study, elementary school teachers were told that a new IQ test administered to their students indicated that certain of these children—called "bloomers"—should have a marked increase in intellectual competence over the ensuing school year. Unknown to the teachers, the children were randomly assigned to the bloomer or nonbloomer categories. All the children in the study were given an IQ test at both the beginning and the end of the school year. The results indicated that the children labeled bloomers acheived a significantly greater gain in IQ than the nonbloomers. There have been many criticisms of this research. For example, Miller and Turnbull (1986) note that although there have been such teacher expectancy effects suggested on academic tasks like mathematics and reading proficiency, IQ gains have not been readily demonstrated. Rosenthal and Rubin (1978) found that some kind of teacher expectancy effect did bring about student gains (IQ and otherwise) in roughly two-thirds of 345 studies surveyed.

Findings of this sort are consistent with the LLT view of human beings, who regularly frame positive or negative assumptions about each other and then unknowingly (unconsciously?) bring them into existence. Teachers have probably assigned higher grades in the face of mediocre performances by the favored children. On the other hand, as Jussim (1986) has proposed, sometimes the favorable context provided by the teacher's attitude regarding the student actually serves as a precedent that seqaciously extends to the student's outlook about him- or herself, which in turn predicates a higher level of performance. This prompts the LLT advocate to recognize that some predicating contexts are actually interpersonal in nature.

There are also negative aspects of stereotypy in human relations to consider. We have reason to believe that racially prejudiced subjects predicate others to a greater degree by race than do nonprejudiced subjects (Stangor, Lynch, Duan, & Glass, 1992). If a negative stereotype prompts the person holding it to exhibit hostile mannerisms in interpersonal relations, the probability is great that this behavior will generate counterhostility from others (Rausch, 1965). On another level of interpersonal relations, if a person expects to be confronted with high levels of competition from others — even though this is not truly the case — he or she will behave in a like manner (Kelley & Stahelski, 1970).

Physical characteristics can also influence other predications of people, as any advertising agent knows. Thus, many research studies have found that physically attractive people are perceived as more sociable, dominant, sexually warm, mentally healthy, intelligent, and socially skilled than physically unattractive people (Feingold, 1992). Even when such physical attractiveness is merely imagined, we can see its influence in the behavior of people. Young women who were described to young men with whom they were unacquainted as physically attractive were more humorous, friendly, and socially adept when speaking with these men on the telephone than young women who had been described as not especially attractive (Snyder, Tanke, & Berscheid, 1977). This interactive facilitation was a response in kind to the conversational styles of the young men, who had nothing but a positive predication to direct their verbal efforts. Here again, what was not real but merely presumptive influenced the eventual reality of a verbal exchange. There are many other such research findings in the literature, some of which will surface as I discuss issues tangential to the matter of the context in human cognition.

Concluding Comment

Chapter 3 presents arguments and considerable evidence suggesting that human cognition is formulative, that it patterns experience to arrive at a product known according to various names but referred to generically as a *category*. Unfortunately, the shift from efficient to formal causation that took place in psychology's cognitive revolution did not extend to its conception of the psychological process active in cognition, which continues to be mediational (efficiently causal) in formulation. The categories are muddled even further by being identified with "intervening variables." From the perspective of LLT, all the categorical concepts ranging from Bartlett's schema to Rosch's prototype represent variations on a theme: the content of the predicational process. That is, they are predicates (noun usage). Predicates abound in psychology, and many interesting experiments are carried out on the structural differences that such patterned meanings assume. None of these experiments contradicts LLT in any way, but neither do they falsify the computer/mediational model on which they supposedly rest. One cannot falsify what is not put to test.

Our very concept of reality is influenced by the knowledge that the individual cognizer frames experience according to his or her contextualized understanding. This is a symbolizing intellect, not a signalizing one. *Symbols* are always more pregnant with meaning than we initially appreciate, because symbols include the contextual ramifications of a wider compass than our focused thought requires at the moment. As Susanne K. Langer (1948) put it so well, "Symbols are not proxy for their objects, but are *vehicles for the conception of objects*" (p. 61; emphasis in the original). The family resemblance phenomenon is fuzzy because it is symbolic in nature. Signs never create meaning contextually because they merely stand as surrogates for that to which they are matched in one-to-one fashion. Computer intelligence is sign-processing—it matches signs to signs in a rigidly literal manner—but human intelligence is always nestled within the rich context of symbols. It is the predicational process that turns a meaning into a symbol. The symbolization is carried by this process, not the (categorical or categorized) content that it produces. And yet, most empirically oriented research psychologists persist in their idealization of engineering lingo by trying to limit human cognition to mediating mechanisms.

4

Cognitive Processing as Logical,
not Mechanical

Chapter 3 has clarified the distinction between context as a content and a process. Chapter 4 takes a closer look at the process to clarify more precisely how it may be said to work. I begin by examining the differences between mechanical and logical processing and then move on to a number of topics providing a clearer description of the latter.

Mechanical versus Logical Processing

There is no term more ill-defined and poorly understood in psychology today than *mechanism*. Logical learning theory is compatible with the following definition of what a *mechanical explanation* represents: "Put negatively, [it is] any explanation which avoids teleology and final causation. Put positively, mechanical explanations stress efficient causation and are reducible to laws covering instances of matter in motion" (Reese, 1980, p. 345). In contrast, LLT suggests the following definition for *logical explanation:* "Put negatively, it is any explanation that avoids reduction to material and efficient causation. Put positively, logical explanations stress formal/final causation relying on demonstrative and dialectical rule following." Recall from chapters 1 and 2 that a dialectical rule like the *one and many* can be considered illogical when judged against a demonstrative rule like the *law of contradiction*. A certain "rule versus law" distinction is violated here in referring to the law of contradiction. This really should be called a rule or a principle.

Although both rules and laws draw on the meaning of formal causation, they are vastly different conceptions. Laws refer to the physically inviolable patterns observed in the processes of the *Bios* (i.e., mediation) and *Physikos* (i.e., gravity). When we eat a candy bar, it necessarily "inputs a calculable number of calories for our mediating digestive system to process. When we drop something, it necessarily falls to the earth. Machines are limited to following laws like this, even though they may process contents according to rules, as computers do (see Rychlak, 1991). Of course, the machine's programmer frames the algorithmic rule. In contradistinction to laws, rules are "taken on" in the processes of the *Logos* (i.e., predication) and *Socius* (i.e., socialization). Rules must be intentionally conformed to by those human beings who participate in rule following, and although promulgators of rules may exhort that they are inviolate, this is never the case. As an old adage asserts, "rules are made to be broken." Nonetheless, the patterning of the logic (process) that frames rules (content) does have a determinate necessity about it.

In fact, we are unable to control or manipulate logical processes in the same way that we control processes in the (efficiently caused) biophysical realm. Predicated meanings (contents) can be supplanted, but the precedent-sequacious force of deduction, inference, and so on (process) is not amenable to controlled direction in the way that we drive our automobiles about or take medications to correct a physical ailment. Kahneman and Tversky (1972; Kahneman, Slovic, & Tversky, 1982; Tversky & Kahneman, 1983) have shown that although people rarely make decisions in the way that logicians, mathematicians, or statisticians do, and although they can easily be led astray by irrelevancies when predicating, there is nevertheless a detectable rulelike order taking place in their erratic and unsound course of mentation (see also Nisbett & Ross, 1980).

The grounds may shift, and the person may forgo a rigid rule in preference of a more flexible semantic formulation; for example, subjects are seen to solve word analogies by means of heuristics rather than inflexible algorithmic rules (Sadler & Shoben, 1993). There is nevertheless a controlling order in such cognition, representing a psychical (*Logos*) rather than a physical (*Physikos/Bios*) determinism. Psychical determinism can be of the "hard" variety, of course, meaning that it is just as intractable as a physical determination (see Rychlak, 1988, p. 245). The concept of will reflects this hard determinism, and, as I noted in chapter 2, a free will notion combines the capacity to select the grounds ("freely") for the sake of which an action is then necessarily carried out ("willfully").

The hard determinism of logical necessity is apparently what convinces psychologists that cognitive processing involves a mechanism. On this assumption, a syllogism, in which meanings framed by the premises extend necessarily (sequaciously) to a conclusion, is to be understood as a mechanism. The major premise is always a position taken (affirmed) by the person. No machine ever takes a position, of course, yet Anderson (1985) has described the biasing nature of the *"Einstellung effect"* as a *"mechanization of*

thought" (p. 226; italics in original). When Watt named the *Aufgabe* (i.e., experimental instruction of the task to be done) as establishing the subject's
Einstellung (i.e., set or bias in the upcoming task), he was, as were so many
of his Wurzburg colleagues, thinking of the person's cognitions introspectively (Boring, 1950, p. 404). The *Aufgabe* was said to reflect the purpose
(telos, end) to be achieved in the task to be done. No machine ever frames a
purpose. Nevertheless, simply because there is a necessity, a sequacious influence following the affirmation of a predicating set, Anderson is prepared
to speak of this process as mechanical.

A related point here has to do with predictability. Many experimental psychologists seem to believe that if they design an experiment in which they
can predict the subject's behavior in the procedure, this proves empirically
that people are mechanisms. The empirical relationship existing between the
independent and dependent variables is interpreted as a law, even though it
could very well reflect a rule. That is, if subjects in an experiment behave according to a logical rule—such as the steps of the experimental design, which
could be "cued" to them by the *Aufgabe*—then the fact that they behave
predictably, extending meaning from their predicating *Einstellung*, is erroneously translated by the extraspective observer into law following. Logical
learning theory, on the other hand, holds that experimental findings reflect
the rule following (i.e., logic) of both the experimenter, who designed a patterned relationship to be enacted as the experimental procedure, and the
subject, who contributes logically relevant variables to the procedure as well
(Rychlak, 1988, pp. 322, 323).

The confusion of efficient-cause mechanical with formal/final-cause logical processing is widespread in psychology. We have to read theorists very
carefully when they begin sounding teleological. We might read on one page
that "the concept of attention . . . brings with it the concept of background
(context, framework, ground), [and] refers to a most important aspect of
the psychological level of organization" (Gilgen, 1987, p. 197). Our interest peaks, for this suggests predication from ground to targeted figure. On
another page, however, we read, "The core-context format further provides
a *mechanism* for retrieving information from the memory store and for directing the attentional process. The attended-to information always brings
with it other information (a variety of contexts) which permits us to consider material *associated* with that to which we are attending" (ibid., p. 196;
emphasis added). We now sadly appreciate that this is really a theoretical
view in which the target and context are associated mechanically—a standard efficient-cause explanation that has been dominant in psychology since
the early years of the 20th century. Here is another variation on the standard mediational theme: "Most psychologists today agree that responses of

the organism to stimulation are mediated by that organism's cognitive state, which provides a context for and an interpretation of the stimulus as it makes contact with the record of his past experiences" (Bower, 1972, p. 85).

So, if a process is automatic, if it is certain, if it necessarily follows from an antecedent or precedent, we are going to find psychologists thinking of this as a mechanism. All these features can be subsumed by a lawfulness conception, making for confusion when we realize that logical processing has these same features due to its rule-following nature. Freud's use of the term *defense mechanism* has added to the confusion in psychology. His willingness to call reaction-formation a mental mechanism demonstrates the point I am now making better than anything else that could be proposed (Freud, 1913/1958, p. 299). No mechanism can possibly effect a reaction-formation. It is true that machines can be thrown into reverse, that their motions can be sent in what a human being would call the opposite direction, but this is not what Freud had in mind. He was referring to a logical misdirection in which the person manifests one seeming goal (target) while unconsciously (unadmittedly) intending its contrary. A person's excessive caution leading to an unfortunate accident may spring from the unconscious desire to wreck that which is supposedly being carefully protected. The logical intent is outside the predicating Euler circle, but it is masquerading as if it were inside.

These kinds of mental strategies can be readily subsumed by the dialectical machinations open to telosponsivity, whereas it is difficult if not impossible to do justice to them with a computer analogue (and its Boolean assumptions) or a stimulus-response format (for a valiant effort in this regard, see Dollard & Miller, 1950, pp. 184, 185). Actually, I think it can be demonstrated that what Freud meant by the mechanisms of thought are mere instrumentalities of the personality structures (id, ego, superego), which always enact their purposes in an intentional manner. Freud camouflaged his teleological formulations with the libido theory and relied on the "mechanics of defense" to convey the intentionality that was actually under description (for more on this, see Rychlak, 1981, chaps. 7 and 10). I will return to LLT's relevance to psychoanalysis in chapter 10.

Constructionism, Contextualism, and Connectionism

I noted in chapter 3 that the notion of construction is often brought in to deal with the unquestioned importance of context in human cognition. This word has the ring of predication because it seems to suggest that the human actually formulates or constructs the cognitive organization. George Kelly's (1955) constructivism is like this. A person is said to construe (process) personal constructs (contents) on the basis of which two targets are alike and different from or opposite to a third (pp. 63, 78). An example would be "Mary and Alice are gentle; Jane is not" (ibid., p. 111). This is an introspectively conceived, "top-down" formulation of cognition in which the cognizer unites two items as sharing a common predication and distinguishes a third target as contrasting with or negating this predication. The associations here are placed on the targets by the construing process, not hooked together in mechanistic (efficient-cause) fashion. Kelly has a Kantian understanding of construction. He employs the verb *construe* as derived from Middle English, meaning "to interpret" (ibid., p. 50).

On the other hand, we have a Lockean usage in cognitive psychology that draws on the Latin roots of *construe*, meaning "to heap together" and "build." When we construct a building we heap together materials to build an edifice. It is this usage that Mandler (1985) has in mind when he speaks of the phenomenal world as follows: "Our phenomenal world is immediate, obvious, and thereby very convincing. Unfortunately, we often forget that it too is constructed, that it is a complex product of our culture and personal histories" (p. 15). Mandler here turns a construct that interprets experience into a mediator that has been shaped by experience.

In the Kantian model (Figure 10), the phenomenal realm is on the inside of the glasses, which frame from above what can be known below. The phenomenal realm is not built up from early experience; it is what makes early (and later) experience possible. Meichenbaum and Gilmore (1984) say the following: "Cognitive processes refer to those processes that shape mental representations, transforming them and constructing schemes of experience and action" (p. 275). The construction here is obviously a content that has been "heaped together" through frequent associative contiguities by a mediating cognitive process. In LLT, as in Kellyian theory, construction is not the result of cognitive processing (a content); construction *is* cognitive processing. We are back to that verb-versus-noun distinction that was drawn in chapter 3 concerning predication.

Theorists sometimes make an effort to resolve the Lockean-Kantian divergence regarding construction or construing by accepting both approaches as legitimate aspects of cognition—one working in a bottom-up and the other in a top-down fashion. According to strict Kantian theory, however, there could be no bottom-up processing without a top-down framing categorical context, and on the Lockean formulation, the top is necessarily cast as a mediating series of contents that has been acquired or input earlier without predication. Thus, the eclectic effort to combine bottom-up and top-down processing through some kind of interaction merely begs the question (Rumelhart, 1977). Furthermore, the postulated interaction invariably ends up being a mediation model, because to get such interactions started, the bottom-up process must first input mediators into the system, which can then process in a top-down (pseudopredicational) fashion.

For example, Tulving (1983) argues that it is a law of cognition that mind contributes to what is perceived or known by the person (I would consider this a rule). He assures us that "there has not been a psychologist or philosopher alive in the last one hundred years who has seriously doubted the veracity of this law" (p. 149). This could suggest a top-down, predicational influence on knowledge. Tulving adds that most psychologists today believe that the "responses of the organism to stimulation are *mediated by* that organism's cognitive state, which provides a context for and an interpretation of the stimulus as it makes contact with the record of his past experiences" (ibid., emphasis added). Tulving's concept of what "mind contributing to knowledge of experience" means is that a context has been input previously, in bottom-up fashion, so that today it acts as a top-down mediator of ongoing experience. This is definitely *not* what at least some psychologists and many philosophers these past 100 years have meant by mind contributing to knowledge.

Sometimes the term *contextualist* or *contextualism* finds its way into discussions of cognitive processing as a supporting philosophy for such theorizing (e.g., see Horton & Bergfeld Mills, 1984, p. 361). This in turn calls to mind Pepper's (1970) philosophical analysis of *world hypotheses*, one of which is contextualism. Some psychologists even cite Pepper as a precedent for their views (e.g., see Jenkins, 1974, p. 786). Contextualism in Pepper's view emphasizes the historical event—the historical context—as establishing the meaning of any human action (Pepper, 1970, p. 232). This strikes many cognitive psychologists as covering what they mean by the framing influences of schemata, plans, prototypes and the like, yet Pepper's explanation of how worldviews are framed is totally at variance with the mediational theories on which these cognitive psychologists actually rely. Thus, in his "rootmetaphor method" of how world hypotheses arise in the first place, Pepper says that the method in principle seems to be as follows:

> A man desiring to understand the world looks about for a clue to its comprehension. He pitches up on some area of commonsense fact and tries to see if he cannot understand other areas in terms of this one. This original area becomes then his basic analogy or root metaphor. He describes as best he can the characteristics of this area, or, if you will, discriminates its structure. A list of its structural characteristics becomes his basic concepts of explanation and description. We call them a set of categories. In terms of these categories he proceeds

to study all other areas of fact whether uncriticized or previously criticized. He undertakes to interpret all facts in terms of these categories. As a result of the impact of these other facts upon his categories, he may qualify and readjust the categories, so that a set of categories commonly changes and develops (Pepper, 1970, p. 91).

This is about as clear a description of predication in telosponsivity as one could hope for. The contextualist root metaphor that Pepper then presents (ibid., chap. 10) is a content framed telosponsively and used as the meaning for the sake of which the person understands life. I see little grounds here for using Pepper as a philosophical precedent for those contextualists in psychology who base their explanations on computer processing and related mediating mechanisms. Pepper theorized in the realm of the *Logos*. He was not a mechanist, although mechanism is one of his postulated world hypotheses (ibid., chap. 9).

Occasionally, the LLT advocate is presented with the possibility that *connectionism* or *parallel distributed processing* (PDP) can somehow account for the dynamics of telosponsivity in human cognition (Rumelhart & McClelland, 1986a). In PDP, individual nodes in the network do not contain specific meaning but attain meaning on the basis of certain relations that they hold to other nodes in the system. The process is distributed in the sense that the computations involved are broken up into separate, relatively independent units or components allowing for parallel processing. The links between nodes take on even greater significance in PDP than in traditional nodal theories (hence the term *connectionism*). The strength of the linking connections are assigned or acquire weights that determine the degree of activation that spreads across the network (playing a theoretical role comparable to the different thicknesses of the paths symbolized in Figure 16). Collectively, the pattern of weighted connections determines what concept will be processed. When a PDP network is just getting underway, it is essentially a tabula rasa mechanism, starting out with linking weights of zero between the nodes. External influence as the PDP system is trained or learns then determines the weights that eventually will be assigned to the links. We have here, in every essential, a bottom-up Lockean model.

Thus, as Fodor and Pylyshyn (1988) point out, the weights are simply a rephrasing of the older associationist principle that "the strength of a stimulus-response connection is a function of the frequency with which the response is rewarded in the presence of the stimulus" (p. 31). Connectionism does not consider the syntactic or semantic aspects of a representation as relevant to the processing of inputs to outputs (ibid., p. 32). Criticisms of the Rumelhart and McClelland (1986b, p. 222) PDP model have been advanced along this line by Lachter and Bever (1988), who consider it to be a complex variant on traditional Hullian learning theory (p. 234). As I noted in chapter 1, we must also keep in mind that PDP models are binary; they continue in the Boolean tradition of hard disjunction (Pinker & Prince, 1988, p. 88).

All things considered, I see no likelihood whatever that PDP will subsume the explanations of learning advanced by LLT. In contradistinction to PDP, LLT embraces a top-down constructivism, a Pepperian contextualism, a soft (non-Boolean) disjunction, and a semantic basis for cognition. Meaning is fundamental to LLT. I next examine in greater detail the various logical aspects of the cognitive process.

Precedent-Sequacious Meaning-Extension

A fundamental assumption in LLT is that the meaning of telosponsivity extends necessarily once it has been affirmed as relevant to the circumstances, although the meaning can be countered by uncertainties, ambivalences, and the like before this affirmation is made. In chapter 2 I noted that the affirmation in telosponsivity is made at the protopoint, which frames the meaning that will be extended tautologically into ongoing cognition. The logical ordering here is from precedent meanings to sequacious (necessary) extensions of these meanings. Time's passage is not relevant here, but if I were to express this process in time-oriented terms, I would say that the meaning-extension is instantaneous.

The research literature has reflected precedent-sequacious meaning-extensions for some time now, with this concept showing up in work on topics such as inference, implication, impression formation, induction, deduction, and so on. I have already noted in this and the previous chapter that the Wurzburg school of imageless thought (circa 1901–1909) pointed to the *Aufgabe* as establishing a precedent *Einstellung* that then extends sequaciously into the findings of the ongoing experiment. Other terms used by the Wurzburgers for such precedent influences were *determining tendency* and *conscious attitude*. The gestalt psychologists (see Rubin, 1921) also proved empirically that figures acquire their form sequaciously from precedent grounds (a point I mentioned in chap. 2).

Asch (1946) conducted an early impression-formation study in which he found that if subjects were told that a person was intelligent, industrious, impulsive, critical, stubborn, and envious, they were more favorably inclined toward this person than if the same characteristics were conveyed in the opposite order. Affirming that the person was intelligent initially framed a precedent set (*Einstellung*) that extended sequaciously into the ongoing impression in the face of some negative counterpoints, which seemed to have been refashioned in terms of this more positive protopoint affirmation. Asch's *primacy effect* has stood the test of time in research on impression formation (see, e.g., Park, 1986).

Heidbreder (1947) then published a famous experiment on concept formation to demonstrate that when subjects had to categorize geometric shapes under quasi-word designations (e.g., Fard, Mank, Dilt), they invariably read into those words meanings drawn from their (precedent) experience that would (sequaciously) concretize them in some way, making them easier to use. Behaviorists of the era viewed these framing efforts as mediators, of course. By this time in the history of psychological experimentation, Ebbinghaus (1885/1964) had framed his dictum that experimentation on memory should eschew studying all spontaneous efforts that subjects make to invent "special associations of the mnemotechnik type" (p. 25). Such spontaneous heuristic (formal/final-cause) efforts on the part of subjects were considered secondary manifestations of memory, and Ebbinghaus was seeking the primary factors—presumed to be found exclusively in the (efficiently caused) frequency of trial repetitions. As we shall see in chapter 5, these mnemonic organizational efforts on the part of subjects are now common topics of research on learning and memory. Ebbinghaus's dictum has faded from view, prompted no doubt by the force of empirical findings establishing that mnemonic organization is more the cause than the effect of acquisition over trials.

Studies on *availability* and *representativeness heuristics* capitalize on the fact that if subjects are given a plausible precedent, they will sequaciously extend this meaning into ongoing behavior (Ross, Lepper, Areack, & Steinmetz, 1977; Tversky, 1977). The *gambler's fallacy* rests on a tautological extension from facts such as that in the past, the ball has landed on the roulette wheel's red squares about as often as on its black ones. The plausible precedent then sequaciously implies that since there has been a long run of red showing up, it is time to bet on the black. If we are interested in the intellectual accuracy of a subject's performance, then it is important for a precedent affirmation to be well-organized and meaningfully appropriate to the circumstances under conceptualization. Along this line, subjects who had to organize information concerning other people have been seen to rely more on "strong" relationship categories (e.g., marriage) than on "weak" relationship categories (e.g., acquaintantship); also, they form these stronger categories at initial "encoding," which suggests what I have been calling a precedent in logical sequence (Sedikides, Olsen, & Reis, 1993). We know in general that if the precedent meanings are not reality oriented, then the sequacious line of cognitive processing may be fraught with error and even irrationality (Sweller & Gee, 1978).

It is also important to realize that personal realities are sequaciously created from precedent meanings that may make *subjective* sense to the person concerned and that this framing context is what ultimately matters. Thus, a paraplegic patient may affirm that "God wanted to teach me a lesson about the importance of my mind rather than my legs"; this precedent affirmation will then result in an "accepting" outlook on life (Bulman & Wortman, 1977). Subjects who are asked to guess a person's occupation based on the latter's personality tendencies generally align personality to occupational stereotype (Kahneman & Tversky, 1973). Establishing an expectation by observing certain behaviors in others extends to what one then recalls seeing in their subsequent behavior, even when this recollection is not totally representative (Stangor & Ruble, 1989).

Asking subjects to read a story involving a house from the perspective of either a home buyer or a burglar influences what they will recall about this house (e.g., a leak in the roof for the home buyer and a color TV for the burglar) (Pichert & Anderson, 1977). Students perform mathematical calculations more easily if they have a meaningful context within which to estimate the computability of certain equations (Kieras & Greeno, 1975). Cross-modality meaning-extensions also occur. Subjects who are shown a relevant picture before reading a vaguely phrased written description of an event understand the description better than subjects who have not seen the picture (Bransford & Johnson, 1972).

Speed of word recognition in a following sentence is sequaciously influenced by similar word meanings in the preceding sentence. Assume we have subjects read "A burglar surveyed the garage set back from the street" *following* either "A cat slipped away from the street lamp" or "The criminal slipped away from the street lamp." We then ask the subjects to indicate whether they have seen the word *burglar* in the experiment (there are several sentence combinations like this given to the subject). The subjects who have read the sequence involving the anaphoric target words (criminal-burglar) recognize *burglar* more quickly than those who have read the other pair of sentences (cat-burglar) (McKoon & Ratcliff, 1980). This suggests that a context has been framed by the first sentence that is then tautologized to the second (I will discuss similar findings on implication and inference later). Such anaphoric word influences have been found in studies using not only text but also sentence pairs (see, e.g., O'Brien, Duffy, & Myers, 1986).

Meaning-extensions can occur to the past as well as to the future. Recall from Figure 4 that the direction of meaning-extension in predication is immaterial. Telosponses are made both to the past and to the future. A person's current intentions act as precedents, which in turn sequaciously reformulate the past, making it conform to the present (Mischel, Ebbesen, & Zeiss,

1976; Ross, McFarland, Conway, & Zanna, 1983). Precedent meanings have been shown to have a sequacious effect on subsequent behavior even though subjects are asked to disregard what they have been told (Wyer & Budesheim, 1987). "Planting a seed" is an old trick in the courtroom, where lawyers know that "stricken from the record" does not mean stricken from the jury's precedent affirmations.

Inference versus Implication

Logical learning theory proposes a distinction in precedent-sequacious processing that captures an aspect of human cognition that the computer analogue finds unnecessary—if not impossible—to capture. Some logicians have recognized that although in one sense an implication and an inference are the same, they are also different (Reese, 1980, p. 270). Both involve the precedent-sequacious extensions of meanings from premises to conclusions, but the conclusion of an implication is more hypothetical or suggestive than is the conclusion of an inference. A logician might present this difference as follows: "Inference cannot be defined in terms of implication, but . . . implication must be defined in terms of inference, namely as equivalent to potential inference. Thus, in inferring, we are not merely passing from the assertion of the premise to the assertion of the conclusion, but we are also implicitly asserting that the assertion of the premise is *used* to justify the assertion of the conclusion" (Johnson, 1922, p. 2).

The reference to a "potential inference" gets at the core of what implication means in the psychology of a person. *Inference* is the belief that the premises in a line of reasoning are true, so that they justify the conclusion reached. *Implication*, on the other hand, although it follows a comparable line of precedent-sequacious reasoning, rests on premises that may or may not be true and hence cannot of themselves justify the conclusion reached. Conclusions in implication are more like hunches or hypotheses. They might, on further examination, become actual inferences, for "the mental process of inference consists in transforming what was *potentially* assertible into a proposition *actually* asserted" (ibid.; emphasis in the original).

From the LLT viewpoint, premises that are not certain are closer to their opposite meanings because they are framed in what is tantamount to an "either/or" context akin to the inside/outside of the predicating Euler circle ("the truth could be this or it could be that"). Inferences are more focused; they dismiss or disregard the meaning realm exterior to the predicating Euler circle in what might be termed a demonstrative manner ("*this* is the truth"). Implications lean more to the dialectical in reasoning quality, and as contents in cognitive processing, they draw on what I named in chapter 1 a delimiting oppositionality. If everything is judged to be sound and truthful in a line of thought, implication becomes inference as the person reaches conclusions that we name beliefs, convictions, deductions, inductions, and so forth (see Gilbert, 1991). The precedent-sequacious flow of meaning-extension during inference is not hampered by the implicative possibilities of contrariety, contradiction, contrast, or negation. Of course, a person might reason according to implication and yet consider this line of thought as inferentially certain, as justifying the conclusions reached.

Let us now turn to some preliminary evidence for drawing a distinction between inference and implication. We know from experiments on sentence memory that subjects do not simply recognize what they have seen previously—the demonstratively given. If subjects are presented sentences like "The rock crushed the tiny hut; the hut was at the edge of the woods," they will later confidently recall having seen the sentence "The rock that rolled down the mountain crushed the tiny hut at the edge of the woods" (Bransford & Franks, 1971). The subjects apparently take the information of the earlier sentence, organize a scenario around it (context), and draw an inference that is not totally justified by what they actually perceived. No mountain was mentioned, but people know that if a rock can crush a hut, it is probably huge and must have gotten its impetus from rolling down a mountain. Thus, they predicate a precedent scenario in organizing their understanding of what they are reading and then later extend this context-meaning sequaciously as what they had seen. There have been several such studies using various types of sentences (e.g., Barclay, 1973; Bransford, Barclay, & Franks, 1972; Johnson, Bransford, & Solomon, 1973). According to LLT, this precedent organizational phenomenon is fundamental to *all* cognitive processing and has been noted empirically in other guises such as *mental models* (Gentner & Stevens, 1983) and *metaphors* (Lakoff & Johnson, 1980).

An even clearer example of this point comes from a study in which subjects read a sentence like "Miss America said that she played the tuba" (Harris, 1974). After reading this sentence, subjects read the following sentence and classified it as true, false, or indeterminate: "Miss America played the tuba." Some subjects made this classification right after reading the two sentences, whereas others did not judge the truth value of the second sentence until they had completed a long list of such sentence pairs. It was found that those subjects who evaluated the second sentence of such pairs directly after reading them were likely to judge them as indeterminate, whereas subjects relying on short-term memory were likely to judge them as true. From the LLT viewpoint, the memorial component turned an initial implication ("Saying that one plays is not actually playing the tuba") into an inference ("I recall something about this; yes, she plays the tuba"). The cognitive organization has moved from a questionable premise to a certain premise based in all likelihood on the predication of Miss America by "tuba playing" in the first sentence of the pair.

Life is fraught with implications balanced against inferences. An example might be as follows: A young assistant professor has been asked to report immediately to the office of her dean, which is a few buildings removed from her present location. It is raining rather heavily outside, and she has no umbrella. She *infers* with confidence that if she leaves immediately, she will show up at the dean's office soaked to the skin. She is dealing in *implication*, however, when she wonders, "What impression will I make on the dean dripping wet?" At this point, since possibilities are under consideration, each thought that "The dean won't think anything of it" is immediately (automatically) opposed by the thought that "The dean might think that I am, literally, a 'drip.' " The automatic opposition here is logical and not mechanical, based as it is on delimiting oppositionality in the cognitive content under processing. But then, it is also true that implications are not always drawn, nor do they necessarily result in such negative concerns. Our young professor might frame the following scenario: "The dean will surely see how responsible I am if I run right over in a downpour." The particular possibility drawn depends on the lifelong style of predicating such circumstances—a style that is not shaped from without but affirmed from within.

Since computers reason demonstratively, they take on their premises as primary and true. This makes it impossible for a computer to draw an implication (in the sense that I have been interpreting this concept). It is therefore not surprising that the information-processing theories that flow from the computer analogue have never drawn the distinction between inference and implication. One example of information-processing theorizing comes from Rothbart and Lewis (1988), who propose a network explanation of inference based on the "activation" of certain nodal patterns, particularly when a prototypical exemplar of this category is encountered by the person who is processing such information. The activated category leads to a more certain generalization (i.e., "inference"), as in assigning the label "conservative" to all members of a college fraternity because one of its number is described as a prototypical example of this political persuasion. This strikes the LLT advocate as a passive explanation of what is clearly an active process, because in the final analysis—unless we sneak a homunculus in here—the degree of activation in a network is always some unilinear mathematical function of past input frequencies. This makes inference an effect, when in fact, it is a cause in cognition. Logical learning theory holds that meanings flow from inferences and implications as the effects of such formal/final causes.

Understanding- versus Action-Intentions

In chapter 2 I established that an intention is behavior for the sake of precedent meanings, hence enlivening or creating the purpose of a concept in words, images, assessments, actions, and so on. If these meanings are restricted to the logical organization of cognition, we have an *understanding-intention*. Glancing out the window as one is eating breakfast and noting that it is a sunny day today is an understanding-intention in which the purposive meaning of certain words (sunny, day, today) are affirmed and extended into ongoing cognition. Nothing overtly discernible takes place. We cannot observe this fleeting impression in the person unless we ask him or her to freely associate aloud as ideas occur. Frequently, however, intentions are overtly observable, in which case I refer to them as *action-intentions*.

There is evidence that both children and adults can observe some targeted event, frame it with meaning (understanding-intention), and then either act or fail to act on the basis of this information (Adams & Hamm, 1973; Yekovich & Thorndyke, 1981). Infants and very young children will not always try to imitate others, especially if they believe that they cannot do what is being modeled for them (Kagan, 1981; Kaye & Marcus, 1981). We know that good intentions are not always enacted. Consider the following intention: I am going to do 25 sit-ups every morning, starting tomorrow. The target in this ambitious statement ("I") is not the predicating source of the intention but the end toward which the intention is aimed. We shall see tomorrow morning whether it becomes an action-intention.

In effect, an understanding-intention is a necessary but not sufficient beginning for any action-intention to follow. Indeed, LLT holds that *understanding-intentions are logical precedents of action-intentions*. Understanding-intentions are closer to implications than inferences. They make sense, but when they intend the purpose of some action, like doing sit-ups, they must also be enacted. As they have this implicative nature, they can also be questioned. We get a good idea and then find loopholes in it after some thought. Sometimes even the good idea is laden with doubt (half inside and half outside the framing Euler circle). Our beliefs require both a construal of the intended meaning (a mental representation) and a confirming assessment of this meaning as sound or true (Bogdan, 1986). If this succession comes off positively we have reasoned inferentially; if not, then an implication has been left hanging. People also play mental games with themselves, framing understanding-intentions but never actually carrying them over to an action-intention. They really intend one meaning (reassuring themselves via an understanding) but not the other (actually carrying out what is implied in this understanding).

The likely reason for this inability to carry out a projection is that the intention to exercise has not itself been targeted by other relevant understanding- and action-intentions. For action to occur we need additional intentions, such as, "Exercise promotes health and longevity" ("exercise" targeted), or "I refuse to get a pot belly" ("I" targeted). Precisely how many additional intentions like this are required depends on their value for the person, from which the action-intention draws its motivation (based on positive or negative affective assessments). This action can be initiated totally within the imagination (Corbin, 1972). In fact, there is some evidence to suggest that simply by imagining exercising the person can avoid the anxiety that might otherwise arise over his or her declining physical attractiveness (Brown & Siegel, 1988). This could delay initiating the exercise program, of course. We really must know what meanings the person is framing and their affective quality before we can predict with any confidence whether understandings will lead to actions. As I noted in chapter 2, it is this proviso that makes teleological description seem unscientific to mechanists. People may or may not do what they say they will do.

When I use a word like *understanding* to describe intention and then suggest that intentions take their logical weight from the predicate and not from the target, it makes it appear that this process will not continue unless all the predications entering into a line of thought are consciously understood. Actually, as I mentioned in the concluding comment of chapter 3, since the predicating context is broader than the targeted meaning to which it extends, it necessarily follows that there will be predicating meanings that are beyond the specific cognition being understood or enacted. Every meaning that we affirm in ongoing telosponsivity is itself subsumable by other patterned meanings that may or may not be relevant to the understanding or action under consideration. Hence, the understanding referred to in the phrase *understanding-intention* must be qualified by the proviso that this be relevant to the targeted item, the very point or purpose of the meaningful intention under affirmation.

The role of pattern in such understanding is of utmost importance. Subjects have been seen to be influenced by a patterned rule even though they cannot name it. For example, subjects who were asked to press a corresponding button after each flash in a series of patterned light flashes decreased their reaction times when the flashes were repeated according to a random (i.e., unpatterned) light sequence (Nissen & Bullemer, 1987). Similarily, given some practice, subjects who were exposed to both quasi-grammatical letter strings and random patterns of letters were able to pick out the grammatical strings at a rate above chance without being able to state the rule (pattern) that they were sensing and following (Reber, 1989). Such "implicit" learning influences have been widely reported in various research designs of this variety (for a review, see Holyoak & Spellman, 1993). According to LLT, these implicit learnings of the patterned in relation to the unpatterned reflect the predicational process, which always works in a global, top-down fashion. Sometimes these implicit learnings are far removed from the targets of awareness. As we shall see when we look at memory studies in chapter 5, some memories take place because of the initial cognitive organization that they enjoy rather than because of the person's understanding-intention to retain the content in question.

The studies on metacognition support this top-down view of cognition. The term *metacognition* was introduced by Flavell (1977), who defined it as "knowledge concerning one's own cognitive processes and products or anything related to them" (p. 232). People can be seen to monitor their knowledge, testing the suitability or correctness of their thoughts and looking for alternatives in light of ongoing results (Brown & DeLoache, 1978; Lovelace, 1984). It is important to know when we do not know something at all versus when we have an inkling of it but just cannot come up with the required answer (Pressley, Borkowski, & Schneider, 1987). When subjects have failed to recall certain items, we can have them rate which ones they have a feeling of knowing; later, in a second attempt, we find that they do indeed recall significantly more of these items than those for which they had no feeling of knowing (Lupker, Harbluk, & Patrick, 1991).

There is some kind of abstract processing going on here that transcends, frames, and evaluates ongoing cognition. Logical learning theory suggests that this transcending process depends on generic oppositionality, a basic sense that things may be as affirmed or they may not . Delimiting oppositionality then occurs as an affective assessment indicating the relative merit of a line of thought. Thus, when college students are presented with general-knowledge items (e.g., "Who wrote *Catch 22*?") but cannot provide the answer, they sometimes feel they know the answer but just cannot state it. In a subsequent recognition task, the subjects correctly identify 76% of these "I feel I know that" items, whereas they correctly recognize only 43% of unknown items lacking this feeling (Hart, 1967). In LLT terms, such feelings are affective assessments and not real emotions. Demonstration Experiment 10 in chapter 7 provides evidence that the affective quality of learnable items (words) is routinely known even before these items are known.

Nisbett and Wilson (1977b) conducted a number of studies in which subjects were given precedents that served to target a subsequent item; after a sequacious influence was demonstrated in their cognitive processing, these subjects could not identify or would not agree to this obvious influence. For example, subjects might first memorize a list of word pairs in which *moon* and *ocean* were joined. Later, they were asked to name a detergent. More subjects in this condition named the detergent "Tide" than subjects who had not learned the moon-ocean pairing. According to LLT, since the context (moon-ocean) was not itself targeted by a predication, the subjects would not be likely to consider its influence—just as, for example, I might use a word to convey an idea without considering the definition (meaning context) that predicates it. Indeed, were I to look up this word in a dictionary, I might find that it does not represent the precise meaning that I wish to convey. In general, when experimental subjects attend to some task, they frame understanding-intentions (*Einstellung*) that are relevant to the specific task defined by the experimenter (*Aufgabe*), so that they are usually unaware of the experimental design's broader ramifications (Davis, 1964).

Viewing cognition this way, we can readily see how so-called unexpected problem solutions might arise as some new pattern that was not initially an aspect of an understanding-intention now accidentally intrudes to give the sudden "aha" insight (Maier, 1931). According to LLT, human reasoning is facilitated by having the proper or relevant pattern qua meaning tautologically extended to the target (i.e., meaning-extension). The role of tautology in framing understanding-intentions can be seen clearly in Einstein's theoretical development, for he essentially tautologized matter with energy (Kondo, 1969, p. 45), inertia with gravity (pp. 69, 70), and gravity with curved space (p. 78).

People frequently search for understanding-intentions even when there are none to be had (Orne, 1962). They try to organize chance events into a fixed, predictable array (Feldman, 1963). People appear to be credulous organisms. They tend to believe what they see and only occasionally question their percepts as an afterthought (Bargh, 1989). According to LLT, whether readily accepting events as experienced or searching for arcane reasons for which such events arise, the person doing the understanding is carrying out a symbolical cognitive process. This symbolical process extends sequaciously from the broader ("fuzzy") to the narrower (targeted) expanse of meaning, and it reflects thereby either understanding- or action-intentionality.

Finally, it should be noted that the principle of meaning-extension, which was presented in chapter 2, has direct relevance to understanding-intentions. That is, we would expect the patterning of meaning that forms into understanding-intentions to extend most readily to the least-known (new, different, strange, etc.) aspects of experiences. People intend to understand what they presently do not know. Of course, as we shall see in chapter 7, there is also the matter of affective assessment, which influences the attention and interest a person will devote to one little-known target over another. All such affective considerations held constant, however, we expect to find the principle of meaning-extension functioning in the framing of understanding-intentions.

Oppositionality in Cognitive Processing

There are many indications of generic and delimiting oppositionality in the process and content of cognition. Although network theories (e.g., Wyer & Carlston, 1979) tend to place "word-nodes" bearing opposite meanings far apart in the network organization—suggesting a longer path for the signal to traverse between such words—findings on word associations reveal that people produce opposites to stimulus words more readily than they do nonopposites (Karwoski & Schachter, 1948; Kjeldergaard, 1962; Siipola, Walker, & Kolb, 1955). This widely cited finding is highly supportive of delimiting oppositionality. No evidence to date has been reported suggesting that it takes longer to traverse network pathways joining antonyms than synonyms. Delimiting oppositionality is consistent with the speed and creativity of thinking. For example, both college students and business executives who rapidly responded to words with opposites were found to score higher on an independent test of creativity than those who did not (Rothenberg, 1973a & b).

Delimiting oppositionality can moderate a stand taken on some position. Thus, subjects who were asked to "consider the opposite" on a number of social issues like capital punishment were found to be less polarized or opinionated than subjects who were asked to "be fair and objective" (Lord, Lepper, & Preston, 1984). In concept formation, transfer is facilitated when both "good" and "bad" examples of concepts are presented to subjects who have to apply them later (Homa & Vosburgh, 1976). People assign responsibility for certain actions according to the opposing intentions of the actor. In one study, a paraplegic couple were described to subjects as having died in an automobile accident after they were denied a cab ride. Although the accident and the cab ride are two separate events, the cabbie's intentional decision to offer or deny the ride was evaluated by subjects in an interesting manner: Subjects perceived the cabbie's refusal to accept the couple's request as a stronger cause of the deaths than if he had granted the rides and then been involved in the fatal accident himself (Wells & Gavanski, 1989).

Delimited opposite meanings are not cut-and-dried alternatives. Westcott (1981) found that college students gave over 200 different words and phrases describing a feeling that was opposite to the feeling of being free. Opposite meanings are definitely not either/or in the sense of Boolean disjunction. Opposing interpretations of the same descriptive statements can sometimes be plausibly defended (Gergen, Hepburn, & Fisher, 1986). On the other hand, alternative *deconstructive* readings of the same text commonly hinge on opposite interpretations of a key sentence or phrase (Derrida, 1985). Studies measuring the reading rate of sarcastic statements, in which a literal expression (e.g., "you're a fine friend") means its opposite ("you're a bad friend"), find that people can immediately grasp the sarcasm without needing additional time to process from the literal to the nonliteral meaning (Gibbs, 1986). Orne (1959) has described what he called "trance logic," in which a hypnotized subject is capable of maintaining simultaneous but contradictory cognitions. Thus, a hypnotized subject might see a hallucinatory and transparent image of person A at the same time that a veridical image of person A is held in view. Findings of this sort suggest both generic and delimiting oppositionality.

Lamiell (1987) has argued that impressions formed of others are not accomplished by normatively (demonstratively) relating the behaviors of person A to the behaviors of persons B, C, D, and so on. Impressions of others are formed by deciding how person A stands in relation to a predicating dimension like reliability (*inside* the Euler circle) against the likelihood that he or she might be otherwise (*outside* the Euler circle). This is a dialectically generated estimation that draws on both generic and delimiting oppositionality. Lamiell's experiments, in which he contrasts personality-impression ratings based on a normatively framed statistical formula with the same ratings based on a dialectically framed statistical formula, clearly establish the superiority of the latter in impression formation (Lamiell, Foss, Larsen, & Hempel, 1983; Lamiell, Foss, Trierweiler, & Leffel, 1983).

People do not always easily manage negation. For example, in concept-learning experiments, even though negative instances of a concept might facilitate transfer of learning, people tend to avoid them in preference to positive instances of a concept (Wason & Johnson-Laird, 1972). This may be another manifestation of the credulity that we have noted in people's behavior. People may wish to base their concepts or beliefs on what is the case and not on what (possibly) is not. Negative information has been found more difficult to process than positive information (Mehler, 1963). Would this disparity occur if human cognition were machinelike? Computers experience no difficulty processing negative information.

Generic oppositionality is suggested in the finding that judgments of sameness are made more rapidly than judgments of difference (Nickerson, 1978; Proctor, 1981). This distinction is the same as that between the inside and outside of the Euler circle, and the judgment is of a difference rather than of a delimiting opposite meaning. In addition, people are ready to tautologize identity rather than to reject this natural proclivity to see the sameness in things. On the other hand, when an experimental task calls for a subject to decide whether he or she has ever been in a city, responding no takes less time than responding yes (Kolers & Palef, 1976). It seems that the nature of the task, not negation per se, accounts for the response-time differences. Taking oneself out of a Euler circle representing a city that one has never been in is apparently easier than placing oneself erroneously into this circle. This is not a simple difference judgment of generic oppositionality; it involves a delimiting oppositionality as well ("I was/was not in").

Incidentally, I should note that in presenting experiments using a time line against which to test the dependent variable, I am not forced into accepting the view that a predicating process is a function of or is somehow caused by time's passage. These temporal measurements occur in the context of experimentation and act as standards against which to test theoretical claims. I can accept these standards as one of the ground rules in scientific method, acknowledging that we can measure a task's difficulty by measuring the time it takes to accomplish it. This methodological finding can stand as a proof without thereby committing me to the view that time has somehow itself brought about the result.

There are also paradoxical aspects of negation. Thus, during a "stream of consciousness" experiment in which subjects freely associated into a tape recorder, those subjects who were asked to think of a white bear had fewer ideas about white bears than did subjects who were asked not to think of a white bear (Wegner, Schneider, Carter, & White, 1987). On the other hand, we know that people can negate physical promptings, such as having a spontaneous urge to move their hand (Libet, 1985, p. 530) or stopping an arm from moving when under cerebral stimulation to move it (Penfield, 1975, p. 77; I will return to such considerations in chapter 8).

All in all, it appears that although oppositionality does not always function in the same way, it most certainly *does* function in cognitive organization and processing. There are indications that investigators of language are becoming aware of this fact. Thus, Gross, Fischer, and Miller (1989) have proposed that predicative adjectives in English are organized in semantic memory by relations of antonymy and synonymy. The basic semantic structure is postulated to be antonymous pairings, with synonymous adjectives clustering around the two antonyms. Validation of this theory has relied on timing subjects' judgments of pairs of adjectives as either directly or indirectly antonymous. Logical learning theory places much greater emphasis on such delimiting oppositionality than confining it to adjectivial organization, but it is nevertheless encouraging to see this modest recognition of an important cognitive heuristic.

Demonstration Experiments: Inference versus Implication

The distinction between inference and implication is extremely important to a teleological theory like LLT, which opposes the computerlike theories of cognition being advanced in modern psychology. If human beings actually have different courses of reasoning, following possible predicating assumptions in a "may be" or "could be" manner, then they accomplish something that no computing machine has achieved and, indeed, cannot in principle *ever* achieve—at least, the computer as presently conceptualized, with its Boolean disjunction and demonstrative reasoning limitations, cannot in principle achieve this metacognitive realization of a hypothetical possibility. Thus, it is important for LLT to establish that something of this sort occurs and that people may even be (meta-)cognizant of their implicational mode of reasoning.

Experiment 2

Hypothesis

Presenting an individual's behavior in the form of an unqualified negation invites subjects to select an explanation of this behavior that is specifically opposite to—rather than simply different from—its meaning.

Rationale

When a subject is told that a person has never done or is not doing something that might predicate his or her behavior, the unequivocal negation of this content under processing is likely to draw the subject's predication out of the Euler circle according to what I have called delimiting oppositionality. That is, since we have a content under consideration here, we are dealing in more than simply generic oppositionality. Implications get at what is not said or what is not made clear in a set of circumstances. What is said delimits this opposite meaning, of course. Often, what is not said is what is not favorable. Hence, the person drawing an implication, as opposed to one drawing an inference, is likely to take a negatively opposite direction in thought. It is important to stress that LLT does not claim that implications are *always* oppositional in meaning-extension. Implications simply have a high probability of being oppositional. Inferences, on the other hand, are nonoppositional by definition.

Experimental Sample

One hundred and thirty-seven college students (70 females, 67 males) served as subjects.

Procedure

Three forms of an Implications Scale were assembled, consisting of 30 items each, to be administered to three different groups of subjects (Forms A, B, and C) (see Barnard, 1989). Each scale item consisted of a brief statement describing a person's action *through a negation* followed by two possible explanations of this action. Each of the three forms had the same statements of action, but there were different pairings of the explanations on each form. These 30 items were selected from an initial pool of 63 items for which three judges had to agree that the alternatives used were appropriately oppositional or nonoppositional. Subjects were instructed to select the more plausible of the two alternatives for each scale item. Here are two items as they appeared on Forms A, B, and C, respectively:

Form A

1. Karen's face reflected an emotional mood, but it was not happiness.
   ____ A. Karen was angry.
   _x_ B. Karen was sad.

2. John never takes his shirt off in public.
   _x_ A. John is ashamed of his physique.
   ____ B. John catches cold easily.

The expected answers to these items have an X placed in the relevant blank. The oppositionality of the first example is directly obvious, relying as it does on strictly antonymical relations between happy and sad. The second example, on the other hand, requires a more covert line of implication suggesting that *if* baring one's chest is a prideful act for a male, then *never* baring it implies that John is ashamed of his physique. There were no significant differences for these two levels (Example 1 versus Example 2) of implication in the data analysis, so the items may be considered as tapping the same process of implication.

Form B

1. Karen's face reflected an emotional mood, but it was not happiness.
   _x_ A. Karen was sad.
   ____ B. Karen was bored.

2. John never takes his shirt off in public.
   ____ A. John sunburns easily.
   _x_ B. John is ashamed of his physique.

Once again, the expected answers are marked with an X.

Form C

1. Karen's face reflected an emotional mood, but it was not happiness.
   ____ A. Karen was bored.
   ____ B. Karen was angry.

2. John never takes his shirt off in public.
   ____ A. John catches cold easily.
   ____ B. John sunburns easily.

In this case, no X appears in the blanks because we have no basis on which to predict which alternative the subjects will select. The subjects were randomly assigned to one of the three experimental conditions and tested in small groups of no more than 10 persons.

Results

When all three forms of the Implications Scale are contrasted, it is possible to compare selections made by subjects when every oppositional explanation has been matched with every nonoppositional explanation. The experimental hypothesis holds that the opposite explanation will be favored on Forms A and B, even when compared to an explanation that has been selected more often by subjects on Form C. For example, assume that subjects had selected "John sunburns easily" significantly more often than "John catches cold easily" on Form C. Even so, the experimental hypothesis holds that the subjects will select "John sunburns easily" less often than "John is ashamed of his physique" (Form B).

To test for the significance of item selections, a chi-square analysis was performed on each item of Forms A, B, and C of the Implications Scale. We accepted the .05 level of significance, which requires that $\chi^2 = 3.841$ with $df = 1$. There were 13 significant chi-squares found on Form A. Ten of these were on items in which the oppositional alternative was selected over the nonoppositional. There were also 13 significant chi-squares found on Form B, but in this case 12 of the selections favored oppositional alternatives. Finally, there were 16 significant chi-squares found on Form C. In 12 of these instances, when compared to an oppositional explanation on either Forms A or B, the latter explanations were selected significantly more often. Indeed, in only *one* instance did a nonoppositional explanation chosen significantly more often on Form C also reach significance over an oppositional explanation on Form A. Thus, in 75% of the cases in which a selection bias favoring one or the other of the nonoppositional alternatives arose on Form C, the heuristic power of oppositionality overrode this preference.

Conclusion

The experimental hypothesis has been strongly supported. The logical weight of an unqualified negation implies that oppositional meanings are involved in the explanations to follow. Our next effort was to see whether information framed negatively is more likely to change an opinion than information framed positively.

Experiment 3

Hypothesis

Subjects who are asked to make an initial judgment concerning the relative presence or absence of a personality trait in the behavior of a target person, and who are then given additional information that contradicts their original judgment, will change their opinion more readily when the contradictory information is framed as a negation than when it is framed as a nonnegation.

Rationale

As a major manifestation of cognitive oppositionality that functions in both generic and delimiting forms of opposition, negation should readily influence an opinion change when additional information is given concerning a target about which an opinion has previously been expressed. Thus, if a subject predicates a targeted person with some meaning, this situates the target in a Euler circle. If subsequent information negates this predication, however, it is reasonable to expect that a change of predication might take place. The target will be moved partially or totally from within the framing Euler circle in the direction of the opposite opinion being delimited as a content in the predicational process. Negation defines "the opposite way" outside the Euler circle with the least equivocation—or, as it also might be termed, with the greatest assertiveness. When we hear that something is not true, or that it never happened, we are beyond merely pondering an inconsistency or a contradiction, wondering whether things go this way or that. Negations finalize things.

Experimental Sample

Eighty-five college students (43 females, 42 males) served as subjects.

Procedure

Subjects filled in an Impression Scale entitled "What Sort of Person Is Cheryl (Greg)?" The target person's sex was randomized across subjects. On page 1 of the experimental form the subjects were given eight facts concerning the target (Cheryl or Greg). These facts referred to the high school behavior of the target, and they were equally divided between extraverted and introverted descriptions. Here is an example of the descriptive facts concerning Cheryl during high school, with parenthetical symbols for both extraversion (E) and introversion (I) indicating the type of fact being presented:

> Cheryl always seemed to be campaigning for a position in the student government or other organizations (E). Although she was always very quiet during class (I), she never failed to talk to others at the lunch table (E). But she never wanted to go out on weekends (I). She liked to read a lot (I). She never seemed to have any difficulty making friends (E). She never attended any of the football or basketball games (I), but she enjoyed acting and always had a part in the yearly school play (E).

The items were pretested by having judges agree on the degree to which they indicated introversion or extraversion. Note that half of the introverted and extraverted statements are oppositional and half are not. The order of the descriptive sentences was rearranged in the paragraph across subjects (to counteract primacy-recency effects). After reading the paragraph relating the target's high school behavior, the subjects were asked to record a judgment concerning the target (in this case, Cheryl) on a rating scale, with the value of 0 labeled *extraverted* and the value of 24 labeled *introverted* (we made certain that the subjects understood these terms).

On the second page of the experimental form the subjects were given additional information concerning the target person several years after graduating from high school. This additional information was contained in five statements, all of which described the target as either extraverted or introverted. The direction that the additional information took depended on the initial predication of the target by the subject in question. If the subject had predicated the target person as an introvert (above 13 on the rating scale), the five additional statements characterized the target as extraverted in nature, and vice versa. However, half of the subjects received these statements in the form of a negation and half received them in the form of an affirmation (nonoppositional).

For example, an affirmative statement of additional information concerning Cheryl's introverted behavior was "She hid her emotions." This same information was conveyed oppositionally as "She did not openly express her emotions." Once again, judges agreed on whether these additional statements indicated introversion or extraversion.

Results

The dependent variable is the difference (*D*) score obtained by subtracting the subjects' second rating of personality from their initial rating. The expected direction here is opposite to the initial rating, and this was true of all subjects. The additional contradictory information influenced all subjects to change their opinion in the reverse direction. The experimental hypothesis, however, held that those subjects who were given the additional information in the form of a negation would obtain a larger D score than the subjects who were given this information in an affirmative, nonnegational form.

The D scores were submitted to a 2 (Sex) × 2 (Negation vs. Nonnegation) × 2 (Introversion vs. Extraversion) factorial analysis of variance. All these variables are between subjects. There was only one significant main effect and no significant interactions. The mean D score for negation ($M = 12.64$, $SD = 3.70$) was larger than the comparable measure for nonnegation ($M = 10.07$, $SD = 4.38$; $F = 8.674$, $df = 1, 72$, $p < .004$). There were several statistical checks run on the possibility of various scaling biases in these data. No such evidence was found.

Conclusion

The experimental hypothesis has been supported, extending the findings on negation in Experiment 2 to include not only an initial influence on the drawing of implications but also an influence on the changing of such predicating opinions. It is possible that the definitiveness of a negation lends reasoning an inferential quality that it does not possess otherwise. Decisiveness is related to such definitiveness and assertiveness. There is now one more question needing an answer: Are people aware that they are drawing implications rather than inferences?

Experiment 4

In the interests of space, I will describe this experiment with less detail. The subjects (99 college students) were administered a form on which four vignettes in the day of two young men and two young women were recorded. All four of these people—potential targets for predication—were described as junior executives working for the local telephone company. Each of these vignettes supplied information (content) about one person that implied something "to the opposite" about the other. For example, in one vignette we overhear the boss of both Lori and Scott say that she is going to give a certain work assignment to Scott because it requires someone who is tough. After reading through such vignettes, the subjects were asked to typify the personality of Scott and Lori (as well as the two other executives) by selecting certain word descriptors made available to them. These descriptors are meaningfully related by synonymy or antonymy to the key word of the vignette—which in this case is *tough*. Thus, *firm* would be presented to a subject as a synonym for *tough*, and *tender* would be presented as an antonym. Independently trained judges selected reliably rated antonyms and synonyms for use in relation to the key words.

The assumption here is that a subject who selects an appropriate synonym describing Scott is drawing an inference. Knowing that Scott is tough, we infer that he is also firm in managerial style. On the other hand, a subject who selects *tender* to describe Lori is drawing an implication. It is not illogical to believe that both Scott and Lori could be tough and that there are other predications beyond just this one leading the boss to make the assignment.

Subjects were also required to rate the extent of confidence that they had in their personality descriptors. Our prediction was that subjects would indeed realize when their cognitions were tentative, giving significantly lower ratings to an implication, and when their cognitions were more certain, assigning higher confidence scores to an inference. This follows from the previously discussed findings on metacognition.

As predicted, we found that our subjects did indeed draw both inferences and implications. Thus, they believed Scott to be firm, but they also were prone to view Lori as a tender person. As expected, they were less confident in their assessment of Lori's tenderness than they were in their assessment of Scott's firmness. This supports the LLT contention that people are cognizant of a difference between drawing inferences and implications. At the close of the experiment we tested subjects to see whether they could recognize the personality characteristics of the target persons. We found that their recognition memory for the implied attributions was equal to their recognition memory for the inferred attributions (Rychlak, 1984).

Conclusion

We have good reason now to believe that, unlike machines, people take on hypothetical possibilities in their cognitions and that such cognitions are frequently induced by oppositionality. When actually cognizing, people seem to know that they are treading on speculative grounds in drawing implications. At the same time, if we carry this forward into brief (recognition) memory, there is the suggestion that implications are retained as well as inferences are. It therefore seems possible that when subjects have to remember their predications of targets, they may confuse what was initially an implication with an inference, arriving thereby at an unwarranted sense of conviction about the past circumstances. This dynamic is reminiscent of the Harris (1974) study presented above.

Concluding Comment

There seems to be nothing in the research literature on cognitive processing that forces us to believe that human beings are cognitive machines. People are seen to take points of view in framing context meanings. They infer with certainty at times, and at other times they begin a more speculative line of implication, including looking to the very opposite of what might be under consideration. They have metacognitive capacities to transcend ongoing thought, putting it to evaluation and, it appears, redirection through negation. Characterizing behavior in terms of final causation—as being done for the sake of some particular line of meaning-extension—seems quite apt. People can project aspirations that are more like self-administered, reassuring pats on the back than true goals. Understanding-intentions always precede, but do not always become, action-intentions. Of course, people can willfully attain their goals as well. To understand and predict people's behavior, we must examine the specific targets to which they actually (introspectively) extend meanings.

5

Predication in Learning
and Memory

Ever since John B. Watson (1913) introduced behaviorism, traditional learning theories have given primary emphasis to efficient causation, with a close second accorded to material causation. Behavioral responses have been conceived as built-in biological mechanisms that occur later than the earlier stimuli to which they are connected, bonded, attached, hooked-up, and so forth, by efficient causation. All such concepts are derived from British associationism—in particular, from the Lockean model to which American psychology has been committed. The associations in a series of contiguous stimuli and responses were said to shape certain patterns of behavior according to the laws of classical or operant conditioning. This patterning brought formal causation into the picture as a third factor in learning theory, but always as the result of the two more "basic" causes. Traditional learning theory did not employ final causation at all. Intentionality was "accounted for" but never taken seriously as a basic cause of human behavior. The ideal in psychology was to trace behavior down to the efficient-cause motions that were presumed to underlie and lawfully direct it.

Gradually, however, a change took place in the study of memory that paralleled the rise of formal causation in modern science. In this chapter we begin with a look at this change in work on both human and animal learning and then turn to a closer examination of what learning and memory involve in LLT, ending with two demonstration experiments that seek to validate the approach taken.

From Frequency/Contiguity to Meaningful Organization in the Study of Human Memory

Memory's central role in the definition of learning was fixed by Ebbinghaus (1885/1964). Following the Lockean model, Ebbinghaus assumed that the basic laws of cognition were to be explained in terms of efficient causation. As I noted in chapter 4, he did not take an interest in the efforts he found himself making to organize the material meaningfully at the outset of learning (he experimented solely on himself). Mnemonic strategies that occurred to him spontaneously as he memorized a string of nonsense syllables were consciously dismissed. This makes good sense from an engineering perspective. If we psychologists are engineers studying "people machines," then it is pointless to consider the meaning (semantics) under processing. Such meanings are merely conveyed by the machine's mediating process and never constitute an intrinsic aspect of it. Even in today's information-processing machines, the meanings of messages conveyed have nothing to do with the engineering characteristics of the process, which deals in halving electrical signals and not with the framing of meanings (Shannon & Weaver, 1962, pp. 3, 99).

It therefore follows that if we are to study learning, we will be studying something like retained information, the associated patterns between contiguous memory units (words, nonsense syllables, etc.), the trials it takes to learn a list, the gains made through practice, and so forth. The guiding rule of learning investigations was therefore to study frequency counts of such units rather than how meaningful understanding is organized cognitively. Organisms do not frame such understanding on their own. To judge whether an organism has understood, count the number of shaping trials and the percentage of retained material that necessarily determines the extent of such "learned" understanding. Meaning is simply another word for the patterns of association that have been shaped into existence by repetitively functioning "natural" (i.e., efficiently caused) laws. Learning is not only assessed through retention; learning *is* retention.

At the outset of the 20th century, Sherrington (1906) provided psychology with a neural machine model to support Ebbinghaus's engineering bias. Microscopic investigation of the (peripheral) nervous system revealed elementary units: neurons connected by synapses, all interlacing and eventually connecting with tracts leading to the brain. Psychologists now believed that they could build on such spatial properties by tracking the engrams or memory traces of associated responses throughout the nervous system. Lashley (1929) was to search for years without finding evidence for a single neural engram in the brain.

Gradually, beginning in the 1930s, the study of memory underwent a change in emphasis. Bartlett (1932) played an influential role here by demonstrating that subjects from the United States recalled a native Canadian mythological tale ("The War of the Ghosts") in terms of their cultural preconceptions. Memory associations were obviously being influenced at their inception by a selective organizational scheme. Because Tolman's (1932/1967) theorizing was known at this time, and Hull's (1937) was soon to emerge, the understanding of what was occurring here followed their mediational modeling, but the fact began to sink in that mental contents were not entirely open to just any kind of association. Certain things associated with certain things and not with others. Could mediation itself be limited by such considerations? Bousfield and Sedgewick (1944) then demonstrated that subjects instructed to recall words tended to cluster them according to certain categorical meanings (for example, recalling all birds together). Bousfield (1953) soon followed up this finding, as did Jenkins and Russell (1952). It was becoming ever clearer that mediated, associative memory depends on its initiating organization. Miller's (1956) extensive coverage of the memory literature then prompted him to speak of mental organizers as "chunks." It appeared that there was an upper limit of seven chunks of information (plus or minus two) that any person could retain in the mediations of immediate memory.

Rock (1957) then presented evidence that struck at the heart of frequency theories of learning. Rock's subjects were asked to learn a list of paired associates assembled from letters, numbers, or quasi words. One group of subjects was required to go through this list repeatedly, memorizing each pairing until the complete list was learned. This was the standard condition for all such experiments, in which it was assumed that as subjects frequently repeated the pairings (efficient causation), they gradually formed associative bonds in the central nervous system (material causation), which resulted in learning. Rock varied this procedure for a second group of subjects. In this case, whenever a subject had not correctly aligned a pairing, the experimenter removed these items from the subject's list and replaced it with a different pairing (all pairs were of equal difficulty).

In other words, these latter subjects were getting replacement pairs for every error they made, trial after trial. They were therefore learning a somewhat new list on each trial, because it contained pairs that were not included on the previous trial. There was no opportunity to practice the unknown pairs (i.e., frequency is removed from consideration). Even so, Rock found that the subjects in his two experimental conditions did not differ in learning rate. Both reached learning criterion in the same number of overall trials. What this finding suggested for the replacement condition was that it was the initial meaningful organization of a pair that enabled learning to take place, not frequency of repetition. A pairing that the subject failed to recall (associate) reflected a poor organization that could be readily replaced with a more meaningful pairing. There was a sort of "one-trial" learning at play in which the organization or pattern either worked immediately or not. Further practice would get it to work—the subjects did eventually manage to organize all pairs to reach criterion in the standard condition—but replacing the item pairs worked just as well as retaining them for additional rehearsal.

Tulving (1962) next gave evidence that learners form idiosyncratic or subjective organizations to facilitate their memory. By the mid-1960s psychologists were suggesting that subjects organize learnable items by employing categorizations of one sort or another. Indeed, it was recognized that *both* the experimenter and the subject have categorical organizers that they attribute to the material to be learned (Mandler & Pearlstone, 1966). Entwined within this developing recognition of cognitive organizers was a gradual shift away from Ebbinghaus's emphasis on the frequency of association for "preformed" items (words, nonsense syllables, etc.) to greater concern for the ways in which the learner frames such items in the first place — including the use of mnemonic devices. Indeed, as Mandler (1967) was later to say, "All organizations are mnemonic devices" (p. 329). I would like to add that all organizations are meanings, and vice versa (see Demonstration Experiment 12 in chapter 8). Could it be that, instead of shaping the learning taking place, frequency and contiguity merely track — as extraspective measurements — the meaningful organization that occurs (introspectively) when a person learns something? Evidence for this theoretical suggestion has emerged in memory research as well.

Important experiments by Brown (1958) and Peterson and Peterson (1959) had subjects first administered a few learnable items such as nonsense syllables, followed immediately by a distracting task such as counting backward. It was assumed that counting backward prevented the subjects from rehearsing, and indeed, it was found that these distracting circumstances adversely affected the ability to recall the learnable items. Control subjects who were permitted to rehearse the items without distraction retained them in memory quite well. Based on such empirical findings, Atkinson and Shiffrin (1968) then proposed their "dual process" theory of two memory stores, *short-term* and *long-term*. This theory holds that items being input are introduced into a limited capacity, short-term store in which they can be retained only by actively rehearsing them. In the absence of such rehearsal, the items are lost to the long-term memory store because they are soon replaced by other traces as experience continues.

This theory of two distinct processes to account for memory retained the emphasis on frequency of associative ties as well as the underlying assumption of some kind of biological imprint. If long-term memory reflected categorical organizations like recalling all birds together, this somehow took place in the repetitions occurring during the progression from short-term rehearsal to long-term retention. The concept of "working memory" was also suggested to account for such transformations through mechanisms like subvocal rehearsal (see Baddeley, 1981, 1986). The Atkinson-Shiffrin dual-process theory has been extremely influential in memory research, for it not only met the initial empirical findings but meshed nicely with the computer analogue. We should not overlook the fact that as the research and theory now under consideration was developing, the so-called cognitive revolution was taking place in psychology.

Craik and Lockhart (1972), however, have challenged the Atkinson-Shiffrin theory, building their initial argument on some findings by Hyde and Jenkins (1969). We will be looking into the Craik-Lockhart theory in great detail in chapter 6, for it forms the basis of an important demonstration experiment. For now, I just want to observe that Craik and Lockhart focused on the initial organization made by a learner rather than on the rehearsal frequency of relatively unorganized items after they had been input. Craik and Lockhart postulated a *levels of processing* theory, which is also called *elaboration* in research on memory. The suggestion here is that at the time of initial input or encoding, a learnable item may be processed at different levels—initially only in terms of sensory attributes (such as the letters combining into a word), but then gradually at deeper levels, such as the import or significance of the word meanings (e.g., whether they are pleasant or unpleasant).

The deeper the processing, the stronger the organization; the stronger the organization, the longer an item will be retained in memory. We now have an alternative understanding of the Brown (1958) and Peterson and Peterson (1959) experiments: The distractor (counting backward) prevented a deeper level of organization from taking place, which adversely affected memory. Rather than two processes, there is only one process occurring, but with different levels. Of course, frequency is retained in the Craik-Lockhart model, for it is assumed that more time must be given to a deeper than to a shallow processing of input information (see esp. Craik & Tulving, 1975). This slight equivocation leaves one wondering whether a real difference in outlook has been effected, but combined with Rock's (1957) findings on one-trial organization of paired-associate learning, there is now at least the possibility that the initiating organization might be the crucial factor in memory and not the sheer frequency of processing.

This suggestion has immense importance for LLT, which, as I noted previously, does not rely on the passage of time to explain learning. Logical learning theory substitutes "predicating meaning" for "time's passage," hence frequency counts are not useful as theoretical explanations, even though they have great methodological significance as a metric, an empirical measure of learning efficiency (e.g., the fewer trials, the greater the Jamesian cash value of the predications under extension, etc.). Thus, according to LLT, memory depends on the cohesiveness and clarity of a richly organized precedent meaning, one that is framed into existence by the predicational process rather than shaped into existence by the frequency and contiguity of fortuitous contacts with an already organized external world. In place of the associationist's dictum that frequency enhances recall, the LLT advocate substitutes the claim that organization enhances recall. *Rehearsal* does not reflect the cutting of deeper and deeper grooves into a brain engram or the placing of preshaped inputs into a memory store; rather, it measures the empirical tracking of the organism's intentional efforts to predicate (organize) the material to be known. The shift from material/efficient causation to formal/final causation here is total and complete.

Does Animal Learning Involve Cognitive Representation or Predication?

There was a time when raising a question of this sort in psychology would have been considered the most horrendous act of anthropomorphization imaginable, but this is no longer the case. Romanes (1883) has been vilified in psychology for his efforts to study the animal mind, which he thought of as the capacity for purposeful adaptation to changing circumstances in individual experience (p. 4). Bouyed by a Darwinian theory of blind natural selection, the early animal experimenters followed a "functionalist" program embracing the traditional notion that any response could be associated to any stimulus. The built-in reflexes of Pavlovian conditioning gradually gave way to presumably learned stimulus-response habits forged through frequency-contiguity and cemented by drive reduction. Skinnerian, or operant, conditioning did away with the drives without giving any greater credence to purpose or intentionality. It is in the formal/final-cause conceptions of purpose and intention that we always find mentalisms being proposed.

There were two important influences that served to reduce prejudice against postulating animal cognition or thought: (1) the increasing knowledge of animal behavior, particularly in naturalistic (rather than laboratory) surroundings, and (2) the rise of information-processing theory, which almost supplanted S-R explanations in animal study. Animal psychologists found that they required an "inside the organism," unobserved but functioning *cognitive representation* to account for their observations. As one investigator put it, "Representation is a central concept in both human and animal cognition" (Terrace, 1984, p. 12). Donald R. Griffin has been a leading spokesperson for the new attitude concerning animal cognition and awareness in psychology. Griffin (1981) pulled together the findings of considerable research to support his contention that animals in the wild might indeed frame expectancies or intentions. Thus, a hungry wolf might believe, "If I chase that deer, I can catch it, and it will taste good," or a defensive-minded squirrel might think, "If I dig this burrow deeper, I can crawl into a dark hiding place" (ibid., p. 15). Comparative psychologists now believe that animals must be understood as actively contributing to their cognitive representations—in an information-processing manner, of course (see, e.g., Roitblat & Von Fersen, 1992, p. 672).

Work on communication with the higher apes has had a significant impact on the changing attitude toward animal cognition. Most of these studies employed American Sign Language, which is used by the deaf in North America (Fouts, 1972; Gardner & Gardner, 1969; Patterson, 1978a & b; Savage-Rumbaugh, 1986; Terrace, 1979), but other means of manual communication have also been introduced, such as colored chips as meaningful signs (Premack, 1976) or a series of geometric figures arrayed on an electronic board that chimps can activate through touch (Rumbaugh, 1977). Using such manual techniques in place of vocal utterance, researchers have produced evidence to support animal cognition and communication. Although this work is controversial, with critics charging that the chimps are merely performing tricks without true understanding (see, e.g., Seidenberg & Petitto, 1979; Sugarman, 1983; Umiker-Sebeok & Sebeok, 1981), the findings are too extensive to be explained away entirely on this basis (for a balanced analysis, see Walker, 1983, chap. 9).

One of the earliest breaks with traditional stimulus-response explanations occurred when Rescorla (1967) suggested that it was not simply a fortuitously contiguous pairing of the conditioned stimulus (cs) to the unconditioned stimulus (us) followed by reinforcement that resulted in Pavlovian conditioning. Rather, it was the *predictability* of the us following the cs presentation that accounted for the associative hook-up. The animal had to see— form an expectancy of—the relationship between these variables. This not only brought Pavlovian explanations closer to Skinnerian explanations, but it greatly liberalized the kinds of constructs that animal psychologists were expected to use in their explanations of learning. Rescorla (1972, 1978) talked of "informational variables" and called for a "cognitive perspective" in Pavlovian conditioning. A. R. Wagner (1978) added concepts of "expectancies" and "priming in short-term memory." And *conditioning* itself was redefined as "the process whereby when an animal is exposed to certain relationships between events, representations of those events are formed, and associations established between them, with the consequence that the animal's behaviour changes in certain specifiable ways" (Mackintosh, 1983, p. 20). Taken from an introspective perspective, this definition could allow predication to be the representational process in question.

Of course, explaining animal behavior from the introspective (first-person) perspective violates a long-standing extraspective (third-person) tradition in psychology. The whole point of mediated associations in conditioning theory was to keep the explanation external to the "psychic apparatus" of any behaving organism. Since Watson's (1913) assertion that the "behaviorist, in his efforts to get a unitary scheme of animal response, recognizes no dividing line between man and brute" (p. 158), the aim has been to explain behavior in a bottom-up, Lockean-Darwinian fashion, accounting reductively for the (higher) person in terms identical to the (lower) brute. But now the tables seemed to be turning, as association theory proved inadequate to the theoretical task. Cries of anthropomorphism were heard in traditional quarters.

About the same time that Rescorla was revising the Pavlovian account, Garcia and Koelling (1966) performed an important series of experiments. They administered saccharin-tasting water to rats, and whenever the rats began lapping it up, lights flashed and a noise sounded. The rats were dosed with X rays during these drinking sessions, which made them physically ill beginning about one hour after ingesting the water. When they had recovered, the rats were tested for acquired aversions to the elements of the compound stimulation. Would they avoid the saccharin-tasting water or water that was accompanied by light and noise? The rats avoided the saccharin water and not the "bright noise." A second experiment was conducted in which shocks to the feet were administered rather than X rays. In this circumstance, rats acquired a conditioned avoidance response to the light and noise and not to the water.

Seligman (1970) then proposed an explanation of this finding in which he held that Pavlovian conditioning theory assumed incorrectly that "any CS and US can be associated with approximately equal facility," and "in instrumental learning [theory], the choice of response and reinforcer is a matter of relative indifference" (p. 407). Actually, Seligman added, the truth is that organisms are *prepared, unprepared,* or even *contraprepared* to learn certain associative relations. Rats are contraprepared to associate exteroceptive events with nausea as well as to associate tastes with footshock. Seligman's rationale was Darwinian (p. 409)—that certain patterns of behavior would be life sustaining and so on—but what I would like to point out is that the preparedness of the rats was remarkably logical.

Stomachaches and malaise seem logically related to something going on inside the organism, and this is where the water is tasted—in the mouth. Shocks of the feet are felt emanating from outside the organism, and this is where the lights and noises were heard and seen. Do we really need a series of blind Darwinian preparatory reflexes to effect such judgments for the rat, or can we theorize that rats and other lower animals participate to some extent in the *Logos* through predication, which involves at least generic oppositionality ("inside vs. outside" the body)? Maybe evolution has actually prepared rats for such predicational logic, even though their cognizance is limited to simple difference rather than implied alternatives via delimiting oppositionality.

There have been many indications that predication occurs in animal behavior. Although Skinner postulated the operant response as a blindly emitted behavior that unintentionally creates a contingently reinforcing state of affairs (see Evans, 1968, p. 19), so-called *auto-shaping* research now establishes that such operant responding takes place even when no contingency has followed its occurrence (Brown & Jenkins, 1968). Thus, consider the following experiment, in which pigeons were exposed to a key illuminated by a flash of light; a food hopper below followed the flash with a bit of food. The pigeons did not have to deliver an operant pecking response to have grain fall into the hopper, as Skinnerian theory demands. Food was contingent solely on the key being lit. Even so, on observing the pattern of a lighted key and food falling into the hopper, pigeons immediately began to peck the key. If the relationship between the lighted key and the food dispensed is random, the pigeons do not condition (Gamzu & Williams, 1973). If a screen is placed between the pigeon and the food dispenser, so that all the animal can do is repeatedly observe the illuminated key followed by the immediate appearance of the food, once this screen is removed, the pigeon walks directly to the key and begins to peck away in obvious expectation that new delicacies will follow (Browne, 1976). It does not require a stretch of imagination to construe these findings as reflecting a predicational process in the pigeon.

Other suggestions along this line have been made in the animal literature. Zener (1937) noted long ago that dogs that have been conditioned in one location and then placed in another will leave the second location and return to the original (predicating?) context when the cs is presented. In his studies of imprinting in chicks and discrimination learning in monkeys, Bateson (1964; Bateson & Chantrey, 1972) demonstrated that if such phenomena are to occur, an animal has to be exposed to an environment containing stimuli that can serve as a background to the target in question. Thus, chicks raised in darkness failed to imprint or to benefit from perceptual learning. Such grounding stimuli are readily conceived of as predicating meanings.

Higuchi (1987) reports that certain green-backed herons practice bait fishing by dropping small objects into the water and spearing a fish that takes the lure. This cannot be a species reflex, because only a small fraction of these birds perform this feat. Similar observations have been made on small groups of bottlenose dolphins, which are seen to herd intimidated mullets out of the water and onto the shore. Once out of the water, the mullets are easily devoured by the dolphins. Other small groups of dolphins less than a mile away are never observed performing this hunting maneuver (Norris, 1992, p. 29). Rats that have previously (precedently) been exposed to inescapable shock are slow to learn at the choice-point of a Y-maze when shock is present (Jackson, Alexander, & Maier, 1980). Pigeons can learn to separate certain pictures into two categories after learning that one of these categories leads to food. One picture may have water or the image of a certain person in it, whereas the other does not (Herrnstein, Loveland, and Cable, 1976). Pigeons may also respond like this to pictures of two different kinds of tree leaves (Cerella, 1979). Here again, the suggestion of grasping difference through generic oppositionality is totally consistent with such data.

I do not want to give the impression that all animal psychologists are in favor of the trend to cognitive theorizing in their area of specialization. Dinsmoor (1983) staunchly defends traditional Skinnerianism. Amsel (1989) has written a most interesting Hullian defense. He tends to blame the Skinnerians for cognizing the field of learning (p. 43). Amsel is especially critical of the demise of drive theory in animal learning (pp. 34, 35). Traditional S-R theory is tied to physiological conceptions of the *Bios* (p. 41). Amsel equates representation with mediation (p. 63). His solution is to propose two systems that operate to strengthen learned associations in the animal—one more primitive than the other. The latter system is a Pavlovian "stamping in" (p. 84). The second system involves incentives, expectancies, and related cognitive representations that early behaviorists like Tolman and Hull anticipated in their mediational models.

The fact that something like Pavlovian conditioning could take place at a very rudimentary level in human beings, and more thoroughly in lower animals, would not in itself threaten the integrity of LLT. Reflexive adaptation (tropisms, etc.) seems plausible enough. Theorists working on *Bios* assumptions may indeed find such patterned reorganizations of reflexive movements taking place. The danger arises when such patterned findings and the mediational speculations they engender are assumed to be the basic source of what LLT describes as predication. The former theoretical process engulfs the latter. We are then back in the 1930s, hoping to account for human cognition in the bottom-up, efficient/material-cause fashion that has led psychology up nothing but a dead-end street.

All in all, the LLT position is strengthened by what has occurred in animal learning. The preliminaries of a predicating intellect are easily seen in the study of lower animals. I will return to animal study in chapter 6, when I take up oppositionality in cognition.

Memory, Prememory, and Time in Human Learning

Logical learning theory views *learning* as reflecting the process of extending recognized or "known" predicated meanings to other or "new" targets of knowledge in ongoing telosponsivity. Learning has occurred when the person feels confident or understands enough to use a former target as a current predicate. To the extent that such precedent meanings sequaciously enhance the person's understanding of ongoing experience, LLT holds that learning is proceeding—even if what is learned is erroneous, biased, or foolish (with such assessments being based on the predicating values of a critic or expert). Thus, in addition to recognizing its role in intention (to mean is to intend), we must appreciate that meaning is to be found in the organization of precedents, some of which are better organized than others.

It is possible to "learn error," because the individual finds such plausibly organized, albeit erroneous, predications (including affective predications) successfully anticipating or predicting events. The predications may engender some interpersonal friction and personal setbacks, but these are not attributed to the predicational stance. The target is the event and not the predication of the event, which works its silent (unconscious) effects into the person's daily routine. It is often a question not of truth or error but merely of interpretation. Two people can observe the same motion picture of an event and yet contradict each other's interpretation of what is taking place on the screen (Hastorf & Cantril, 1954). In LLT we are interested in the learner's introspective perspective. How does he or she learn the supposed truth? Errors in interpreting experience can be costly on other counts, but they are not directly relevant to an understanding of how this process takes place.

A comparable issue is to be seen in the interpretations given to the empirical literature cited in this book. The LLT advocate accepts the same empirical evidence that mechanists garner to support their view of learning but interprets such findings teleologically. This is entirely consistent with good science and stems from the limitations that the fallacy of affirming the consequent imposes on the use of empirical evidence to verify scientific theories. I think LLT is extremely consistent with the findings that have elevated organization at the initiation of learning over contiguity and frequency of input mediators. But then, I speak from certain predicating assumptions that direct what I can and will know. Whether the reader accepts LLT or the mechanist position will depend on assumptions of this nature. All arguments come down to decisions based on such precedent understanding-intentions. Once these are settled, the sequacious extension of meaning follows automatically (*not* mechanically).

This matter of predicating assumptions is directly relevant to the LLT view of memory. To speak of *memory* in LLT is to take three factors into consideration:

1. An initial assumptive meaning (i.e., a predicate) must extend to a target (this is a telosponse);
2. a period of (what is called) time passes; and

3. a recurrence of the initial meaningful organization is effected or approximated (this is also a telosponse).

Point 1 obviously refers to learning. In chapter 2 I argued that an infant can tautologize a perceived item (e.g., "a nipple is a nipple") but that eventually analogical extensions are telosponded ("a thumb is a nipple" in the sense that a thumb is *like* a nipple and also *unlike* a nipple). (*Note*: Given that fetuses have been observed to suck their thumbs in utero, if we assume that cognition is underway before birth, the very same telosponsive explanation would hold, except that now the course of learning would be from "a thumb is a thumb" to "a nipple is a thumb," and so forth.)

Logical learning theory holds that the very first concept formations at Point 1 are gradually lost to memory as they gain the status of prototypical knowledge. As the person confronts an ever-expanding experience, the precedent meanings (e.g., "nippleness") at Point 1 are used assumptively as a cognitive *prototype*. In this way, predicated experience follows predicated experience in a long, increasingly abstract succession of meaning-extensions. Logical learning theory does not admit the possibility of a completely unpredicated experience, although vaguely understood experiences are commonplace.

In the course of this developing succession, the *initial* meaning formulated at Point 1 becomes increasingly abstract in cognitive organization, so that it comes to take on the status of an *assumption*. Memory is essentially a top-down process. Assumptions are extended to the targets that memory is said to retrieve or produce. Thus, it is not necessary to remember what *bird* means assumptively to remember seeing a bird in the backyard yesterday. When we first learned what the word *bird* means, this concept itself had to be targeted in memory. Now, however, as *bird* becomes a predicate and is extended to other targets, to new Point 1 formulations, we no longer cognize it in the way that we did when we first learned its meaning. The bird prototype is part and parcel of seeing this animal in the new experience—that is, a new Point 1 item in memory.

We might now call this assumptive framework at Point 1 the *prememory*. In coining this term I am simply recognizing the role that initial predicating assumptions must play if a learned relationship in the *Logos* is to occur. Memory requires a preliminary formulation, a prememorial context from which the learning to be remembered takes root. Ultimately, our prememory is equivalent to what we call our commonsense, which frames procedural evidence. As the logical progression of predications takes place in experience, the prememory formulation need not itself be remembered for a memory to occur at Point 3. The prememory has receded to an assumptive status. We do not remember how or when we learned what *bird* means, but we do know what a bird is—albeit in a global, Wittgensteinian (1968) sense of family re-semblance—and can recall seeing one yesterday.

Logical learning theory thus draws a clear distinction between knowing and remembering meanings. It follows that we can know without remember-ing. When we know, we have a predication relevant to the target that we are attempting to remember. Knowledge deals in predications, the most abstract of which we consider to be universals. These predications do not have to be remembered, for they literally create what is to be remembered. The concept of remembering therefore places emphasis on the target under predication. To remember a past event or object is to extend meaning from the best pos-sible approximation (at Point 3) of the initial predication (at Point 1) relating to the target we intend to remember. This predication at Point 3 can occur spontaneously, so that unintended rememberings also occur.

The principle of meaning-extension is obviously involved here. A famil-iar example of knowing without remembering is in driving an automobile. When we first learn to drive, the targets of the meaning-extensions to be remembered are all the details of this task, such as turning on the engine, setting the gears, depressing the gas pedal, carefully steering, observing the traffic, watching for traffic signals, and so on. Later, when we know how to drive, these patterned movements are no longer the targets of our predi-cations as we slip behind the steering wheel. These former targets serve as predications framing the concept of driving as an instrumentality that we enact (action-intention) in furthering new targets to be remembered, such as where we are to meet a friend. Alternatively, the predications under affir-mation as we drive someplace may be on different targets entirely, such as our job concerns, vacation plans, and so forth.

The principle of meaning-extension suggests that our attention will be likely to turn to such anticipated but unknown eventualities—unknown in the sense that they have not yet occurred. (Indeed, they may never occur, so that these eventualities include those considered in daydreams). In fact, our focus of attention might be so tightly organized on such nondriving con-siderations that we actually forget—having never targeted them—the details of our drive home from work. This can happen because our "learned habit" of driving involves moving former targets to current predications, and it is not thereby necessary to remember everything that we know predicationally to target (hence remember) other aspects of our experience.

Evidence for the claim that we can know without remembering can be seen in research on amnesiac patients (Warrington & Weiskrantz, 1970). Such patients recognize and recall words much more poorly than do nor-mals. However, these patients perform as well as normals in completing fragments of words that have been presented before but are now introduced as a new task. For example, amnesiacs accurately complete the fragment *tab* more readily when they have seen the word *table* previously in the experimental context than when they have not. This suggests that there must be some kind of implicit memory functioning even when the patients cannot do well in recalling or recognizing the precise words (for many examples of this phenomenon, see Roediger, 1990).

Logical learning theory suggests that such performances of implicit memory reflect Point 1 prememory. Completing word fragments takes the person back to very basic initial learnings in his or her life history. Such rudimentary knowledge of letter forms and word units predicates the amnesiacs' reading capacities in the prototypical manner discussed above, or they would be unable to read the listed words in the first place. I recall observing an Alzheimer's patient who was asked to name a picture of a rhinoceros. He glanced at it, mumbled "bush," and then diverted attention from the task because he could not name the animal in the picture. According to the present analysis, his prememory framework of "animals in the bush" seemed to be functioning, at least to some extent. He had this largest, most abstract Euler circle labeled "bush animals" properly aligned with the targeted rhinoceros, but he could not also affirm the less abstract predication of the name. If these most abstract assumptions were lost completely, the patient's capacity to function mentally would presumably be lost completely.

Evidence for prememory may also be drawn from research on the so-called memory-independence effect in reasoning (Ackerman, 1992). Children in grades 2 through 6 first listened to stories composed of short sequences of sentences. They were then tested on their retention of the sentences, as well as on their capacity to discern true from false inferences based on the stories. It was found that performance and improvement on these two tasks were independent. Children could infer correctly from the stories without remembering the specific sentences of these stories. According to LLT, such children had learned the sentence content to a greater or lesser extent, turning the initial targets (i.e., subjects) of some sentences into predicates (i.e., objects) for yet other sentences to be framed in ongoing cognition regarding the stories. As a result, the children framed a context of meaning for the story enabling them to draw inferences without relying on the precise sentences (representations) initially administered to them. The exact reproduction of the sentences was, in effect, logically irrelevant at this point. Such independence between memory and reasoning has been found in the identification of concepts (Kellogg, Robbins, & Bourne, 1978), social judgments (Shedler & Manis, 1986), and attitude changes (Hastie & Park, 1986) of adults. For a mediational, "fuzzy-trace" theoretical explanation of such findings, see Brainerd and Reyna (1993).

Although understood entirely differently from LLT, Tulving and Thomson's (1973) "encoding specificity" concept takes prememory into consideration. Research has shown that it is easier to recall something if the context circumstances at the time of recall (Point 3) are identical to the circumstances at the time of initial encoding (Point 1) (Smith, Glenberg, & Bjork, 1978; Tulving & Osler, 1968). This phenomenon may be seen at class reunions, where names long forgotten begin springing to mind as the old school context is revived by mixing among formerly significant friends and associates. The context includes not only the physical situation—including whether on land or water (Godden & Baddeley, 1975)—but also the kinds of terms used to characterize the initial situation. Recall that telosponsivity occurs in both temporal directions, to the past and to the (immediate and distant) future. For example, in recalling an automobile accident, if it is initially characterized as involving "smashed" rather than "bumped" automobiles, subjects will recall far more damage in the accident than actually took place (Loftus & Palmer, 1974). In addition, characterizing people as friendly or unfriendly at initial learning biases a subject's recall of the behaviors that these people supposedly manifested at the time (Rothbart, Evans, & Fulero, 1979).

Tulving and Thomson (1973) interpret such findings according to the mediation model. They suggest that for good memory to result, correct retrieval cues must be encoded at the time of and along with what is also being input and stored in memory (p. 369). Note that both retrieval cues and information to be stored in memory are thought of as shaped by efficiently caused influences external to the mediation process. In contrast, the LLT interpretation of ongoing memory builds on what we have said about the growing number of predications that are aligned over a life. As the very first predications become knowledge prototypes, new organizations of meaning are framed at ever arising Points 1, and these prototypes in turn facilitate reconceptualization at newly occurring Points 3.

If the person's initial predication lending meaning to some experience at Point 1 can be precisely reaffirmed at Point 3, the memory of this experience will be detailed and accurate. The memory will, in a sense, be a virtual repeat of the Point 1 experience—somewhat like observing an ongoing scene across eyeblinks and considering it "memory" from pre-eyeblink to post-eyeblink. On the other hand, if an experience that has been predicated one way at Point 1 is now predicated another way at Point 3, the possibility of complete and accurate recall diminishes. This is surely the more likely outcome in human behavior, for we almost never reconceptualize Point 1 exactly at Point 3. This would amount to a match, and as I have noted previously, predication is *not* matching. Computers match (Rychlak, 1991); people predicate.

Thanks to generic and especially delimiting oppositionality, interpretation always rears its head in human predication.

Turning to Point 2, how are we to understand this phenomenon of time's passage? If learning through predication occurs outside of time, why do we sense this sequential course that events seem to take in our lives? Traditional s-r psychology was founded on the Newtonian assumption of a linear flow of *absolute time*, a completely independent course of motion against which changes in events could be measured. The behaviorist's concept of the stimulus is as an event occurring earlier on this linear time dimension, with the response following later. The formulation here is extraspective and underwritten by efficient causation, in which an earlier antecedent stimulus triggers, impels, or cues a later consequent response. Remove time from this equation and there is no possibility of describing anything. The input-output sequence of computer modeling is equally bound to the efficiently caused passage of time.

The Newtonian assumption of absolute time flowing along according to equally divided, linear units was a useful mathematical fiction, but it could not be sustained in the face of empirical evidence supporting relativity theory (Hawking, 1988, pp. 18, 33). It is routine today to read that "there does not exist one 'really true' time scale. There are only different natural processes that may be compared by time measurements" (Fraser, 1987, p. 64). Time is a construction—which translates into "a predication"—that is framed according to arbitrary units of measurement (Slife, 1993). Empirical studies find that there is no single, natural temporal code involved in human memory; rather, a person's chronological past depends on active, repeated construction (Friedman, 1993). Ross (1989) has shown how recall of personal facts such as the severity of past pain is jointly determined by the person's present state and his or her theory of consistency over time. Logical learning theory follows this modern understanding of time, giving this concept a formal-cause rather than an efficient-cause interpretation. The fact that a person can select alternative scales for the sake of which time is to be measured adds a final-cause feature to this concept as well.

The sense of a flow of time is due to the succession of predicating contexts that are continually being extended, one to the next, in logical order. Each protopoint identifies a new framing of such affirmed meanings, and since one meaning extends to another in precedent-sequacious fashion, a logical flow is sensed. As with the principles of contiguity and frequency, time is best thought of as a unit of measurement employed to logically array (organize, pattern, plan, etc.) events. People logically arrange events by years, months, and weeks, not to mention by using the sun's daily passage across the sky to define units like morning, noon, evening, and night. Clocks define hours, minutes, and seconds. Finally, there are the conceptualizations of biological maturation to consider, like the period of pubescence, which call for a recognition that significant events are taking place—events that are very meaningful (tightly organized) and hence readily recalled (i.e., reconceptualized). It is the patterned organization and order in such events that register in memory and that the person uses to frame events ("That happened three years ago, when I was 17 years old," etc.).

I noted above that information framed at Point 1 influences recall at Point 3. Because we can telospond to the past, however, the reverse is also true. The recall of earlier information framed at Point 1 may be recast by later, logically relevant information at Point 3 (Dooling & Christiaansen, 1977; Spiro, 1980). Fish stories about the "one that got away" are a familiar example of this phenomenon. A context in which a target was extended meaning several predications ago (in logical sequence) and is now reconceptualized is said to be a memory. To speak this way is obviously to use the word *memory* as referring to a content rather than a process. Sometimes this content is framed as an old memory and sometimes as a more recent memory, depending on both the meaningful vividness with which the reconceptualization is predicated at Point 3 and the predicated date (calendar time) of the memory's occurrence (all of which can be in error, of course).

Natural events like the sun's daily movement across the sky lend support to the Newtonian formulation of time. Such temporal patterning enables the person to organize experience and to predict from past or present to the future, which is actually a reflection of precedent-sequacious meaning-extension rather than something under the direction of time. Time is frequently hypostatized based on such logical ordering ("Time heals all wounds"). When we are unable to frame a predication for some target, we call this *forgetting*, although there may not have been any actual meaningful organization taking place at the outset. Sometimes there is nothing to forget. At other times, so much has occurred in the logical sequence between the initially framed meaning (Point 1) and the point of reconceptualization (Point 3) that it is extremely difficult to recapture the initial predicational organization. Further, if this organization is weak, then memory is weak.

This mass of intervening experience is akin to the distractors given to subjects in the previously mentioned Brown (1958) and Peterson and Peterson (1959) experiments, but on a longer and broader time frame. These interventions weaken the Point 1 organization, making it more difficult to reconceptualize at Point 3. On the other hand, there are certain memory organizations framed at Point 1 that are retained for long periods of time. For example, an individual may be able to recall aspects of a foreign language

(Spanish) learned 50 years ago but not practiced since (Bahrick & Phelps, 1987). Presumably, in the intervening years the person framed few predications to interfere with (i.e., rearrange) the strong linguistic organization affirmed initially.

Such long-term memories are probably the prototypical assumptions that LLT considers assumptive knowledge. The transcendent capacity of thought allows one to explore one's fundamental assumptions and to find that they are there for identification and hence are remembered. Such identification arises through the self-reflexivity of cognition. The knowledge function of such basic prototypes is reflected in the fact that elderly, senile individuals generally retain in memory their earliest life experiences but lose what occurs in the present. Logical learning theory suggests that, as with the amnesiacs, what is being retained here relates to the most basic, prototypical knowledge (including assumptions) employed conceptually throughout a lifetime—often refashioned or distorted (a "false memory"), but identifiable enough to be considered a remembrance.

In the cognitive research literature, remembering (recall, recognition, etc.) is said to occur at Point 3. Such remembering is usually referred to as *retrieval* because it is assumed that the pattern that has been shaped at Point 1 and stored over Point 2 can be activated at Point 3 by using a portion of the Point 1 pattern to trigger the complete pattern (see Johnson & Hasher, 1987, p. 637, for an argument of this type). Precisely how the activation is initiated without an executive (telic) decision being rendered is never clarified. This Lockean theoretical language may be plausible for computer processing, but the LLT advocate finds it quite unsuitable as a description of what takes place in human memory, particularly since it does not capture the active role that unique and logically distinctive meanings play at Point 1.

How Is Memory Initiated and Sustained?

Why is it that a person remembers things? According to LLT, it all depends on the meanings under processing at the protopoint (which is detected as the moment when remembering comes into play). The physical context within which a person finds himself or herself living invariably has certain demands calling for what we might consider an exercise of memory. As one rises from a night's sleep, a number of memories can be said to be called for, such as the location of the bathroom, one's grooming articles, one's closet, the kitchen, and the exit from the home. We do not ordinarily consider these to be memories, of course, for we are in the context of our home situation and—as when we remember our sight across eyeblinks—actually doing what the predicating context calls for. In terms of the distinction drawn in the previous section, LLT considers these routine morning practices as reflecting knowledge and not memory. It is only when some item is misplaced— when the logical pattern is broken—that we invoke memory: "Where did I put that hair brush the last time I used it?"

In other instances, of course, we are asked to use our memories. People ask us questions. Our employers give us work assignments demanding that we have some grasp of what is taking place and how today's efforts tie into yesterday's. In these cases, we intentionally strive to remember. Aristotle (1952d) would have called this *recollection* rather than *remembering* (p. 692). To remember is already to have a consciousness of the item in question, but to recollect we must infer, and we therefore rely on such mnemonic devices as similarity, contiguity, or contrariety (oppositionality) to prompt our memory (ibid.). There is an understanding-intentionality being worked out in recollecting. Centuries later, in devising their "laws of association," the British associationists (Locke, Hobbes, J. S. Mill, etc.) were to argue that sheer similarity, contiguity, and frequency (contrariety was dropped) accounted for what was associated with what in the mind (Boring, 1950). But this efficient-cause interpretation of association was never Aristotle's view. He was a teleologist who essentially defined association as follows: "'Why does one thing attach to some other?' . . . We are inquiring, then, why something is predicable of something . . . the inquiry is about the predication of one thing of another" (Aristotle, 1952c, p. 565).

In line with Aristotle, LLT contends that in recollecting what others ask us to bring to mind, we are not responding or retrieving associatively but telosponding predicationally. The evidence is rather clear that having an intention to learn something or making a personal effort to recall something leads to good memory (Blaxton, 1989; McDaniel, Waddill, & Einstein 1988; Slamecka & Graf, 1978; Tulving, 1966). Sloppy, indifferent, unintended learning efforts do not result in a good memory performance. We also can learn and remember without consciously intending to do either (Danner, 1976; Postman, 1964), but when this occurs it is due to the well-organized predications to which the indifferent learner is exposed (Mandler, 1967). Such effective organization acts as a mnemonic device, a cue that works even when the person may not intend to remember anything at the moment (Cermak, 1976). A well-organized predication is often a familiar one. Thus, chess masters can recall the layout of a chess board much better than nonplayers when this pattern reflects an actual chess game, of which they are naturally very familiar. When the pattern (context) is random, however, they lose their memorial superiority over the nonplayer (Chase & Simon, 1973).

I have already noted that enriching the target by way of a highly meaningful context is called *elaboration* (Craik & Tulving, 1975; Hyde & Jenkins, 1969). Memory can be facilitated by using bizarre mnemonic devices or (affectively) personal meanings (Rogers, Kuiper, & Kirker, 1977). Long-term memory in particular is aided by such elaborations (Rundus, 1971). Students have been known to use salacious allusions as mnemonic predications to aid in recalling otherwise dull lists of examination material.

In line with LLT's concept of understanding-intention, the more understanding there is in a predication, the easier it is to recall, because of the plausible (internally consistent) organization of the meanings involved. For example, a statement like "the doctor cured the patient" is better remembered than "the doctor fired the janitor" (Rosenberg, 1969). Aristotle would have said that only doctors can be predicated of cured patients, whereas many professions can be predicated of fired subordinates. Hence, the organization of the former incident is clear and precise, making it easier to recall (or recollect). This is probably why, when a person's current belief conflicts with a memory, this past experience is distorted in the direction of the current belief (Cordua, McGraw, & Drabman, 1979; Signorella & Liben, 1984). Present beliefs are good organizers of the fading past.

In the section above on animal learning I noted how conditioning is being defined today as involving a prediction from the CS to the US. We can readily construe this as the CS predicating the US. This precedent-sequacious extension of a meaningful relationship occurs in human learning as well. Fully 90% of the hundreds of experiments conducted on this topic establish that conditioning does not occur unless the person being conditioned is aware of the relationship—the patterned organization—existing between the CS and US in Pavlovian (classical) conditioning, or between the operant response and contingent reinforcer in Skinnerian (operant) conditioning (Brewer, 1974; Chatterjee & Eriksen, 1962; Dawson, 1973; Dawson & Furedy, 1976; Dulany, 1961; Levin, 1961; DeNike, 1964; Spielberger & Levin, 1962). This is not simply a matter of getting a clear "input signal" tying the CS to the US, for a second requirement in human conditioning is that the person being conditioned comply with what is indicated by the signaled relationship (Page, 1969, 1972). If the person is uncooperative, conditioning will not occur. What this means in LLT terms is that cooperation follows from the subject's developing intentionality. An understanding-intention must become an action-intention before conditioning occurs.

There are interesting order effects to be noted in memory. A classic finding is that for items in a series, those learned first (primacy effect) and those learned last (recency effect) are easier to remember than those learned in the intermediate positions (Howard, 1983, p. 51). According to LLT, this preference for the first and last items in a series is due to the teleological nature of this logical array. The beginning and end of a directed series are clearly represented here, effecting a tight cognitive organization due to the delimiting oppositionality heuristic of the notions of "first" and "last." Primacy and recency are not simply practice effects during short-term memory. There are long-term manifestations of primacy and recency. Rugby players who were asked the names of opponent teams over the past season reflected a large recency effect in their recall efforts (Baddeley & Hitch, 1977). Primacy effects seem to be influenced by education (D. A. Wagner, 1978), leading one expert to suggest that they "may be due to some active memorization strategies that are encouraged in the formal educational setting" (Howard, 1983, p. 101). A strategy obviously combines both understanding- and action-intentionality.

It has been empirically established that a recognition task is easier to perform than a recall task (Anderson, 1985, pp. 157–160). Logical learning theory interprets this difference in terms of the experimental instructions (*Aufgabe*) that the examiner (or experimenter) gives to the subject. In recall the subject must provide the complete (predicating) organization of the materials to be remembered, whereas in recognition the task amounts to completing the predicating intentions of the examiner. In a multiple choice recognition test, for example, the student has to pick out the correct answer from among the incorrect distractors. In an experimental recognition task, subjects might first view several words and then later select them after they have been mixed in with an equal number of other (distractor) words. Since meaning extends from context to target, having a clear-cut context provided by the examiner frequently aids recall. Predication in recognition often involves simply judging an item as "in" or "out" (i.e., previously encountered in this experiment or not). If the examiner's instructions provide a weak context with confusing distractors, the subject's recognition performance declines significantly (James & Hillinger, 1977).

If subjects intend to learn the material presented to them (words, cvc trigrams, etc.), they show greater gains on recall than on recognition tests of performance (Eagle & Leiter, 1964). Intentionality is related to recall because it plays a role in the initial organizational effort (Point 1, above), which is even more vital to memorial retention in free recall than recognition (because there is no help provided by the tester/experimenter in a recall task). The intending person brings to bear personalized mnemonic precedents to effect a clear organization that extends sequaciously in later recall. This has sometimes been called the *generation effect*. Memory is facilitated when subjects in a learning task generate the organization of the material to be learned (i.e., organize it themselves) rather than have it organized for them by the experimenter (Crutcher & Healy, 1989; Nairne, Pusen, & Widner, 1985). There is no evidence that the familiarity of learning units (e.g., high-frequency words) determines generation (Gardiner, Gregg, & Hampton, 1988). Logical organization at the outset (Point 1) is what matters. Along this line, a logically meaningful relationship among words in a list facilitates recall but not recognition (Kintsch, 1968).

If subjects expect one kind of task (e.g., recall) but receive another (e.g., recognition), their performance level tends to be adversely affected (Greene, 1984, 1986). Findings like this have been attributed to the additional processing time it takes to rearrange the initial organization into a new one. Logical learning theory makes a similar argument but attributes nothing causally relevant to the length of time taken per se. If the predication at Point 1 is not suitable to the memorial task at Point 3, then obviously a reconceptualization is called for. Time may *track* the decrease in performance as this organizational adjustment is made conceptually, but as I have noted earlier, it cannot explain the process involved, which is entirely logical. Some evidence has been presented that a recall expectation on the subject's part can facilitate both recall and recognition, whereas expecting recognition does not facilitate recall (Balota & Neely, 1980).

Cueing the Memory Process

If human memory involves the retrieval, recollection, or remembering of some previously conceptualized experience, then whether it was intentionally or unintentionally organized in the first place, it should be possible to assist this reconceptualization. What this comes down to is providing the subject in a memory task with certain *meanings*, termed *memory cues*, that somehow facilitate the reconceptualization of Point 1 at Point 3 in the logical sequence. Logical learning theory holds that meaning (construed in formal-cause terms) always extends from some predicate to a target in ongoing cognition. Of course, the words used to capture these meaningful contents can change locations in any statement or sentence (e.g., "a person is like a tree" vs. "a tree is like a person"). It is therefore of great interest to the LLT advocate to examine this cueing process in an effort to determine whether, as LLT implies, cueing the predicate meaning is more important to recall than cueing the target meaning.

Linguistically considered, the target is the subject of a sentence, normally lying to the left in English sentences (for example, *John* in "John is reliable"). In trying to remember a forgotten statement like "John is reliable," which word would be more useful as a cue to help us reconceptualize the full statement, *John* or *reliable?* Undoubtedly, either cue would be helpful. John has

other predications lending him meaning besides reliability, and once reconceptualized, these interpatterning meanings might well help us to recapture
the full statement. It follows from LLT, however, that the meaning of reliability, having been previously extended to John, should be more helpful.
"Past" and "present" are themselves predicating meanings in the telosponsive succession under consideration.

Actually, I prefer Aristotle's concept of recollection in this context, because when we are intentionally searching about in our memory to recall
something, we are actively looking for the context qua predication of our targeted memory. We use various mnemonic strategies (including the rules or
laws of associative organization like contrast, similarity, and so on). Logical
learning theory's suggestion at this point is that in doing so, we are trying
to hit on an even more abstract predication (organizing context) that targets
the predication of the statement we are trying to recall. We struggle, saying
something like "John is, John is . . . something good . . . he is the kind of
person you can count on . . . John is reliable!" The references to "good" and
"count on" in such efforts are actually wider contexts within which the concept of "reliable things" is positioned as a target. Meaning flows from the
wider context to the targeted item. It follows from all of this that a *memory
cue* is a meaningful referent that can extend this meaning to a target, which
in turn suggests that it serves predominantly a predicational role in cognition. There are many such potential predicates available to the person.

The "tip-of-the-tongue" (TOT) phenomenon is interesting in this regard
(for a review, see Brown, 1991). Most people experience a TOT about once
weekly. They are unable to recall something but are sure that they know it
and will be able to come up with the memory in due course. About half the
time they are able to do so. Often, the first letter of the target to be recalled is
remembered. We apparently have a tenuous predicating organization here,
but it is strong enough to assure the person that the content can be recovered.
Sometimes the name of the forgotten item is lost but the pictorial image is
clear (i.e., the person "sees" what cannot be named). This latter instance is
suggestive of a dialectical frame of mind—knowing (visually well organized)
yet not knowing (verbally poorly organized). See chapter 8 for other findings
on such conflicting predications held at the same time (esp. Figure 18).

As I have noted previously, every concept we have in mind, whether functioning as a target or a predicate in the ongoing cognitive process, is itself
under predication by more than one meaningful framework. This is why we
sometimes cannot remember something, only to have it pop into mind later
when we do not intend it to do so. We probably have been trying to press
a poor organizing context onto the target—like using an improper mnemonic—and now that this misconstruing framework is removed, we can re-

place it with an effective framework that is probably cued by an analogy from whatever it is that we are now cognizing in ongoing activity.

In one notable historical incident of this type, the French mathematician Poincaré (1929) had struggled with a problem in his field for some time, but nothing he tried worked. He decided to put the problem aside and take a holiday. As he was strolling along the beach one day, a solution to his problem suddenly and clearly popped into mind, one that framed a tautological identity between two seemingly different mathematical formulations (p. 388). From an LLT perspective, Poincaré's well-organized precedent knowledge enabled a variant problem solution to extend sequaciously via what is sometimes called an "incubation effect." Was there an additional cueing here? Possibly, as in Poincaré seeing—hence conceptualizing—identities in natural events (two identical sea gulls or sailboats analogized to the formulas, etc.). This is an oversimplification, of course, but it is how the LLT advocate would begin a study of such amazing occurrences. The *Logos* is multifaceted and open to such unintended intuitions.

The role of meaning has always been important to learning, but it has not always been studied directly. Traditional explanations of learning and memory substituted frequency estimates based on the assumption that the number of times an engram or associative pathway had been repeated ("strengthened") is what determines the organization in cognition called meaning. A clear distinction was drawn between *meaningfulness* and meaning. Meaningfulness is a measure of the extent (applicability, utility, etc.) of meaning contained within learnable items, which is assessed by determining the frequency with which words are used in the standing language structure (Thorndike & Lorge, 1944) or what percentage of people will find a CVC trigram (GUC, HIB, LAT, etc.) looking or sounding like a word or usable in a sentence (Archer, 1960). Thus, a word like *baby* has the same associative strength or "association value" as the words *egg*, *guess*, and *taste*. The trigrams PAM, TOW, and GIT are equally high in meaningfulness, whereas QEX, GYC, and HIJ are all low. The experiments run on such linguistic or quasi-linguistic units have focused on such nomothetic frequency considerations rather than on the idiographic meanings that subjects might have expressed concerning these individual units.

It was not that idiographic differences were overlooked by the mechanistically oriented frequency theorists. They realized that people had unique, personal associations to words and trigrams. Given that the way in which these unique organizations presumably worked was identical to the way in which the nomothetic measures worked, however, why should we single them out for study? All learning and memory was a question of associative strength based on the frequency and contiguity of such verbal inputs, organized externally and carried along in the mediation process. Why then single out such idiographic factors like personal meaning for study? What would they teach us about this mechanistic process that we do not already know? This has been the predominant attitude in verbal learning and memory.

It is easy to understand why traditional mechanism has avoided directly tackling *meaning*, for, as I noted in chapter 1, the concept takes Anglo-Saxon roots from teleological precedents such as intending, wishing, expressing a purpose, and so on. This is the definition that LLT employs. Meaning is intrinsically tied to patterned organization. Meaning is a relational tie of one conceptualized item to another—as the predication to the target. The LLT formulation embraces the symbolical aspects of meaning, which address the creation of such ties. As I noted in chapter 3, symbols express meanings. Traditional learning theories have employed the signalizing interpretation of meaning, which assumes that a meaning arises when one item stands surrogate for another. When *seven* stands for "1 1 1 1 1 1 1," we have signal meaning taking place; when it conveys luck, we have symbolical meaning taking place. Logical learning theory relies on symbolical meaning to explain cognition, for this is obviously an alternative way of speaking about predicational activities like analogy, metaphor, and so on.

It has been repeatedly found that meaningfulness influences learning rate more significantly when it is varied at the response, rather than at the stimulus, side of the paired-associates unit (Cieutat, Stockwell, & Noble, 1958; Goss & Nodine, 1965; Kothurkar, 1963; Sheffield, 1946). The customary explanation here holds that subjects must generate the response but merely have to recognize the stimulus. Actually, the initial stimulus is always presented by the experimenter, but the succeeding response is not exactly freely concocted by the subject. However, there is a requirement here somewhat comparable to the difference I discussed in the previous section concerning recall and recognition. Consider a paired-associates task in which, after the initial presentation, a subject is placed in a kind of free recall task regarding the succeeding term. It becomes a target, so to speak, but can also serve as a predicate for the initial (stimulus) term. I have found in my studies over the years that subjects routinely search for some meaning that logically ties the two terms together. Using something like the memory strategy discussed above concerning "John is reliable," they pair *HIB* and *LAT* with a statement like "HIB was LATE for the appointment." The response term is important here because this is where the predication is most likely to be framed.

Predicate cueing has been employed in experiments without specifying its role in recall. When subjects are asked to memorize both words (e.g., *cow*, *rat*) and categories (e.g., four-footed animals), cueing them with the categories facilitates recall (Tulving & Pearlstone, 1966). Of course, the theory here follows encoding specificity, which holds that the categorical cues are input at initial learning and later serve as "retrieval cues" (Tulving & Thomson, 1973). The real issue here is that subjects organize their recall according to the categories even when they are *not* being cued by them. This seems to support LLT's contention that the categories are not simply *content* cues but also reflect a predicational process.

Predicate cueing has been matched to a contiguity explanation in memory. Thus, subjects in one study were first required to memorize sentences of the following sort: "Children who are slow eat bread that is cold" (Weisberg, 1969). The subjects subsequently were asked to associate to the word *slow*. They almost always replied with *children* rather than with *bread*. Contiguity would suggest that since *bread* is closer to *slow* in this sentence, it should have a higher representation in the associations (due to the shorter distance that the electrical signal has to take in the associative network from the "bread" to the "slow" node; see Figure 16). In contrast, LLT points out that *slow* predicates—lends meaning to—*children* and not to *bread*.

Dong (1972) presented 50 categorizable words (5 words in each of 10 categories) to subjects in either a random or a blocked (i.e., organized by categories) fashion. Memory was tested by free or cued recall (i.e., cued with a category name akin to Tulving and Pearlstone, 1966). There were no differences between free and cued recall when the words were initially presented randomly, but cued recall exceeded free recall when this initial presentation was blocked. This finding is consistent with the LLT view that a clear initial predication provides an excellent framework for recall. Jacoby (1973) then demonstrated that cued recall in this general form was significantly improved when subjects expected to be tested in this fashion. Free recall was not affected in this way. It thus appears that expecting organizational assistance from the experimenter facilitates the task if this assistance is indeed relevant to the memory test.

Relevance is important at initial learning as well. Providing subjects with a grounding predication greatly facilitates the recall of ambiguous sentences. For example, subjects remember sentences like "The streak blocked the light" and "The man saw his face in the body" much more easily when we provide them with appropriate predicate (context) meanings (i.e., "dirty window" and "new car," respectively) (Johnson, Doll, Bransford, & Lapinski, 1974). The overall meaning of a statement is obviously crucial to memory. If it makes sense, then it reflects a good organization. The word meanings as understood by the predicating subject are crucial here. Thus, subjects asked to recall sentences like "The container held the apples" and "The container held the cola" were found to perform better if certain words were used as cues. The cue *basket* was very effective for the sentence about apples, and the cue *bottle* was excellent for the sentence about cola (Anderson & Ortony, 1975). Obviously, subjects had pictured apples being contained in a basket and cola in a bottle—a clear reflection of predication. Once again, predicate cueing was vital to memory.

This matter of picturing a predication is very important to LLT, and I will return to it in chapter 8 when I take up perception. Along this line, Baker and Santa (1977) read off a list of 24 words to their subjects. Some subjects were instructed to learn these words in any way that they wished. Others were asked to form images of four successively presented words. Cueing at recall of the 24 words was achieved by presenting a highly normative associate to the word in question (e.g., *nurse* for *doctor*). It was found that free recall was aided significantly by imagery encoding, whereas cued recall was not. This again appears to reflect the fact that the organization provided by the experimenter in cued recall sufficed to keep the performance of those subjects who had not initially organized the task via imagery on a par with those who had. Since there was no way to provide this assistance in the recall task, a significant difference favoring those subjects who patterned their initial targets via imagery was inevitable.

In an experiment that is a clear precedent to the demonstration research of this chapter, Stein (1977) administered 24 similes to subjects of the following sort: "A pliers is like a crab," or "A pin is like a nail," or "A bumper is like a statue." Stein was investigating levels of plausibility, but what interests the LLT advocate is the matter of cueing recall. Ratings were obtained to see which similes the subjects understood and which they did not. Stein cued recall of the similes with the left-hand term (i.e., the subject of the sentence, or *pliers*, *pin*, and *bumper* in the preceding examples). He found that his experimental subjects recalled about half of the 24 words overall in cued recall—that is, combining understood and not understood similes. This figure jumped to 78% when only those similes that were understood were calculated, and it fell to 35% when only those similes that were not understood were calculated. The LLT advocate would point out that to understand a simile, the subject has to conceptualize a meaningful tie of predicate to targeted subject in the sentence. Hence, here again, predication definitely played a role in recall. But what about looking specifically at the role of cueing predicates versus subjects in memory for sentences?

Demonstration Experiments: Predicate Cueing and Memory

Experiment 5

Hypotheses

1. An experimental group cued for the predicate nouns of unrecalled *sentences* will reconceptualize more of these sentences than will a group cued for the subject nouns.

2. A control group given the nouns of hypothesis 1 in *word-associate pairings*—with the left-lying (stimulus) noun considered to be the subject and the right-lying (response) noun the predicate—will not reflect the predicate over subject superiority predicted by hypothesis 1.

Rationale

When people are given many sentences to memorize, followed by a free recall, there are always some sentences that they do not successfully reconceptualize. If predication is the source of meaning-extension (i.e., the predication effect occurs; see Table 1 in chap. 3), it follows that cueing the predicate word (noun) of the unrecalled sentences should lead to more reconceptualizations of the sentences in memory than cueing the subject word (noun) of the unrecalled sentences. Subject cueing is expected to facilitate memory for sentences as well, but not to the extent of predicate cueing (see Stein, 1977).

We first established that people do not simply recall more subject nouns than predicate nouns in remembering sentences (Rychlak & Rychlak, 1984). Subjects ($N = 62$) were asked to read 26 sentences of the following sort: "The baby chased the puppy" or "The lawyer waved to the mailperson." They then freely recalled as many sentences as possible before being asked to fill in sentence blanks reflecting either a missing subject noun ("The _____ chased the puppy") or predicate (object) noun ("The lawyer waved to the _____"). The initial, freely recalled sentences were not scored in the sentence completion task. We found no differences between memory for subjects ($M = 6.03$, $SD = 2.65$) or predicates ($M = 7.03$, $SD = 3.12$) in this completion task ($t = .745$, $df = 60$, N.S.).

Experiment 5 is a partial cross-validation of an earlier experiment in which hypothesis 1 was confirmed (Rychlak & Rychlak, 1985). However, a control group was added in this cross-validation to strengthen the LLT interpretation of the data. In the control condition, the key nouns of the sentences are used in the memory task without the predicational alignment occurring—that is, as simply two associated words ("ladder-bookshelf") rather than being tied together through predication ("A ladder can be used as a bookshelf"). A traditional view of association would suggest that the frequency of contiguous bondings of one word to another accounts for memory, not the logical organization of the predication effect. It follows from this traditional view that we should get the same cueing effects whether we use a sentence or simply a pairing of the two key nouns of the sentence. Logical learning theory challenges this experimental prediction.

Experimental Sample

I will use the word *participant* in place of *subject* in discussing Experiment 5 so that no confusion will arise between the subjects of sentences and the people who participated in the study. Eighty participants drawn from an undergraduate research pool were randomly assigned to either an experimental or a control group (20 males, 20 females per group).

Procedure

The procedure used in the experimental condition was based on an experiment suggested in Bransford (1979, pp. 56–58). As a demonstration experiment in retrieval processing, the recommended design employed subject cueing. This design was modified to include predicate cueing as well. The memory task consisted of 26 sentences of the following type: "A brick can be used as a doorstop. A ladder can be used as a bookshelf. A pan can be used as a drum. A sheet can be used as a sail. A rug can be used as a bedspread. A balloon can be used as a pillow." There were two filler sentences, one placed at the beginning and one at the end of the list, to counteract primacy-recency effects. These fillers were not scored. The sentences were also presented in two different randomized orders to offset any categorical biases that might exist between them.

The participants were instructed to read the list of 26 sentences just once, but carefully, because they would be asked to remember as many as possible. When they finished reading the sentences, the participants were administered a blank sheet of paper on which to record all the sentences they could remember. This was the *free recall* step of the experimental design. Following the free recall, participants were administered a form on which 26 words were listed, half of which were subjects and half predicates of the experimental sentences (all predicates and all subjects were used in random combinations of 26). This was the *cued recall* step of the experimental design. Participants were instructed to read each word listed to see whether it facilitated recall of a sentence. If so, they wrote out the sentence recalled (including those that they had spontaneously recorded during free recall) on the cued recall form.

Hypothesis 1 held that in cued recall, those sentences that were recorded but had not appeared initially in free recall would be more likely to emerge through predicate cuing than through subject cueing. Sentences were scored for precise recall (i.e., word substitutions were not permitted). The order of sentence recall was irrelevant, and spelling errors were ignored. It should be noted that participants occasionally failed to recall a cued-recall sentence even though they had remembered this sentence correctly in the free-recall aspect of the experiment. An item of this sort would not be included in the cued-recall mean score, even though it would be represented in the free-recall mean. As a result, subject-cued and predicate-cued means need not sum to the precise difference between the free-recall and cued-recall means.

The participants in the control group followed exactly the same procedure except that they were administered *only* word pairs. Thus, whereas an experimental-group participant was asked to memorize the sentences "A ladder can be used as a bookshelf. A rug can be used as a bedspread. A balloon can be used as a pillow," and so forth, a participant in the control group was asked to read through and memorize the pairings "ladder-bookshelf, rug-bedspread, balloon-pillow," and so on. The word array at cued recall was identical for control subjects to that of the experimental subjects. Order of recall and misspellings in the control condition were ignored, but word-substitutions (synonyms etc.) were not permitted. If the pair was "rug-bedspread" and a participant recorded "bedspread-rug," this was considered an error (it happened rarely). No credit was given for recalling only one of the words of a pair in the free recall.

Results

The first dependent measure of interest was the number of sentences/word pairs recalled under the free- and cued-recall conditions. This score can tell us whether we obtained a cueing effect. Note that in this case we are using all the sentences recorded on the cued-recall form, including those that might also have been recorded on the free-recall form. These scores were entered into a 2 (Sex of Participant) × 2 (Sentences vs. Word Pairs) × 2 (Free vs. Cued Recall) factorial analysis of variance. The first two variables are between subjects and the third is within subjects. A significant cueing effect was found, with the free recall $M = 9.56$ ($SD = 3.56$) and the cued recall $M = 16.13$ ($SD = 6.03$) ($F = 258.21$, $df = 1, 76$, $p < .001$). This establishes that cueing did have an effect on the reconceptualization of forgotten sentences and paired-associates. There were no sex differences. There was a significantly larger increase from free to cued recall for sentences than for word-associates, but I will not detail these figures.

The predication effect we were out to test is found using the scores drawn solely from the cued-recall phase of the memory task. How many additional

Table 2   Mean and standard deviation of recall score for subject and predicate cueing, arrayed by sex and sentence/word pairs

	Subject cueing				Predicate cueing			
	Males		Females		Males		Females	
Materials	Mean	SD	Mean	SD	Mean	SD	Mean	SD
Sentences	4.00	1.49	3.10	1.80	5.15	1.60	4.65	3.03
Word pairs	3.70	1.95	3.00	2.18	3.80	2.35	2.70	1.92

Note: Predicate cueing means for sentences are significantly different from all other means ($p < .05$).

sentences were recorded on the cued-recall form that did not appear on the free-recall form? These scores were entered into a factorial analysis of variance having the characteristics of a 2 (Sex of Participant) × 2 (Sentence vs. Word Pair) × 2 (Subject vs. Predicate Cueing), with the first two variables between and the third within subjects. There was a main effect for sex, with males performing higher ($M = 4.16$, $SD = 1.85$) overall than females ($M = 3.36$, $SD = 2.32$) ($F = 4.04$, $df = 1, 76$, $p < .05$).

There was also a main effect favoring sentences over word pairs, as follows: for sentences, $M = 4.17$, $SD = 1.65$; for word pairs, $M = 3.30$, $SD = 2.13$ ($F = 5.40$, $df = 1, 76$, $p < .05$). There was also a main effect for subject versus predicate cueing, as follows: for subject cueing, $M = 3.45$, $SD = 1.88$; for predicate cueing, $M = 4.08$, $SD = 2.43$ ($F = 6.49$, $df = 1, 76$, $p < .05$). That this difference is due to the sentences and not the word-pairings is made clear in the significant interaction between "sentence versus word pair" and "subject versus predicate cueing" ($F = 8.74$, $df = 1, 76$, $p < .001$). Table 2 presents the recall data for subject/predicate cueing, arrayed according to items memorized and sex of participant. Tests of simple effects (combined sex) on the data of Table 2 revealed that predicate cueing of the sentences resulted in a significantly higher level of recall than the other three subgroupings represented (i.e., subject cueing of both sentences and word pairs and predicate cueing of word pairs).

Conclusion and Discussion

The findings of Table 2 make it clear that predicate cueing leads to greater recall than subject cueing does in both sexes and that no such distinction can be drawn for the word pairings. This experimental design was used in several additional studies. In one study, the sentences were varied so that they did not have "can be used as" linking subject to predicate meaning. All sentences were four words in length. Some examples follow: "An owl loves silence. A judge admires honesty. Newspapers stretch the facts. The waiter proved clumsy. The politician tasted victory." Once again, predicate cueing was found to enhance recall significantly better than subject cueing ($p < .05$; Rychlak & Rychlak, 1986). However, when even more complex sentences were attempted, the predication effect could not be demonstrated. Doubtless the range of meaning in more complex sentences limits the utility of such a basic and simple strategy as we used.

We were more successful in cueing metaphors. Recall that Stein (1977) found that cueing subjects facilitated memory in forgotten similes. Similes and metaphors are variations on the analogical capacity of human beings, a capacity that stems from (partial) tautological meaning-extension in telosponsivity. In the experiment under consideration, we used a list of metaphors (e.g., "a prison is a cage," "a school is a ladder") and found, consistent with the above research, that predicate cueing was superior to subject cueing in memory for forgotten metaphors (Rychlak & Ulasevich, 1987). All in all, the predication effect is made apparent in these experiments. Considering the huge number of predications that can target cognitions (words, images, etc.), enabling all manner of reformulations to be made in human thought, it is almost surprising to find that we can demonstrate the predication effect in experiments of this type.

Experiment 6

Hypothesis

Cueing the word with the broadest meaning in a previously read but un-recalled triplet will result in better recall of other words in this three-word unit than cueing words with a narrower range of meaning.

Rationale

It is important to demonstrate that the cueing effects reported thus far are not simply linguistic conventions learned in the acquisition of English. Predication is reflected in English syntax, of course, but LLT contends that this is due to the semantics involved in communication. We therefore decided to employ three-word units, or *triplets*, in which one word would be broad in meaningful reference relative to the other two words in this unit. As such, this broader word would be the "expected" predicate meaning in the organization of memory. We would then treat the triplets as we had the sentences in Experiment 5, to see whether a predication effect could be demonstrated even though no syntactical organizer such as a sentence was involved.

We make the assumption here that in reading a triplet, the subject organizes this unit in "top-down" fashion, thereby taking the broadest word meaning as the framing predicate. For example, in the triplet "nose, face, smile," the word *face* would be the most probable predicate meaning, sub-suming the other two words as targets to which this meaning is extended. If this triplet were read and then not recalled initially—comparable to the for-gotten sentences of Experiment 5—we would expect a cueing of *face* to more readily help the subject to reconceptualize one or both of the other words in the triplet than if *smile* or *nose* were used as cues. These latter words do not have the implicit and ready-at-hand range to cover the full extent of the triplet's meaning. The words of the control condition in Experiment 5 were equally plausible as predicates, and so we did not find a predication effect without an organizing sentence structure assisting, but we expected to find the predication effect in our triplet arrangement.

Experimental Sample

Forty-eight undergraduate college females participated in this experiment (Stilson, 1988).

Procedure

In this study we wanted to examine predicate cueing when the level of association value (AV) of the words used in the triplets varied. Three ex-perimental conditions were devised, to which subjects were randomly as-signed (16 subjects per condition). Association value was drawn from the Thorndike-Lorge (1944) tables of word frequency. These tables include three categories: words that appear between 1 and 49 times per million in English publications, which are listed with their frequencies (for example, *alert* is listed as appearing 14 times per million); words (e.g., *giant*) that appear between 50 and 99 times per million, which are given the code "A"; and words (e.g., *public*) that appear 100 or more times per million, which are coded "AA."

The triplets were not simply words tossed together randomly within AV levels. Each triplet had a core meaning, captured by the predicate (i.e., the meanings of *nose* and *smile* have relevance to *face*). Three judges had to agree that one of the three words was likely to be the predicate before we actually used the triplet in the study. The three experimental conditions were named "higher," "same," and "lower." This referred to the AV of the expected predi-cate word in relation to the other two words of the triplet. Here are examples of triplets in the three conditions:

Lower (expected predicate, italicized, lower in AV than other words):
  wallet (6) picture (AA) money (AA)
  noise (A) *traffic* (26) motion (A)
  address (A) note (AA) *envelope* (22)

Same (expected predicate same in AV as other words):
  face (AA) smile (AA) nose (AA)

seat (A) *theater* (A) play (AA)
tent (A) fire (AA) *camp* (AA)

Higher (expected predicate higher in AV than other words):
railroad (AA) schedule (14) luggage (10)
carrot (9) *garden* (AA) rake (13)
peg (9) flap (16) *tent* (A)

Note that no real distinction was drawn between A and AA words. Essentially, we tried to find words that were as low as possible below the 50 per million mark and words that were above this level. Thus, in the lower condition, 66% of the words in a triplet were A or AA; this figure in the same condition was 100%; and in the higher condition it was only 33%.

The subjects were instructed to read a list of 18 triplets carefully, but just once. The first and last triplet of a list were fillers to counter primacy-recency effects. Thus, 16 triplets (between groups) entered into the scoring. As in the examples given above, triplets were presented in three different orders, so that the expected predicate did not appear in any one location on the experimental form. The subjects were told that they would be asked to remember as many of the triplets as they could. Order of triplet recall was irrelevant, and spelling mistakes were overlooked. However, if a subject substituted one word for another (e.g., replacing *suitcase* for *luggage*) this was considered an error.

We followed the same procedure as in Experiment 5. After subjects read through the list of triplets, they were given a blank sheet of paper on which to record as many triplets as they could remember. Following this, subjects were given a form on which 16 randomly arrayed cues were listed. Half of these were expected predicate words, and half were expected nonpredicate words. Different combinations of the triplet words were used in the cued recall from participant to participant. All the expected predicates and nonpredicates were used as cues in the sample of participants.

Results

A "hit" (correct score) was given when the subjects recorded one or more correct words to the cue. Most of the subjects recalled the entire triplet when cued. However, 35% of the subjects did not remember both words in all cases. We decided that since the sentences in Experiment 5 required only one word to be recalled to a cueing, we should give equal credit (a "hit") for one or two correct word recalls on the triplets. (Incidentally, the findings to be reported were no different when we ignored these partial recollections and analyzed the resultant data; see Rychlak, Stilson, & Rychlak, 1993.)

The hit scores were entered into a 3 (Higher, Same, Lower) × 2 (Predicate vs. Nonpredicate Cue) factorial analysis of variance, with the former a

Table 3 Mean and standard deviation of words recalled, arrayed by triplet type and word cued

	Triplet type		Word cued	
	Expected predicate		Expected non-predicate	
	Mean	SD	Mean	SD
Higher:	2.56*	1.21	0.81	0.83
Same:	2.06	1.29	1.56	0.89
Lower:	2.25	1.18	1.50	0.89

*Significantly different than expected nonpredicate mean, $p < .01$.

between-subjects and the latter a within-subjects variable. Table 3 presents the mean and standard deviation of the recall scores, arrayed according to type of triplet and word cued.

There was no main effect for experimental condition (Lower, Same, Higher). However, a main effect for cueing was found in that the expected predicates led the subjects to reconceptualize twice as many "hits" ($M = 2.93$, $SD = 1.23$) as expected nonpredicates ($M = 1.29$, $SD = .873$) ($F = 12.45$, $df = 1$, 44, $p < .001$). There was no significant interaction between condition and word cued. Note in Table 3 that it was the higher condition that led to the greatest difference between (expected) predicate ($M = 2.56$) and nonpredicate ($M = .81$) cueing. This difference between cueing means was significant ($t = 4.87$, $df = 15$, $p < .01$). The comparable differences between means for the same and lower conditions were not significant.

Conclusion and Discussion

The expected predication effect materialized in the triplets data, so we cannot explain it as due to syntax (i.e., sentence structure). The range of meaning being wound together in cognition plays a role in memory independent of such linguistic conventions. Of major interest is the fact that the higher condition resulted in the clearest differences across words cued. This is as it should be, because in this instance the predicate had considerable meaning compared to the other words, which presumably could not extend as much meaning when under cueing. Neither of the other conditions combined such enriched predicate words and pallid nonpredicate words, so that even though they do reflect a predication effect, the contrast in meaning-extension is not so pronounced as in the higher condition. This suggests that predication is not essentially a function of AV—a frequency estimate of meaningfulness—but that it does adapt to such frequency considerations. There is also some support indicated here for the principle of meaning-extension, which predicts that the flow of meaning is greatest between the best-known and the least-known items being patterned (organized, related, etc.) in cognition.

Concluding Comment

The shift in emphasis from sheer frequency of contiguous inputs to organization at the point of input (as well as at the point of retrieval) has surely proven beneficial to LLT, which bases its explanation of learning on the patterning of such meanings. This reflects the same shift from efficient to formal causation that has taken place in physical science. Even so, I note in the research literature a tendency to hang on to frequency as a principle of explanation. Although organization is being emphasized, the average cognitive theorist seems always to bring in something like extent of response time or processing time, which is a variant form of frequency estimate, to account for the improved retention to be seen in rich organizations. Elaboration, which we will be looking at in chapter 6, is given this twist: The stronger the elaboration, the more time spent in processing the inputs, etc. Hence, due presumably to the time commitment making up the elaborated meaning, memory is facilitated. I doubt that this style of explanation will change in the near future. The formal causation of one-trial learning is not likely to replace the efficient causation of frequency-contiguity in our mechanistic psychological accounts.

The flow of meaning from predicate to target is nicely demonstrated in the cueing studies of this chapter. Doubtless something like cueing is what psychologists mean by the "association of ideas." I like Aristotle's (1952c) suggestion that ideas attach to each other because one meaning is predicable of the other (p. 565). Most cues establish an extended context of predication. We think, see, or hear of something or someone framed by a context that not only lends a meaning to the target but also extends to targets other than the one in cognizance. We do not always willfully intend to think of these other targets. The ideas just pop into mind automatically as understanding-intentions. But this automatic cognitive action is not a mechanism, particularly since some of the things that pop up are opposite in meaning to the target that was initially framed. Machines do not deal in oppositionality. Chapter 6 will teach us that human beings (and certain animals too) have this unique cognitive ability to turn the "is" into the "is not," and vice versa.

6

Oppositionality in Learning
and Memory

It would not be an exaggeration to say that LLT must ultimately stand or fall on the claim that oppositionality plays a fundamental role in cognition, in both its generic and delimiting manifestations. Oppositionality is not some arcane principle of explanation defying empirical investigation. It is not a mere "feature" of linguistic usage. It is fundamental to human behavior and can be shown to have had a continuing, albeit unrecognized, influence in many experiments from the very beginning of psychology as a science. In the present chapter I will review a number of topics having relevance to oppositionality's role in learning and memory and then present three demonstration experiments that assess the merits of LLT's claims.

Oppositionality: The Overlooked Dimension in Experimentation

It is not necessary to present a detailed history of the many ways in which oppositionality has been wound into the empirical investigations of psychology, much less of human affairs more generally (for the latter, see Ogden, 1967). I stress *empirical* here because it is actually easier to demonstrate the role of oppositionality in nonexperimental investigations, such as the analytical approaches of Freud or Jung (for such an analysis, see Rychlak, 1981, chap. 10). Nevertheless, we should appreciate that oppositionality has been active for a long time in psychology's empirical research without receiving the recognition that it deserves. Indeed, Wilhelm Wundt, who is credited with founding experimental psychology in 1879, studied human feelings in terms of the oppositional dimensions of pleasant-unpleasant, tense-relaxed, and excited-depressed (Watson, 1978, p. 289).

One area of study that has had and continues to have a large percentage of oppositional concepts under empirical investigation is personality assessment. Bipolar dimensions of assessment have always abounded in personality scaling, including such classical examples as extraversion-introversion (Eysenck, 1947), excitement-depression (Stagner, 1948), and anger-love (Leary, 1957). Such examples could be multiplied ten times over. Since personality descriptors are adjectives, it is impossible for an investigator to avoid relying on delimiting oppositionality in such characterizations. Another highly visible application of oppositional dimensionality occurred in Osgood's worldwide investigation of language systems, which he found could be arrayed according to the meanings of *evaluation, potency,* and *activity.* These three concepts were measured, respectively, along dichotomous dimensions like good-bad, powerful-weak, and active-passive (Osgood, Suci, & Tannenbaum, 1957). Social structures have been assessed cross-culturally along dichotomous dimensions such as abstract-concrete (Foa & Foa, 1974) and intimacy-formality (Triandis, 1977). In all such efforts to classify, one pole of the dimension delimits and to that extent subtly enters into the definition of its opposite. Nonetheless, oppositionality is never given credit for the important role that it plays in such classification schemes.

As far as cognitive research is concerned, there are many examples of oppositionality playing an unrecognized role in the experiments of this specialty. For example, using words with either strong or weak associations to each other, McCullers (1965) was surprised to find less associative interference (i.e., confounding one pair with another) in a paired-associates task for his strong than for his weak conditions. He had expected the reverse finding, because it would seem to follow that words that are strongly associated would intrude on each other in a memory task and hence lead to errors in paired-associates learning. However, when we look at his lists, we find that two-thirds of his "strong" pairs reflected delimiting oppositionality (e.g., different-bad, same-nice) and none of his weak pairs are oppositional (e.g., long-real, strange-old). It did not seem to occur to McCullers that strength of association between words that are oppositional represents a special case of semantic bonding—framing a dimension of common meaning by bipolar difference—not to be equated with comparable nonoppositional associations.

There are countless studies in the cognitive literature in which strongly associated words are used as an experimental condition in contrast to weakly associated words without mentioning the fact that the former condition is full of opposites. I can speculate along this line because, as I mentioned previously, we know for certain that when a word has an opposite, this opposite is one of the strongest (i.e., most frequently given) responses to it in a word-association task (Karwoski & Schachter, 1948). Hence, unless a specific effort is made to control for this factor, we can confidently assume that any list of strongly associated words will be stacked with oppositionality. In a related strategy, Watkins and Tulving (1975) reported data in which a cueing procedure was used. The "strong cue" condition was loaded with about 40% opposites (e.g., dark-light, closed-open), whereas the "weak cue" condition had no such opposites. Although the results are interpretable in terms of an influence based on delimiting oppositionality, no such formulation is forthcoming because of the assumption that a count of sheer associative strength is what determines the strong and weak conditions of the study. Oppositionality is not seen as a possible semantic determinant going beyond sheer frequency considerations to influence the observed findings.

Oppositionality was silently involved in Thomson and Tulving's (1970) oft-cited research on encoding specificity. In this research, subjects were administered "strongly associated" word pairs (with "white-Black" given as an example by the authors) or "weakly associated" word pairs (with "train-Black" given as an example). After learning a list of either of these pairings, subjects were then cued at recall with a strong or a weak word associate. Encoding specificity states that the information provided by this cue must appropriately match the initial context of learning. Thus, as encoding specificity predicts, when subjects initially learn a strong association like "white-Black" and then are cued with *white*, they recall a high percentage of the other words in the associated pairing. On the other hand, when subjects initially learn a strong association like "white-Black" and are subsequently cued with a weak association to *Black* like *train*, they recall a significantly lower percentage of the other words than subjects cued with *white*. Finally, when subjects initially learn a weak association like "train-Black" and then are cued with *train*, they perform at essentially the *same* level as subjects who initially learn this weak association and then are cued with the more strongly associated *white*.

Technically, LLT would not define white as the opposite of black, but in point of fact people routinely consider these two words to be opposites. It is, of course, up to the person to name what she or he takes to be opposite meanings of this sort (see Westcott, 1981, 1982). In this case, it would be more accurate to speak of light and dark hues as the opposite meanings under consideration. Nevertheless, it is clear that within the findings of Thomson and Tulving's (1970) encoding specificity experiment, we have evidence that oppositionality greatly facilitates original organization (input encoding) as well as cued recall. Even when the initial learning was "train-Black" (a weak association), cued recall relying on the oppositionality of "white-Black" (a strong association) performed very well.

In explaining their findings, Thomson and Tulving were thinking exclusively in terms of the strength of word association, but the delimiting oppositionality of word meanings was surely involved as well. This criticism does not imply that the encoding specificity hypothesis is wrong. In fact, LLT is highly compatible with the findings on encoding specificity, except that instead of relying on presumed mechanistic input traces that have to be matched at output, and so on, LLT explains the findings as due to the predication process, which necessarily involves generic oppositionality and in turn capitalizes on the delimiting oppositionality of the word meanings under processing.

Another way in which oppositional organization shows up in the cognitive research literature is as a presumed control for association strength in transfer during the learning of successive lists of paired associates. In these studies, which unite words with quasi words (e.g., slow-corlep), oppositionality is arrayed on the stimulus (left-hand term) of the paired-associate unit because of the efficient-cause assumptions made by such traditional mechanistic formulations (i.e., the stimulus cues and hence supposedly causes the response occurrence in efficient-cause fashion). Thus, Ryan (1960) demonstrated that learning paired associates like "slow-corlep" facilitates the subsequent learning of pairs with "highly associated" stimuli and identical responses like fast-corlep. The undoubted facilitation of "slow-fast" oppositionality here goes unrecognized. Gough, Odom, and Jenkins (1967) later demonstrated the same phenomenon using what they called "bidirectional associates" as stimuli (e.g., "hard vs. soft," "king vs. queen"). Responses were the digits 1–4, resulting in successively arrayed paired associates like "hard-1, soft-1" and "king-3, queen-3." Once again, no credit was given for the increased transfer effects as being due to the heavy loading of delimiting oppositionality in the bidirectional stimuli.

The point should now be clear that, although oppositionality cannot account for all the findings of the previously cited research, it most certainly can be said to have made a significant contribution to the results. Logical learning theory contends that this is a distinctive contribution, one that cannot be reduced to frequency counts underlying strength of association. Oppositionality must be seen as an aspect of the predication process and the contents it processes.

Oppositionality in Research on Lower Animals

Before we look more closely at some of the research topics in human cognition, it is appropriate to ask the following question: Is there any evidence for oppositionality in lower animals? If, as I suggested in chapter 5, the behavior of animals below *Homo sapiens* on the evolutionary scale is nevertheless consistent with what we know about predication, then we would expect to find indications of oppositionality in their behavior as well. As we shall see, it appears that lower animals manifest primarily the generic oppositionality of sheer difference—more so, at any rate, than they show the abstractly more difficult capacity to see alternatives by way of delimiting oppositionality. Nevertheless, there are intimations of a delimiting oppositionality going on in the cognitions of the higher apes.

Although Darwinian arguments are overdone in psychology, I think that some comments along this line may be in order. My suggestion is that cognitive oppositionality is increasingly evident in the behavior of the more "highly evolved" organisms, particularly delimiting oppositionality of the sort that underlies transcendence and self-reflexivity. The theoretical suggestion here is that, although lower animals may grasp oppositionality in their cognitions, it is only the more evolved, or "higher," organism that employs this bidirectionality of meaning in self-referencing (see chap. 9 on self-predication in identity). Whether this occurs at or below the level of the apes or exclusively at the level of *Homo sapiens* is a question for future research to determine.

Thus, according to an LLT Darwinian formulation, it was when an animal could employ oppositionality self-referentially, realizing that it was a continuing identity doing one thing or living one way when it could be doing or living quite the opposite, that a truly higher cognitive processor emerged on the ladder of evolution. This animal could grasp intrinsic ties of seemingly disparate experiences using generic oppositionality. The "it" soon became an "I," of course, because self-referencing gave birth to an introspective cognition. The appreciation of alternatives based on a non-Boolean form of disjunction permitted this higher organism to begin laying plans for a change in circumstances (e.g., shelter, location, food supply, etc.) framed by the bipolarity of what is currently taking place versus what is not (but could be).

For example, it was when this animal realized that it was an identity living in a tree or in a valley—which meant it then appreciated that existence in the opposite direction (on the ground, up the side of a mountain) was also possible—that a new kind of intelligence was born, one that broke free from "natural" selection to generate alternatives that might even intentionally counteract this unintentional selective process. I picture this evolutionary advance as initially involving generic oppositionality, followed in time by the possibility for a delimiting oppositionality that was greatly enhanced with the formation of a pictorial-linguistic symbol system. Note that here I depart from Mead's (1934) symbolic interactionism, in which self-reflexivity is said to arise *along with* the acquisition of language. The evolving organism who has a language system can now enter into symbolic communication with his or her "self" as if this were an object. Because there is no introspectively conceived reflexivity here, I take Mead's thesis as a variant of Lockean reflectivity rather than as Kantian reflexivity via dialectical (oppositional) transcendence. My Darwinian scenario is highly speculative, however, so it is incumbent on me to demonstrate that there are at least intimations of oppositionality in the behavior of animals other than language-using human beings.

In looking for possible references to oppositionality in experimental research, the lowest level on the evolutionary scale I found mentioned was in Yerkes' (1912) study of learning in the earthworm. An earthworm was taught to turn right in a T-shaped tube by shocking it whenever it turned left. After about 100 trials the worm learned to turn right when inserted into the tube. Heck (1920) then reproduced this experiment, adding the feature of reversing the direction to be turned following initial learning. Thus, after learning to turn right, the same earthworm had to turn left or be shocked. The worm now learned to turn left in fewer than half the number of trials required to learn the initial right turn. Such savings are attributed to previous learning, of course—but in what sense does this process take place?

Logical learning theory's suggestion is that a "same" versus an "other" (not-same) generic oppositionality could play a role in such learning. Negating an already learned pattern hastens the process of learning the next (essentially different) pattern. Of course, there is no claim here that earthworms transcend or reflexively reason dialectically, much less demonstratively. Still, a *Logos* perception of environmental circumstances in which generic oppositionality is involved need not be limited to the human being. Logical learning theory considers the *Logos* from an introspective perspective, but it is also possible to think of such patterned organizations extraspectively, and an organism like an earthworm might engage this layout of oppositionality without conceptualizing it—behaving, so to speak, within the oppositional pattern rather than for its sake (i.e., intentionally). To do the latter would require representational contents of a delimiting oppositionality that the earthworm does not possess.

A more complex manifestation of oppositionality might be seen in *deception*, which is quite prevalent in the animal kingdom. To deceive is to mislead or to somehow make another organism believe in the truth of what is not true. Thus, deception relies on the deceiver's capacity to oppose the apparent circumstance through a form of negation. In scorpion flies, a male can copulate with a female only if he first provides her with a dead insect (Thornhill, 1979). Some males catch insects on their own, whereas others steal insects by approaching males that already have them and adopting the posture and behavior of females. Birds have been observed giving alarm calls in the complete absence of danger so as to cause a rival bird to break off the pursuit of a desirable insect that it was just about to capture, leaving the prey open for their devouring (Munn, 1986).

Pepperberg (1987) taught an African gray parrot to discriminate more than 80 different objects by vocalizing English words and to respond to questions concerning categorical concepts of color and shape. The parrot might be shown two objects (e.g., pieces of wood or rawhide) that were of the same color but different in shape, or two objects that were of the same shape but different in color. The experimenter then asked "What is same?" or "What is different?" The parrot answered "color" or "shape" correctly over 70% of the time for pairs of unfamiliar objects (not used in training) and better than 80% for pairs involving objects whose combinations of colors and shapes were familiar. Because the parrot responded accurately in novel pairs of items, its responses were not stimulus specific. It thus appears that the parrot had learned to organize experience according to generic oppositionality (i.e., same-different).

Rats that are rewarded for making different responses to two different stimuli will learn this discrimination more readily if one response is rewarded by food pellets and the other by sucrose than if both responses are rewarded exclusively by either of these nourishments (Trapold, 1970). The sucrose versus food pellets reinforcer reflects a difference based on generic oppositionality, of course. This same facilitation in discrimination learning has been observed when rats are rewarded for one response by large food rewards and for the other response by small food rewards (Carlson & Wielkiewicz, 1976). In research on observational learning or "auto-shaping" of cats, it has been found that the cat learns more easily when it can see both the right and the wrong way to solve a manipulation problem than when only the right way is shown (Herbert & Harsh, 1944). Such results suggest that generic oppositionality is functioning in these animals, but delimiting oppositionality— within which right-wrong alternatives are spontaneously conceptualized— is apparently limited. Language content (word meanings) would definitely prove helpful to learning here.

This issue can be seen in the discrimination learning of chimpanzees (Savage-Rumbaugh, 1986). In one series of experiments, food was dispensed from two vending machines with clear plastic containers that allowed the chimps to see when they were empty. The chimps were required to signal (by touching the appropriate symbol on an electronic board) for different foods in two different vending machines placed to the left and the right of the animals. For example, pieces of banana would be placed in the vending machine to the right, and pieces of beancake would be placed in the vending machine to the left. Banana is the preferred food in this instance. The sensible thing here is to signal for the preferred food in the right-hand dispenser, eat it, signal again, eat, and so forth, until the dispenser is empty, and then to begin signaling for the food in the left-hand dispenser.

Although there was a delimiting oppositionality suggested here in the original arrangement of the vending machines (left versus right), the chimps did not readily catch onto the contrast. They would continue activating the same symbol that worked initially (e.g., the symbol for banana) as they looked expectantly at the dispenser filled with beancake. Occasionally, a chimp would stumble onto the correct change in signal, but the experimenters activated a noise each time a dispenser was turned on to facilitate such learning. One dispenser made a high noise and one made a low noise (p. 94). With this clear delimiting oppositional contrast in place, the chimpanzees learned the task rapidly. Having noises at the same level would not be as effective. We know that, in general, it is almost impossible to condition animals when there is no distinctive feature present to signal the discrimination under investigation (Jenkins & Sainsbury, 1970). In this case, the contrast in noise level seems to have played this distinctiveness role.

Monkeys have been studied in an indoor-outdoor enclosure that allowed some of them to be temporarily separated from the group. On seeing a predator, adult females gave alarm calls more often when they were with their juvenile offspring than when they were with an unrelated juvenile of the same age and sex (Cheney & Seyfarth, 1985). Males gave more alarm calls when they were with a female than they did when they were with another male. This pattern still seems heavily influenced by generic oppositionality, but there are suggestions of delimiting oppositionality in ape behavior as well. For example, dominant rhesus monkeys, which often behave aggressively toward subordinates that fail to respond to their threats by becoming more submissive, will usually restrain their aggressivity if the subordinate appears not to have noticed their initiating threats. Certain subordinate monkeys have been observed acting as if they had not seen the dominant monkey's initial displays of aggression by sitting very still and looking down at the ground or up in the sky when they almost certainly had seen the threat (de Waal, 1982). The subtlety of this strategy suggests that the nondominant monkeys had framed a more reasoned alternative and that the dominant monkey had discounted its hostile outbursts accordingly. The complexity of this interaction suggests delimiting oppositionality.

Tinklepaugh's (1928) classic study also suggests a delimiting oppositionality issuing from an expectation (predication) that had been formed by a monkey. A monkey under restraint is shown a preferred food (banana) being placed under a cup, but this is a subterfuge; actually, a nonpreferred food (lettuce) is placed under the cup. The monkey is then released, runs to the cup, and turns it over. Finding a leaf of lettuce, the monkey looks at it and ignores it (unless very hungry) and then initiates a search for the piece of banana. The monkey examines the cup carefully and after a time shrieks at the experimenter in evident anger for being deceived. This reaction is more than just a sign of noting that a difference has taken place. It suggests that the monkey had a clear sense of what should be taking place and that it could draw implications to the opposite by way of delimitation.

Baboons have been observed concocting deceptive sexual scenarios to their advantage (Whiten & Byrne, 1988a). Thus, a male baboon recruits three other males to confront a rival in order to obtain the latter's female. The male approaches the rival and then screams as if he had been attacked. Three other males converge on the rival, screeching until the rival chases them in aggressive retribution. In the meantime, the male baboon that started the fracas chases the desired female off in the opposite direction. A male chimpanzee has been observed concealing his erect penis when trying to approach a female without attracting the notice of the dominant male, which is almost certain to attack if he sees what is going on (de Waal, 1986). In another example, a male chimp that was injured in a fight was observed limping for a week afterward—but only when his rival could see him. All these strategies suggest a move away from exclusive reliance on generic oppositionality and toward delimiting oppositionality.

Chimpanzees are deceptive with their own kind and also with humans. They are capable of forming a cognitive representation of a terrain, and if shown where food is hidden on this terrain, they can either lead other chimps to this location or intentionally refrain from doing so (Menzel & Halperin, 1975). In one case, a chimp that had walked past an area in which the experimenters had buried some grapefruit did not show any outward sign of being aware of this fact (de Waal, 1986). This led the experimenters to believe that he had not seen the location of the hidden fruit. However, three hours later, when the other chimpanzees were asleep, this chimp walked directly to the spot, dug up the grapefruit, and enjoyed his repast. In another instance, during a feast in which older, dominant chimps were eating most of the bananas, a young chimp was observed to stride with dramatic haste and seeming purpose into the woods, drawing the older chimps along, only to circle back quickly and obtain a better share (Whiten & Byrne, 1988b).

As I suggested above, since delimiting oppositionality involves the contents of the predicational process, it follows that a symbol system would greatly facilitate this cognitive activity. Consistent with this suggestion, there are many examples of oppositionality to be seen in the research on hand-signing with chimps, but my favorite is the one reported by Patterson (1978a, 1978b) in her work with the female gorilla Koko. As I noted in chapter 5, this research is controversial (e.g., see Sugarman, 1983), but Patterson

(1978b) reported that Koko had a playful streak, as follows: "She seems to relish the effects of her practical jokes, *often responding exactly opposite* to what I ask her to do. One day, during a videotaping session, I asked Koko to place a toy animal under a bag, and she responded by taking the toy and stretching to hold it up to the ceiling" (p. 443; emphasis added). I cannot find a more beautiful example of reasoning via delimiting oppositionality in the higher apes than Koko's frequent displays of playfulness. It seems evident to me that Koko takes a position on what is required of her in the hand-signing communication, doing what is called for or its opposite depending on her inclinations at the time.

All in all, therefore, the LLT advocate can take reassurance from the fact that just as we found evidence for predication in lower animals, we now find evidence for the practical benefit of (much generic and some delimiting) oppositionality in the cognitions of lower animals. Oppositionality need not be thought of as limited to human cognition. The human factor seems to enter in the more self-reflexive, transcendent aspects of cognition, which in turn seem to make judgments of worth (values, etc.) possible—judgments that are greatly expanded by the verbal facilities of *Homo sapiens* (see chap. 10). Assuming that the work with higher apes continues to be improved (it is still under fire), we may yet establish that generic oppositionality can generate delimiting oppositionality in subhumans. Just how far down the evolutionary ladder this may extend is an open question, but the heuristic and practical benefits of opposition in animal behavior seem worthy of study in their own right.

Oppositionality in Human Cognitive Organization

There is plenty of evidence supporting the LLT contention that oppositionality plays a crucial role in the cognitive organization of humans. As I have noted previously in other contexts, people readily produce opposite meanings to stimulus words in a word-association task (Karwoski & Schachter, 1948; Kjeldergaard, 1962; Siipola, Walker, & Kolb, 1955). Network theorists presume that such delimiting oppositionality is simply another manifestation of associative patterning among word nodes forged by learning the language syntax, but the significance of meaning in human cognition frequently intrudes on such presumptions. Meaningful oppositionality has been shown to be a semantic rather than simply a syntactic or lexical feature of learned words (Brewer & Lichtenstein, 1975; Grossman & Eagle, 1970). In one study, 2- and 3-year-old children were seen to acquire the oppositional orientation of "front-back" before they learned the meanings *front* and *back* (Levine &

Carey, 1982). Further, in performing a lexical decision task, adult subjects have been found to employ or "activate" both ends of a dichotomous personality construct (e.g., aggressive and passive) when primed by the name of a familiar person under predication by such a personality descriptor (Millis & Neimeyer, 1990). Thus, "spreading activation" often follows an oppositionally meaningful pathway within the network.

Similar findings have emerged in studies of antonymy, where subjects are seen to respond with greater rapidity in identifying antonymical words having increasingly clearer delimiting oppositionality (Herrmann, Chaffin, Conti, Peters, & Robbins, 1979). Generic oppositionality is suggested in the greater rapidity of identifying sameness than difference in categorical decisions (Smith, 1977) or in synonym recognition (Hermann, Papperman, & Armstrong, 1978). Glass, Holyoak, and Kiger (1979) found that sentences in which direct antonyms were falsely related as subjects and predicates (e.g., "All boys are girls") were disconfirmed more rapidly than sentences with indirect antonymical relations (e.g., "All boys are sisters"). This finding occurred even though the direct antonyms (boy-girl) used in these sentences were rated as less similar in meaning than the indirect antonyms (boy-sister) and should therefore—according to network theory—have been easier to disconfirm.

Network theory predicts that associated words rated as low in similarity have weaker associative ties and therefore should take longer to process in a disconfirmation task. But the facts are otherwise. We know that, in general, antonymy makes rapid recognition of differences possible without the processing time required of nonantonymic word pairings (see also Hampton & Taylor, 1985; Schvaneveldt, Durso, & Mukherji, 1982). Another peculiar thing about opposite word meanings in networks is that, although they may be strongly related, sometimes opposites cannot be shown to have any word associations in common. For example, in a study using a large sample of college students, Deese (1962) found that although the words in the pair "soft-loud" associated to each other, they had no other word to which they were related jointly (like *music*, for example). It is difficult to conceive of an associated network of interlacing and spreading meanings when such findings emerge.

Oppositionality in Human Learning and Memory

Although it is not always singled out for special consideration in research on human learning and memory, oppositionality has frequently been recognized as a significant—and even troubling—factor in this literature. One of the earliest troubling intrusions of acknowledged oppositionality occurred in the findings on transfer. Charles Osgood (1949) had proposed a widely studied "transfer surface" that predicted certain likelihoods of facilitation or inhibition across lists of words to be memorized. This surface predicted that oppositionality would lead to antagonistic responding from list to list and hence that positive transfer would be inhibited. However, a series of subsequent experiments established beyond doubt that oppositionality facilitated positive transfer (Bastian, 1961; Mink, 1963; Ryan, 1960; Weiss-Shed, 1973; Umemoto, 1959; Wickens & Cermak, 1967). It is still difficult for traditional learning theories to account for such findings. How can a learner mediate words having such diametrically opposite meanings yet attain a facilitation from one list to the other? It is as if a *difference* in meaning functions as a *similarity* in the generalization process across lists. This goes against the law of noncontradiction underwriting Lockean theorizing.

A comparable puzzle arose in schema theory when it was found that material that is inconsistent with a schema—including, of course, meanings in opposition to the schema—are enhanced in memory. For example, subjects in one study were given trait descriptions establishing that a certain person was honest (the schema) and then given additional information about this person that was consistent with, inconsistent with, or irrelevant to the question of honesty (Hastie & Kumar, 1979). Subjects recalled significantly more inconsistent information than consistent or irrelevant information.

In an alternative format, subjects were asked to study the layout and contents of an office or a preschool classroom because they were going to be asked questions about it later. These environments were made consistent or inconsistent with customary (i.e., schematic) expectations. It was then found that subjects recalled more items in environments that were inconsistent (e.g., an ashtray in a preschool classroom) than those that were consistent (e.g., colored crayons in the classroom) (Pezdek, Whetstone, Reynolds, Askari, & Dougherty, 1989). A predicational theory can explain these findings only by appealing to the outside of the Euler circle along with the inside (see Figures 2 and 6). The schema predication is the inside of the circle, the meaning of which extends to the target. Because contrast or negation is an aspect of every predication, however, even when information (content) is inconsistent with such a framing meaning, it contributes to this meaning through the meaningful ties of delimiting oppositionality.

There is some evidence that such inconsistencies in personality trait descriptors are aided by value judgments. For example, since the opposite of honest behavior is dishonest behavior, information inconsistent with the former would borrow from the valuations of the latter, valuations that would themselves hinge on judgments like good-bad or desirable-undesirable. Evidence suggests that these value differences may well account for the enhancement of remembered information that is inconsistent with the original schema (Wyer & Gordon, 1982). In fact, there is even evidence that if the person has a strong evaluative commitment to the initial schema, inconsistent — in LLT terms, "negating" — information loses its advantage in memory (see Stangor & Ruble, 1989). The person remembers primarily what he or she is affectively committed to and thus expects to encounter in the future (ibid.). The point here is that such affective commitment is itself based on a delimiting oppositionality in cognition (good-bad, like-dislike, etc.). In chapter 7 we will look into such affective influences on cognition in great detail.

A common way in which traditional theorists explain the findings on memory enhancement via schematic inconsistency is to adopt the Tulving and Thomson (1973) theory of encoding specificity. Given this encoding assumption, it is then suggested that inconsistent material receives special attention during initial encoding, giving it stronger associative links to material stored in memory (see Srull & Wyer, 1989, for an example of this kind of theorizing).

There is evidence that newborns in the first weeks of life already orient themselves according to a "left-right" delimiting oppositionality. Papoušek (1967) had infants taking a dextrose solution from a nipple that required them to turn their head to the right. When the flow of dextrose was suddenly terminated, rather than rooting all the more vigorously to the right, the infants quickly turned their heads to the left in search of an alternative food source. Although 6-year-old children are unable to single out oppositionality per se in their learning, by the time they are 10 years old they know that learning words with opposite meanings is easier than learning words lacking this intrinsic semantic relationship (Kreutzer, Leonard, & Flavell, 1975). Even when they are younger than 6 years, however, children can be seen organizing their learning based on oppositionality. Thus, Carey (1978) made the following request to nursery school children who were already familiar with the color red: "Bring me the chromium tray, *not* the red one, the chromium one" (emphasis added). There were only two trays visible, a red one and a chromium tray of an olive-green color. Recall from chapter 4 that in a universal negation of this sort, delimiting oppositionality is likely to come into play via implication. Since the child knows that red is a color, and this color is being entirely negated as a predication for the target *tray*, it follows that he or she would draw the implication that chromium is a color.

Stated in terms of the Euler circles of Figure 2, red is the larger circle in which a smaller circle labeled "tray" is framed. If the other tray is not-red, then the implication is drawn that what falls outside the red circle is under consideration as a nonred, *not* a noncolor. Although red and chromium green

are not truly opposites—that is, they do not delimit each other's meaning—
the children did not know this. Hence, they reasoned according to a delimitation of "this color" versus "that color" predication. The children's precedent framing of color difference was difficult to correct. Even after six weeks
they spontaneously referred to the color green as "chromium," despite the
fact that they had repeatedly been corrected. We can say that the children
had made a "category mistake" in their initial framing of experience, having
been misled by the experimenter from a color to a metallic predication of
the tray in question.

Many studies have been reported in which subjects are presented with
negations like "The coffee is not hot" or "The book is not on the table,"
only to remember having heard "The coffee is cold" or "The book is off the
table" (Brewer & Lichtenstein, 1975; Harris, 1974; Johnson, Bransford, &
Solomon, 1973). Such reorganizations of meaning in memory are common,
but inhibitions of meanings also occur thanks to negation. Thus, when a subject reads the phrase "no bread" in original learning, he or she will be seen
later to inhibit responses to *bread* in a probe task (MacDonald & Just, 1989).
When misleading suggestions are given to subjects, negating what they are
told, or even what they see in a picture, this influence reduces their ability to
remember details of what is conveyed or distorts their memory concerning
what they actually saw (Lindsay, 1990; McCloskey & Zaragoza, 1985). This
processing influence suggests that generic oppositionality was involved via
the initial negation.

In LLT we look for the origins of so-called unconscious behavior in such
oppositional capacities to negate or deny—not admit—actual events and
occurrences. Especially when the meaning requiring predication is affectively negative and has pronounced implications for the individual's life, is it
possible for a negation of the "called for"—that is, reality-oriented—predication to take place. As examples of hysterical blindness demonstrate, people
do not have to see what is there for the seeing. I will return to this question
of unconscious cognition when I take up motivation in chapter 7.

Subjects have been shown to take longer to decide that an item is *not* a
member of a large category (e.g., the name of a certain animal in the animal kingdom) than of a smaller category (e.g., the name of a team in an
athletic conference) (Landauer & Freedman, 1968). Differences such as this
are frequently interpreted as reflecting a cognitive mechanism's processing
time (see, e.g., Johnson-Laird, Gibbs, & de Mowbray, 1978). In LLT we look
at such findings as a measurement of the complexity involved in the task at
hand. That is, since we can show this complexity independently of any subject's cognitive efforts to deal with it (i.e., we can count many more names
of animals in the animal kingdom category than athletic teams in the ath-

letic conference category), there is no need to postulate an unobservable mechanical process as the reason for the differential rate of task accomplishment. Measuring the task's formal complexity by counting the units to be dealt with is in effect the same as counting the timed units that pass during this supposed mechanical process.

Problem solution is another area in which psychologists have overlooked the important role that oppositionality plays. The concepts of "trial" and "error" are classical descriptors in problem solution. To know that one has made an error, however, is to know that one is wrong, which means that one must recognize a negation of the expected or correct outcome (Miyake & Norman, 1979). Questions and answers are often used in problem solution; this tactic involves delimiting oppositionality because the meanings framed in effective questions point to possible answers or solutions. As the saying goes, a question well framed is a problem half solved. A learner who does not know that he or she does not know when an error is being made faces an insurmountable block to learning (Brown, 1978; Collins, 1977). As I noted in chapter 4, this self-reflexive capacity in reasoning is referred to as metacognition.

Children in the first grade can distinguish between test items that they are almost certainly answering correctly and those that they are probably answering incorrectly (Pressley, Borkowski, & Schneider, 1987). By the second grade they know which parts of a text are easier to learn than others (Danner, 1976). By the sixth grade most students prefer a semantic (i.e., conceptual or meaning-based) strategy in problem solution and learning rather than a rote strategy (Justice, 1985). A developmental trend of this sort suggests to the LLT advocate that a Kantian form of self-reflexivity is an important aspect of problem solution and general learning. Only a self-reflexive and potentially transcending intellect knows that it does not know and consequently selects its preferred learning strategy—which can be modeled as being inside or outside the proper Euler circle.

As I have noted in previous chapters, all learning is a matter of extending meanings tautologically from what is known (precedently) to what can be known (sequaciously). This process involves the opposite knowledge, however, the contradiction of what is under predication or, in the case of analogical meaning-extensions (e.g., "this is 'like' that"), the negation of the analogy or the disanalogous (e.g., "this is both 'like' and 'not like' that"). When cognitive psychologists refer to analogies as enriching experience, they are not likely to consider the disanalogous aspects of such partial tautologies (e.g., see Eysenck & Keane, 1990, p. 412).

There has been no concept in psychology more involved with learning than that of conditioning. For some years psychologists believed that classical and operant conditioning were unintentional, automatic processes. Thanks to the findings of hundreds of experiments, however, it was finally made clear that this is not true (see Brewer, 1974). As I noted in chapter 5, it is necessary for a person to be aware of certain patterns if conditioning is to occur, which is comparable to the previous findings on metacognitively knowing when a response is probably right or wrong. In *classical conditioning* the person must grasp the pattern between the conditioned and unconditioned stimulus, and in *operant conditioning* he or she must grasp the pattern between an emitted response and the contingent reinforcement that may or may not follow. If the person does not grasp these patterns correctly, conditioning is not going to occur (at least, it did not occur in 90% of the cases studied). Even if the person grasps these patterns, conditioning still does not occur unless she or he intentionally carries out what is being suggested in this pattern. In the typical experiment, this means that the subject must carry out the experimenter's intention (via the *Aufgabe*). No cooperation, no conditioning—it is as simple as that.

Such cooperative intentionality strikes the LLT advocate as reflecting oppositionality in behavior. The person does or does not cooperate. As suggested by LLT, the person is an agent, a factor in what will eventuate in the conditioning format. The literature provides us with two marvelous examples of precisely such oppositionality, one drawn from an operant conditioning format and the other from a self-selection experimental design. In the conditioning format, Monte M. Page (1972) conducted a series of experiments in which he was able to identify subjects who had caught on to the pattern obtaining between the operant response and the contingent reinforcement. The operant response to be reinforced was that of making up sentences beginning with the pronoun *I*. The reinforcement was delivered by Page, who said "good" each time a subject made up a proper sentence. Subjects had 75 trials, the first 15 of which were not reinforced (i.e., this is the base rate). On trial 16 Page began delivering his reinforcements for "I" sentences.

Page found that, consistent with the literature on conditioning, not all his subjects became aware of the patterned relationship between an "I" sentence and his saying "good." These unaware subjects continued to produce "I" sentences at their base-rate level (i.e., they did not become conditioned). But he also found two kinds of "aware" subjects—those who complied with what was being indicated by "good" and those who were aware but did *not* comply (refused to go on making up "I" sentences). Page could identify the aware but uncooperating subjects because they actually declined to a zero response rate after they had become aware of what the experiment was about. The fact that they fell below their base rate operationally defined them as intentionally avoiding what was called for.

To prove that he had different types of subjects in his experiment, Page briefly interrupted the procedure on one of the later trials and asked his two kinds of aware subjects to make him do the opposite of what he was then doing (i.e., either saying or not saying "good"). Thus, to the aware and co-operating subjects he said "Make me stop saying good," and to the aware and uncooperating, as well as to the unaware subjects, he said "Make me start saying good." This is all he said, and then the procedure continued on as before. Immediately, with the very next verbal statements, the operant graph lines of his aware and cooperating subjects and his aware and uncooperating subjects *crisscrossed*, so that he did not even need to use statistical tests to determine that these subjects knew precisely what to do and what not to do as the procedure unfolded. Knowing what was implied in the experimental design, they could become conditioned or not at will. In the meantime, the unaware subjects who were challenged in midexperiment to make the experimenter say "good" fumbled on as before without increasing their base rate level of "I" sentences. Clearly, negation qua oppositionality played a role in this study.

The other experiment directly testing oppositionality is from the series of "peanut-eating" experiments conducted by George S. Howard (see esp. Howard, Youngs, & Siatcynski, 1985, as cited in Howard & Conway, 1986, p. 1246). In the self-selection design followed by Howard, college students are given jars containing precisely 16 ounces of peanuts. They are instructed to take the jar of peanuts back to their room and over the next several weeks to eat or not eat the peanuts based on certain experimental conditions required by the experimenter (e.g., whether the jar is in or out of sight) or decided by the subject him- or herself. In the study under consideration, subjects were given the choice of following experimental instructions on the eat or not eat days scheduled by the experimenter or doing the opposite. Subjects kept a record of what they had decided to do on the stipulated days (affirm or negate experimental instructions). Each day, at a prearranged hour, an experimenter showed up to weigh the peanut jar and to refill it to precisely 16 ounces. The ounces of peanuts eaten per 24-hour period represented the dependent variable of this research. As predicted, subjects ate considerably more peanuts on "eat" days when they had chosen to follow instructions (135 g vs. 10 g), as well as on the "not eat" days when they had opted to negate the instructions (120 g vs. 3 g).

In chapter 5 I noted the contribution that *elaboration* makes to memory. To elaborate a target for memory is to enrich it by combining it—LLT would say "predicating it"—with several contexts, making the target increasingly meaningful. The more meaningful we can make the target, the better it will be remembered (Bobrow & Bower, 1969; Ozier, 1978). Elaborations are usually relevant to the target, of course. It is not just a question of tying more and more concepts of any sort to the target. If we were going to elaborate a targeted food concept (e.g., "bouillabaisse"), it would be best to enrich this meaning through related meanings of food, cooking, dining, and so forth, rather than to tie it to computer terminology. I have found that there is sometimes an unmentioned oppositionality in research on elaboration. For example, in their classic study, Hyde and Jenkins (1969) found that "pleasant-unpleasant" served as the best context of elaboration for words that were targeted for recall. Stein and Bransford (1979) showed that if "The fat man read the sign" is elaborated as "The fat man read the sign warning of thin ice," recall of "fat man" is facilitated. The delimiting oppositional contrast of fat and thin obviously played a role here.

In sum, there is surely enough evidence to suggest that oppositionality plays a role in human learning and memory. There is no disputing this fact. Of course, as we have seen previously, the traditionalists in learning and memory view this finding as due to contiguous singular targets being joined through frequent association. It is the fortuitous but accidental association of certain unipolarities like this that sometimes results in an oppositional bipolarity taking shape. In the demonstration experiments of this chapter and the next, evidence is presented to cast doubt on this Lockean, bottom-up formulation of human cognition. Oppositionality, LLT contends, is intrinsic to the cognitive process in a Kantian, top-down fashion.

Demonstration Experiments: Concerning Oppositionality

Experiment 7: Oppositionally Predicating Targeted Names Facilitates Learning

Hypothesis

Subjects who learn to predicate targeted names on the basis of two descriptors differing in meaning accomplish this task more readily when these predicating descriptors are opposites than when they are nonopposites.

Rationale

Since, as was demonstrated in chapter 5, meaning extends from predication to the target, the way in which predication is organized should have a demonstrable effect on the ease with which the target is endowed with meaning. The clearest form of predication seems to follow the Euler-circle-based logic of inside versus outside the predicating circle. That is, a clear delimiting opposition between the predicate meanings being extended to the target would be like a Euler circle organization in which one pole of a predicating bipolarity (e.g., reliability) is extended to the target even as its opposite meaning (e.g., unreliability) is also lending a contrasting meaning to the target, resulting in a richer, more elaborated organization of the targeted content (recall the discussion in chapter 2 concerning how we violate the law of noncontradiction by taking oppositionality into consideration). This combined effect of an oppositional organization—a "double predication"—should facilitate learning more than an organization in which the predicate meanings lack such delimiting oppositionality.

Experimental Sample

Undergraduate college students ($N = 160$, divided equally by sex) were the subjects of this study.

Procedure

The subjects were asked to learn predications of either eight male or eight female target names. All names consisted of seven letters. The following male names used were: Charles, Douglas, Francis, Michael, Phillip, Raymond, Timothy, and William. The following female names used were: Valerie, Melissa, Lynette, Sherrie, Deborah, Barbara, Cynthia, and Theresa. As predicates for these targets, four words were selected from Anderson's (1968) normative list of socially descriptive personality words. The four descriptors selected had to meet two criteria: (a) The descriptors had to have the same level of familiarity and likability in the ratings, and (b) when combined, the four descriptors had to form either two oppositional or two non-oppositional pairs. The predicate descriptors settled on were *quiet, outspoken, cautious,* and *bold.*

The experimental conditions were arrayed based on the following combinations of predicates: quiet-outspoken, cautious-bold, outspoken-bold, and cautious-quiet. Note that when used as predicates to target a list of names, the first two of these pairs (quiet-outspoken, cautious-bold) involve delimiting oppositionality, whereas the latter two pairs (outspoken-bold, cautious-quiet) do not. Because both male and female names were used as targets for these predicate pairings, eight different lists were arrayed for the learning task. For each of the lists, 10 men and 10 women performed as subjects.

The target names and their predicates were presented to subjects in a paired-associates format, using eight name-predicate pairings displayed in the windows of a standard memory drum set on a 2-second cycle. Four of the name-predicate pairs had one of the descriptor meanings (e.g., outspoken) and four of the pairs had another descriptor (e.g., quiet or bold, depending on the experimental condition). The name (e.g., *Valerie*) was presented first for 2 seconds, followed by a 2-second delay in which the subject was instructed to say *is,* and then the predicate descriptor (e.g., *cautious*) appeared for 2 seconds.

Subjects were instructed to anticipate the descriptor by stating it aloud before it was flashed in the memory-drum window ("Valerie is *cautious*") as the learning trials proceeded. Three different orders of the list were administered to a subject, thereby removing list-dependent serial-learning cues from the task. Learning criterion was two consecutive correct anticipations of the entire 8-pair list. When this occurred, the subject was dismissed.

Results

A score was the anticipation trial on which a subject achieved learning criterion (two consecutive correct anticipations of the entire list). The lower this score was, the more rapidly learning was achieved. The basic design lent itself to a 2 (Sex of Subject) × 2 (Gender of Target Names) × 2 (Oppositional vs. Nonoppositional Predication) factorial analysis of variance (ANOVA). All variables were between subjects. Statistical analysis of the data resulted in only one main effect and no significant interactions. This significant main effect revealed that the opposite predication condition resulted in faster learning ($M = 12.04$, $SD = 6.29$) than the nonopposite predication condition ($M = 16.20$, $SD = 6.29$) ($F = 17.49$, $df = 1, 152$, $p < .001$).

Conclusion and Discussion

A predicate context framed by oppositionality clearly facilitated the learning of the lists. To counter any suggestions that this result was due to the predicate words per se, rather than the oppositional relationship between these words, we conducted a further experiment in which consonant-vowel-consonant (CVC) trigrams were used as targets and predicates in the place of actual words. Subjects learned a series of predications of the following sort: HIB is always VIC, HIB is sometimes YAT, and HIB is the opposite of JOQ. Note that the target (HIB) remains constant across the predications. The focus here is entirely on the joining relationship of *always*, *sometimes*, and *opposite*. We found that *opposite* rank ordered as the best condition of all (Rychlak, Williams, & Bugaj, 1986). This supports LLT's contention that oppositionality is an excellent heuristic in organizing cognition.

Experiment 8: A Learning Curve for Oppositionality

Hypotheses

1. Subjects who are exposed to a series of sentences will, when subsequently tested, recognize the opposite meaning of these sentences as readily as a paraphrased meaning.

2. The recognition of opposite sentence meanings predicted by hypothesis 1 will increase with practice.

Rationale

In addition to manifesting its heuristic properties in learning, oppositionality should be demonstrable in tests of memory. Actually, it has already been so demonstrated. For example, we have evidence that subjects can actually hear the phrase "not hot" but later remember having heard "cold" (Brewer & Lichtenstein, 1975). This involves delimiting oppositionality in the reorganization of memory (i.e., negating the "hot" Euler circle realm and moving outside it to what is then remembered as "cold"). According to LLT, it should be possible to demonstrate that delimiting oppositionality is routinely involved in all memory efforts—that to learn one thing is to learn its negation as well. To my knowledge, there has never been an effort made to frame a "learning curve of oppositionality" in which the capacity to recognize such reversals of the meanings initially learned is shown to improve with practice. Experiment 8 was designed to correct this oversight.

Experimental Sample

Fifty-four subjects, divided equally by sex, were drawn from introductory psychology courses. They were put through the recognition task individually.

Procedure

The recognition task used involved memorizing 24 brief sentences, each of which was printed on an individual 3-by-5-in. card. Examples of the sentences include the following:

> The ant crushed the rock.
> The cabbage shook its head no.
> The diamond pinched its pennies.
> The elephant climbed the ladder.
> The moon had insomnia.
> The suitcase missed its train.
> The chair leaned back and dozed.

During the original exposure trials, each card was placed before the subjects for 5 seconds. The subjects were required to read the sentence aloud during this time. They could then memorize the sentence until a new card appeared. Subjects were instructed that they would be asked to recognize these sentences later in the experiment. They were also given a warm-up procedure involving a few sentences that were not used in the actual task.

Eighteen subjects were randomly assigned to each of the following recognition conditions: *identical* (subjects received exactly the same sentence presented during original exposure); *paraphrase* (subjects received a sentence conveying the same meaning as the original sentence, but in a different form);

and *opposite* (subjects received a sentence conveying a meaning directly opposite to the original sentence). Here is an example of the three recognition conditions for the sentence "The elephant climbed the ladder":

> *Identical:* The elephant climbed the ladder.
> *Paraphrase:* The elephant went up.
> *Opposite:* The elephant went down.

Within each of these recognition conditions, six subjects were assigned to either 1, 3, or 5 trials during original exposure (totaling 18 subjects per recognition condition). During the recognition test, 24 cards were added to the original 24. Each of these additional 24 cards presented an alternative sentence matched to a sentence on the original card. For example, the original sentence, "The elephant climbed the ladder," had the sentence "The elephant danced a jig" matched to it. Hence, it was not possible for subjects simply to recognize that an elephant had been mentioned in the original sentence. They had to recognize the specific action carried out by the elephant as well. Subjects were instructed to say yes if a card placed before them was contained in the original deck. As the experimenter placed a card before a subject in the recognition task, a stopwatch with a 10-second sweep hand was activated, and the time that the subject took to say yes for an accurate recognition was recorded.

After subjects had been exposed to the original 24 cards for 1, 3, or 5 trials, they were given a recognition instruction. Subjects in the identical condition were told that they would now be presented with the original sentences mixed in among 24 other cards. If they had seen one of these sentences in the original presentation(s) they were to say yes. Subjects in the paraphrase condition were told that their original cards were replaced by cards that had "essentially the same meaning" mixed in among the 24 new cards. They were to say yes when those paraphrased sentences appeared. Finally, the subjects in the opposite condition were told that their original cards were replaced by cards that had the "directly opposite meaning" mixed in among the 24 new cards. They were to say yes when these delimiting oppositional sentences appeared. The identical condition was taken as a form of control or standard of comparison against which to assess the other two conditions.

Results

The dependent variable of this experiment was a recognition score determined by totaling the number of cards that a subject had correctly identified as having been seen before in the experiment. These scores were entered into a factorial ANOVA having the characteristics of a 2 (Sex of Subject) × 3 (Experimental Condition) × 3 (Trials). All variables were between subjects.

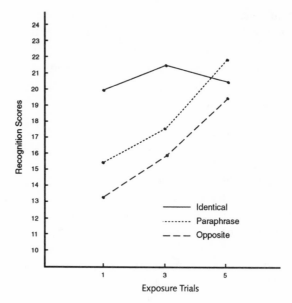

Figure 17   Recognition scores arrayed by
experimental condition across exposure trials

There was no main effect for sex of subject. There was a main effect for experimental condition ($F = 7.36$, $df = 2, 44$, $p < .001$), with the data arraying as follows: identical, $M = 20.78$ ($SD = 2.34$); paraphrase, $M = 18.44$ ($SD = 4.42$); opposite, $M = 16.22$ ($SD = 4.57$). Simple effects tests established that the opposite condition did not differ significantly from the paraphrase condition, but it did differ from the identical condition ($p < .05$).

There was also a main effect for trials ($F = 5.67$, $df = 2.33$, $p < .001$), with the data arraying as follows: one trial, $M = 16.50$ ($SD = 5.09$); three trials, $M = 18.44$ ($SD = 3.79$); five trials, $M = 20.50$ ($SD = 2.60$). Simple effects tests revealed that all three of these means differed significantly from each other ($p < .05$). Although there was no significant interaction between experimental condition and trials ($F = 1.25$, $df = 4, 44$, N.S.), the pattern of the data here is of interest. Figure 17 presents the recognition scores arrayed by experimental condition across exposure trials.

It is obvious that the task was too easy in the identical condition, but we do have a nice three-step increase for the paraphrase and opposite conditions across trials. There is no significant difference between the latter two conditions. Recognizing paraphrases was no different from recognizing oppositional rephrasings of the memorized sentences.

Conclusion and Discussion

We now have evidence that the recognition of meanings that are opposite to those committed to memory can be facilitated by additional practice. The only explanation that I think is possible is for there to be a paralleling sense of negation, reversal, or contradiction of the meaning being learned even as it is being learned. Although there is evidence in certain experimental designs that it takes longer to reframe an opposite than a paraphrase of a sentence, we have also found in other designs that no such time differences obtain (Rychlak, Barnard, Williams, & Wollman, 1989). Thus, subjects recognize the oppositionality of linguistic terms (antonymy) as readily as they recognize their meaningful identity (synonymy) (ibid.). The final demonstration experiment of this chapter confronts LLT with a widely cited experiment in which oppositionality played a significant but totally overlooked role.

Experiment 9: Oppositionality as Elaboration or Depth of Processing

The presentation of this experiment requires some background discussion. When the emphasis in learning and memory shifted from sheer frequency of contiguous events to organization at input, cognitive psychologists began emphasizing the operations carried out by the learner in organizing memory rather than the repetition of items submitted to memory. A significant influence here was Hyde and Jenkins's (1969) experiment on the organization of electronically recorded words in subsequent recall. Hyde and Jenkins had subjects perform in three experimental groups, all of which listened to the same 24 words recorded in a single order. In a recall experimental group, the subjects were told to listen to the words with the expectation that they would be asked to recall them later. An incidental group was asked to perform certain tasks with these words, but no mention was made of a subsequent recall. Finally, an incidental + recall group of subjects was both given these preliminary tasks and told that they would have to recall the words. The dependent variable was therefore the number of words recalled.

There were three incidental task instructions: one asked subjects to estimate the number of letters in a word, a second asked them to estimate the number of times the letter *e* was used in a word, and a third asked subjects to rate each word along a pleasant-unpleasant dimension. In effect, Hyde and Jenkins were using an oppositional predicating context similar to the one used in Experiment 7 and contrasting it with predications lacking in oppositionality. As LLT would have predicted, the findings were that evaluating the targeted words by the oppositional context of pleasant-unpleasant led to greater recall of words than either of the letter-counting predications.

In explaining these findings, Hyde & Jenkins followed Tulving's (1966) suggestion that the traces of the words themselves that are stored together facilitate organization in recall, forming thereby a strongly related semantic tie. Hence, the more meaningful tie of actual words (*pleasant, unpleasant*) to the presented words resulted in a better organization than nonsemantic letter counting. The recall instruction then activated a better organization in storage, leading to the observed differences (Hyde & Jenkins, 1969, p. 480).

Another early study that was important in furthering this organizational thesis was that of Bobrow and Bower (1969), whom we considered in chapter 5 concerning subject/predicate cueing in sentence memory. These experimenters asked subjects to read a series of sentences such as "The cow chased the rubber ball." Some subjects were asked to check on the spelling of certain words in the sentence, such as *ball*. Others were asked what meaning was intended in the use of the word *ball*—a "dance" or a "round object." Later, without being prepared to do so, subjects were given the first significant word (*cow*) of each sentence and asked to recall the second (*ball*). It was found that subjects who had looked for misspellings recalled the second word only 18% of the time, whereas those who had answered questions about the word meaning recalled the second word 49% of the time. Bobrow and Bower suggested that the latter subjects had performed a "deeper" processing on the sentences than had subjects who merely checked the spellings of words. Hence, this depth of processing made a greater recall possible.

In a subsequent analysis of Hyde and Jenkins, Craik and Lockhart (1972) defined depth as involving a "greater degree of semantic or cognitive analysis" (p. 675). The Craik and Lockhart depth interpretation of Hyde and Jenkins has received wide coverage in textbooks on cognitive psychology, virtually making it into a modern classic (e.g., Anderson, 1985, pp. 170, 171; Bransford, 1979, pp. 77–79; Howard, 1983, pp. 144–146, 153; Mandler, 1985, p. 103; Stillings et al., 1987, pp. 77, 78). How does this semantic enrichment take place? Craik and Lockhart (1972) suggest that "after a word is recognized, it may trigger associations, images or stories on the basis of the subject's past experience with the word" (p. 675).

This reference to past experience is typical of traditional psychological explanations relying on efficient causation, and it smacks of the frequency-contiguity thesis. Frequently encountered experiences are strongly situated in the network of associations, and so on. Because of their complexities, such strong associations may also take more processing time in the ongoing cognitions of the network, which, as I noted in chapter 5, is yet another variation on the frequency thesis. Organizations that take longer to process are presumably retained longer because of their numerical superiority across the seconds and subseconds of the (efficiently caused) cognitive process. At this point we can legitimately ask whether it is the organization of cognitions that influences memory or the sum of past experiences connecting today with a related item. I think psychologists are still uncertain about this.

Craik and Lockhart equate their notion of a triggering of associations with Tulving and Madigan's (1970) phrase "elaborative encoding." Craik and Lockhart are aware of the research evidence suggesting that elaborative encoding is not necessarily hierarchical, as the concept of "depth" seems to be (Macnamara, 1972; Savin & Bever, 1970), but they like the depth usage nevertheless. Gradually, the term *elaboration* began to be used in the literature as equivalent to depth. In fact, some cognitive textbooks have recommended that the latter term be dropped in favor of the former (Anderson, 1985, p. 170; Stillings et al., 1987, pp. 77, 78). Craik and Lockhart (1972) actually use the phrase "elaborative encoding" as synonymous with depth (see p. 675). They admitted that " 'spread of encoding' might be a more accurate description [of encoding], but the term 'depth' will be retained as it conveys the flavor of our argument" (ibid., p. 676).

It seems clear that Craik, the leading theoretician here, wished to retain a "levels of meaningful significance" notion in the concept of depth. What interests me is that whether we speak of elaboration or of depth, the point under consideration is meaning. Organization is essentially a code word for meaning. In another paper Craik had this to say: "Thus greater depth of processing is characterized by qualitative differences (greater meaningfulness), by a greater number of possible elaborations, and thus, typically, by richer and more distinctive encodings of events" (Craik & Jacoby, 1979, p. 152). Depth thus encompasses qualitative differences, as well as clarity or distinctiveness of the meanings under processing. Even so, the source of this richness in meaning is presumed to be external to the cognitive process.

Thus, as mediational modelers, Craik and Lockhart (1972) suggest that in organizing word materials for memory, the subject begins with the more superficial aspects of a perception, such as the slanting lines of the letters in word recognition. As this analysis moves from the superficial appearance of a word to the elaborating associations of memory traces in a network, however, the likelihood of recalling this word increases. Craik and Lockhart sum up their view as follows: "We suggest that trace persistence is a function of depth of analysis, with deeper levels of analysis associated with more elaborate, longer lasting, and stronger traces. Since the organism is normally concerned only with the extraction of meaning from the stimuli, it is advantageous to store the products of such deep analyses, but there is usually no need to store the products of preliminary analyses" (ibid., p. 675). To round out their account, Craik and Lockhart postulate a "flexible central processor" that functions at various levels to keep words in consciousness through rehearsal at a fixed rate or, at a deeper level, to connect with learned cognitive structures that contribute semantically to the words under processing (ibid., p. 679).

I do not think such theorizing is related to the empirical findings. What we observe in our experiments is that meaningfulness is related to retention. We are not observing mechanical central processors. We are not tracking traces or opening up "stores." We are observing people using more or less meaningful frameworks within which they order other meanings (i.e., words) that they are called on to retain in memory. The evidence on the primacy of meaning in this retention effort grows with each experiment, yet our traditional theoretical accounts of such findings do not focus on meaning. They invent all these other supposed mechanisms to describe what is not observed in place of what is observed. The data force us, again and again, to consider meaning per se, but traditionalists cook up these substitute concepts of elaboration, depth, distinctiveness, and so forth, which are themselves mere elaborations of the concept of meaning and not underlying producers of meaning. What we require is some direct consideration of meaning, yet it only seeps into the traditionalist's account secondarily or unknowingly—as when we read that "distinctiveness is not an absolute quality but is relative to the background of other relevant encodings" (Craik & Jacoby, 1979, p. 159). I suggest that this is a reference to predication made without appreciation—or acknowledgment—of this fact.

We now move on to Experiment 9, which is designed to show that Craik and Lockhart's (1972) understanding of Hyde and Jenkins' (1969) results completely overlooked the possibilty that delimiting oppositionality rather than depth of processing accounted for the findings.

Hypotheses

1. Subjects whose preliminary incidental task involves judging a target word in light of opposite comparison words will subsequently recall more of the target words than subjects whose incidental task does not involve such oppositionality.

2. Hypothesis 1 will hold even when the same comparison words of the oppositional task are used as a rearranged, nonoppositional task within which the target words are to be judged.

Rationale

The hypotheses predict that a subject is more likely to recall a target word that is predicated by the meaning context of "pleasant-unpleasant" or "important-unimportant" than one that was predicated by a combination of such meanings resulting in a nonoppositional predicate context like "pleasant-unimportant" or one framed by a count of the number of *e*'s or the total letters that it contained.

If depth of processing is the crucial variable in the recall of words, then, according to Craik and Lockhart (1972), a combination such as pleasant-unimportant should be even deeper than the more limited oppositional context of pleasant-unpleasant. There would have to be an extensively elaborated triggering of two entirely different semantic complexes in the pleasant-unimportant context of the cognitive network, resulting in a greater likelihood of retention in memory. A person judging *decisive* to be both pleasant and important should activate more associative pathways connecting to this word node than someone judging the word to be simply pleasant. Hence, the former judgment should be more elaborate or deeper than the latter, leading to greater retrieval for the more richly endowed nodal complex. This kind of theorizing flows from the Lockean constitutive theorizing of mediational modeling.

On the other hand, LLT predicts that—as in Experiment 7—an oppositional context is a powerful heuristic; it lends a broad and clear meaning to a targeted item. It is as if the word *decisive* is placed in a Euler circle labeled "pleasant," even as it is delimited by a much wider range of meaning, labeled "unpleasant." The resultant dual predication focuses meaning along a clearly singular, albeit bipolar, dimension of meaning, leading to a greatly enriched target. But the enrichment is distinctive, and not likely to be confounded in memory, as when two nonopposite—hence intrinsically nondimensional—meanings are extended to the same target. A clear and distinctive organization is produced by the affirmation of the target within the rich context of delimiting oppositionality, which consequently facilitates memory, as per the experimental evidence presented in chapter 5. Effective organization at the outset of predicating the target is the key issue here, and not the depth of some form of networking process.

Experimental Sample

The sample consisted of 190 college students, randomly assigned to one of 10 experimental conditions. Sex of subject was balanced within these conditions.

Procedure

The procedure followed is a modification of the Hyde and Jenkins (1969) design. All subjects listened to the same tape recording of 28 target words, with a 2.5-second interval between word presentations. The first two and last two words heard by subjects were simply fillers used to counteract the effects of primacy and recency on memory. Hence, the crucial list for the memory task was the 24 target words arrayed between the fillers. The words were taken from the intermediate range of familiarity on Anderson's (1968) list of personality-trait words; some examples are *religious, idealistic, cautious, blunt,* and *rash.*

Subjects were randomly assigned to small groups in which one of 10 instructions was administered: nine of these were experimental conditions in which an incidental task was administered, and one was a control condition lacking an incidental task. A warm-up demonstration was given to the subjects in the experimental conditions. The instructions for the experimental and control conditions were as follows:

1. Pleasant-Unpleasant: the subject was asked to strike a mark through a 3-in. line separating *pleasant* from *unpleasant,* depending on how closely the word meaning in question approximated one or the other of these opposite meanings.
2. Important-Unimportant: same as (1), using these different opposite meanings.
3. Common-Uncommon: same as (1), using these different opposite meanings.
4. Pleasant-Unimportant: the subject was asked to draw an *X* in a space on the answer sheet if the word meaning in question was both pleasant and unimportant. If it was not *both* pleasant and unimportant, the subject was asked to record a zero.
5. Common-Unpleasant: same as (4), using these nonopposite meanings.
6. Important-Uncommon: same as (4), using these nonopposite meanings.
7. E Counting: the subject was asked to estimate the number of *e*'s in each word and to record these in a space provided on the answer sheet. Twenty of the 24 experimental words had between one and three *e*'s.
8. Letter Counting: the subject was asked to estimate the number of letters in each word and to record these in a space provided on the answer sheet.
9. E + Letter Counting: subject was asked to place a checkmark on the answer sheet if the word in question had at least one *e* and contained 10 or more letters. Ten of the words on the experimental list fulfilled this requirement.
10. Control: the subject was asked to listen to the words and concentrate, for on completion of the list he or she would be asked to recall as many of the words as possible.

Conditions 1 through 9 had 20 subjects (10 males, 10 females) performing in each. Half of the subjects in each of these nine conditions were instructed that they would be asked to recall the words under presentation. The other half of the subjects in a condition were not told that a recall of the words would be required of them. Of course, if we tell subjects that they are going to have to recall the target words, they are performing not in an incidental learning task but rather in an intentional one. Actually, Hyde and Jenkins (1969) found no difference across their told and not told conditions. Only ten subjects performed under the control instructions, because these subjects (5 males, 5 females) were necessarily told to expect a recall task. The sample size for this experiment was 190 subjects (95 females, 95 males). The subjects recorded the words recalled in writing. Spelling errors did not invalidate a word recollection.

Results

The dependent variable of this experiment was the number of correct words recalled. A factorial analysis of variance was run on these data, having the characteristics of a 2 (Sex) × 2 (Told, Not Told) × 9 (Experimental Instruction); all variables were between conditions. A main effect was found for sex, with females ($M = 6.19$, $SD = 2.37$) outperforming males ($M = 5.66$, $SD = 2.28$) in the recall of words ($F = 2.70$, $df = 1$, 162, $p < .05$). There were no significant interactions of sex with the other between conditions. There was no main effect for told/not told (F = less than unity, N.S.), but incidental task instruction and told/not told did interact significantly ($F = 2.05$, $df = 8$, 162, $p < .05$).

There was a significant main effect for task instruction ($F = 2.73$, $df = 8$, 162, $p < .001$). Table 4 presents the means and standard deviations of the target words recalled, ranked across task instruction (10 males, 10 females per condition) by recall scores (i.e., from highest score [most recall] to lowest score [least recall]).

Note in Table 4 that, in support of the hypothesis, the three oppositional instructions stand at the top of the array. The means of Table 4 were submitted to a Duncan's multiple range test, and it was found that the pleasant-unpleasant instruction differed significantly ($p < .05$) from the following six instructions: pleasant-unimportant, letter counting, important-uncommon, *e* counting, *e* + letter counting, and common-unpleasant. The important-unimportant condition differed significantly ($p < .05$) from the following two conditions: *e* + letter counting and common-unpleasant. The common-uncommon instruction failed to reach significance in the first Duncan test but did so in the second.

That is, since there was a significant interaction between told/not told and the nine task instructions, it was possible to array 19 subgroup means

Table 4   Mean and standard deviation of target words recalled, ranked across task instruction by recall score

Task instruction	Target words recalled	
(20 Subjects in each)	Mean	SD
Pleasant-Unpleasant	7.55	2.24
Important-Unimportant	6.65	2.25
Common-Uncommon	6.15	2.39
Pleasant-Unimportant	5.95	1.85 [a]
Letter Counting	5.60	1.79
Important-Uncommon	5.50	3.22
E Counting	5.35	2.16
E + Letter Counting	5.15	2.21 [b]
Common-Unpleasant	4.95	1.96

[a] All task means at or below this point are significantly different from Pleasant-Unpleasant ($p < .05$).
[b] This task mean and the one below it are significantly different from Important-Unimportant ($p < .05$).

(5 females, 5 males in each subgroup) and submit them to a Duncan test. The additional subgroup here was the control condition ($M = 6.80$, $SD = 2.90$). The top rank in this array of 19 means was the pleasant-unpleasant told subgroup ($M = 8.00$), and the bottom rank was the *e*-counting told subgroup ($M = 3.90$). As suggested in this finding, there was no noticeable pattern for the told instruction to be superior to the not told instruction among the 19 subgroupings. The top two scores and the bottom two scores were both told subgroups.

The second highest score in the subgroup ranking was the important-unimportant told subgroup ($M = 7.60$), followed by the pleasant-unpleasant not told subgroup ($M = 7.10$), the control subgroup ($M = 6.80$), and the common-uncommon told subgroup ($M = 6.60$). All these subgroups differed significantly ($p < .05$) from between 1 and 11 of the nonoppositional subgroups. The control subgroup differed from two nonoppositional instructions, common-unpleasant told and *e*-counting told subgroups. In no case did a nonoppositional instruction result in a significantly greater level of word recall than an oppositional arrangement.

Conclusion and Discussion

Once again, delimiting oppositionality has proven to be a strong heuristic in organizing memory. All the oppositional instructions reflected at least some significantly better results, over the two Duncan analyses, in comparison to the nonoppositional instructions. None of the nonoppositional instructions reflected superiority in recall over any of the other experimental conditions, oppositional or nonoppositional. There is no evidence for "depth" in these findings. The told/not told condition did interact with the nine experimental conditions, but there was no pattern of findings to suggest that anticipating recall can be counted on to facilitate such recall. This cross-validates Hyde and Jenkins (1969) and falls into line with other findings mentioned in chapter 5 that although intentionality facilitates recall, it is not essential to recall. That is, intentionality seems to facilitate organization at initial conceptualization (input, etc.), which in turn facilitates recall. But a strong organization at initial conceptualization can result in good recall even though intentionality did not bring it about. Predication and its attendant oppositionality undoubtedly play a prominent role in all such cases of unintended remembering, just as they do in the case of intended remembering.

Concluding Comment

The preceding demonstration experiments present sound evidence that traditional psychological investigation has overlooked the important role of oppositionality in cognitive organization. Something like elaboration undoubtedly takes place in cognition, but it is how this takes place that matters. What LLT contends is that although some of the elaboration seems to be nonoppositional, as when we predicate apples by the color red, generic oppositionality is always involved, which in turn permits a delimiting oppositionality to take place as contents of a more symbolic abstractness appear.

Demonstrative reasoning does occur, of course, but it proceeds by limiting generic oppositionality to difference, thereby dismissing the alternatives implied by delimiting oppositionality. In other words, the delimitation can itself be negated as the person focuses exclusively on what is the case (demonstrative singularity) rather than contemplating what else might be the case (dialectical alternatives). Indeed, a person cannot become enmeshed in what I discussed in chapter 4 as the oppositional implications of every thought. To do so would seriously counter the course of thinking, negating not only its suggestive hunches and hopeful wishes but also its conviction through fundamental belief. Even so, as psychologists, we must study the entire range of cognitive processing—the demonstrative and the dialectical. Chapter 6 has given many proofs that the oppositionality of dialectical reasoning operates in both human and subhuman cognition. It does not further the field of psychology to go on acting as if *only* demonstrative reasoning takes place. This is an unacceptable negation of the truth.

7

Motivation: Affection versus Drive/Emotion

We come now to motivation, a topic of historical importance in learning theories. Many psychologists have complained that the cognitive revolution has essentially overlooked motivation's role in behavior, referring to the activation of networks without explaining the motivating causes of such activity. In this chapter I will discuss the LLT concept of affection, or affective assessment. This concept, which I introduced in chapter 2, has special relevance to motivation; to show this connection, I will contrast this concept with the drive theories of old, as well as with some of the major theories of emotion that have been advanced more recently.

From Drive to Affection

The early theories of learning, originating with such luminaries as Thorndike, Watson, Tolman, Skinner, and Hull, were all framed in an exclusively extraspective manner. Although drives were not integral to the others, Hullian learning theory placed great emphasis on this motivational concept. The 1940s and early 1950s were dominated by Hullian learning theory, which drew on Pavlovian conditioning to frame a highly sophisticated explanation of learning encompassing drive stimulation and reduction (Hull, 1937, 1943). Drive conceptions like Hull's make a good deal of sense when we frame behavior as taking place "over there" (i.e., extraspectively), in efficient-cause fashion. Since it is assumed that there is no intention or purpose directing the observed motion of the organism, we require some basis on which to explain how behavior gets going, as well as to describe how the units of behavioral motions (i.e., stimuli and responses) become patterned into sequences (S-R attachments, habits, bondings, hook-ups, etc.). If a rising drive level impels the organism to activate potentially rewarding behavior (e.g., foraging when hungry) and then falls off following satiation (e.g., eating), we have a way in which to describe how behavior is patterned through past pushes rather than future pulls of an aim, target, or goal.

Hull thus succeeded in fixing the drive conception in psychological theorizing. Stimuli attached to responses because of the elevated drives that were reduced when appropriate, albeit unintended, behaviors occurred. Skinner (1938, 1953) was also influential during this period, but he really did not achieve dominance in the field until the later 1950s and on into the 1960s, due in part to the fact that his operant theory was more compatible than Hullian theory with expectancy's growing importance as motivational theorizing ceased to be focused on the ubiquitous white rat and was directed instead to the descriptions of people. This change, which occurred in the latter half of the 20th century, was to influence explanations of motivation greatly, shifting interest from the past push of a drive to the future pull of a goal. Goals for Tolman's (1932/1967) animals were ensconced within their cognitive maps, but these were intervening variables that were etched on the animal's tabula rasa cognitive apparatus in efficient-cause fashion (for a discussion of Tolman's nontelic purposivism, see Rychlak, 1988, pp. 150–154). As psychology expanded into a broad profession, theorizing was increasingly focused on the behavior of people without the obligatory bow to the "basic" laws of rat behavior. This meant that theoreticians found themselves relying on intentionality in a new way, one that was not so easily reduced to efficiently caused impulses from the past—although they still attempted (and attempt) this effort in various guises.

To get some idea of the shifting focus in motivational accounts, we can glance at some major theorists of the post-midcentury decades. A prototypical example of the shifting locus in motivation theorizing is McClelland and Atkinson's achievement motivation, which burst on the scene in the 1950s to emphasize the incentive value of future goals, as well as estimations of the possibility for achieving these goals (McClelland, Atkinson, Clark, & Lowell, 1953). At about the same time, and drawing on Lewinian findings concerning *levels of aspiration* (Lewin, Dembo, Festinger, & Sears, 1944), Rotter's (1954) social learning theory held that motivation stems from a person's *expectancy* concerning a projected goal, as well as from a judgment of the worth of this goal.

Festinger (1957) added that conflicting expectancies or beliefs act like an aversive cognitive drive state (p. 18), inducing the person to reduce this level of *dissonance* by ignoring threatening facts or arguments, concocting unlikely alternatives, and so on. We see here Festinger's effort to retain the older drive-reduction formulations. *Equity theory* (Adams, 1965) was similar in that it suggested that people are motivated to achieve a balance between their perceived contribution to a social exchange and the rewards they receive in turn; any imbalance (inequity) between these two factors creates a tension (qua drive) that must be relaxed. Brehm's (1966) *reactance theory* enlarged the motivation concept to include instances in which a person can back off from pressures applied by others to resist their hard sell or lust after an item that is no longer available for purchase simply because it is not there (note the delimiting oppositionality here).

Although they retain the traditional notion of rising and falling motivating instrumentalities (achievement motive, expectancy, dissonance, inequity, reactance, etc.), these post-1950 theories do not rest on biologically based drives. There was no opportunity to theorize in this fashion when the white rat was the object of study. The growing emphasis on psychological (*Logos*) rather than physical (*Bios*) bases for motivation was even extended to an *economics* rationale (see Kukla, 1972) in which a person supposedly makes a cost-benefit analysis in deciding whether an effort should be expended; this analysis includes the probability of success as well as the task's estimated level of difficulty. A unique adaptation of motivational theory is Apter's (1982, 1989) *reversal theory*, which relies on oppositionality in a way different from Festinger's usage. That is, reversal theory allows a person to interpret a rising level of arousal as being motivationally either positive (e.g., excitement) or negative (e.g., anxiety), and vice versa for a falling level of arousal.

All the accounts in this selective overview broaden the earlier drive conception to include personal evaluations made by the individual under motivation, tilting the focus of explanation from the already lived past to the predicating meanings of both the ongoing present and the expected future. On such accounts, the human being may find his or her drive level rising *after* a challenging goal has been framed, setting a course of expected achievement that moves life along in a final-cause manner rather than it being pushed from out of the past in an efficient-cause manner. This shifting locus of motivational influence might have led to a more introspective formulation of motivation in psychological theorizing, but unfortunately, no one took the crucial step, and the predominant stance of these theories therefore remained extraspective and mediational. Hence, although at times such theories read as if they are moving to the (introspectively conceived) predications of the human beings under motivation, careful reading makes it obvious that they still use the traditional style of explanation. Logical learning theory takes the step called for by simply extending the process of predication to include affection, or affective assessment.

As I noted in chapter 2, affective assessment is due to transcending telosponsivity—that is, a person's innate capacity to evaluate reflexively the meanings of his or her cognitions, characterizing them as either liked (positive evaluation) or disliked (negative evaluation). Since affective assessment focuses on the contents being cognitively processed, it relies on delimiting oppositionality. Thus, a liked content is not simply or precisely different from a disliked content. The liked content is opposite from, albeit dimensionally related to, the disliked content.

Logical learning theory contends that affective assessments are rendered in all telosponsivity, so that the person not only frames meanings in telosponding but, pari passu, takes a position on the contents of these telosponses within an even wider realm of positive or negative affection. It is possible, in principle, to avoid rendering an affective assessment, but this is extremely rare. As I noted in chapter 2, if a person is truly indifferent about some item of meaning under affirmation ("I don't care about this one way or the other"), the affection is probably slightly negative. When a person cannot state a clear affective preference, this is often because of *ambivalence*, in which case there is both a positive and a negative valuation of the item in question. Affections are ultimately arbitrary, in that they can always go either way. The person takes the affective position based on a conceptualization of whatever item or event is being processed at the time. Although they are arbitrarily grounded, affections are extremely important in directing the course of learning and memory once they are affirmed.

Logical learning theory claims that infants are born with this innate capacity to render affective assessments of experience, organizing it in the ways that we have been reviewing in chapters 3 thru 6. Indeed, LLT holds that affective assessments are the most basic and abstract cognitions carried on by a human reasoner. Framed in Euler-circle terms, the "like" and "dislike" circles are therefore always the broadest meanings extended in any cognitive act.

Affection was the very first Kantian concept to be studied in LLT. The term *affection* is used as a synonym for *emotion* in psychological writings, of course, but there was also a precedent for adopting the notion of an evaluative cast to all cognition. Thus, Titchener (1909) had distinguished between affection as the "characteristic element in emotion" (p. 277) and as an "emotion proper," which would include all those distinctive feeling states we name anger, joy, and so forth. Continuing in the vein of his teacher, Wundt, Titchener held that there are only two forms of affections: Either they are pleasant, or they are unpleasant (ibid., p. 226). Although he theorized extraspectively and in no way was thinking of predication, there was a suggestion that a person naming certain bodily feelings as this or that emotion might also be evaluating the pleasantness or unpleasantness of the emotion in question, even as it was being registered cognitively in a certain context.

Thus, rather than assume that an emotion has the "pleasant-unpleasant" label affixed to it biologically, LLT proceeds on the assumption that a cognitive evaluation establishes this relative preference. The same emotion can therefore be judged liked in one context and disliked in another. The athlete who believes in "no pain, no gain" during exercise is not rendering the same kind of negative evaluation of pain in this context as she or he would render if the pain being felt were a stomachache following a meal. People feel "righteous" anger at times, but at other times they are ashamed of their "sinful" anger. A sexual feeling in an inappropriate context does not carry the same emotional tone that it does in an appropriately romantic context. Thus, it seemed reasonable to believe that an affective assessment is rendered cognitively over and above the sensations experienced as emotions. Logical learning theory has followed this assumptive belief. I will return to the question of emotions below, but first I will review the findings on affection as a distinctive cognitive process.

Operationalizing Affective Assessment

Having postulated transcending telosponsivity in human learning and memory, it became necessary to operationalize this concept. How could one prove that framing affective assessments of meanings in experience distinctively and uniquely influenced what the cognitivists refer to as their acquisition, retention, and retrieval? Based on a method of assessment used by Berg (1957), it was decided to have subjects rate learnable items—potential cognitive contents—for likability along a 4-point scale: *like much, like slightly, dislike slightly,* and *dislike much.* This measure was originally called *reinforcement value* because of my belief that we should always have a methodological term to parallel our theoretical term, thereby keeping the realm of method conceptually distinct from the realm of theory (see Rychlak, 1988, chap. 9). The interpretation given to *reinforcement* in LLT was different from traditional usages of this term, however, and considerable confusion resulted.

In LLT terms, a *reinforcement* is said to occur when understanding- or action-intentionality flows from a premise that successfully (effectively, helpfully) conceptualizes a circumstance for the individual employing it. The meaning-extension has constructive relevance; it works by endowing life with "true" meaning (even though this meaning may be objectively false). It is this precedent meaning that is reinforced or not. Positive reinforcements extend meanings that are affirmed in positive predications, and negative reinforcements extend negative meaning affirmations. Given the inevitable confusion resulting from this usage, it was decided to drop reinforcement value as a methodological term altogether. Hence, LLT now employs affective assessment or affection as a theoretical construct and operationalizes this concept methodologically by ratings of likability.

Note that the likability scale has no midpoint. This followed Berg's strategy and was quite suitable to the LLT position on oppositionality. In effect, we force our subjects to rate in one or the other of opposite directions. No fence-sitting on a midpoint is permitted. Over the years, my students, collegues, and I have used this 4-step scale of likability in many studies, having subjects rate dozens of learnable items or tasks such as words, consonant-vowel-consonant (CVC) trigrams, paralogs, names, sentences, designs, paintings, pictures of faces, IQ subtests, personality scales, modeled actions, toys, family members, acquaintances, and so forth (ibid.).

To see the evaluative nature of this procedure, consider some studies that required subjects to affectively assess a series of CVC trigrams (e.g., ZIB, HIL, CAS; Archer, 1960) or words. Extensive preliminary study of such ratings demonstrated that about a third of them would flip-flop on the 4-point scale, moving from the liked to the disliked side or vice versa. Hence, the practice was adopted of always readministering the items to subjects after a delay (usually of several hours or a day, but occasionally just one hour) and then employing only the reliably rated items—preferably, those falling at the two extremes—in the experimental tasks. Thus, after selecting a number of reliably rated liked and disliked trigrams or words, we could ask subjects to learn them in either a serial or paired-associates format, using the number of trials it took to memorize the list as our dependent variable. Note that the entire approach here is idiographic. We rely as much as possible on the subject's personal assessments. After the subject has practiced the lists over several trials, we can test the relative performance of learning across liked or disliked materials.

When we do a study of this sort on a random group of people, we find that they perform better on their liked material than on their disliked material (Rychlak, 1966). This finding has a long history dating back at least to Tait (1913), who drew on Wundtian theory to prove that pleasant words are more readily recalled than unpleasant words. Actually, this does not always hold (as I will discuss later in this chapter), but even when it does, how are we to explain the superiority of the liked or pleasant over the disliked or unpleasant? Traditional learning theory would suggest that liked items are sought out and hence encountered more often; therefore, it is the frequency of such past contact (contiguity) that accounts for the finding. Alternatively, it may be suggested that the learner expends more energy memorizing a positive item than a negative item, resulting in a stronger associative bonding and hence better memory for the former than for the latter. We see the frequency-contiguity thesis and the drive (energic) conception rearing their heads in such explanations.

Great care was taken to frame experiments proving that affective assessments of learnable materials could be demonstrated when frequency-contiguity considerations were held constant in the experimental task. Several studies had subjects rate learnable items such as CVC trigrams, paralogs, and real words for both affective preference and for assorted frequency instructions such as whether the items were wordlike, familiar, usable in a sentence, easy or hard to learn, pronounceable, and so forth (Rychlak & Nguyen, 1979; Tenbrunsel, Nishball, & Rychlak, 1968). In study after study it was made ever clearer that an affective assessment is not identical to a judgment of the strength of association of learnable items. Indeed, in cross-validating factor analyses, judgments of word associative strength or familiarity were essentially orthogonal to judgments of affective preference (Rychlak, Flynn, & Burger, 1979).

Another way of proving that association value (i.e., frequency measures like word similarity or word familiarity) and affective assessment are independent dimensions of meaningfulness is to have subjects learn lists of verbal materials that have been equated on both dimensions and then to examine the respective roles of these dimensions in a subsequent learning task. In a typical study using CVC trigrams, a subject would be asked, "Does ZOS look like a word or sound like a word, or can you use it in a sentence?" (adapted from Archer, 1960). If the subject answered yes to this question on two separate occasions, a "presence" scoring for association value was assigned. If the subject answered no on two occasions, an "absence" scoring for association value was recorded. The same CVC trigram (ZOS) would then be rated for affective assessment on two occasions with the same reliability considerations given to the resultant like/dislike scorings that were given to the association-value judgments. After several trigrams had been idiographically rated in this fashion, a list comprising trigrams with different combinations of association value and affection were submitted to subjects for memorization to see whether an independent role for each of these factors could be demonstrated. As predicted by LLT, an independence of this nature was found on several occasions (Abramson, Tasto, & Rychlak, 1969; Rychlak, 1975b; Rychlak, Hewitt, & Hewitt, 1973). Sometimes the two dimensions did not even combine into an interaction on memory tasks. Given this early work, there is no doubt that affective differences in learning cannot be accounted for, reduced to, or explained away by differences in the association value of liked versus disliked learnable items.

Affective Assessment in Motivation

From the LLT point of view, *motivation* is an evaluation of the relative advantage that an affirmed premise—one encompassing a predicated target—makes possible in the telosponder's life. This advantage can be leveled by the telosponding individual or by an observer who presumes to know what the intentions being enacted comprise and what they will therefore result in relative to the telosponder's total situation. A crucial consideration in estimating any such advantage is the affective assessment of the target(s) under predication during ongoing telosponsivity. The man affirming "If I work on the job for one week, I'll have a paycheck to take home" is seen trudging off to work with the expected advantage of having some money in a few days. Hunger may be "driving" him to work, but not necessarily. He may have been receiving financial assistance from the government, food supplies from relatives, and so forth. He may even be independently wealthy but is seeking a sense of achievement by earning his money for a change. This "achievement motive" reflects a positive affective assessment for the targeted goal. The only way we can know what the motivation is in any instance is to grasp the meanings under (introspective) affirmation by the person involved, including their affective quality.

Affection therefore plays an important role in motivation, because when people deal in advantages, they are dealing in what they perceive is good for themselves (hence liked). The other side of the coin is that they are sensitive to occasions when they lose out on a potential advantage (a disliked event). Gain necessarily involves loss. Sometimes people even expect the worst for themselves and get it, just as the self-fulfilling prophecy predicts. There are three points to be made concerning affective assessment as a motivational concept.

1. Affection occurs according to the same predicational process that all telosponsivity relies on, except that its content is self-reflexive. The target of such affective predication is the meaning under affirmation in cognition (i.e., the specific contents of ongoing telosponses). For example, the infant learns the word *mama* in relating to his or her mother and concurrently assesses mama as positive or negative. In doing so, the infant is organizing his or her initial cognitions. A generic oppositionality is basic to this process, as it is in all telosponsivity, but because affection is always concerned with the specific contents of this process, it necessarily involves delimiting oppositionality. We might say that, generically, liking delimits disliking; additionally, however, each cognitive content is itself delimited by these contrasting values. Through such delimiting oppositionality, the person can affectively assess

sheer differences (e.g., brown versus blue colors) brought about by generic oppositionality. Affection is surely one of the first, if not the first, cognitive organizers in the human experience of reality (see Experiment 10). Furthermore, it plays a significant role in directing thought because it always implies that a quality or level of value different from what is under consideration can be carried out.

2. At certain conflicting points in life, affection orients the person to the future through choice. Cognition is valuational at its core. To speak of *choice* is a nontechnical way of referring to the affirmation or targeting of one of two equally desirable (or undesirable) alternatives. According to LLT, another way of speaking about meaning is to talk of selecting or choosing from among many patterned congeries of oppositionally framed possibilities, signifiers, implications, and so forth. The person continually makes such selections, and it is only when the affirmation is difficult (i.e., affectively ambivalent and hence conflict-laden) that a decision or choice is cognized. We usually do not think of getting up in the morning as making a choice, even though it would always be possible to remain in bed. However, when we have to affirm only one of two or more possibilities bearing similar affective qualities, we sense that a choice is underway: Should I major in medicine or law? Do I order apple pie or chocolate cake for dessert? Which of these two treatments for my heart condition should I accept?

As I noted previously, reinforcement occurs when understanding-intentionality or action-intentionality flows from a premise that successfully conceptualizes a circumstance for the individual employing it. The meaning-extension works, in the sense of what James (1907/1943) called the pragmatic cash-value (p. 46) of ideas. But ideas always have an affective cash value as well. A positive or negative reinforcement is not a reinforcement until the individual makes it so based on precedent affective assessments (Muller & Rychlak, 1979). Sometimes yesterday's positive reinforcement can be today's aversive stimulation because of the person's changing affective assessments (Buchwald, 1960). Also, many reinforcements are based on long-term affective projections into the future that are not influenced by short-term deficiencies in reward (Baum, 1973).

Therefore, according to LLT, it is not drive reduction that shapes a behavioral pattern but rather the sense of affective satisfaction of the person who finds her or his precedent assumptions paying off with the successful attainment of expected or predicted outcomes (positive and negative reinforcers). White's (1959) construct of *competence* makes this same point. He believed that, rather than there being many different drives, there is one overriding motive in human behavior: to attain competence in all of life's challenges. Some psychologists still give this a drive interpretation, but LLT says that competence rests on the capacity to know beforehand whether what follows in behavior logically supports what is expected to follow.

In contrast, although it has similar overtones, Bandura's (1986) *perceived self-efficacy* concept does not capture this sense of competence, for it is said to involve "people's judgments of their capabilities to organize and execute courses of action required to attain designated types of performances" (p. 391). The focus here is more on outcome, on the success estimations of already completed performances rather than on the evaluative predications that motivated such past efforts and made satisfactions possible in the first place. I find that theorists are relying increasingly on the definition of *attitude* as "a symbolic representation of one's *evaluation* of an attitude object" (Tesser & Shaffer, 1990, p. 497; emphasis in original). This could easily serve as a variant definition of affective assessment.

3. Affection facilitates moving from an understanding- to an action-intention, because it is when a certain pattern falls into place, assessed as "good" (liked) or "bad" (disliked), that some kind of action is likely to be called for. Critics often charge that teleologies fail to explain just how a freely made intention is arrived at and how it translates into action. When they level this criticism, they usually want the teleologist to resort to underlying material and efficient causal description to say how a decision is triggered. But the LLT advocate is committed to explanations in the *Logos* realm alone and is not about to permit reductionism to seep into the account. What triggers action is the recognition and affective assessment of a certain pattern in relation to a certain target (end). Sometimes this is clearly understood by the person, as with the chess player who analyzes the board and sees that the pieces are organized perfectly, so that a specific move simply "must" be made.

At other times, however, the person may not actually grasp a well-organized pattern of meaning, but the affective assessment alone insinuates a mood, hunch, or impulse to carry out a certain action. People have such intuitions; they are caught up in patterns that they do not really see but nevertheless sense (I employ these terms in a logical and not a biological manner). We touch here on the unconscious aspects of motivation and cognition. Rather than positing a blind mechanism initiating behavior, LLT has affirmation and affection initiating it, selecting it, and intending that it go the way it is being meaningfully understood or affectively intuited. Often, this latter form of action is termed a feeling. The person says, "I don't know why I did that, except that it felt like the right thing to do." This confounds the motivational picture because it appears that a biological feeling made the choice, which suggests to many that an emotion is involved. Emotions are readily conceived as driving forces, and hence we are right back into the drive-reduction kettle of fish.

Emotion versus Affection

No concept in psychology is more challenging and controversial than emotion. Psychologists have been disputing the nature of emotion since the James-Lange theory gave it prominence in the literature; this theory attempted to unite *Bios* and *Logos* assumptions into one account. James believed that every object in experience that excites an instinct also excites an emotion (James, 1890/1952, p. 738). James believed not that cognitions known as emotions bring about bodily expressions like fear, love, and anger but rather that the perception of instinctively stimulated bodily changes result in emotion (ibid., p. 743). Thus, if we see a bear while strolling through the woods, we are instinctively moved to flee, and our perception of our bodily changes such as heavy breathing, palpitation, and rapidly pumping legs is the emotion of fear. Fear is thus the perception of a pattern of instinctive responses. Cannon (1927) subsequently attacked Jamesian emotion theory using several arguments, such as the fact that the very same pattern of visceral reactions occurs in more than one emotion and sometimes when no emotion is felt at all. Although James had argued that one must consider the entire context of any emotional reaction—including the predicating meanings being framed by the emoting individual—Cannon's criticism seriously damaged the James-Lange theory.

From the LLT perspective, the confusion regarding emotion stems from the fact that theorists in this area are trying to solve the long-standing problem of how to unite body and mind. Has this problem been solved? Surely the answer is no. Lacking such a solution, it is better to keep the *Logos* and *Bios* realms separate and distinct (Rychlak, 1993). It is for this reason that LLT distinguishes *affection*, which is a transcending telosponse, from an *emotional feeling*, which is not a telosponse but rather a content targeted for predication by a cognitive representation (the type of emotion experienced) and an affective assessment (whether it is positive or negative). We all know what it feels like to be depressed, angry, elated, thankful—the list of descriptors for the emotions is endless—but does the emotion per se explain anything, except that a human being has lent order to a series of physical feelings in a given context of life? Thus, as follows from Cannon's criticism, a macho hunter who finds himself running from the third bear in his hunting experience may be feeling shame rather than fear. To explain the emotion, we must always look for the meaning framed by the telosponding organism involved in the emotional incident.

In an early paper, we find James (1884) discussing emotion in a way that LLT considers to be affection. Thus, he speaks of the "intellectual feeling" (ibid., p. 201) that occurs as we are thrilled at the justice of some act or the perfection of a musical form, in which case "our mental condition is more allied to a judgment of *right* than to anything else. And such a judgment is rather to be classed among awarenesses of truth: it is a *cognitive* act" (ibid., pp. 201–202; emphasis in the original). Although he goes on to stress that this feeling of rightness (*Logos*) "hardly ever does exist" (p. 202) independent of bodily feelings (*Bios*), it would not be a great stretch to say that he has recognized something like affection in this characterization. We do use the word *feeling* in the intuitive sense of "it felt like the right thing to do," or "I was feeling my way through the problem on hunches, but they proved correct." Logical learning theory holds that this kind of feeling is an effort to describe the direction being taken in ongoing telosponsivity by using a metaphorical allusion to bodily feelings when in fact it is affection that is involved. This kind of feeling is like feeling one's way along a darkened hallway in the conviction that it is the way out. Affection's role as a form of intuition is central in these cases.

It was inevitable that emotions would be wedded to drive theory, since it is immediately apparent that our emotions do convey a mood in relation to whatever we do. Do we strive for success driven by the emotional need to feel happy, or is happiness a feeling that follows from that sense of competence we experience when we meet our intentions? Recall my discussion of competence in the previous section. Some people are sorry to reach their goal, to experience the happiness of success, because they found their greatest satisfaction in the struggle to attain their end. They want to do it over again. The theorist relying on emotional motivation might well say that we have misunderstood this person's goal, which was not to complete the effort but to carry on the effort. Arnold (1970) referred to emotions as "physiological appraisals" (p. 174) of the circumstances of life. Logical learning theory would say that any such appraisal occurs as a transcending telosponse, in affective assessment, and that emotions per se do not generate meaning.

Here, then, is the LLT definition of emotion:

> *Emotion* refers to the pattern of physiological feelings in a certain situation, the sum of which is targeted and thereby organized into meaning by the predications of the person experiencing these feelings and living through the situation. Emotions are not telosponses, but they are affectively assessed via such transcending telosponses. Emotions are not arbitrarily generated by oppositionality but occur in unidirectional fashion, as do all biological and physical circumstances in experience. Emotional feelings can be stimulated by certain drugs or by having the person recall (relive) an emotion-provoking circumstance.

This definition is framed so as to apply no matter how emotions are said to function, as the result of precedent cognitive appraisals or as cognitive efforts to categorize a pattern of already occurring bodily reactions. Thus, having a positive outlook might well engender positive moods, for this is how predications extend into lived experience. There is no guarantee, however, and one cannot pretend that something is liked when it is not; at least, one cannot pretend it is liked and make it so. Nor can one manufacture a genuine emotion through an intention to have it. To capture an emotional mood we must place ourselves back into a situation that we have already experienced in which the emotion came on us. Just as inanimate physical events intrude on our behavior—as when we are suddenly caught in a cold downpour of rain—so too do biological intrusions occur, as when a person is swamped by a strange sensation.

Some theorists would consider such emotional intrusions to be communications to the person experiencing the emotion, as well as to others who observe this display (e.g., see Buck, 1991; Oatley & Johnson-Laird, 1987). According to LLT, however, any message being communicated would have to be framed by the person caught up in the emotional feelings. The person who is affected by an emotion must make sense of the total context, which is identical to the task of endowing targets with meaning through predicational organization. Logical learning theory has been helped by the fact that modern theories of learning tend to stress the evaluative and preparatory functions of emotions, which are obviously consistent with a teleological image of human behavior (see Frijda, 1986; Oatley & Jenkins, 1992).

Research and theory on emotion have frequently been controversial. In a classic study, Marañon (1924) injected subjects with adrenaline and found that most experienced this as a negative state in which they should have been experiencing an emotion but were not clear about what it was supposed to be. When they did feel a clear emotion, such as sadness, it was tied to their recollection of a specific incident, such as the death of a loved one. Marañon concluded that emotions consist of both a bodily and a psychological or subjective component. Schachter and Singer (1962) adapted Marañon's design in their classic investigation, adding proper controls and the ingenious strategy of having subjects who were injected with either epinephrine or a saline (control) solution placed in a social situation that was either positive or negative in mood. This atmosphere was created by having confederates either act in a clownish manner or complain bitterly for having to answer personally insulting questionnaires. Experimental subjects given epinephrine who associated with the clownish confederate experienced mirth or euphoria, and those who associated with the bitter confederate experienced anger. The control subjects reflected a similar disparity; that is, they were influenced by the confederate's mood to have a comparable emotion even though they had been administered a placebo.

Schachter (1964) theorized that to have the subjective experience of an emotion, the individual must both perceive a physiological arousal and label this arousal in accordance with cognized situational factors. Without this broader situational context, the person is unable to pinpoint the meaning of the feelings underway even when noticeable biological changes are occurring. The cognized social context predicates what the physiological pattern will be called, whether anger, joy, fear, and so on. For example, residual sexual arousal has been shown to be misjudged as anger in the presence of anger-provoking cues (Tannenbaum & Zillmann, 1975; Zillmann, 1978).

Evidence has continually accrued supporting the view that although people may feel many different emotions, these feeling states are all associated with similar patterns of visceral arousal and hormonal secretions (Duffy, 1962; Frankenhaeuser, 1975; Levi, 1972; Patkai, 1971). Occasionally, slight differences in blood pressure or heart rate for different emotions are found (e.g., Schwartz, Weinberger, & Singer, 1981), but the more common finding is that something in addition to physical responsivity defines the emotional state. Schachter therefore goes beyond a narrow definition of the Jamesian theory to suggest that it is not the apperception of bodily changes that constitutes the emotion but the total (predicating) context that does so. All this is highly consistent with LLT.

A spirited exchange occurred in the literature when Zajonc (1980) proposed the existence of stimulus features he called *preferenda;* these features, he said, combine with emotions (affects) and allow people to make evaluations of the sort known as attraction, repulsion, pleasure, and so forth, in 800 milliseconds or less (see also Wells, 1925). This reactive evaluation has nothing to do with cognitive inference, discrimination, categorization, or recognition (Zajonc, 1980, p. 159). In effect, Zajonc locates what LLT calls affective assessment in the determining stimulus, making all such judgments mechanical (efficient-cause) responses rather than telic (final-cause) predications. Zajonc first had subjects rate items (e.g., polygon designs) for likability and then arranged a task in which they had to identify polygons that they either had seen before (old) or were seeing for the first time (new). He found that they could make the latter judgment only when dealing with their liked polygons (p. 163). Although Zajonc does not consider this an act of categorization, since he has the external stimulus triggering judgments like attraction or repulsion, LLT would easily account for the empirical findings in terms of an affective assessment that lent an initially meaningful organization to what was then more readily recalled.

Zajonc was answered by Lazarus (1982), who contended that cognition is central to emotion. Lazarus noted that Zajonc's view of emotion, which relied ultimately on a computer analogue, does not give sufficient credence to the role of meaning in emotions (p. 1020). Lazarus defines an emotion as a *cognitive appraisal*, which involves interpreting one's circumstances in terms of thoughts, action impulses, and often somatic disturbances (p. 1019). People define both their own and others' emotions in terms of such appraisals (see Weiner, Russell, & Lerman, 1978). Lazarus (1982) minces no words when he states that "cognitive appraisal is *always* involved in emotion" (p. 1023; emphasis in the original). Zajonc (1984) retorted with a series of arguments based on empirical findings such as the fact that appraisal and affect are often uncorrelated and disjointed (Garcia & Rusniak, 1980), that separate neuro-anatomical structures can be identified for emotion and cognition, that new affective reactions can be established without any apparent participation of appraisal (Kunst-Wilson & Zajonc, 1980), and that affective reactions like emotional facial gestures show phylogenetic primacies and similarities across cultures (see, e.g., Ekman, 1992; Ekman, Friesen, & Ellsworth, 1972).

Lazarus (1984) responded with more on the role of meaning in emotion, including the observation that an emotion arises out of a sensory state when the organism perceives that this sensation signifies a favorable or a damaging outcome to its well-being (p. 126). Additionally, the remarkable self-control that can be achieved over activities of the visceral organs through biofeedback was brought in to support the influence that cognition has over emotion (Anchor, Beck, Sieveking, & Adkins, 1982). In a subsequent paper Lazarus (1991b) went on to refine his concept of cognitive appraisal to include both primary and secondary varieties (p. 827). He also reaffirmed the importance of the molar person-environment relationship in framing emotions and suggested that certain states like being startled or feeling pain or pleasure are best thought of as innate reflexes rather than emotions (p. 820). Logical learning theory is in broad agreement with Lazarus's treatment (see also Lazarus, 1991a) because he places emphasis on both meaning and an evaluating intelligence rather than on the mechanistic models of stimulus propulsion or cybernetic mediation.

The theory of emotion advanced by Bower (1981) is a prime example of the latter, mechanistic form of theorizing. Bower relies on associative network theory to account for human memory, including the role that mood or emotion plays in it. The basic unit of thought is said to be a proposition, which in turn is said to be *activated*, on the analogy of "an electrical network in which terminals correspond to concepts or event nodes (units), connecting wires correspond to associative relations with more or less resistance, and electrical energy corresponds to activation that is injected into one or more nodes (units) in the network" (p. 134). Emotion is a node on this model. Thus, in a diagram, Bower has a connecting link extending to a node labeled "joy," which has been activated in the processing of a proposition transmitting "Mary kissed me" (see ibid., p. 135, Fig. 5). Bower notes that the "semantic-network approach supposes that each distinct emotion such as joy, depression, or fear has a specific node or unit in memory that collects together many other aspects of the emotion that are connected to it by associative pointers" (p. 135).

Bower has done considerable research on mood-induced learning, and I will be taking up many such findings in the next section of this chapter. Bower found that a subject who has been hypnotized and placed in a certain mood before learning a task will recall this task more readily if placed in the same mood at recall than if placed in a different mood. This finding is consistent with Tulving and Thomson's (1973) encoding specificity hypothesis, which LLT subsumes as an instance of predication. Bower (1981), however, gives his emotion node a kind of drive status, as follows: "Activation of an emotion node . . . spreads activation throughout the memory structures to which it is connected, creating subthreshold excitation at those event nodes" (p. 135). Thus, a weak cue may combine with the activation of an emotion node to "raise the total activation of a relevant memory above a threshold of consciousness" (ibid.), bringing an emotionally toned memory to awareness that would not have made it otherwise.

Bower's style of explanation is, of course, not compatible with LLT. It seems to be an attempt to unite traditional drive theory with computer terminology, as when Bower notes that "when activated above a threshold, the emotion unit transmits excitation to those nodes that produce the pattern of autonomic arousal and expressive behavior commonly assigned to that emotion" (ibid., p. 135). This effort to combine *Physikos* and *Bios* concepts into an explanation of what are essentially *Logos* considerations strikes the LLT advocate as misguided.

Experimental Findings on Affection: Background Considerations

As I noted previously, the findings on affection trail back at least to Tait (1913), who drew on Wundt's theory that emotions were either pleasant or unpleasant to explain the positive influence of affection on learning. Shortly thereafter, Tolman (1917) found that retroactive inhibition was facilitated when the material to be learned had a positive meaning. Occasionally, words with unpleasant meanings were learned more readily than words that subjects judged as indifferent. This was unfortunate, because the practice then arose of lumping pleasant and unpleasant words into a single category of "emotional" and comparing the learning rate on these words with the words judged as being indifferent (Bunch & Wientge, 1933; Jones, 1929; Lynch, 1932; Smith, 1921).

In the 1930s several studies were published in which subjects were asked to learn a list of words that had been prerated by others (i.e., nomothetically) as to pleasantness (Carter, 1935, 1937; Carter & Jones, 1937; White, 1936; White & Powell, 1936; White & Ratliff, 1934) or that the subject had rated for him- or herself (i.e., idiographically) (Silverman & Cason, 1934; Stagner, 1933; Thomson, 1930). The finding of a learning superiority of pleasant over unpleasant and indifferent words continued to show through these collective results, particularly when the prejudgments were handled idiographically.

The general topic of affective influence on learning then fell from view for over a decade, until the "perceptual defense" studies rekindled interest in the 1950s. Much of the work done at this point centered on the relative contribution of association value to this influence—the sort of issue that I discussed earlier in this chapter (Cromwell, 1956; Johnson, Frincke, & Martin, 1961; Koen, 1962; Sarbin & Quenk, 1964; Staats, 1959). The drift of these findings suggested that an affective dimension is at work in verbal meaning, often correlated with but still independent from sheer frequency measures of association value. A major boost to the study of affection was Zajonc's (1968) research on the so-called *enhancement effect*, which claimed that sheer frequency of a subject's exposure to materials (e.g., Chinese figures) increases the likelihood that these materials will be considered positive. This finding seemed to reduce affection to frequency of exposure. In time, however, Brickman, Redfield, Harrison, and Crandall (1972) demonstrated that positive enhancement occurs only when the material exposed to subjects is initially neutral or positive; that is, negative (disliked) materials fail to be enhanced or made more positive through frequent exposure. I later cross-validated these findings (Rychlak & Nguyen, 1979).

Another boost to the study of affection was the vast effort that Osgood (1952) and his associates devoted to the measurement of meaning. Osgood's evaluation rating of good/bad was found to load on the like/dislike rating of affective assessment (Rychlak, Flynn, & Burger, 1979; Rychlak, Tasto, Andrews, & Ellis, 1973). There are continuing reflections of affective assessment in studies issuing from all corners of the psychological literature. I will now present under four subheadings research evidence that is consistent with and enlarges on empirical findings that LLT advocates have been placing into the literature for some time.

Positive Affection in Behavior

As I previously noted, from my very first studies on affective assessment I found that college students learned their liked cvc trigrams more readily than their disliked ones (Rychlak, 1966). It was then necessary to prove that this measure of likability was not simply a variant measure of association value. As I detailed earlier in this chapter, I think we proved that it is indeed a unique dimension of meaningfulness. My students and colleagues then went on to demonstrate the applicability of affection to all manner of material in human learning. Subjects were shown to recognize or recall paintings, abstract designs, faces, and names that they liked more readily than those that they disliked (Rychlak, 1975a; Rychlak, Galster, & McFarland, 1972; Rychlak & Saluri, 1973). Masculine or feminine subjects were found to learn masculine and feminine word meanings according to their personality tendencies. That is, masculine subjects reflected the "liked over disliked" learning rate only when they were learning masculine words and vice versa for feminine subjects (Rychlak, Tasto, Andrews, & Ellis, 1973). Subjects who prerated their study topics in an introductory psychology course at the outset of the semester were subsequently found to obtain better grades in study areas that they liked than in those that they disliked (Slife & Rychlak, 1981).

Matlin and Stang (1979) named this pervasive influence of positive over negative meaningfulness the *Pollyanna principle;* they explained it based on an information-processing theoretical rationale in which the processor considers material of a negative quality as "discarded" (p. 3) information (note the hard disjunction here). Matlin and Stang contacted me for reprints of my work when they were writing their book, and I pointed out to them that there is both a positive and a negative side to affective learning (see the next section), but my warning fell on deaf ears. Delimiting oppositionality was completely overlooked, so the pessimistic side to human nature was left out of their theoretical account.

When we survey the literature in many areas, we find obvious manifestations of the role of positive affection in human behavior of all types. As we saw in chapter 6 regarding the work of Hyde and Jenkins (1969), who used "pleasant-unpleasant" as a cognitive organizer, the role of affection sometimes goes unnoticed in an experiment (see also Einstein & Hunt, 1980; Hummert, Crockett, & Kemper, 1990). Subjects have been found to identify "good" (liked) words correctly at a faster tachistoscopic exposure rate than "bad" (disliked) words (Johnson, Thomson, & Frincke, 1960). It is reasonable to suggest that the "feeling-of-knowing" or "tip-of-the-tongue" phenomenon stems from an affective assessment (Brown & McNeill, 1966; Hart, 1965). These self-monitoring hunches are reflective of that feeling one's way along the right track that I took up earlier in this chapter.

Subjects will place photographs of liked persons closer to their own photograph than they will photographs of disliked persons (Kleck, 1967). Children who draw a picture of a liked peer give it more detail than a drawing of a disliked peer (Lott & Lott, 1970). Children with a positive affective

outlook extend help to others to a greater extent than children with a negative affective outlook do (Strayer, 1980). Adults tend to see themselves as
causes of positive outcomes more than they perceive themselves as causes of
negative outcomes (Mirels, 1980; Sherman, 1980). They also overestimate the
likelihood of personally experiencing positive outcomes in life and underestimate the likelihood of experiencing negative events (Weinstein, 1980;
Weinstein & Lachendro, 1982). Preteenage females with a positive self-image
were less likely than females with negative self-images to become ill when
challenged by something positive in their lives (Brown & McGill, 1989).

Negative Affection in Behavior

As LLT was fleshed out, it became apparent that some people might actually be prone to learn more along the negative than the positive. People who
(precedently) predicate themselves (their self-image), the task facing them,
the materials to be learned, and so on, in a negative way should be seen
to (sequaciously) extend this meaning more readily in a negative than in a
positive direction. An LLT view of maladjustment was elaborated in these
precedent-sequacious terms, and a series of experiments was designed to
validate it.

In time, we proved that adult patients carrying diagnoses such as schizo-
phrenia, depression, and alcoholism (Mosbacher, 1984; Rychlak, McKee,
Schneider, & Abramson, 1971; Slife, et al., 1984); elementary, high school,
and college students with negative self-images (August & Rychlak, 1978;
August, Rychlak, & Felker, 1975; Rychlak, Carlsen, & Dunning, 1974); and
high school students who were forced to perform a learning task that they
disliked (Rychlak & Marceil, 1986, 1992) collapsed the learning superiority
for positively assessed items or reversed it in the direction of favoring negative items. In fact, we demonstrated that a person could learn along a positive
affective line when learning words drawn from an area of confidence and reverse this by learning along a negative affective line when the targeted words
were taken from a conflict area of life.

Not all these subjects had significantly better performances for their disliked than their liked material. Some merely collapsed the difference between
the liked and disliked items, so that there was no longer a significant advantage for liked items; we called this a *diminution* of the customary positive
effect (e.g., Rychlak, Carlsen, & Dunning, 1974). Others achieved what we
called a *reversal*, meaning that they actually learned significantly more disliked than liked items (e.g., August & Rychlak, 1978). Sometimes one sex subgroup of our sample would achieve a reversal, whereas the other would simply
reflect a diminution (August, Rychlak, & Felker, 1975; Rychlak, McKee,

Schneider, & Abramson, 1971). In one study on high school students, we combined the factors of high versus low self-image with liking versus disliking in an enforced paired-associates learning task. We found that although neither of these factors alone achieved a reversal, when subjects were both negative in self-image and forced to take a disliked learning task, they did indeed learn significantly more disliked than liked cvc trigrams (Rychlak & Marceil, 1992). Thus, it appears that a combination of factors enters into precisely how far the advantage swings from positive to negative in affective learning style.

Just as we found many indications of positive affection in the broader research literature, so too are there many examples of the role that negative affection plays in human behavior. People who experience test anxiety are prone to dwell on their deficiencies rather than focus on the task at hand (Wine, 1971). Both children and adults who are negative self-evaluators tend to punish themselves more for failures and give less credit to themselves for successes than positive self-evaluators do (Reschly & Mittman, 1973). Novices who predicate computers negatively learn editing tasks more slowly and make more errors than novices who predicate computers positively (Walther & O'Neill, 1974). Negative information may have a stronger influence on impression formation than positive information; for example, character weaknesses can outweigh achievements in forming impressions of a political candidate (Klein, 1991). According to llt, many errors are extended sequaciously from predicated meanings that intentionally distort what is under study. The Jamesian cash value here is being paid off in negative coin.

Depressed people, who are by definition negative self-evaluators, are sometimes said to be wise in a way that the nondepressed fail to be. This claim is made because depressed people are supposedly more realistic in assessing their performance, chances of attaining some goal, or controlling events (Alloy & Abramson, 1979; Alloy, Abramson, & Viscusi, 1981; Lewinsohn, Mischel, Chaplin, & Barton, 1980). This realism, however, is surely rooted in diminutions or outright reversals of the typically optimistic, positive affective assessments that people make in their lives. After all, if the nondepressed person were pessimistic, little would be attempted and few chances would be taken. "Aim high so that you achieve something even when you fail" is a common strategy among nondepressed people. Depressed people underestimate how well they have performed in a task (Buchwald, 1977) and believe that they have minimal capacities to meet life's demands (Kanfer & Zeiss, 1983). Apparently, this negative outlook adversely affects the depressed person's interpersonal relations as well. That is, associates of victimized people are likely to avoid them because of the victim's depression, which is predicated negatively by the nondepressed (Coates, Wortman, & Abbey, 1979). Severely depressed individuals have been found to engender rejection by others (Coyne, 1976). Following a successful psychotherapy series, the depressed person's bias for the negative gives way to a more normal affective pattern of cognition (Slife, et al, 1984).

Mood Induction Research

Mood induction is a vast area of research having relevance for affective predication in learning, memory, and behavior. The lingering influence of drive theory is to be seen in the fact that some studies in this area are said to reflect "state-dependent" memory, as if an emotional state had been activated to propel the behaviors observed (Blaney, 1986). There are two general strategies employed in mood induction research: (1) Studies using a *mood-congruence design* manipulate a subject's mood either positively or negatively and then show the effect on the rate of learning either positive or negative materials; (2) studies using a *mood-state-dependent design* match the initial mood with a later mood (e.g., positive with positive) to see how this influences memory for initial learning at recall. Moods can be induced by having subjects read a series of statements like "I feel happy" (positive) or "I feel sad and blue" (negative) (Teasdale & Russell, 1983; Velten, 1968); recall happy or sad incidents from their past or simply imagine comparable incidents (Nasby & Yando, 1982; Salovey & Birnbaum, 1989); receive rewards such as gifts, money, or good reports on a test that they have taken (Forgas & Bower, 1987; Isen, Shalker, Clark, & Karp, 1978; Isen & Simonds, 1978); smell pleasant or unpleasant odors (Ehrlichman & Halpern, 1988); listen to sad/happy music (Parrott & Sabini, 1990), or answer questions on rainy or sunny days (Schwarz & Clore, 1983).

With only a few exceptions, such research has uniformly found that the mood created influenced what was learned initially, recalled later, or proffered as an evaluation in subsequent events. Pleasant moods facilitate initial learning of positive items, and a matched pleasant mood later facilitates recall of positive items; negative moods matched with earlier negative moods facilitate recall of negative items; happy subjects form more positive impressions of others than sad subjects; getting a gift raises the positive evaluation of services to follow in a shopping mall, and so on. All such findings are consistent with the precedent-sequacious style of explanation that LLT advocates. A mood is clearly a context meaning that the person involved predicates, and once affirmed, its meaning extends to what is then under continuing cognitive formulation ("processing").

The question regarding the role of induced activation (as a quasi drive) versus an affirmed predication can be addressed by comparing the work of Bower (1981, 1983) with that of Lewis and Williams (1989); these studies by

Bower employed hypnotism to induce a pleasant or unpleasant mood in the subject. Bower found that subjects given hypnotically induced happy moods retrieved many more pleasant memories than unpleasant memories, they remembered more words having the same positive mood connotation as the moods they learned them in, and so forth. The reverse is true for sad subjects. His theoretical explanation of such findings is that since emotions are nodal units within the cognitive network, if the person's emotion node is activated via the experimental instructions, then it will link with the items being encoded at the time; later, at the point of retrieval, such appropriate activation will facilitate recall.

Working within the framework of LLT, Lewis and Williams (ibid.) had their subjects, while under either a positive or a negative hypnotically induced mood, listen to a list of words controlled for word association, familiarity, and so forth. Previously, half of these words had been reliably rated as positive by each of the subjects and the other half had been rated as negative. After listening to the words, the subjects were asked to recall as many as possible, in any order. During the recall phase of the study, however, mood was varied so that its effect on recall could be tested in the light of the word ratings and not simply in the light of the dictionary definition of what nomothetically constitutes a positive or negative word meaning.

Lewis and Williams found that when the words learned in a positive mood are favored in recall by a positive mood, the facility in recall is due to the words rated idiographically positive by subjects and not just any nomothetically positive words exposed to the subjects initially. Not all subjects rate the same nomothetically positive word meanings positively (e.g., one subject may find *punctual* positive, whereas another finds it slightly negative). Alternatively, when the words learned in a negative mood are favored in recall by a negative mood, the facility in recall is found only with the idiographically negative words and not just any nomothetically defined negative words (e.g., one subject may find *sloppy* quite negative, whereas another finds it moderately positive). Activation per se is surely not driving such selective facilitations in memory. It thus appears that affective predication is playing an unrecognized role in yet another realm of psychological investigation.

More than just memory is affected by a positive mood. Studies have demonstrated that an individual in a positive mood is more likely to be altruistic, helpful, and interested in caring for others (Isen & Levin, 1972; Maccoby & Martin, 1983; Mischel, Ebbesen, & Zeiss, 1973; Rosenhan, Salovey, Karylowski, & Hargis, 1981). Positive mood increases the advocacy level of a persuasive communication (Petty, Schumann, Richman, & Strathman, 1993). All such results are consistent with LLT. Thus, if the person approaches life with many understanding-intentions of a positive affective quality, it is likely that such precedent meanings will be translated into action-intentions in all corners of his or her life. Arguments of this sort demonstrate that personality scaling can be facilitated by taking affection into consideration. Thus, if a well-adjusted subject likes the personality dimension being tapped by a scale, this positive affective predication increases the predictability of the test scoring over what it would be if this dimension is disliked (Gruba-McCallister & Rychlak, 1981). Normals more readily enact the personality styles for which they have a positive affection in precedent-sequacious fashion.

It is quite another thing for abnormals, who proceed on a pervasively negative assumption about themselves and everything else. This tendency to extend life's meaning along the negative on any scale given to them was once called the *complaint factor* in the study of maladjustment and has more recently been referred to as *negative affectivity* (Watson & Clark, 1984). This adverse tendency explains why scales testing abnormality work. Any one of several scales that allow the person to be harshly self-critical (affirm a negative self-predication) will pick up on this tendency—a tendency that also creates the very criterion of maladjustment *in vivo* that the test is supposedly predicting. Once again, the process here involves a precedent-sequacious extension of meaning. Negativity creates negativity as a variation of the self-fulfilling prophecy.

Sundry Findings Relevant to Learning Theories

There have been a number of studies on affection done by LLT advocates having relevance for concepts in traditional theories of learning. Positively assessed words in a list facilitate the primacy effect (i.e., remembering the first few words in a list), whereas negatively assessed words do not (Apao, 1979). Even if we remove trigrams on trials when they are not being recalled and replace them with other trigrams of the same affective quality, the superiority of liked over disliked trigrams persists (David, 1977). This reproduces the same type of finding that Rock (1957) reported in removing words that subjects were not recalling (see chap. 5). It is the organizing heuristic at the outset of learning that ensures solid learning and long-lasting memory, not sheer repetition of such cognitions. Affection is a major cognitive organizer of this nature. Affective clustering has been found, with liked words both clustering together and being recalled sooner than disliked words (Nguyen, 1975). Looking at studies with an attribution format, we found that liked traits were more apt to be clustered in describing others than were disliked traits (Bugaj, 1984).

One of the more interesting findings on affection concerns nonspecific transfer. The task here involves learning two unmixed lists of trigrams or words, either or both of which may be liked or disliked. We found that when subjects move from disliked to liked lists, they reflect a dramatic *positive nonspecific transfer* (i.e., they do much better on the second list even though there are no common linguistic or stimulus qualities between lists). This is not the case when the subjects learn lists in the opposite affective direction. In one study, all 32 subjects moving from a disliked to a liked list of trigrams reflected improvement in performance on the second list, whereas only 13 of the 32 subjects moving from liked to disliked lists reflected this improvement (Rychlak & Tobin, 1971). In a follow-up study we contrasted idiographic judgments of trigram meaningfulness (association value) with affection and showed that moving across lists of varying meaningfulness (low to high, high to low) produced no differences in transfer, whereas moving from disliked to liked lists did indeed produce significantly greater improvement than moving in the opposite affective sequence of liked to disliked lists (Rychlak, Tuan, & Schneider, 1974). I think these findings are relevant to Premack's (1965, 1971) widely discussed studies in which subjects were shown to perform a less preferred activity in order to engage in a more preferred activity. Also, it has been reported that the termination of a stressful event (negative affection) leaves people in better moods (positive affection) than if these events have not occurred (Bolger, DeLongis, Kessler, & Schilling, 1989). This sequence essentially reproduces the disliked-to-liked ordering, since the termination of stress means by definition that things are now more positive.

We conducted an operant conditioning study in which rather than giving just one response in a reinforced condition, subjects were permitted to select one of two responses. Thus, we reinforced either adjectives or nouns by saying "good" when subjects selected them from a card. There were two nouns and two adjectives on this card, however, and the subjects had prerated one of the nouns and one of the adjectives as liked and the other noun and adjective as disliked. As predicted by LLT, even though the subjects were presumably "shaped" by the reinforcer into selecting either nouns or adjectives, they (almost always) selected the word they liked significantly more often than the one they disliked (Campbell, 1983). Given that to be operantly conditioned a subject must know the relationship between the operant response and the contingent reinforcer, and thereby intentionally comply with what is indicated (see chap. 6), we can ask whether findings on operant conditioning reflect an "automatic shaping" or a maneuvering within the constraints of the design to maximize what the subject personally intends to take place. Pursuant to this point, we found in a "sharing" study that children share candy that they do not especially like and keep their strongly preferred candies for themselves (Mosbacher, Gruen, & Rychlak, 1985).

The final area of study in which affection has shown its influence is that of modeling. We followed the Bandura, Ross, and Ross (1963a, 1963b) design in which young children are exposed to filmed models who aggress against an inflated plastic "bobo" doll. The models used various toys (a jumping rope to strangle the doll, a gun to shoot it, etc.). After observing the modeled acts of aggression (I prefer the term *hostility*), the children were left alone to play. Control subjects who had not been subjected to the model's influence also played with the doll. Of course, children under modeling produce behaviors like the model at least twice as often as the controls.

Using first- and second-graders as subjects, we had them rate both the aggressive acts and the toys they were exposed to for affective preference. Control subjects rated only the toys for affective preference. We found that the experimental group of subjects, who had witnessed the modeled aggression on videotape, performed significantly more aggressive acts against the bobo doll than did the control subjects (Slife & Rychlak, 1982). However, the aggressive acts performed by subjects in the experimental group were those that they had rated as liked; also, in performing these aggressive acts, they used only those toys that they had rated as liked. The children in the control condition also played with their liked toys significantly more often than with their disliked toys. The question remains: Are the children's behaviors really being shaped into hostile acts, or are children astute enough to see the demand characteristics of the task and conform to these even as they also involve themselves in their preferred activities and toys? I do not believe this to be a case of mechanical modeling any more than we had mechanical shaping of noun and adjective words in the study discussed in the previous paragraph. At the very least, these results clearly show the precedent-sequacious extension of meaning that we have seen occurring in behavior of many types throughout this chapter.

Demonstration Experiments: Concerning Affective Assessment

Experiment 10: Affection at "Encoding": Knowing the Positive/Negative Quality of a Word Before the Word Is Known

Hypothesis

Subjects who cannot recall a (positive or negative) word that predicates a person's behavior in a (positive or negative) situation will be more likely to recall the correct affective quality of this unrecalled word than an alternative word with a similar meaning.

Rationale

Logical learning theory holds that affection *is* predication rendered by a process that operates from birth. Predication is not learned. Even before the infant learns anything, this native evaluative judgment is available to organize experience along positive or negative lines (via a transcendent delimiting oppositionality). This means that, framed in traditional computer lingo, affection works at the point of encoding. Logical learning theory, however, does not cast this as a question of input, a term that suggests an already organized item being taken in from an unpredicated external source. From the LLT perspective, encoding is active organization, including affective assessments rendered by an evaluating intellect and brought to bear on what can and will be known.

It follows that we should be able to demonstrate that affection is actively underway even before semantic learning takes place—affective knowledge before semantic knowledge, so to speak. This would be the LLT equivalent of Zajonc's (1980) previously mentioned claim that preferences need no inferences. Previous LLT work on affection did not address this question directly but merely assumed that certain subject populations might be found to rely more on affective predication than others do. For example, if we were to consider the association value (AV) of CVC trigrams to be a form of meaningfulness based on linguistic conventions (word fragments, etc.), and the affective assessments of these same trigrams as a natively engendered form of meaningfulness, then relevant experiments might be conducted. I am using "meaningfulness" here as a reflection of cognitive organization—the drawing of either linguistic or affective distinctions in whatever is known.

In a group of people whom we have good reason to believe do not highly identify with the broader cultural (i.e., "middle-class") values, we should find a greater tendency to rely on affection relative to AV in undertaking any learning effort that is typical of such valued cultural standards. Such individuals may be expected to continue organizing their learnings along their native affective propensities rather than along the lines provided by the culture's linguistic distinctions, patterns of expression, and so forth. Following this hypothesis, we indeed found that both African-Americans (O'Leary, 1969; Rychlak, Hewitt, & Hewitt, 1973) and Hispanics (Garza, 1975) organized their learning tasks more along affective preference (like/dislike) than along linguistic distinctions (wordlike/nonwordlike). We argued that this finding was based not on genetic differences but on the contrasting identification of these groups with the values of a culture that stressed achievement in school-like tasks involving memorizing intellectualized discriminants (words, word fragments), time pressures, and so forth. In support of this sociocultural

argument, in one study we found that when African-Americans and Cauca-
sians were grouped within socioeconomic levels, the lower-class subjects as
a group relied significantly more on affection than did the middle-class subjects (Rychlak, 1975b).

Though these findings are suggestive, they are no substitute for a more
direct test of the LLT claim that affective organization accompanies and can
even precede semantic organization in learning. We needed to show that
people who have learned certain words (content) serving as predicate meanings (process) in a sentence will tend to be able to name the affective quality
of these words before they can name the words themselves or words similar in meaning to them. This takes us back to my discussion of how a person
may feel his or her way along a learning path. Much of language no doubt
occurs following the affective assessment of the situation in which a certain
word is to be appropriately employed. As the title of this experiment suggests, the typical information-processing description of what we are now
involved with would be termed "encoding." Experiment 10 predicts that affective assessment is fundamental to so-called encoding, for it will be seen to
influence the input of learnable items before these items have been encoded.

Experimental Sample

Fifty-one undergraduate students (30 females, 21 males) served as subjects for this experiment, receiving course recognition for their participation
(Ulasevich, 1991).

Procedure

A learning task was presented to the subjects as the "Judging John" experiment. The study used a series of 14 descriptive sentences consisting of a
stem and a word completion, as in the following examples:

> When others are rude, John is (impolite, polite).
> When watching a movie, John is (loud, quiet).
> When life gets strained, John is (relaxed, tense).
> When attending a party, John is (timid, outgoing).

Half the stems framed a negative context (rudeness, stress, etc.) and half
framed a positive context (watching movies, attending parties, etc.). This
established a predicating context within which the specific target ("John")
was to be further predicated, thereby completing the sentence. The concluding sentence phrase—"John is _____"—involves predicating John in
terms of some meaning within the context established by the stem. Note
that the words completing the sentences always predicate John and that they
can be either positive (polite, quiet, relaxed, outgoing) or negative (impolite,

loud, tense, timid). These words were selected for affective quality from the Anderson (1968) likableness ratings and equated for familiarity in the standing language structure (Thorndike & Lorge, 1944). In addition, three raters had to agree on the alignment of a positive/negative stem to a positive/negative word predicate before we used this combination as a sentence.

The learning task was administered via an IBM microcomputer, for which a special program was written. Subjects were instructed that they were to learn a list of 14 statements concerning John. A brief practice list was administered. The task involved reading through the list (practice trial) and then immediately taking a recall trial in which the stems were presented on the computer screen and subjects were given time to complete the sentence with the correct (predicating) word. For example, on the practice trial, a subject would see "When others are rude" on the left-hand side of the screen for 2 seconds, and then either "polite" or "impolite" would appear for 2 seconds on the right-hand side of the screen while the stem continued to be presented (i.e., the stem was on screen for 4 seconds, and the full sentence was on for 2 seconds). After a 2-second delay, the next sentence stem would be presented, and so forth, until all 14 sentences had been completed.

On the recall trial, the word stems ("When others are rude, John is") were presented on the screen. A counter also appeared to the right, numbering down from 5 to 0 seconds; the subjects had to begin typing the correct predication ("polite" or "impolite") during this time. There was no penalty for slow typing. When they finished typing the answer, the subjects hit the enter key to continue the list. If at the end of 5 seconds a subject had not begun typing, the computer screen presented one of two (between-groups) instructions: (1) "If the word you cannot think of is Positive or Negative, hit the P or N key," or (2) "Type a similar word to the one you cannot think of."

Subjects were given 10 seconds to hit a P or N key or begin typing at this point; if they did not respond within 10 seconds, the program moved on to the next sentence stem for recall. Misspellings were not penalized, but word substitutions were not allowed. After the recall list had been completed, the subjects were taken back through the 14 sentences once again as another practice trial. Two successive recall trials without error constituted a completed task. As it turned out, the task did not prove very difficult (the range of trials to completion was 2 to 9).

Five raters who were blind to the purpose of this experiment were asked to judge the predicating word completions for affective quality or a meaning similar to the correct predicate. All words were judged for affective quality, even when they were not given credit as being similar to the correct predicate. Four out of the five raters had to agree on the appropriateness of a similarity answer. For example, if the stem "When competing with others, John is" was presented and "passive" was the correct (negative) answer, but the subject had typed "unmotivated," four of the five judges were likely to agree as to the appropriateness. If the subject had answered "slow," however, even though the affective quality was appropriate, it would not be scored as correct.

Since subjects varied in the number of trials it took to reach criterion, a ratio score was employed as the dependent variable. The number of correct responses, or "hits," given by the subject was divided by the number of opportunities she or he had to score such hits in guessing either the affective quality of the unrecalled word or a word with similar meaning. For example, if a subject reached criterion (i.e., learned all 14 sentences twice in a row) in 7 trials, there would have been several unrecalled word completions during the first 5 trials when the subject was learning the sentences. Assume that the subject attempted either to judge the affective quality of the unknown word or to offer a word similar to it 35 times. Assume that on 19 of these occasions the subject was correct. The value of 35 would thus be taken as the denominator of the ratio score, and the number of actual hits (19) would become the numerator. Hence, the score for this subject would be 19/35, or 54 (decimal removed). The score therefore directly reflects the percentage of correct guesses the subject made regarding the affective quality of, or a word similar in meaning to, the unrecalled word.

Results

The ratio scores were submitted to an arcsine transformation to equate for distance between the data points. However, since the subsequent analysis did not affect the findings, the data presented here are the raw ratio scores. The ratio scores were submitted to a 2 (Affection vs. Similar Word) × 2 (Positive vs. Negative Stem) × 2 (Positive vs. Negative Word Predicate) ANOVA. The first variable is between and the latter two are within subjects.

There was one main effect and no interactions. The ratio score for affective assessment was significantly higher ($M = 78.80$, $SD = 31.81$) than the ratio score for similar words ($M = 44.02$, $SD = 44.90$) ($F = 8.87$; $df = 1, 44$; $p < .005$). Since there were no interactions in the analyses, this superiority of affect over similarity did not differ whether the stem or the word predicating John was positive or negative in affective quality.

A critic might suggest that our procedure was seriously biased because subjects could obtain a ratio score of 50 simply by depressing either the positive or the negative key each time they could not recall a word. Actually, the probability for positive and negative answers depended on the pattern of misses for each subject, some of whom did more missing along the negative than the positive, and so on. Correct ratio scores were not therefore based on a clear-cut 50–50 split. However, to test the possible role played by simply responding either positively or negatively on the ratio scores, the sample was arrayed on three separate bases preliminary to two nonparametric analyses.

Subjects were arrayed from high to low on (1) number of times they had depressed the positive key, (2) number of times they had depressed the negative key, and (3) their ratio score. It was then possible to divide the sample at the median of these rank orderings and run two (2 × 2) chi-square tests. If a high ratio score could be obtained by depressing either the positive or negative keys several times, then a significant chi-square could test for this by showing that high ratio scorers were also high positive or negative key depressors. Actually, the chi-square analysis on the positive key depressions failed to reach significance. The analysis for the negative depressions did reach significance (χ^2 = 4.89, df = 1, p < .05). However, the sample array in this case went against the criticism in that those subjects who depressed the negative key *fewer* times (i.e., fell below the median) had the highest ratio scores, and vice versa. Consequently, the findings cannot be an artifact of key depression.

To provide an additional check on the heuristic power of affection, we looked at the errors made by subjects in the similar word condition. For instance, assume that a subject typed *wonderful* to the stem "When solving problems, John is" but that the correct word should have been *fast*. The word *fast* is affectively positive. If four or more judges agreed that the word *wonderful* was positive, then we scored this as an affectively appropriate answer even though it was semantically incorrect. We found that there were significantly more affective matches of this sort than would be expected on a 50–50 chance basis (χ^2 = 21.04; df = 1; p < .01). Hence, even when subjects made incorrect word guesses, the affective tone of these erroneous words was frequently correct.

Conclusion and Discussion

The experimental hypothesis has been supported. Subjects are more likely to grasp the affective quality of a word that they do not yet know than they are to produce a word that has a similar meaning to it. Also, even when subjects produce similar words that are incorrect, these words *are* affectively correct. It seems clear that affection is a significant heuristic at the initial point of meaningful organization—that is, at what has been called in cognitive psychology the point of encoding information. The LLT equivalent here is "affirmation at the protopoint" in the act of predication. As the person grasps the situation that the sentence stem has established in terms of the target, the affective quality of the predicating word meaning is itself targeted within the broader expanse of an affectively positive or negative affirmation. This affirmation aligns the target to the situational circumstances even as—and frequently before—the semantic meaning of the word is grasped. A reasonable suggestion here is that affection plays a role in encoding, a role that is unappreciated and uniformly overlooked in cognitive research and theory. The other side of the coin is whether there are any indications that affection is active in what cognitive psychology has called "retrieval."

Experiment 11: Affection at "Retrieval": Remembering Unrecalled Words by Changing the Positive/Negative Predication That Targets Them

Hypothesis

After having the opportunity to recall as many secondary (adjectival) predicates as possible under the influence of a primary (like/dislike) predication, subjects who are asked to shift this affective predication (from like to dislike or vice versa) will recall secondary predicates that had not been previously recalled bearing the same affective quality as the newly affirmed primary predication.

Rationale

Demonstration Experiments 5 and 6 (see chap. 5) established that the meaning extending from the predicate to a target within the scope of this predicate can act as a cue in the recall of sentences and triplets that have been lost to short-term memory. If a subject cannot recall the sentence "A pan can be used as a drum," cueing the subject with *drum* is more likely to facilitate retrieval of this sentence than cueing with *pan*. If a subject cannot recall the triplet "nose, face, smile," he or she is more likely to retrieve it when cued with *face* than when cued with *nose* or *smile*. In these earlier experiments we were dealing with word meanings as both the broader predicate (largest Euler circle) and the more focused target. However, according to LLT, the same "broader-to-narrower" process occurs when affective assessment serves as the predicate and extends to the target. Indeed, affective assessment is considered the broadest predication open to human experience, since this evaluative frame is extended to literally everything in cognizance. Experiment 10 supports the LLT contention that affective assessment is crucial to the learning of word meanings. Word meanings are assessed affectively by those who use them, and often enough the users can recall this affective predication before they can recall the word they are trying to produce.

Suppose that we were now to ask subjects to think of a person that they like (or dislike). By definition, this means that the subjects would affirm a broad realm of affect (like, dislike) within which they would target the person in question. Next, let us ask these subjects to select from a list of adjectives any that would describe the personality of this target. In effect, we would be asking subjects to select adjectival predicates for the targeted person (e.g.,

"Person X is intelligent, suspicious, quiet, etc."). Let us call the initial affective assessment the "primary" and the adjectival descriptors the "secondary" predications in this task. These secondary predications would also be targets of the primary predication. Recall that according to LLT, any predicate meaning can itself be the target of an even broader or more abstract predication. In terms of our model, the broadest Euler circle would represent "liked people," within which we would find smaller circles labeled by positive adjectives, collectively encircling the smallest circle of all—the targeted person.

In other words, to capture the person selected in terms of the primary predication, the subjects would be expected to select as secondary predicates predominantly those adjectives that would extend the meaning of this broadest realm of all. Liked person targets should be given more liked than disliked secondary predications, and vice versa for disliked person targets. Moreover, in a subsequent free-recall task, we would expect to see that more liked adjectives would be remembered for liked targets, and vice versa for disliked targets (since the quality of the primary predication is what extends through the secondary predications to the person targeted). The research cited earlier in the present chapter makes these predictions a foregone conclusion. We could add nothing to this literature by reporting such findings.

However, assume now that after we give the subjects the opportunity to record in writing all the recalled adjectives serving as secondary predications of the target, *as well as* any other adjectives that they can remember in the task, we then asked our subjects to *reverse* the target of their primary predications. Those subjects who had initially framed a liked target would now think of someone disliked, and vice versa. Once the repredication has been accomplished, we then ask our subjects to reconsider the list of adjectives and to try to recall any adjectives that would suitably apply to the new target. Would they retrieve any previously unrecalled adjectives, and would these newly recalled adjectives be consistent with the affective quality of the new primary predication?

The present experimental hypothesis predicts that subjects would indeed be likely to recall adjectives that they have not recorded in the procedure to this point but that have relevance as secondary predications to the new primary predication. That is, additional framing of a person as disliked and as situated as a target within the scope of a negative predication would help the subject to retrieve previously unrecorded ("new") words from memory of a predominantly negative meaning, and vice versa for additional framing of a person as liked. A finding of this sort *would* add something to the literature, because it demonstrates that affective assessment is involved in memory retrieval.

Experimental Sample

Sixty-four undergraduate students (38 females, 26 males) served as subjects for this experiment and received course recognition for their participation (Hughes, 1993).

Procedure

The experimental task was presented to subjects as the study of personality characteristics of people that we may like or dislike. Each subject received a packet of forms consisting of six sections, a 3-by-5-in. index card, and a pen. Small groups of from three to eight subjects were taken through the six sections of the study together, with the experimenter playing an active role in timing the procedure. Subjects first thought of a person that they either liked or disliked (between-groups condition) and recorded the initials of this person on their form. In the next section of the study, they were given a brief practice list of adjectival descriptors (e.g., efficient, good-tempered, prideful, annoying, etc.), which they were to check if applicable to the person they had selected.

Because pretesting had suggested that some subjects are reluctant to assign many secondary predicates to their targets, the procedure was adopted of having subjects select one or the other of a pair of descriptors. The task thus became to select the adjective from a pair that was "more characteristic" of the target (e.g., optimistic/skillful; lazy/incompetent). Both adjectives of a pair were either positive, negative, or ambivalent in meaningfulness. Thirty such pairs were administered to the subject. The adjectives were taken from the Anderson (1968) norms for personality-trait words and thus could be equated for association value. Of the 60 words used in the 30 pairs, 20 were from the high likability levels of Anderson's norms, 20 were from the low levels, and 20 were from the medium levels. This final pool of items was arrayed after five independent raters had agreed that the adjectives in each of these designations were indeed high, low, and medium (or ambivalent—i.e., neither clearly positive or negative in likability). Thus, the affective quality of the adjectives was determined nomothetically. We did not have each subject prerate these words for idiographic affective assessment, as we did in many other experiments.

The word pairings were administered to subjects according to three different random orders to counteract any sequencing bias. The index card was used by all subjects as a control on the amount of time given to the reading of the adjectives. It was placed on top of the first item pairing and then brought down to expose the two adjectives. The experimenter read the two adjectives aloud for the group, allowed subjects 10 seconds to place a check alongside the more relevant adjective, and then instructed the subject to move the index card beneath the next pair. In this fashion, all subjects moved through the 30-item task at the same rate.

In the next section of the experiment, subjects were confronted with a blank sheet on which they were asked to write down all the adjectives that they could recall attributing to their targeted person. Pretesting had established that five minutes was an adequate period for this free recall. Subjects then turned to another blank sheet in their packet and were instructed to record all the *other* adjectives that they had *not* assigned to the targeted person (presumably this would include adjectives that fell outside the primary predicating Euler circle). Once again, five minutes was allotted to this task. At the completion of this second effort, subjects had exhausted their memory for the adjectives. Retrieval within the affirmed predication was complete.

However, to see whether further retrieval was possible when the primary predication was reversed in affective quality, subjects next moved into the final section of the experiment. They were now instructed to think of a person who was opposite in likability to the original target and to record this person's initials on the experimental form. Subjects who had initially targeted a liked person now targeted a disliked person, and subjects who had initially targeted a disliked person now targeted a liked person. They were then given an additional five minutes to search their memory and try to recall as many words from their experimental task as they could that characterized this second target. These secondary predications were recorded in writing. Following this, subjects were debriefed and dismissed.

Results

The dependent variable of this experiment was the number of words recalled that fell into one of the three categories of positive, negative, or ambivalent. As expected, and in line with previous research on affective assessment, subjects did recall significantly more liked than disliked adjectives when the target was liked, and vice versa for disliked targets. They also recalled more positive than negative adjectives that were not used as secondary predications, but this proved significant only in the disliked target condition. As I noted in the rationale section, these findings are routine, and I will not take up space to give the specifics.

Turning to the experimental hypothesis, the newly retrieved adjectives were totaled for each subject. These data were entered into a 2 (Liked, Disliked Target) × 3 (Positive, Negative, Ambivalent Adjective) ANOVA. The first variable is a between-subjects comparison and the second a within-subjects comparison. The experimental hypothesis can be tested in the 2 × 3 interaction, which reached significance ($F = 50.76$, $df = 2, 124$, $p < .001$).

It was found that when the new predication was a liked person, the means for newly retrieved adjectives arrayed as follows: positive, $M = 1.52$ ($SD = 1.29$); negative, $M = 0.03$ ($SD = 0.18$); ambivalent, $M = 0.39$ ($SD = 0.62$). When the new predication was a disliked person, these values were as follows: positive, $M = 0.15$ ($SD = 0.36$); negative, $M = 1.45$ ($SD = 1.20$); ambivalent, $M = 0.33$ ($SD = 0.54$).

We can also consider these findings in terms of the percentage of subjects who retrieved adjectives that they had not previously recalled. When the new target was liked, 71% of the subjects recalled between one and five additional positive adjectives (Mode = 2). Only one subject (3%) recalled a (single) negative adjective when the new target was liked, and 32% of the subjects recalled either one or two ambivalent adjectives that could predicate the newly framed liked target (Mode = 1). When the target was disliked, 79% of the subjects recalled between one and six negative adjectives (Mode = 2). Fifteen percent of our subjects recalled 1 positive adjective when the new target was disliked. Finally, 26% of our sample recalled one or two ambivalent adjectives when the target was disliked (Mode = 1).

Conclusion and Discussion

The experimental hypothesis has been supported. Affective assessment does indeed play a predicating role in so-called memory retrieval. As a context cue, the affective quality of a realm of meaning can facilitate reconceptualization of previously encountered targets. The new affective context (liked to disliked or vice versa) enhances previous word meanings that initially were not relevant descriptors but later served such a role. The newly recalled adjectives were both targets to the wider context of affection and also secondary predications of the targeted person. Thus, when the new predicating context was affirmed, this served as the same kind of memory cue that we have observed taking place in studies using word meanings (see Demonstration Experiments 5 and 6). The new affective context enhanced the relevant meaning of the targeted adjective, which in turn could serve as a (secondary) predicate of the targeted person. This is an entirely top-down, precedent-sequacious process.

Concluding Comment

Logical learning theory places great emphasis on the role of affection in human behavior of all types. The human being is a valuing animal because of this capacity to render an affective assessment of literally everything that is encountered in experience. As telosponders, humans cannot avoid making affective judgments of their experience, which comes down to the meanings they frame in ongoing life. There are purely biological (*Bios*) aspects to behavior, of course, but we do not advance our understanding of the complete human condition by reducing behavior to such drive-ridden accounts. Drives must be conceptualized (*Logos*) and dealt with in specific ways. This lending of meaning to drives is not a machinelike process, for it brings an individual (and subjective) judgment into the process that is foreign to machines. Judgments are affirmed predications, and machines do not predicate. As the demonstration experiments of this chapter reveal, affective alignments play a fundamental role in both initial learning and memorial retrieval.

Demonstration Experiment 10 gives some support to LLT's contention that precedents function from the very outset of learning—at birth or at the initiation of cognition. That is, in the same way that our adult subjects had an affective inkling of the meanings they were learning even before they could express these meanings in words, so too, I contend, do infants have an affective inkling of what they are learning for the first time but do not yet literally know. In this sense, affective assessment can be thought of as the initial prememory of the human learner—a precedent that extends sequaciously before there is anything to remember. I will take up this contention about the learning of infants in more detail, with accompanying empirical support, in chapter 9.

It should not be thought that affective assessment in reasoning is the same as emotional reasoning. When we say that people reason emotionally, we are usually rendering a judgment of the suitability of their line of thought. People who reason with their "hearts" and not their "heads" are presumably affirming premises (encompassing predications) that are poorly thought out. They are being impetuous, following hunches or implications too readily, without suitable reflexive examination. Often, this occurs in circumstances that hold great personal significance for the individual concerned—religious commitments, economic pressures, love entanglements, and so on. Affection is most certainly involved here, but this does not mean that we should equate affective assessment in reasoning with emotional reasoning per se. To do so would be to make it appear that affection is not involved in "unemotional reasoning"—which is most assuredly false. Logical learning theory holds that affective assessment occurs in all forms of reasoning—sound, unsound, emotional, unemotional, and so on.

8

A Look at the *Bios:* Perception
and Brain Function

I have asserted several times in this volume that there is no need to reduce LLT's explanations—which are grounded in the *Logos* realm—to some supposedly more fundamental realm of explanation such as the *Bios.* Even so, I realize that any approach must conform reasonably well to the empirical findings of biologically based areas of study in psychology. In this chapter I will consider two such areas of study—perception and brain function—to see whether there is anything here to contradict the claims of LLT, either theoretically or empirically.

Perception

Two Interpretations of Perceptual Processing

A survey of the field of perception quickly uncovers a basic divergence in how this phenomenon is understood. The two wings of this divergence might be named the *direct/ecological* and the *constructive/representational* views of perception. The field of perception was dominated initially by Helmholtzian representationalism, which held that perception depends on inferred organizers lending continuity to the strictly sensory aspects of the nervous system. Helmholtz considered such "unconscious inferences" to be the contents of a mediating process rather than a pro forma Kantian process (Boring, 1950, p. 309). Helmholtz's theory drew a distinction between sensory signals or raw input on the one hand and a perceptual representation on the other. Our modern divergence continues to reflect this issue: Is the organization of meaning directly perceived in the natural (ecological) environment, or is it somehow constructed by the perceptual process through representations of the input stimuli?

The initiator of the direct/ecological view of perception was J. J. Gibson

(1979). He contended that information could be picked up directly from the surrounding or ambient optic array (ibid., pp. 56–58, 62). Gibson rejected the dualism of the perceived external object or event on the one hand and the biophysical mechanism through which information about such objects or events is made known to the perceiver on the other (Gibson, 1966). What the organism sees is not some signal carried by the optic nerve and requiring a representational organizer but the actual, real-life environmental circumstance. This direct perception enables the organism to pick up information concerning important experiential possibilities without a preliminary organizer like the Helmholtzian inferences. Gibson (1979) termed these directly perceived possibilities *affordances* (p. 18). Affordances occur from birth and reflect such immediate perceptions as knowing that an object is reachable, that a pathway is walkable, that a defile in the surface of the earth can serve as a hiding place, and so on.

Neisser (1991a, 1991b) has been a major supporter of the Gibsonian view of perception. Since affordances are predominantly tied to motility, to the movements of the organism in relation to the shifting environment, Neisser (1991b) limits the concept of direct perception to *orientation*, to the layout of an orienting system (p. 11). Perception is "immediate knowledge" (ibid., p. 10). This theory relies on a realism in which the environment as experienced is assumed to exist independently of the perceiver (ibid., p. 27). Direct perception is not recognition. To recognize is to match a current event with some past memory (Neisser, 1991a, p. 20). There may be room for the Helmholtzian theoretical line here, but perception in the Gibsonian sense is immediate; it captures what is really there in the ecological surround, the ambient optic array.

What interests the LLT advocate in Gibsonian theorizing is that Gibson seems to base much of his argument on the patterned organization of what could in fact be the *Logos*, considered now extraspectively rather than introspectively. Thus, Gibson notes that physical reality has a structure at all levels of scale, "from atoms to galaxies" (ibid., p. 9). Smaller structural units are nested within larger units, so that "there are forms within forms both up and down the scale of size" (ibid.). Oppositionality is suggested in the fact that the natural units of an animal's "space of movement" always include an "intrinsic polarity of up and down" (ibid., p. 18). Predication is clearly indicated in Gibson's analysis of the optic array, as when he observes that "each star can also be located by its inclusion in one of the constellations and by the superordinate pattern of the whole sky" (ibid., p. 68).

Although he eschews gestalt formulations (ibid., p. 140), this kind of talk is highly reminiscent of Rubin's (1921) work, in which it was demonstrated that contour has a one-sided function, a figure always taking its shape from the wider realm of the ground (see chap. 1). Indeed, as Gibson (1979) acknowledges, in his earlier writings he actually took the position that the "character of the visual world was given not by objects but by the background of the objects" (ibid., p. 148). This would admit predication to the perceptual process. In his later formulations, Gibson referred to this ground as the *layout of surfaces*, by which he meant "the relations of surfaces to the ground and to one another, their arrangement" (ibid.).

This seems a modest theoretical revision. It is still entirely possible for a wider referent-surface to influence the perception of a narrower referent-surface, particularly since the structures of the physical world are presumed to be arranged in this manner. Gibson's discussion of structure takes on a clearly Heraclitean tone when he says, "Let us suppose that a kind of essential structure underlies the superficial structure of an array when the point of observation moves. This essential structure consists of what is invariant despite the change" (ibid., p. 73). When Heraclitus used the term *Logos*, he meant precisely the same thing—that although one never steps in the same flowing river twice, there is an invariant pattern of the river discernible at all times. Although framed supraindividually, in extraspective fashion, this Gibsonian style of explanation is not essentially different from the more introspectively framed concepts of LLT, which suggests that stimuli are stimuli only because predication makes them so.

Gibson's advocates and opponents both have criticized his theory. O'Connor cited research findings on intrinsic cognitive imbalance (Berlyne, 1960) and readiness, or set (Swets, 1964), to suggest that a subject's perceptual attention is not controlled by sensory inputs and that it may not be triggered by a stimulus in the first place (O'Connor, 1981, p. 123). Heil (1983), a supporter of Gibson, became convinced that perception is not only influenced by mental representations but is also "essentially cognitive" (p. 120). Sensations are direct signals based on bodily mechanisms, but perception is an indirect function and, as such, inferential (ibid., p. 5). Heil also recognized that to have a cognitive representation implies that the perceiver can distinguish when this belief is *not* applicable (ibid., pp. 43, 118)—thereby endorsing a role for generic oppositionality in perceptual functioning.

Critics of Gibson tend to focus on such issues as the fact that not everyone directly perceives the same affordances in the ambient optic array, that errors occur in such perceptions, and that the concept of "pick up" is a dubious metaphor for what actually takes place (Fodor & Pylyshyn, 1981; Reed & Jones, 1978; Ullman, 1980). Considerable support for internal representations stems from research by Shepard (1975) and Kosslyn (1975) demonstrating that perceivers not only form analog mental representations of the environment but can rotate or change the shape of these representations in a continuous fashion, create three-dimensional images from flat pictures, and so forth.

The theory that is most compatible with LLT is Rock's (1983) formulation, in which perception is viewed as a problem-solving process. According to Rock, a perceiver can be said to construct ongoing events and then to test out these constructions as experience unfolds. Perception has a logic to it, one that may be inaccessible to conscious, declarative knowledge. Of course, LLT uses the term *predication* rather than *construction*. Rock also employs information-processing terms like encoding and so on, which LLT eschews (except informally, as in Demonstration Experiment 10). The general thrust of this view, however, has the person bringing to bear meaningful groundings in perception that are not always elements of the stimulus array per se. This is highly compatible with LLT. As I noted in chapter 2, LLT claims that learning begins in the perceptual act of tautologizing a patterned item with itself; once the person is confident enough regarding the item in question (e.g., a nipple for an infant), he or she uses the pattern as a predicate meaning to be extended to targets elsewhere in ongoing experience (to thumbs, toys, etc.). When a former perceptual target can be used as a current perceptual predication, a representation has been formed and learning has taken place.

Unconscious Perception and Belief

Bowers (1984) has distinguished between *perceiving* and *noticing*, suggesting that the former can occur without the latter. For example, we perceive the pattern on a clock's face (and hence know the time) before we notice that the clock has Roman numerals. To notice an item of experience, we must selectively attend to it. *Conscious perception* is selectively attended perception; *unconscious perception* lacks this attentive quality. *Intuition* involves a "perception of an emerging coherence which is not yet noticed" (ibid., p. 228). These refinements of the perception concept are compatible with LLT. Indeed, the LLT advocate would suggest that in addition to noticing, a person can negate such selectively attended materials to not notice, resulting in unconscious or "unadmitted" (i.e., negated) knowledge.

Based on LLT principles we can therefore accept the psychoanalytical dictum that what is not known (consciously) is known (unconsciously), although we should avoid reifying different cognitive realms ("levels of mind") in doing so. That is, as our Demonstration Experiments (2, 3, 4) on implication suggest, the unqualified negation (repression, denial, etc.) of one meaning delimits its direct opposite. The latter meaning does not then simply go away and may in fact bias understanding- and action-intentions, thereby intruding on behavior in what can be a paradoxical fashion. We would expect affection to be involved here, since what is denied frequently involves a negative valuation of some meaning under processing.

To speak of *awareness* in LLT is to suggest that the person knows that something other than what is now taking place might or could occur:

> Perception is not enough for awareness. To have a grasp of what is taking place demands a broader frame of reference, within which we see not only that which stands before us as reality but (at least some of) the possibilities and likelihoods not yet "there" for perceptual delineation. Telic animals are aware animals because they are constantly looking forward to such nonliteral aspects of experience. (Rychlak, 1988, p. 354)

Awareness is more than simply consciousness, a concept that is confounded by such *Bios* characteristics as being awake, vigilant, responsive, and so on. Awareness extends beyond the active predications taking place in consciousness to include patternings we see to be possible or likely. An individual is aware to the extent that he or she is cognizant that things could be other than they are. This is another manifestation of transcendent reflexivity, the capacity to see beyond the given to new possibilities on the horizon that are not yet encompassing the target. Delimiting oppositionality makes such alternatives possible. This sensitivity to the nuances of perceived possibilities is why it is so difficult to separate perception from motivation (perceptual defense, etc.; see Dixon, 1971).

The possibility that meanings opposite to those that are either affirmed or denied consciously can function unconsciously has relevance for the occurrence of perceptual imagery in dreaming (Rychlak, 1988, pp. 356–359). Dreaming has been called thinking in pictures. According to LLT, what occurs in dreaming is that the predicating assumptions are expressed in an uncertain relationship to the target(s) as the dream unfolds. The thinking in dreaming is not as clear as it is in waking thought, because the predication involved extends simultaneously from both inside and outside the Euler circle, or equivalently, it interfuses both the B and non-B of Figure 14 into a single telosponsive affirmation. We must never forget that, as both Kant and Freud appreciated, in such free thought—unconstrained by the demands of clearly perceived reality—the law of contradiction does not hold.

Unlike awareness, in which an item falling outside the predicating Euler circle is consciously understood as a contrasting possibility to what is taking place at the moment (i.e., an implication), the outside and inside meanings are one in a dream sequence. This violation of the law of contradiction is why "illogical" events abound in dreams (e.g., person A has the face of person B but remains person A). Dreams can also reflect an implied attitude change concerning some item of experience that the person does not want to affirm.

For example, the person unexpectedly sees a respected friend steal something in a store (placing the friend outside the predicating Euler circle of honesty) and negates (represses, etc.) this perception, only to dream that very night that this person has died or dramatically changed appearance. Psychoanalysts have capitalized on the essentials of the dream process to gain insights into what the person is trying to avoid. Such nonaffirmed themes are wound into patients' dreams and provide insight into the dynamics of their personalities.

There is another side to unconscious or unadmitted cognition. This exceedingly rigid form of cognition appears during wakefulness and manifests itself as sensory *hallucinations* and conceptual *delusions*. Logical learning theory suggests that these states are unyielding because they do not interfuse the inside and outside of the predicating Euler circles, as the dream state does. They are exclusively the discarded (outside the circle) meanings that have been previously rejected as unacceptable, frightening, and literally unthinkable predications. These discarded alternatives are one-sided Jungian contents returning as demonstrative assertions and expressing a singularly threatening (albeit often fascinating) meaning. Following a temptation to do so, the psychiatric patient may have once sworn, "I won't steal," only later to suffer from the unyielding obsession (the thought that "I am a thief" or hallucination (a voice saying "You are a thief"). Naturally, there are many other predicating implications and inferences under affirmation in the cognitions of this patient leading him or her to this unfortunate point in life—not the least of which was some sort of demonstrative either/or style of reasoning about life to begin with.

I might note in passing that the line of theorizing I am now following has relevance to the classic issue of Janet's (1920) notion of the *fixed idea*, which Breuer and Freud (1893/1955) later wrestled with in their conflicting theories about the origins of hysteria. Breuer favored a *Bios* explanation in which hysteria was said to be due to an inherited *hypnoid state*. Freud, on the other hand, proposed a *Logos* explanation of *defense hysteria*. As Freud would have it, the person offers an unqualified negation of something seen (or capable of being seen) only to be visited by its opposite, "I am blind." The blindness solves a problem by shifting the focus of a psychological concern (i.e., some terrifying affectively negative vision) to a physical dysfunction. This hysterical idea (understanding-intention), which cannot be worked over by countering (oppositional) ideas, is—as Janet said—"split off" from the rest of the mind into a demonstratively unyielding action-intention. Logical learning theory can readily subsume the Freudian explanation as long as we remain on *Logos* grounds. Freud's problem was that he had to provide a quasi-*Bios* explanation to placate his medical colleagues, which resulted in the clumsy libido theory.

Research Evidence for Predication in Perception

There is no shortage of empirical evidence for the belief that perception is influenced by a predicational process. In this section I will survey three general topics in support of this claim.

Visual Attention and Intention

Modern research in vision has revolutionized our understanding of the newborn's perceptual capacities. Although this was not believed to be true at mid-20th century, we now know that the human newborn has a functioning visual system capable of delineating colors, shapes, and the edges of objects (Bower, 1974; Cohen & Salapatek, 1975). Within a few months, infants can sort out familiar objects from novel ones (Haith, Bergman, & Moore, 1977). Evidence suggests that at this time, infants have a clear capacity to attend, remember, and form expectations in perceptual experience (Haith, 1980). Harris, Cassel, and Bamborough (1974) found 8-week-old infants tracking an object visually only when it moved relative to a background. If the background moved along with the object, the tracking was discontinued. These results clearly suggest predication. Cohen and Younger (1983) found infants in the first few months of life employing prototypical categories by forming concepts based on perceptual similarity. Five-month-old children display anticipatory perception by following an object visually as it passes behind a screen and emerges on the other side (Gratch, 1979). Such findings suggest intention, which is relevant to all learning. Preschool children have been found to focus their attention on a television's picture and to ignore its sound. As a result, they tend to remember a video transmission's visual information much better than its auditory information (Hayes & Birnbaum, 1980).

Perceptual organization is an important consideration at all age levels. Adults who focus eye movements on the relevant visual factors of a task are better learners than adults who do not (Itoh & Fujita, 1982). Limiting one's attention to a specific visual target restricts the possibility for learning alternatives (Potter, 1975). Acoustical cues like the sound of a word can be attended to and prove even more effective as a memory prompt than the word's meaning (Fisher & Craik, 1977). Of course, people can recall and even use words that they do not understand. Newtson (1976) found that people perceive the meaning of one another's actions by inferring or drawing implications regarding the intentions involved.

Perceptual Organization in Recall/Recognition

We find predication to have the same heuristic benefits on perceptual recall and recognition that we have found it to have on learning and memory
generally (see chap. 5). Most of this work has been done on vision, but all
sensory modalities reflect the influence of predication. After all, as Haber
(1983) has noted (p. 202), each moment of perception is a continuation of
the previous one. This perceptual flow is readily understood as a precedent-
sequacious extension of meaning. For example, we do not appreciate the fact
that we continually infer across eyeblinks, working on pure assumption that
what we perceive after blinking is what we were perceiving before blinking.
We also do not think of the perceptual organization of up-down and left-
right as oppositional frames of reference. Bargh (1989) has pointed to a kind
of perceptual credulousness in that people immediately believe what they
see as being true and then, occasionally and secondarily, question what they
have perceived. But perceptions can be questioned and denied. Hysterical
blindness is a most dramatic example of such denial.

According to LLT, the initial (protopoint) perceptual organization reflects
the meaning that a subject lends to what is being observed. How much can
subjects lend such meaning, and how much of this organization is merely
imprinted from without? We are back to the Kantian-Lockean distinction.
Hume claimed that people acquire the notion of cause-effect (efficient causation), but Michotte's (1963) study of launching and entraining effects suggested that people natively and directly perceive such causation. Leslie (1982;
Leslie & Keeble, 1987) has found the Michottean effects in infants from 3 to 6
months of age. Conceptual organization is adversely affected if subjects have
to read a color name (e.g., red) when the letters of this word are presented in a
different color (e.g., colored green) (Stroop, 1935). Paralleling Rosch's (1973a)
work on prototypes, Berlin and Kay (1969) found that native speakers of 20
different languages formed a reliable consensus about the best exemplar of a
color. All such findings suggest that human perceivers lend meaningful organization to what is perceived at least as much as they take in such meanings.

Such perceptual organization greatly facilitates learning and memory.
The imageability of a cue word is more helpful than its linguistic frequency
when the task is to give an association to this cue rapidly (de Groot, 1989).
Images are essentially pictorial organizations *in toto*. Framing a face globally facilitates later recognition better than focusing on specific aspects of
the face (Sporer, 1991). Recognition is enhanced even if a subject's perceptual memory is organized through extrafacial features, such as targeting a
face by a predicating occupation (Klatsky, Martin, & Kane, 1982). We know
that any effort a subject makes to unite two words through imagery facili-

tates their recall (Howard, 1983). It has been suggested that the reason that concrete words (e.g., *boat*) are easier to recall than abstract words (e.g., *justice*) is because the former can readily be elaborated by imagery, whereas the latter cannot (Paivio, 1971).

If a visual pattern is complex but meaningless, recognition memory is not enhanced (Potter, 1975), but even brief exposure (e.g., 3 to 10 seconds) to hundreds and even thousands of meaningful pictures results in better than 90% accuracy in recognition memory (Shepard, 1967; Standing, 1973; Standing, Conezio, & Haber, 1970). The length of fixation time on a picture part does not seem to be as important to such memory as the number of fixations made per picture (Loftus, 1972). Picture memory is considerably better than memory for words or sentences (Gehring, Toglia, & Kimble, 1976). Memory has been shown to be influenced by the organizing perception of a picture. If two small circles linked together by a straight line are described as "eyeglasses" to one group of subjects and as a "dumbbell" to a second group, in subsequent memory tests these biasing predications are readily apparent in the subjects' drawings of what they saw (Carmichael, Hogan, & Walter, 1932).

Predicational influences like this have been shown in sensory modalities other than vision. People recall hearing *eel* as heel, wheel, peel, or meal, depending on the audiotaped sentence in which this sound is vocalized (e.g., "The _____ was on the axle" versus "The _____ was on the shoe") (Warren & Warren, 1970). Subjects who memorized adjectives with the odor of chocolate present subsequently recalled more of these words when this odor was present than when it was absent (Schab, 1990). Experiments show that when subjects are given minimal time for perceiving every word in a sentence, the meaning gleaned from initially grasped words influences the perception of successively encountered words (Potter, Moryadas, Abrams, & Noel, 1993). There is no doubt that such predicating context effects are at play in perception.

Biasing Predications in Perception

As I have already noted, there are many experiments supporting the view that motivation enters the realm of perception through predicational strategies. Spectators observing the same athletic contest can literally see either many or few rule violations being committed by the teams depending on their allegience (Hastorf & Cantril, 1954). It is also possible for the person who finds him- or herself in a boring situation to create perceptually satisfying meanings through daydreaming. The person's eyes at this point take on an unfocused quality, as if the attention has shifted from "out there" to "in here" (Holland & Tarlow, 1975).

No area of investigation in perception is more debated than the one known variously as subliminal perception, perceptual defense, or vigilance (Dixon, 1971; Erdelyi, 1974). The question remains: How do such biases come about? We know that if words are aligned in a series, the one occurring first primes those to follow so that they will be identified more readily as a word. This priming effect has been shown to occur even when the first word of the series is flashed so quickly that it is not consciously perceived (Marcel, 1983). A finding of this sort suggests to the LLT advocate that the *Logos* pattern obtaining between words is being conceptualized even though the specific word meanings are not yet delineated, which is rather like the advantage obtained in globally framing the face rather then focusing on parts of the face (Sporer, 1991). The initial (protopoint) word, affirmed as a precedent meaning, sequaciously extends the meaningful organization to what follows.

If meaning is patterned organization, then it is possible that the more global aspects of a word are framed before its specific details are delineated, as when we read and understand a word but cannot yet spell out the letters constituting the word. On this point, it has been demonstrated that, under viewing conditions that leave simple detection at a chance level, the semantic content of a word is accessible even before its physical properties are perceived (Fowler, Wolford, Slade, & Tassinary, 1981). We must not overlook the possible role of affective assessment in framing new or unknown words. It is but a short step to understand how people reorganize such word meanings to say or not say what they would like to perceive rather than confront perceptions they dislike knowing or admitting.

Conclusion

The theories and empirical findings of the field of perception offer no challenge to LLT. Indeed, LLT is supported by the fact that the perception of patterned organization or meaning takes precedence over the specifics of sensory stimulation. Leading scholars in the field of perception and brain function find no difficulty in the top-down *Logos* formulations of LLT (although they may not agree with all of our tenets, of course). Pribram (1991) has presented a *holonomic* theory of brain functioning that is friendly to the concepts of LLT. Pribram's theory is computational, relying on Fourier transforms of nervous signals, but the essence of holonomic theory is its holistic view of brain functioning in figural processes such as those used in vision. Pribram concludes from extensive research evidence that vision is not based simply on external stimulations entering the brain through bottom-up processing of sensory inputs. Rather, as such sensory input occurs, a top-down categorizing and evaluating procedure immediately preprocesses the perception of object forms. This meets the requirements of a Kantian (predicational) view of perception, in which the entering inputs are immediately framed and transformed by the native structures of the visual or cognitive system.

Of course, as it is in all such treatments designed to capture the totality of cognition and perception, the phrasing is usually broad enough to allow a mediation model to sneak into the reader's understanding of the theory. That is, if the top-down processes triggered by inputs occur from birth, from the onset of perceptions, then we have a clear predicational model under employment. Any learning through experience would from that point onward be influenced by this native predicational process. Hence, when a theorist like Pribram refers to the fact that the top-down processes are themselves dependent on prior experience (including developing genetic determinants), this does *not* mean — at least, not necessarily — that they are simply yesterday's bottom-up (i.e., unpredicated) inputs acting as (quasi-) top-down mediators today. Pribram, like many other workers in visual perception, makes reference to such earlier experiences that result in the learning of top-down processing schemes, and so on — which leaves the issue somewhat clouded if no further comments are made concerning the nature of learning. Nonetheless, it is clear that an LLT formulation of learning could be situated within such explanations of perception without contradiction.

Brain Functioning

There is no area of study in psychology that brings the mind-body problem home more directly than the study of brain function. Indeed, brain studies underwrite the reductive presumptions of psychology. It is impossible to have a dialogue with a colleague who insists that since "the brain thinks," there is little point in speculating on such mysterious (i.e., nonmaterial) concepts as LLT employs. One would like to point out to such a colleague that the concepts of LLT are as relevant today, when the brain is being interpreted as a computer, as they were fifty years ago, when the brain was being interpreted as a telephone switchboard. Furthermore, LLT concepts will still be relevent in another fifty years, when the brain may be understood as a chemical system.

Mapping the *Logos* directly onto the *Bios* has a long tradition in psychology. William James (1895/1952) can be credited with establishing this style of explanation probably more than anyone else, although the founders of psychology like Helmholtz and Wundt ensured that something of the sort would eventuate when they adopted their particular strategy of empirical investigation (Boring, 1950). At midcentury it was Hebb's (1949/1961) brain cell-assembly theorizing that greatly promoted this reductive approach. Hebb (1974) made no bones about his commitment to the *Bios,* as when he stated flatly that "*psychology is a biological science*" (p. 72; emphasis in the original). Given this grounding predication, it followed for Hebb that "free will has a physiological basis" (ibid., p. 75). Bunge (1980) continued in the Hebbian mode when he then asserted that "the laws of thought are neurophysiological laws, not logical ones" (p. 161). Logical learning theory challenges such *Bios* assertions on the grounds that the empirical research on brain functioning fails to support them. I will survey three such areas of brain research.

Brain Stimulation: Penfield

Penfield (1975) is the father of direct brain stimulation. In 1933 he stumbled onto the remarkable effects of electrically stimulating the brain. During operations on patients with epilepsy, in which abnormally firing portions of the cortex were severed or removed (ibid., p. 13), Penfield inserted an electrode administering 60 pulses per second into various portions of the cortex to see whether brain functions could be induced. These operations are done with the use of local analgesics, so that the patient is conscious throughout. The cortex has no pain receptors, so the patient feels no discomfort when electrodes are inserted. After years of such research, Penfield concluded that all he ever dealt with was the physical hardware of the brain and that he never influenced the mind per se. Thus, he could say with confidence that "there is no place in the cerebral cortex where electrical stimulation will cause a patient to believe or to decide" (ibid., p. 77). In fact, quite the opposite suggestion leaps out at us from Penfield's clinical examples.

Thus, when he would stimulate a patient's motor cortex, causing a movement in the hand, Penfield would ask the patient about this motion. Invariably, the patient's response was "I didn't do that. You did." (ibid., p. 76). Sometimes, the patient would reach over with the other hand and stop the motion entirely (ibid., p. 77). When made to vocalize, the patient would add "I didn't make that sound. You pulled it out of me" (ibid., p. 76). All such behaviors are consistent with a delimiting oppositionality. Penfield identified an "interpretive cortex" lying near the speech area, along the temporal lobe (ibid., p. 32), and he found that some inexplicable things occurred when it was stimulated. For example, a young South African patient described himself as both laughing with his cousins on a farm in South Africa and also being on the operating table with Penfield in Montreal. This is a clear violation of the law of contradiction, but it is consistent with what might occur if the bipolarity of generic oppositionality is expressed concurrently.

Since he did not entertain oppositionality as fundamental to reasoning, Penfield framed a dualistic theory of brain functioning that held that "the mind may be a distinct and *different essence*" from the brain (ibid., p. 62; emphasis in the original). Elaborating on this point, Penfield tells us that "a man's mind, one might say, is the person. He walks about the world, depending always upon his private computer [i.e., brain], which he programs continuously to suit his ever-changing purposes and interests" (ibid., p. 61). The mind directs, and the mind-mechanism executes. The mind is like the program writer, relying on the memory bank of the brain. The brain is like the hardware, carrying out the directions of this higher brain source.

Although LLT makes no such dualistic theoretical claims, surely there is nothing in Penfield's basic findings to contradict its tenets. No claim is made in LLT that there are two streams of consciousness or two realms of being. Logical learning theory places its emphasis on the duality of an oppositionally patterned *Logos* in which affirmation versus contrariety (negation, contradiction, contrast) functions in directing behavior as the person continually must take a position on what occurs next. As Penfield suggests, the brain can be considered an instrumentality rather than the originator of thought. It is in the active patterning of taking a position that thought occurs. To *think* is to take a position in the light of a certain predication relating to a targeted referent, as well as the meaning-extension that follows. Directed thought is relevant, well-focused position-taking and meaning-extension.

Readiness Potentials: Granit, Eccles, Libet

A vast area of brain research has centered on Kornhuber and Deecke's (1965) discovery of the *readiness potential* (RP), which is an endogenous slow negative potential that appears in the brain's cortex up to 800 *milliseconds* (ms) prior to the execution of a motor response. The RP gradually peaks just prior to a person's making an overt movement, then shifts rapidly in the positive direction. About 50 to 150 ms before contraction of a muscle group, a more precise and brisk motion potential is observed over the part of the motor area belonging to the muscles called up for service. Granit (1977), a brain researcher who describes himself as a teleologist (pp. 7, 9), has argued that the RP is an anticipatory brain process and that it in all likelihood reflects a mounting motor command, a kind of volitional effort being put forward intentionally (p. 165).

Eccles (1977) has also relied on the RP findings to underwrite his theory of brain functioning (see pp. 364, 365). Eccles has gone far beyond Granit in the direction of teleology, for he has a *dualist-interactionist* theory (p. 226) in which he introduces a self-conscious mind as an agent in thought. Here we have a completely introspective, formal/final-cause theoretical formulation under development. The self-conscious mind is more than simply an organization of the physical parts of the brain. It is *not* part of the physical and biological realm *at all*, and we are unable in principle to say where it is located (ibid., p. 376). Of course, LLT would suggest that we are dealing with pure *Logos* at this point, but according to Eccles, the RP phenomenon is a reflection of the ongoing process of the self-conscious mind, as follows: "Another temporal property of the self-conscious mind is displayed by the long duration of the readiness-potential [i.e., 800 ms]. . . . It can now be proposed that, when willing brings about a movement, there is continuous action of the self-conscious mind on a neuronal field of great extent" (ibid., p. 364).

Mountcastle (1975) has proven that the neurons of the brain fire holistically, in response to a total pattern of activity, rather than individually to create such patterning in bottom-up fashion. The suggestion is that formal causation takes precedence over efficient causation. Borrowing a phrase from Campbell (1974), Eccles argues that the RP reflects a "downward causation," or what might be seen as a Kantian "top-down" influence, *from* the identity or self-conscious mind *to* the brain structure, where the holistic pattern of neuronal firing serves an instrumental role during a measurable period of time. This formulation is consistent with LLT's claims of precedent-sequacious extensions of meaning. Libet (1973) has found that even the most rudimentary "raw feel" type of experience requires 0.5 seconds of patterning among the neurons of the cortex before it is experienced consciously as a sensation. Eccles holds that the self-conscious mind can influence this formal-cause pattern, thereby aligning overt behavior according to its intentions.

It is not difficult to imagine a fundamental role for generic oppositionality in cognition given what we know of the brain's structure. There are two kinds of neurons in operation in cerebral tissue, one that forms excitatory synapses and one that forms inhibitory synapses (Eccles, 1977, p. 232). Granit (1977) has suggested that the central nervous system works on the basis of such oppositional functioning (p. 138). A large number of the brain's neurons—in the cortex roughly half—*do not have axons*, so there is no real question of input-to-output taking place at this level. This dendritic cellular network serves on the inhibitory side of the ledger in the processing of nervous signals (where negations could be implemented). The corpus callosum has fibers joining brain halves that are in a mirror-image relationship with one another (Eccles, 1977, p. 241). The prefrontal lobes are in reciprocal relationship with the limbic system (ibid., p. 349). The brain is anything but a model of machinelike precision and clarity. The press of seemingly excessive elements in the system, crisscrossing each other, is tremendous. For example, "there are about 50 million cells per cubic centimeter in the human visual cortex, as against 10 million in the motor field, which has larger neurons" (Granit, 1977, p. 41).

As Mountcastle's (1975) work helped establish, the basic organization of nerve cells in the brain is modular. The modules contain up to 10,000 nerve cells locked together by mutual connectives into a mind-boggling organization of zigs and zags that fire in patterns. Each of these modules takes electrical power from its neighbor once given the chance to be activated. Eccles (1977) says, "We think the nervous system always works by conflict—in this case by conflicts between each module and the adjacent modules" (p. 234). A conflict model of brain function meshes well with oppositionality and therefore presents no difficulties to LLT. Contradictions, negations, contrasts: These are at the very heart of cognition as framed by LLT.

Libet (1985; Libet, Gleason, Wright, & Pearl, 1983) has conducted a number of fascinating experiments in which two electrical recordings are taken: RPs from the subject's scalp and electromyograms (EMGs) from the wrist and fingers. Since the aim of the experiment is to study endogenous responses, subjects are instructed to avoid planned responding in favor of acting only when they have a spontaneous urge to move their hand or to flex their fingers. As they are waiting for this spontaneous inclination to arise, subjects are also instructed to observe a moving spot of light revolving in a circle on the face of a cathode-ray oscilloscope. The only requirement is to recall where this spot was when the subject was first aware of wanting to move the hand or flex the fingers. Forty such self-initiated acts were measured for each subject.

It was now possible to relate brain activity as measured by the RP both to overt motion, as measured by the EMG, and to the instant of conscious awareness of wanting to make this motion, as indexed by the moving spot. Libet (1985) found that the RP had its onset approximately 550 ms (p. 532) before the motor act occurred. Subjects reported becoming aware of wanting to move approximately 200 ms before this movement was recorded. These findings led Libet to conclude that "the performance of every conscious voluntary act is preceded by special unconscious cerebral processes that begin about 500 ms or so before we act" (ibid., p. 536). This might appear to be evidence for biological determinism without agency. However, a crucial finding reported by Libet is that *all* subjects reported *frequent* instances of the urge or initial decision to act, only to *oppose* such inclinations and abort the action (ibid., p. 530). There is no way in which to measure such negations, but they obviously arose during the 200 ms preceding the overt motion recorded by the EMG. Libet concluded that there is nothing in his experimental findings to exclude the potential for individual responsibility and free will in human behavior (ibid., p. 538).

By the same token, there is nothing in Libet's findings to contradict the formulations of LLT, which places emphasis on the role of negation in accounting for free will or human agency. It is common to think of free will as an *initiating capacity*, as the force that aligns events according to some preconceived plan. The image here is that of the decider, chooser, or intender who aligns events by careful design and preselection. Although it is true that initiation of action is an aspect of free will, the larger truth seems to be that such initiations of understanding- and action-intentions frequently occur through *negating* alternative possibilities that have relevance to the point being ordered by understanding or the end being sought by action. These possibilities are generally thrust onto the person by unexpected circumstances. Sometimes the first possibility arising is the one affirmed, but the person can also reject possibilities until the one that seems most likely to attain the end being sought is hit on. Even when the person has long-term plans, there are many ways in which to achieve the hoped-for goal; hence, negation is always needed to redirect strategies from the lesser to the greater possibility (i.e., the "better" or "correct," etc., alternative generated by delimiting oppositionality).

Split-Brain Research: Sperry, Gazzaniga

The final area of research in brain functioning that I will look at has to do with the remarkable series of *split-brain* experiments and clinical studies carried on by Sperry and his colleagues (Myers & Sperry, 1953; Sperry, 1961; Sperry, 1985). I also want to look at some findings by Gazzaniga (1985), who once worked with Sperry but departed over theoretical differences.

Myers and Sperry (1953) found that when the corpus callosum, anterior commissure, and optic chiasma of the cat's brain are sectioned, visual discriminations taught to one brain half are unknown by the other. If a sectioned cat with its left eye covered was required to learn to push a panel with a triangle on it to obtain a food reward, the cat could learn to do this task. However, when later tested with the right eye covered, it could not do it. Knowledge concerning the task located in one brain hemisphere failed to transfer to the other brain hemisphere. The cat's brain could in a sense have been said to be split in two parts. Similar operations have been done on human beings suffering from epilepsy as early as 1940, with the therapeutic aim of avoiding overt epileptic seizures (Gazzaniga, 1985, p. 32). That is, an epileptic attack frequently begins as a series of firings in one hemisphere that then spread to the other. If the brain hemispheres are disconnected, this spreading of the abnormal discharges can be prevented, thus leaving one half of the brain free of the seizure and in control of the body.

In the case of human beings, only the corpus callosum is sectioned in either one or two stages. The full extent of the sectioning has sometimes been in question in this line of research, but Sperry's careful work and startling findings have left little doubt that the split-brain phenomenon is genuine. Human beings are not noticeably changed in their routine daily activities by the fissuring of the corpus callosum. It is only when we place them in a controlled experimental context that significant changes are noted. As with the cats, people are found to be unable to bring information framed by one brain half into a common understanding with information framed by the other half.

The oppositional organization of the brain is such that sensory receptors on the left-hand side of the body go to the right-brain hemisphere, and vice versa. Similarly, the motoric actions (touching, grasping, pointing, etc.) on the left side of the body are under the control of the right brain, and vice versa. The optic chiasma (where some of the retinal nerve cells cross over and hence enter both brain hemispheres) is not severed in operations on epileptics, but the arrangement of the retina allows us to send information into one brain half or the other by positioning what is observed in the visual field either to the left or right of a point located in the midvisual field while the split-brain patient is under instructions to focus on this midpoint.

Through ingenious experiments of this type, Sperry, Gazzaniga, and their colleagues were able to send visual information into one hemisphere without knowledge of this input by the other hemisphere. The left hemisphere in most cases is concerned with linguistic matters, whereas the right hemisphere cannot enter into speech communication. Only the left hemisphere can talk, offer a point of view verbally, and so on. Thus, if a split-brain subject sees a word (e.g., *screwdriver*) flashed onto a screen in the left visual field, thereby entering the right hemisphere, the subject typically reports seeing nothing. However, if this subject's hand were to be placed underneath a table where various objects are located (a screwdriver, hammer, wrench, etc.), after tactilely examining the various objects, the correct item (i.e., the screwdriver) represented by the "unseen" word would be picked out. The right hemisphere obviously did see something, but it could not put what it saw into words, because that is the province of the left hemisphere. The left hemisphere is therefore "speaking" when the person says, "I saw nothing." Nevertheless, the right hemisphere can make its viewpoint known on the matter of what has been seen by using touch, a nonverbal form of communication.

This kind of finding can be shown to support LLT's claim that predication

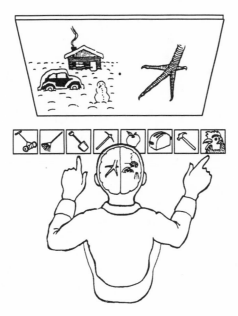

Figure 18   Split-brain patient confronting
two different tasks simultaneously

is fundamental to cognition. Figure 18 presents a drawing of a split-brain patient in one of Gazzaniga's studies looking at a point in the midvisual field on a distant wall (from Gazzaniga & LeDoux, 1978, p. 149). Projected to the left on this wall is a winter scene (i.e., snow-covered house, yard, automobile, snowman) and to the right, a huge bird's claw.

Placed within easy reach before the subject are several pictures, including a grass cutter, a rake, a shovel, a pick, an apple, a toaster, a hammer, and a chicken's head. After the images are flashed onto the more distant wall for a fraction of a second, the patient is asked to use both hands in pointing to those pictures immediately in front of him that go along with these wall flashings. A typical performance on this task was that of a split-brain patient named Paul, who pointed concomitantly to the chicken with his right hand and the shovel with the left. Gazzaniga (1985) asked him why he made these selections and received the following explanation without a moment's hesitation: "Oh, that's easy. The chicken claw goes with the chicken and you need a shovel to clean out the chicken shed" (p. 72).

An LLT analysis of these findings would go as follows: The winter scene to Paul's left was made available for predication by the right-brain hemisphere. The claw of a bird was flashed to his right, which meant that it had to be predicated by the left-brain hemisphere. The two brain halves cannot communicate, owing to the severed corpus callosum. It seems reasonable to expect the snow scene on the left wall to frame a context within which the shovel would be targeted from among all of the pictures available. And so it is that Paul's left hand, under the influence of the right-brain hemisphere (perceiving the left wall), pointed to the shovel. A bird's claw, however, frames an entirely different context within which to select a picture, and since there is a chicken head available, this is what the right hand—under the influence of the left-brain hemisphere (perceiving the right wall)—singles out. So far so good.

But now Paul is asked to rationalize and verbally state why a chicken and a shovel are being pointed to at the same time. Only Paul's left hemisphere has the capacity to verbalize, however, which means that he is limited to the left hemisphere's framing predication. The result is that Paul elaborates his explanation around chickens and the shoveling out of chicken sheds, making up a total explanation in the light of the left-brain predication. The predication of the right brain goes unmentioned. But why should it be mentioned? Who is to benefit from such "truth," except a third-person observer who now claims dictatorial powers over naming the reality taking place. From the left-brain's perspective, the predication voiced has Jamesian cash value, which is all that matters in the psychological realm. In fact, from this perspective, the predication is true. There is no better example of the fact that, even though there is a reality "out there," the human mind has a conceptual capacity lending it organization from "in here." It is hard to accept a naive realism with such empirical findings staring in one's face.

These findings are also important because they suggest that predication is not an isolated function carried on in a localized region of the cortex, within a predication center or node. Each hemisphere has its unique slant on perceived events and makes logical sense of them accordingly. Predication must be understood as a fundamental process reflecting itself uniformly in all cortical functions that have been variously localized as the higher mental processes, visual perception, auditory perception, and so on. This is not to deny the possibility that reflexes are mediated by structures in the brain (framed now via a *Bios* formulation, of course).

As I noted above, Sperry and Gazzaniga differ in their theoretical explanations of brain functions. Sperry (1985) is a self-proclaimed mentalist (p. 31) and nonreductionist (p. 41) who suggests that mind and consciousness are dynamic emergent patterns or configurations in the living brain (p. 32). He accepts free will and self-determination, believing that the person can select a course of action from among a large number of ongoing possibilities in behavior (ibid, p. 40). Sperry poses no threat to LLT. Gazzaniga (1985), on the other hand, embraces the mechanistic formulations of cognitive science, referring to mind as a "confederation of mental systems" (p. x). This involves the typical modular arrangement of a network with connecting pathways and the like. Each module is a mechanism that can bring about behavior automatically, without the person's intending to carry out what is activated. A special module named the *interpreter*, which is located in the dominant (usually the left) hemisphere, computes all the activities of the network to form a belief about what is being enacted (ibid., pp. 5, 6, 28, 187). No explanation is given for the special mechanism of this interpreting module, which apparently does not have to compete for energy with other modules as in conflict theories of brain modularity. The interpreter just works differently from the other, noninterpreting mechanisms. Obviously, LLT departs from Gazzaniga to a considerable extent when it comes to explaining findings on split-brain patients like Paul.

Conclusion

As was true of perception, there is nothing in the empirical findings on brain functioning to dissuade the LLT advocate from proceeding on course. There is no contradiction to be found in believing in a *Bios* realm on the one hand and a *Logos* realm on the other. Strictly speaking, the architectonic structure of the brain is aligned appositionally rather than oppositionally, but the logic that such physical processes convey can easily be understood as involving oppositionality. This dialectical logic unfolds in large measure during the preaffirmations of telosponsivity. As long as the formal cause holds supreme in scientific accounts, the possibility remains open that the *Logos* is a realm of explanation separate and distinct from the physical realm. As students of the *Logos*, we do not have to wait on those who study the *Bios*. Even so, it is important to know that investigators relying on these different theoretical groundings can address the same empirical data when called on to do so (Rychlak, 1993). There is no empirical embarrassment awaiting LLT in the evidence on brain function.

Demonstration Experiments: Concerning Perception and Brain Functioning

Experiment 12: Meaning as Perceptual Organization

Hypotheses

1. Ratings of variously patterned dots in a confined space will be highly comparable whether they are based on judgments of organization or of meaning.

2. Hypothesis 1 cannot be accounted for by the imageability of the dot patterns per se.

Rationale

This little perceptual study arose in response to a colleague's question. After reading a book (Rychlak, 1991) in which I discuss the central role of meaning in the predicational process, a prominent researcher in perception asked me where meaning comes from. My immediate reply was, "Meaning is organization. Where does organization come from?" I was thinking, of course, of meaning as a formal-cause conception. The present study was designed to test the assumption that meaning is what we refer to when we want to typify or characterize—lend a name to—a perceptual or conceptual organization (Rychlak & Ulasevich, 1991). Intention is central here, of course, for a formal-cause organization is always the "that," or goal, aspect of final causation. The pattern is the reason ("that") for ("the sake of") which meaning is being expressed.

We therefore decided to arrange a series of dot patterns and have independent groups of subjects rate these same dots according to two different criteria : (1) extent of organization and (2) extent of meaning. The latter subjects would also be asked to record what meaning they thought of when they rated a pattern as highly meaningful. We did this to check on the role of imageability in ratings of meaning.

Experimental Sample

Fifty-eight introductory psychology students (evenly divided by sex) served as subjects; this group was randomly sorted into two subsamples. There were 30 subjects who rated for the meaning of the squares and 28 who rated for organization.

Procedure

Fifty dots were arranged in a square with 2-in. sides. Forty-eight such squares were drafted. The arrangement of 50 dots varied from a totally random display through increasingly differentiated patterns. At no point did we attempt to portray a specific target in the dotted array, such as a plant, building, or person. An effort was made to have four levels of dot patterning—from minimal to well organized—with 12 squares at each level. A 12-page questionnaire was assembled, with four squares arrayed on the left-hand side of each page. During administration the order of these 12 pages was randomized across subjects.

On the right-hand side of the page, alongside each of the squares, there was a 7-point scale ranging from *minimum* (1) to *maximum* (7). Subjects circled the value they judged appropriate to the square in question. Subjects were randomly assigned to either a meaning- or an organization-instruction condition. They were tested in small groups of from 4 to 10 subjects. The meaning instruction asked subjects to rate for meaning, that is, for any sense of purpose that they believed was suggested by all the dots in the square. The organization instruction asked subjects to rate for organization, that is, the extent of patterned arrangement that they believed there was in all the dots in the square.

Subjects were given two practice squares to familiarize themselves with the task before beginning; they were then asked to glance over the 48 squares to get a sense of the differences among them. At the completion of the meaning ratings, subjects were asked to go back over the squares and record next to the relevant square anything that they felt they had perceived there.

Results

To derive the scores for a correlational analysis, the ratings were collapsed across subjects in each group for each square. In other words, we averaged the meaning and organization scores and then correlated them. The resultant Pearsonian value between our two groups was .88 ($p < .001$). This extremely high value of the correlation supports hypothesis 1.

To test hypothesis 2, we devised an "imageability score" as follows: The number of items perceived by subjects in the meaning condition was totaled. Thus, if for a certain square 25 subjects recorded that the dots looked like or reminded them of a cloud, mountain, island, or whatever (i.e., the content need not be uniform), the imageability score for this square was 25. If only 15 of the subjects had recorded that the dots in the square looked like or reminded them of something, the score would be 15. These imageability scores were then correlated against the average meaning scores for the squares, resulting in a value of .25 (N.S.). This finding supports hypothesis 2, in that it was not just those squares that "looked like something" that determined our meaning ratings. Interestingly, when we next correlated the imageability scores with the organization scores, we found a slightly higher value of .30 ($p < .05$).

Conclusion

The experimental hypotheses have been supported. A reasonable conclusion is that when people see or infer meaning in perceptual events, they do so based on the patterned organization in such events. They perceive some purposive reason for the sake of which the organized or organizing perception has taken or is taking shape. Therefore, I can now answer my colleague based on data to suggest that meaning comes from organization. I believe this holds conceptually as well as perceptually.

Experiment 13: Predication in Brain-Lateralization: Recognition of Verbal or Pictorial Materials with Contrasting Affective Qualities

Hypotheses

1. Subjects who are asked to affectively assess verbal (cvc trigrams) or pictorial (abstract paintings) material that is exposed to either the left or right brain hemisphere *first* will on subsequent testing for recognition reflect the typical facility of liked-over-disliked material.

2. When the left hemisphere is exposed to material first, there will be a larger disparity favoring recognition of liked-over-disliked pictorial (abstract painting) contents than there will be for verbal (cvc trigram) contents.

3. When the right hemisphere is exposed to material first, there will be a larger disparity favoring recognition of liked-over-disliked verbal (cvc trigram) contents than there will be for pictorial (abstract painting) contents.

Rationale

This experiment combines the theory and empirical findings on affective assessment in learning (see chap. 7, esp. Demonstration Experiment 10) with the work on brain lateralization. Logical learning theory holds that affective assessment plays a crucial role in the initial learning of infants, organizing cognitions according to likes and dislikes even as the very first items are being tautologized of themselves. Affection is therefore the very first cognitive organizer. It takes the place of prememory in infancy. To the extent that the person has no other framing predication to lend organization to cognition, he or she will fall back on the discriminations of positive or negative affection. It follows that the less the person knows about some realm of experience, the more likely it is that affective assessment will play a role in framing meaningful discriminations regarding this realm. As learnable material becomes more difficult (abstract, complex, unclear, etc.), the person will be forced to rely increasingly on affective assessment relative to the intellectualized discriminants and verbal organizers of so-called information.

If the left hemisphere is forced to recognize pictorial materials, it will rely more on affection than when it processes verbal materials. Similarly, when the right hemisphere processes verbal materials, it too should reflect a larger affective disparity than when it processes pictorial materials. By placing the hemispheres in circumstances contrary to their accustomed realm, we ensure that they will rely more heavily on affective predications in a recognition task (this is similar to findings cited in chap. 7 on judgments of lower socioeconomic subjects; see esp. Rychlak, 1975b). Fortunately, Gazzaniga devised a procedure that enabled us to test this line of theorizing.

The Gazzaniga (1970, pp. 90–93) procedure adapted for use on normals (i.e., individuals with an intact corpus callosum) is as follows: Subjects are asked to fixate on a point in midvisual field, and material is presented to them through a tachistoscope. Brief exposure times (0.1 to 0.01 seconds) ensure that each side of the retina scans only the material exposed to it. The anatomical arrangement of the retina causes material exposed to the right visual field to register first in the left brain hemisphere, and vice versa. Of course, these neural impulses traverse the intact corpus callosum in milliseconds to bring the other half of the brain into play, but there is an *order of entry* factor in this sequence that has a proven effect on the processing of materials.

Thus, when a subject is asked to make either a nonverbal or a verbal response to signals presented tachistoscopically in this manner, the nonverbal response comes more quickly when these signals are sent into the right hemisphere first (Filbey & Gazzaniga, 1969). It has been found that words projected in the left visual field (going to the right hemisphere first) are not recognized as readily as words projected in the right visual field (going to the left hemisphere first) (McKeever & Huling, 1971). Normal subjects recognized more cvc trigrams when they were flashed into the left hemisphere first rather than the right hemisphere, and the reverse facilitation occurred when faces were employed (Hilliard, 1973; Klein, Moscovitch, & Vigna, 1976). Memorizing digits is easier when these items are flashed into the left hemisphere first than when they are presented to the right hemisphere first (Dimond & Beaumont, 1974). Pictures of faces with emotional expressions at variance with the mood of a subject were more difficult to recognize when presented initially to the right hemisphere than to the left (Gage & Safer, 1985). Logical learning theory holds that the order of entry is a *logical precedent* influencing what will follow in the typical sequacious fashion of all predication. Time is not a factor here. The initial organization of the logical sequence is what matters, just as the initiating (formal-cause) organization in all of learning and memory is what matters.

Experimental Sample

Sixty-four high school students (evenly divided by sex) were put through the experimental procedure. All these students were at least 16 years of age and right-handed.

Procedure

Subjects were tested individually in the tachistoscopic procedure taken from Gazzaniga (1970, pp. 90–93; see Rychlak & Slife, 1984). Each subject was seated at a table on which a chin-rest apparatus was fixed at a constant distance from a white projection screen (45.5 cm × 40.5 cm) taped securely to the wall. In the center of the screen a 3-mm dot was evident. This dot was the fixation point for the subjects as they put their chins on the rest to keep their distance from the screen constant. The chin rest was adjustable, so that each subject's eye level was kept on the same plane as the dot. The tachisto-scopic projector was fitted into a special stand that kept its projection level in this same plane, thereby reducing the distortion of slides flashed to the visual field on either the right-hand or left-hand side of the fixation dot.

With a subject's eyeball 108 cm from the screen, a projection approxi-mately 5 cm to either side of the fixation dot ensures that the subject will frame material from the left visual field by the right hemisphere first, and vice versa. This assumes that the subjects are fixating on the dot, of course, and to ensure compliance with the instructions, the experimenter sat facing the subject, off to one side of the projection screen. It was easy to establish the subject's visual fixation on the dot in the warm-up procedure. Eye-movement during the slide flashes was never observed (see comparable findings by Gef-fen, Bradshaw, & Wallace, 1971; White, 1968). Material was presented at the rate of 0.2 second. Pretesting had established that this exposure time enabled subjects to read the cvc trigrams and rate their affective preferences accord-ingly. The cvc trigrams were taken from the middle ranges of Archer's (1960) norms, and the pictorial materials were abstract paintings selected from the slide collection of the New York Museum of Modern Art.

A subject's affective preference for the material flashed was conveyed to the experimenter via a single-pole, double-throw, spring contact switch that controlled two lights. This switch was placed on the table next to the chin rest. Throwing this switch one way activated a green light (signifying "like"), and throwing it in the reverse direction activated a red light (signifying "dis-like"). The pole returned to the upright position after the switch had been thrown. The red and green lights were installed behind and above the subject, so that as the experimenter faced a subject (monitoring subject's eye fixation on the dot), the red and green lights were also in the line of the experimenter's vision. Subjects used the hand identical to the visual field in which material was being projected to throw the switch (i.e., contra the hemisphere exposed to the material first). The direction of like versus dislike signaling was ran-domized by rotating the placement of the contact switch among the subjects.

Subjects were put through three experimental sessions at the identical hour on successive days. They were randomly assigned by sex to four experi-mental conditions: trigrams–right hemisphere, trigrams–left hemisphere, paintings–right hemisphere, and paintings–left hemisphere. These condi-tions signify materials used and the hemisphere that was first exposed to the flashed materials (i.e., the one opposite to the location of a slide projection: left-side projections entered the right hemisphere first and vice versa). On the first two experimental days 30 trigrams or paintings (identical for all subjects) were flashed at the 0.2 second rate, with 5 seconds between flashes. Subjects affectively assessed these materials using the control switch, and the experimenter recorded their judgments. The experimenter randomly selected four trigrams or paintings that had been liked on the first and second experimental days and four trigrams or paintings that had been disliked on both days. In addition, four ambivalent trigrams or paintings (e.g., liked on one day, disliked on the other) were randomly selected as material that had been seen before but was not actually to be used in data analysis. The dependent variable was thus the disparity in recognition between liked and disliked materials.

These 12 trigrams or paintings (i.e., 4 reliably liked, 4 reliably disliked, 4 ambivalent) were randomly mixed among 12 other slides of trigrams and paintings that the subject had not confronted previously in the experiment. This list of 24 slides was presented on the third day, and subjects were asked to indicate which trigram or painting they recognized as having been presented before in the experiment. The procedure for judging recognition on the third day was to have subjects place their chin on the rest and fixate the area just above the center dot. The slides were then flashed in this area, directly in the line of vision. Using the same hand as on the first two days, subjects operated the switch to indicate whether they had seen (green light) or not seen (red light) the trigram or painting on the first two days of the experiment. Slide exposure time was again 0.2 second, and presentations were on a 5-second cycle. Direction of moving the bar on the contact switch was also randomized. The experimenter sat in the same location as before.

Results

Two scores were employed in the data analysis. The first was termed the *preference* score, which reflected the number of trigrams or paintings that a subject reliably liked and also those that he or she reliably disliked during the presentation of the 30 slides over the first two experimental days. Hence, the preference score could range from 0 to 30 for both liked content and disliked content. A subject had to reliably rate at least 4 slide presentations as liked and 4 as disliked to continue the recognition phase of the experiment. No subjects were dropped because of this requirement.

The second score enabled us to test the hypotheses. It was based on the subject's third-day performance and hence is termed the *recognition* score. This score could range from 0 to 4, for it reflected the number of trigrams or paintings that a subject reported as having been seen before in the experiment. As with the preference score, there were two values of the recognition score, one for liked materials and one for disliked materials. Both the preference and recognition scores were entered into separate factorial ANOVAS having the properties of a 2 (Sex) × 2 (Trigrams versus Paintings) × 2 (Left versus Right Hemisphere First Exposed to Slides) × 2 (Liked versus Disliked Slides). The first three variables are between subjects and the last variable is within subjects.

Considering the preference scores first, two main effects and no interactions were found. More paintings were reliably rated ($M = 11.21, SD = 3.23$) than trigrams ($M = 8.01, SD = 3.10$) ($F = 62.54, df = 1, 56, p < .01$). Secondly, there were more reliably liked materials (trigrams and paintings combined) found ($M = 10.69, SD = 3.45$) than disliked materials ($M = 8.52, SD = 3.34$) ($F = 10.17, df = 1, 56, p < .01$). No sex differences were found for the preference scores.

Turning to the test of the experimental hypotheses, the factorial ANOVA done on the recognition scores revealed two significant main effects and one second-order interaction. There were no sex differences on the recognition scores. More paintings ($M = 3.04, SD = .90$) than trigrams ($M = 2.42, SD = .81$) were recognized by all subjects ($F = 13.94, df = 1, 56, p < .01$). Also, in support of the first hypothesis, more liked ($M = 3.11, SD = .67$) than disliked ($M = 2.35, SD = .97$) materials (trigrams and pictures combined) were recognized by all subjects ($F = 7.16, df = 1, 56, p < .01$).

The second-order interaction occurred between trigrams vs. paintings, left vs. right hemisphere exposed first, and like vs. dislike ratings ($F = 7.16, df = 1, 56, p < .01$). In support of hypothesis 2, when paintings were presented to the left hemisphere first on days 1 and 2, the recognition scores on day 3 reflected a larger disparity between liked ($M = 3.48, SD = .63$) and disliked ($M = 2.37, SD = 1.09$) paintings than between liked ($M = 2.73, SD = .50$) and disliked ($M = 2.25, SD = .93$) trigrams. Simple effects tests established that the difference between means for paintings in the left hemisphere was significant ($p < .01$), but the difference between means for trigrams was not (N.S.).

Conversely, in support of hypothesis 3, when trigrams were presented to the right hemisphere first on days 1 and 2, the recognition scores on day 3 reflected a larger disparity between liked ($M = 2.87, SD = .72$) and disliked ($M = 1.82, SD = .75$) trigrams than between liked ($M = 3.37, SD = .50$) and disliked ($M = 2.94, SD = .93$) paintings. Simple effects tests found the difference between means for trigrams in the right hemisphere to be significant ($p < .01$), whereas the difference between means for paintings was not (N. S.).

Conclusion

All three experimental hypotheses were validated. These findings clearly support the claim that precedent-sequacious logic plays a role in each hemisphere. Whether we are dealing in perceptions or conceptions, the predicational nature of cognition is readily discernible.

Concluding Comment

Although LLT does not seek to base its tenets on the findings in the *Bios* realm, it is gratifying to observe that there is considerable room here for a complementarity with the *Logos* description of cognition (Rychlak, 1993). Since we find a range of theoretical outlooks among the researchers in the *Bios* realm, such as the conflicting views of Sperry and Gazzaniga, it seems virtually certain that there is always going to be room for the teleologist in this arena. Indeed, an impartial assessment of the circumstances at present would probably conclude that some form of teleology is currently the predominant view in brain functioning. The attitude in perceptual research is probably more evenly divided between mechanism and teleology than are attitudes elswhere. There is this unfortunate tradition in psychology to speak of the "mechanisms" of perception and brain function—indeed, of cognition per se. If we could limit such Newtonian lingo to *Physikos* and *Bios* formulations, and accept complementing telic conceptions in the *Logos*, it would greatly facilitate the advancement of psychology as a discipline (ibid.).

9

Predication in Development: Concepts, Language, Self-Image

A major area of psychological science is dedicated to the study of human development. This concept of a developing organism has been tied historically to physical development, to the capacities that human beings acquire as their bodies mature. As such, the emphasis has been on material/efficient-cause influences in human behavior. In his immensely influential theory, Piaget (1952, 1971, 1978) framed a kind of *evolutionary rationalism* that went beyond the strictly biological to an advanced or higher level of functioning where logical reasoning played an important role. Organisms were said to pass through biological stages in which the maturation of certain capacities enabled behaviors that were not possible at earlier developmental periods. This "stage theory" form of explanation was very important to early developmental theories and dates back to G. Stanley Hall (1906), who was one of the first to introduce this style of theorizing in psychology (see Rychlak, 1982, chap. 3, for a critical analysis of stage theories).

Logical learning theory has no developmental theory to offer, if we mean by this a stage theory. The reason this is so can be seen in the distinction between *vehicular* and *discriminal* theorizing (Rychlak, 1981, pp. 243–248). Logical learning theory is a vehicular formulation, which means that it aims at capturing a process that will explain events regardless of the specific differences in the contents that this process conveys at different periods of maturation. Differences are understood as being due to the different meanings of the contents being formulated by the vehicular process. Traditional learning theories are vehicular in nature, so that the concepts of stimulus, response, reinforcement, and so on, obtain no matter what we are attempting to explain in terms of them. These concepts are the vehicles that carry the explanation of how children learn their first words, delinquents learn to steal automobiles, or nations learn to trust other nations (for an example of the latter, see Osgood, 1962). In like fashion, LLT advances process constructs like telosponsivity via predication, meaning-extension, and so forth, which have relevance to human functioning at all developmental periods.

A discriminal theory is devised to account for differences in behavior per se. It therefore involves a somewhat lower level of abstraction than does a vehicular theory. To theorize discriminally is to look for what makes things different. Why do children in kindergarten behave differently from children in the third grade? This is what stage theory aims to do, and if such an account is based on a *Bios* formulation, then the theory in question must postulate a process that presumably brings about the differences in behavior because it involves capacities that mature and expand over time. It is assumed that human learning alone cannot account for the differences to be seen in a maturing child. Without this fundamental biological maturation, the behavior would be impossible.

Logical learning theory assigns the vast majority of these variations in behavior to learned psychic contents of the telosponsive process. Children in third grade behave differently from children in kindergarten because they have had the opportunity to frame more and varied conceptual contents than the younger children have, contents that affect their so-called level of development. It is not biological maturation but learning that accounts for the difference. This learning of psychic contents takes influence from the social context in which a child is reared (i.e., socioeconomic, cultural, ethnic, etc., differences). Of course, it is foolish to deny any influence on behavior whatsoever from biological maturation. For example, children acquire secondary sex characteristics and consequent sexual urges at certain points in their biological development. They cannot "learn" to have such urges without the biological development taking place.

Logical learning theory does not dismiss such biological realities of the human experience any more than it denies the biological importance of the brain in human cognition (see chap. 8). The question, however, is whether this biological factor accounts for the psychological factors in behavior, such as learning. It makes no difference to LLT when a cognitive capacity develops into a functional unit of behavior—in utero, at infancy, in the early years of life, or during pubescence. The point of importance is that when such functioning is underway, it will reflect the process that LLT claims is fundamental to all human behavior: predication in telosponsivity.

For example, it has been noted that children who are roughly 3 years of age misuse grammatical forms even though they recognize that they are doing so. It is entirely possible that the child says "Mommy goed to the store" because that form is easier to enunciate than "Mommy went to the store." But this maturational influence—if it exists—cannot account for the fact that the child knows he or she is misusing language or expressing this circumstance differently from how an adult would say it (see Bever, 1975; Slobin, 1978). A theory of behavior must take such occurrences into consideration in its explanations. The present chapter is devoted to a review of important developmental themes. The aim here is to see how well the process advocated by LLT meets with the empirical findings on human development.

Predication in Infancy: From Passive to Active Organism

There has been a significant reconceptualization of the newborn infant taking place in psychology from roughly the late 1960s onward. Previously, traditional learning theories had painted the newborn as a passively manipulated, tabula rasa type of organism, but as developmental researchers began to take an interest in the exploratory behavior of the infant, the picture began to change. The young child was gradually understood as an organism actively searching for cognitive control of the environment rather than passively being shaped by the environment (see, e.g., Berlyne, 1966). Of course, it was recognized that such efforts to learn the environment require maturing physical capacities like crawling, walking, and so forth. There was also the child's sense of confidence gained from an *attachment* to the mother while exploring the environment (Bowlby, 1969; Rheingold & Eckerman, 1969). Bruner's (1973) studies on the attainment of *competence* did much to advance the image of an active human organism. Bruner also began to use the term *intention* (ibid., p. 1) in his description of how competence was attained (see also Kalnins & Bruner, 1973). This led to a number of research studies on intention; unfortunately, the theoretical account of such intentional actions invariably dissolves into typical mediational theorizing. But at least there was now an opening for an alternative, teleological description of such experimental designs. As we shall see, the findings of these studies have been a boon to LLT.

In this section of the chapter I pose a series of questions aimed at putting the assumptions of LLT to work in explaining the burgeoning findings on infant and early childhood behavior. Infancy (the first year of life) is a crucial period in any theory of human learning. As has been noted previously in this volume, the difference between LLT and other learning theories must be seen in the way that they explain events beginning right from birth—or whenever it can be said that cognition gets underway (i.e., presumably there could be intrauterine manifestations of this process). Traditional mediational theories view the newborn as a tabula rasa, as taking in externally patterned influences. Such theories assign behaviors that LLT takes to be natively teleological (e.g., intentional selections and evaluations) to past or earlier learning as it was shaped by this process of input and mediation. Language plays a major role in such mediational theorizing, and I will look at the study of language in the next section of this chapter; for now, there are a series of questions that can be posed regarding how well LLT measures up to the empirical findings on infants and children.

Are Infants Tabula Rasa or Natively Intentional Learners?

One does not have to read very deeply into the literature on infancy and children for the tabula rasa bubble to burst. The orientation capacity of newborn infants, which lets them adjust themselves to their environment at the outset of life, clearly indicates an intentional learning process. Thus, shortly after birth infants are seen turning their heads relative to (for the sake of) a voice. Breast-fed infants turn toward the voice, since that is where they find their nourishment, and bottle-fed infants turn away from it, since that is the direction from which their nourishment originates (Alegria & Noirot, 1978). This orienting effort occurs much too early in life to be attributed to shaping. This phenomenon suggests a natively framed understanding-intention leading to an action-intention. In the first few days of life infants reflect an unlearned defensive pattern (head retraction, blinking, etc.) when an object approaches their face (Bower, Broughton, & Moore, 1971). In the first few weeks of life they can reach toward and sometimes grasp objects on which they have fixated visually (Butterworth, 1978); more importantly, when they are capable of bringing an object to their mouth, infants open their mouths *before* it arrives (Butterworth & Hopkins, 1988). This suggests a coordinated action-intention (see also Bower, Broughton, & Moore, 1970).

In a remarkable series of experiments, infants in the first weeks of life (Meltzoff & Moore, 1977) or even in the first hour of life (Bower, 1989, p. 31) have been observed imitating the facial actions of an adult model (e.g., their mother). Mouth openings and tongue or lip protrusions by the adult are matched by the infant. Studying babies as young as 3 days old, Bower (1989) had them look at a film depicting a face with 15 small light points arranged on an adult's face (mouth, chin, eyes). The adult was photographed in a dark environment with only these points of light illuminated. All the child could see in the film was a pattern of 15 lights moving about to create images similar to a facial expression (a mouth opening, etc.). Even in this circumstance, the infants were found to imitate the facially organized light movements.

In an equally fascinating series of studies, it has been demonstrated that twelve-month-old children who are shown slides of other children of both sexes are prone to look predominantly at those of their own sex (Lewis & Brooks, 1975). Little boys look more at little boys than at little girls, and vice versa. This visual preference continues if we videotape the actions of children who are dressed in a cross-sex fashion. Aitken (1977) videotaped a boy model dressed in frilly attire and holding a doll, as well as a little girl dressed in dungarees and banging a drum. Even so, the 1-year-old subjects continued to look at their inappropriately attired same-sexed model. If 12 lights are attached to the joints of the models (one at each shoulder, elbow, wrist, hip, knee, and ankle joint), and then videotapes are taken of the models walking about against a dark background with only the lights visible, the sexual identity preference continues (Johansson, 1973).

Based on such findings, Bower (1989) argues that the fundamental consideration for the newborn is movement: "The baby can see the movement of another and *feel* the movements of his own face" (pp. 31, 32; emphasis in the original). This also holds for identification with the movements of same-sexed models. Bower suggests that in this latter instance, "babies are aware of their own pattern of movement. Presumably they are directly aware of their own patterning through information from joint receptors" (ibid., p. 132). And in what the LLT advocate would consider an allusion to tautological meaning-extension, Bower next suggests that "the source of the preference [for same-sex observation] . . . was the mapping of a pattern known via joint information onto a similar pattern fed in through the eyes" (ibid., p. 138). Thus, whether the child is imitating a facial motion or looking at a bodily motion that is somehow familiar, the principle of explanation here seems to be a tautological extension from the known (my pattern) to the knowable (someone I see like me) rather than input or external stimulation. Although Bower falls prey to mediational theorizing (ibid., p. 151), his findings and theoretical suggestions are readily subsumed by LLT.

Additional evidence for intentional learning in infancy stems from a series of studies in which infants were allowed to control the appearance of an interesting visual display or sound. This work has frequently been explained as operant conditioning. I reviewed some of the shortcomings of conditioning theory in chapter 5; at this point it should merely be noted that there are just as many questions about the validity of conditioning in explaining infant behavior as there are about its validity in explaining adult behavior (see Sameroff & Cavanagh, 1979; Cameron & Rychlak, 1985, pp. 33–41). Infants seem to have remarkable control over the learning process, so much so that one wonders whether external stimuli and reinforcers are controlling the newborn or whether the opposite might not be the case. Papoušek (1969) has opined that the infant in a so-called operant conditioning situation is actually formulating and testing hypotheses. This is the view of LLT as well, for *hypotheses* encompass predications as suggested premises that might or might not extend meaningful understanding. The cash value of a hypothesis is still in doubt.

In the studies now under consideration, a recording instrument was attached to a rubber nipple. This instrument can record the infant's sucking rate, which in turn can be related to some independent measure such as the slide projection of a cartoon, a human face on a screen, or the activated recording of a voice or tune. Sucking rate was found to vary as a function of the screen flashings: Infants as young as 3 weeks of age were found to increase their sucking rates to maintain the slides' appearance (Siqueland & DeLucia, 1969; DeCasper & Fifer, 1980). In fact, infants will even raise their sucking rate to effect a better focusing of a projected picture (Kalnins & Bruner, 1973). During the first four weeks of life, infants will selectively suck to bring forth a recording of their mother's voice (Mehler, Bertoncini, Barriere, & Jassik-Gerschenfeld, 1978). Three-day-old infants were observed to increase their sucking rate to turn on a recording of someone singing; moreover, they became upset when their efforts were thwarted (DeCasper & Carstens, 1981). It is difficult to think of such actions as shapings from external sources. This type of behavior is what people mean when they speak of the human will. Telosponsivity can subsume this notion without sacrificing scientific rigor.

Sucking is not the only manifestation of such intentional behavior. Infants have had cuffs attached to their wrists or ankles, which in turn were connected to items of potential interest. Moving a limb activated the item in question. In an apparatus of this sort, infants 10 to 16 weeks of age learned to manipulate the movements of a crib mobile with their foot kicks; once again, they became distressed when their kicking failed to enliven the mobile (Mast, Fagen, Rovee-Collier, & Sullivan, 1980). Bower (1989, pp. 58–69) reports similar findings using a procedure in which infants broke an electronic beam with their foot. Infants as young as 8 weeks of age learned to pull their arms to activate a color slide of a smiling infant (Lewis, Sullivan, & Brooks-Gunn, 1985). Facial study of these subjects established that they were happy when pulling led to slide projection and unhappy when it did not. Indeed, when the flashes of a smiling infant were discontinued, arm pulling increased by 376%. Controls showed no such effects. This certainly suggests both understanding- and action-intentionality to the LLT advocate.

Such native organizational capacities in the infant's cognitive processing are sometimes far beyond what Piagetian theory led us to expect. In a study on musical phrase structure, infants 4 and 6 months of age sat on their mother's lap and were free to turn their head in the direction of one or the other of two loudspeakers. When the infant turned to one, the other loudspeaker was turned off. One of these loudspeakers played musical passages with segmental organization, whereas the other did not. As is true of adults, the infants at both age levels listened significantly more often to the appropriately segmented music (Krumhansl & Jusczyk, 1990). When two movie films were presented along with a soundtrack that was appropriate for only one of them, 4-month-old infants were seen to attend to the film that co-ordinated with the soundtrack (Bahrick, Walker, & Neisser, 1981). Michotte's (1963) procedure for studying causation has been adapted to the study of infants. Infants who are 30 weeks old can perceive two temporally ordered movements combining into a launching effect (Leslie, 1984). If we disrupt an 8-month-old child's understanding of cause and effect, he or she will in-variably show surprise (Frye & Moore, 1991, p. 24).

Studies of infants playing with adults have also provided evidence of in-fant intentionality. Thus, in a turn-taking game with 12-month-olds as sub-jects, if an adult delays taking a turn for 10 seconds, the child looks back and forth from adult to toy, makes truncated motions to take a turn, holds up his or her hands as a sign to continue, and so on (Ross & Kay, 1980). There is evidence that children younger than 9 months are incapable of such co-operative and coordinated play with an adult (Trevarthen & Hubley, 1979), but the point remains that the very same intentional capacity seen in in-fant behavior before 9 months is part and parcel of this capacity to arrange circumstances in a give-and-take manner at 9 months. This anticipatory ca-pacity continues to influence the child's behavior over the early years of life. It is ever clearer that infants learn more according to such pro forma inten-tions and expectations than they do according to tabula rasa inputs.

Is There Evidence for Childhood Predication?

Up until the 1960s most developmental psychologists were working under the Piagetian assumption that children could not categorize (predicate, in LLT terms) experience until they had reached the stage of concrete opera-tions (roughly 5 to 7 years; see Gelman, 1978). Studies then began appearing that challenged Piaget. For example, Ricciuti (1965) reported that 1-year-olds could categorize various toys into groupings such as "balls" and "babies." Nelson (1974a) subsequently replicated these findings on 20-month-olds. Categories such as these have been termed "basic-level" categories because they refer to the macroscopic level of description whereby a perceptual refer-ent is fairly uniform (e.g., dogs, chairs) (after Rosch, Mervis, Gray, Johnson, & Boyes-Braem, 1976). In linguistic terms, basic-level categories are those that adults use to name objects. Superordinate categories become increas-ingly general and complex (e.g., animals, furniture). Subordinate categories are specific and complex (e.g., small dogs, rocking chairs). It is an empirically established truism that children learn basic-level categories first.

An interesting procedure was devised for testing whether preverbal in-fants were categorizing experience. This experimental design capitalizes on the fact that infants tend to prefer novel over familiar visual stimuli (Cohen

& Gelber, 1975; Fantz & Yeh, 1979)—a finding, incidentally, that lends support to the LLT principle of meaning-extension. A typical experiment of this type might involve giving infants several familiarization trials with pictured items from a specific category (e.g., faces) followed by either a novel member of this category (a new face), a novel member of a different category (an animal from an unfamiliar animals category), or both at once. The expectation is that the infant will spend more time looking at the novel picture of the unfamiliar novel category (animal) than at the novel picture of the familiar category (face). We might think of the infant as reasoning, "Oh, here is another one of those that I have seen before. But over there is something new/different!" Using a format of this type, it was shown that 30-week-old infants could form the categories "female face" (Cohen & Strauss, 1979) and "stuffed animal" (Cohen & Caputo, 1975).

Other designs have also been used to prove that infants and children in the second year of life do indeed cognize through the formation of categories (e.g., Strauss, 1979; Sherman, 1985). Of course, such findings are not explained in terms of a predicational model, but LLT is surely not injured by the fact that very young children are seen framing their cognitions according to wider realms of meaning, within which variations on the theme framed are reliably recognized.

The childhood experience is one of actively exploring the environment. It has been reported that about 90% of the waking hours of 1- to 3-year-olds is spent in self-initiated nonsocial efforts; about 50% of their time is spent in exploring, seeking information, and gaining mastery of the environment (White, Kaban, Shapiro, & Attanucci, 1977). If we track the developing child from roughly 8 to 18 months of age, we find that initially a category is formed based on physical properties (e.g., all items that look like a pacifier). In short order, however, the functional utility of items subsumable by the category (e.g., sucking of pacifiers) is added, and those which do not conform are rejected (Benelli, D'Odorico, Levorato, & Simion, 1977; Mervis, 1985). This empirically observed sequence is entirely in line with my discussion in chapter 2 of tautology, analogy, and disanalogy in early learning. There is evidence that as children mature, their attention becomes less stimulus controlled and more intentionally controlled as they direct their actions according to interests, affective assessments, and the like (Lane, 1979).

Piaget (1929) found that children under 10 years of age predicate physical phenomena anthropomorphically, assigning intentions to inanimate objects. For example, a 6-year-old might claim that the sun is hot because it wants to keep people warm. Younger children believe that cars, clocks, bicycles, and the wind all know where they are and that they can feel a pin prick. Piaget referred to this anthropomorphic predication as *childhood animism*, which is readily understood as tautological meaning-extension from the personally known self to the inanimate object. The parent does not have to teach or model such inferences for the child to frame them. Logical learning theory views such findings as evidence that the human being is natively teleological in cognitive outlook.

Piaget concluded that mechanical causality becomes distinguished from intentional causality only late in the first decade of life. Investigators have since brought Piaget's claims into question. It has been found that preschool children do not lack an appreciation of mechanical causation. These children can interpret events in terms of physical forces, as in knocking things over and so on (Bullock, Gelman, & Baillargeon, 1982; Shultz, 1982). The view now is suggested that children may, at least occasionally, actually choose to predicate inanimate events anthropomorphically rather than mechanically because it is highly meaningful and hence easy to do so, just as adults explain such functions as computer processing in anthropomorphic terms ("The computer doesn't allow that to happen," etc.).

During the second year of life, most children spontaneously begin categorizing objects without instructions from parents to do so. Kagan (1981) has referred to this as a "basic process," one that is not shaped or modeled for the child (pp. 88, 89). There appear to be two major themes reflected in early categorizations. Children 6 or 7 years old will place objects into *taxonomic* categories, such as putting all vehicles (cars, coasters, trains, etc.) together in a sorting task. Younger children sort on a *thematic* basis, such as putting a man and a car together as a category because the former drives the latter (Markman, 1989, p. 21). Here again, as in the case of anthropomorphic causation, it has been found that 4-year-olds knew the principle behind taxonomic categorizations, yet they apparently preferred to continue sorting objects on the grounds of a thematic category (Smiley & Brown, 1979). I shall return to this topic of category formation when I take up language formation.

The general pattern of taxonomic predicational development seems to be for the child to extend through direct comparison from the known to the unknown, just as LLT's principle of meaning-extension suggests. Thus, a pre-school child will decide whether an object in experience belongs to an animal category by comparing it to a person-exemplar. In time, and age 10 does seem to creep up quite often as the critical point in development, the maturing child will define a distinctive category that can stand apart from these earlier exemplars (see Carey, 1985). By this time, of course, the child has learned that all animals eat, breathe, have "babies," and so on. The similarities and differences have doubtless been worked out between plants, cars, dogs, and cows.

This reference to similarities and differences suggests that generic oppositionality is at play in childhood learning, which of course (according to

LLT) it must be, because it is an intrinsic aspect of predication. But there is even more obvious evidence of delimiting oppositionality in the learning of children. Kagan (1984) has observed that the 2-year-old child not only formulates categories but is "disposed to invent their complement" (p. 189), by which he means the opposite meaning, as in delimiting *down* following *up* and *low* following *high* (Kagan here follows a Boolean characterization of opposition). Children as young as two or three years old know the oppositional orientation of "front-back" even before they have learned the words *front* and *back* (Levine & Carey, 1982). Children of this age also employ deception, including the telling of lies, which reflects their capacity to delimit experience in terms of truth and falsehood (Chandler, Fritz, & Hala, 1989).

Children at 6 years make category mistakes based on negation. If the experimenter asks children who know the color red to select one of two trays—either a wooden red tray, or a chromium olive green tray—and does so by saying "Bring me the chromium tray; not the red one, the chromium one," these children will learn that the color of the nonred tray is chromium (Carey, 1978). I mentioned this study in chapter 4 because it is very much in line with LLT's interpetation of implication. By age 10 children know that it is easier to learn a series of words that can be arrayed oppositionally than a series that cannot be (Kreutzer, Leonard, & Flavell, 1975). In a true sense, the categories of "things/people/actions I like" and "things/people/actions I dislike" may be seen as categorical organizations. I have termed this phenomenon affective assessment, but surely it can be seen now that when elementary school children primarily enact the behaviors of a model that they like, they are manifesting a delimiting oppositionality in their ongoing behavior (Slife & Rychlak, 1982).

How Well do the Findings on Adult Memory Apply to Children?

Since LLT is vehicular in formulation, so that the person is thought of as a telosponder from the outset of cognitive life, it follows that we should see roughly the same findings on children's memory that we observed for memory in adulthood. Is this the case? There is ample evidence that memory improves steadily over childhood (Kail, 1990), but of what does this improvement consist? Interestingly, the same shift from frequency to categorical organization in adult memory that I reviewed in chapter 5 holds true for modern theories of childhood memory. At the middle of the present century, explanations of learning and memory in childhood were exclusively of the tabula rasa variety. Children were believed to pass through biological stages that predetermined their memorial capacity or were conceived as passive receptacles for external inputs. In response to the findings of many studies on children, this theoretical image of organismic passivity has gradually changed to that of an actively conceptualizing organism that produces the categorical organization leading to its memory stores. Even so, and in line with research on adult memory, information processing has emerged in the study of childhood memory as the "most influential theoretical perspective" (Schneider & Pressley, 1989, p. 20).

There is a direct parallel between the research findings on children and adults. The more tightly organized and clearly patterned the child's initial predication of an item or topic to be retained in memory is, the better the chances are that such contents will indeed be recalled. Thus, if the attention of a 1-year-old or even slightly younger infant is gained, and an experimenter then models a pattern of behavior with a toy just once, the infant can reproduce this patterned action 24 hours later (Squire, Knowlton, & Musen, 1993, p. 465). Two- and 3-year-olds in item-recognition studies are seen using rudimentary mnemonics, like touching an item (e.g., a cup) that they are supposed to remember before leaving a room (DeLoache, Cassidy, & Brown, 1985; Wellman, Ritter, & Flavell, 1975). This "touched/not touched" predication (reflecting delimiting oppositionality) facilitated subsequent recognition of items in the room. Based on the study of story grammars, it has been suggested that children as young as 2 years old may organize their memories according to *scripts* fashioned about their daily activities (Mandler, 1982).

Given toys that can be sorted according to either taxonomic (animals, utensils, etc.) or color (red, blue, etc.) predications, 4- and 6-year-olds who were instructed to play with the toys and also to try to remember them have been compared to children of the same age who were instructed to sort the toys and also to try to remember them (Sodian, Schneider, & Perlmutter, 1986). The 4-year-olds recalled more toys when they had sorted these items than when they had simply played with them. There was more clustering in recall for the taxonomic than for the color categories. Taxonomic classification is more efficient than color classification (which cuts across natural distinctions like animal vs. utensil). There were more such taxonomic clusters for the older children, who reflected better memory on the task than their younger counterparts did. This finding, that children use more categorization strategies and better categories as they mature, has been demonstrated in many studies of memory covering ages 7 to 12 years (e.g., Kreutzer, Leonard, & Flavell, 1975; Melkman & Deutsch, 1977; Moynahan, 1973; Schneider, 1986). The children's growing reliance on heuristics is obvious here. An interesting demonstration of the powerful role played by organization is to be seen in the fact that elementary school children who are expert chess players have been found to recall the placements of chess pieces on the board better than adults, although in a digit span task the adults outperformed the children (Chi, 1978).

According to LLT, a rehearsal or practice trial is legitimate only if the person is intentionally affirming the relevant meaning in the task confronted and bringing it forward into ongoing behavior (i.e., telosponding). There has to be some meaning affirmation or no learning will eventuate. As research demonstrates, unintended learning is possible, such as in incidental learning. Unintended learning is not very efficient, of course, but as long as there is some organization at the initiation of a task, there will be some retention—at least for a brief period. For the longer-lasting outcome, however, the person must have framed a reliably clear and stable organization of meaning capable of serving as a framing *memory cue* for some time. Logical learning theory holds that a memory cue works in recall because it takes on the role of a predication. The closer a memory cue can approximate a relevant predication for the target to be recalled, the better it will serve as a memory prompt (see Demonstration Experiments 5 and 6).

Consistent with this line of theorizing, it has been found that preschoolers who are good at remembering things intentionally exert effort to recall them by using, among other strategies, such mnemonic devices as visually examining potential targets and determining what they look like or could be (Galbraith, Olsen, Duerden, & Harris, 1982; Baker-Ward, Ornstein, & Holden, 1984). It is possible to teach first graders to use heuristic strategies such as these, which in turn facilitate memory (Moely, Olson, Halwes, & Flavell, 1969). Effective rehearsal appears to involve choosing and assembling such cognitive organizers, a skill that increases in complexity with age. For example, in a word-recall task, third graders put few words together, whereas sixth and eighth graders combine several words to aid memory (Ornstein, Naus, & Liberty, 1975). Here again, an unintentional contribution to memory is to be seen in the fact that when the words were blocked (organized by listing words in a given taxonomic category together), the third graders' recall was improved. Children who have been instructed in rehearsal will sometimes be seen to reject this effort if left to their own devices (Keeney, Cannizzo, & Flavell, 1967).

It is difficult to prove that children rehearsing in rote-memory fashion have absolutely no organization in their remembrances. Linear order is itself an organization. Frequency of rehearsal definitely promotes good memory, but this practice must be conducted in a certain manner if it is to be maximally helpful. The evidence suggests that children ranging in age from 2 to 12 years who intentionally make the effort to rehearse and who select appropriate organizers demonstrate good memory (Schneider & Pressley, 1989).

This finding obtains over and above any evidence suggesting that memory may receive a contribution from physical maturation or fortuitously organized material per se.

Preschoolers asked to recall or recognize the contents of pictures reflect greater recognition than recall of picture contents (Perlmutter, 1984; Perlmutter & Myers, 1979). This is a consistent finding at all ages up to and including adulthood. In chapter 5 I offered an LLT explanation for this phenomenon having to do with the fact that in recognition, the task is at least partially predicated for the subject, whereas in recall, a predicating organization is left entirely up to the subject. Giving preschoolers a category cue relevant to the items under memorization (e.g., cueing with the word *animal* when a child is trying to recall seeing a picture of a bear) facilitates memory, which is another finding that also holds for adults (Morrison & Lord, 1982). Elementary school children soon learn that the presence of several members of a given category in a learning task makes the task easier to accomplish (Moynahan, 1976; Tenney, 1975). Clustering is then likely to appear in a child's free-recall lists.

Do Infants and Children Affectively Assess Their Experience?

In Chapter 5 I introduced the concept of a prememory to capture the LLT view that human reasoning is assumptive. Cognition functions from framing meanings to targeted items in ongoing experience according to the principle of meaning-extension. Prememories are not subject to recall or recognition unless they become the targets of a transcendent self-examination, as when we explore our deeper assumptions concerning some topic of interest. Once the person has learned how to read, there is no need to remember the meanings of letters, words, and paragraphs before recalling what these lexical ingredients conveyed in yesterday's newspaper. Memory is required to remember yesterday's news, for it was a target, something to learn about, but the letters and words used to convey yesterday's news story were an aspect of patterned predication—they were the known making the knowable possible.

In chapter 2 I argued that at the outset of learning, the infant predicates a target of itself—as in the tautological extension, "a nipple is a nipple." With this identity established, the nipple is then employed as a (known) predicate—learning has taken place—and the infant goes forward through analogical extensions of this predicate meaning to learn more and more about this "nipplelike world" (much of which is then found to be not nipplelike). "Nippleness" now functions as a prememory in the infant's ongoing cognitions (e.g., "This thing here has more nippleness than that thing"). Of course, many other items in experience are also initially framed as tautological identities and then subsequently extended as predications (mother's face and behavioral pattern, texture of a blanket, foodstuffs, etc.). Recall that such predications also function analogically. We cannot overlook the remarkable findings discussed above concerning tautological identities between mouth openings, the visual identification of a same-sex infant, and so forth. The concept of precedent-sequacious meaning-extension is not strained by such empirical findings.

As a Kantian formulation, LLT challenges the traditional Lockean learning theories of psychology that have held that the newborn person begins life with certain reflexive capacities but is otherwise cognitively a tabula rasa. There is no need for prememorial influences in a tabula rasa cognitive process, which takes in external influences passively. As I have noted several times in this volume, this is a fundamental point separating LLT from its opponent theories, many of which claim that the organism interacts with the environment, presumably from the outset of life (see, e.g., Bandura, 1986, pp. 23, 24). If there is such interaction with the environment at birth, what is the unique contribution of the newborn to this two-way street?

An answer might be that the native reflexive (hard-wired) physical equipment of the newborn works to interact with the external stimuli—as in the apparatus of perception. This physical equipment interacts with the externally perceived environmental influences. This is not a very satisfying answer, because no theory denies that such innate physical processes occur at birth. The challenge is to delineate a cognitive process enabling the person to make a difference here, to actively and freely influence what is attended to perceptually in the first place rather than act as a conduit for influences originating over time in the external environment. A mechanical process that works at the dawning of life is still a tabula rasa process. I have found that, if pressed, the traditionalist inevitably falls back on the suggestion that there is an initial input from experience, and in time such cumulating inputs serve mediating roles to influence ongoing learning in what is then an interactive manner. There is no real cognitive interaction being postulated in such accounts at the initiating moment of cognitive life. Kant felt that he had to postulate (actually, he believed that he had deduced) the categories of the understanding to account for such "person-environment" interactions occurring in the first moment of life, when the initial cognitive organizations (representations) were already underway. We might say that the categories were Kant's unlearned "prememory conceptions" functioning to organize life experience at its inception. Since LLT does not follow Kant here, is there some other native capacity that the person has available to effect these earliest of all cognitive organizations?

The answer is yes. The capacity for affective assessment is taken as an unlearned capacity to evaluate, by way of delimiting oppositionality, any contents that are being targeted by generic oppositionality. If we now combine generic and delimiting oppositionality, we have formulated a truly Kantian image of the cognitive process. Ideas here are both formulators and evaluators of life experience. In this sense, affection is the first prememory, for it provides the same organizing background that subsequent prememories will make possible. An interesting question is whether positive (liking) or negative (disliking) is the predominate affective quality at the outset of life. Some psychologists (e.g., Rankians) would probably hold that the birth trauma argues for a heavily negative evaluation first, delimiting in turn the positive aspects of life to follow. Logical learning theory leaves this "chicken-and-egg" question open, since it is plausible to believe that either affective emphasis might be given to lived experience at its inception. The main point is that LLT does not claim that such value estimates at life's outset are biologically determined or externally shaped into existence. The infant qua affective assessor renders the evaluations given to all relevant circumstances under targeting in the life context.

How does one prove that a newborn infant is already making affective assessments? Well, we know that newborn infants display distinct and stable visual preferences (Banks & Salapatek, 1983). At 10 weeks of age infants smile at an approaching face, and at 12 weeks they smile differentially at a familiar versus an unfamiliar face (Izard, 1978). By 3 months of age they selectively scan and focus and discriminate among colors, features of figures or objects, and different organizations of features (Cohen, DeLoache, & Strauss, 1979). I have already noted that infants like to observe novel stimuli. If we have a 3-month-old look at an orange ball moving up and down on a pulley mounted against a black background, the child will watch it move with obvious interest. If this process is repeated a day later, however, this infant will give indications of boredom and look away (Super, 1972). Note the suggestion here of the principle of meaning-extension, as well as of affective assessment. Infants extend their (meaningful) affective preferences away from that to which they have already lent such meaning (i.e., the ball) in favor of other possibilities yet to be assessed in their experience.

As I have stated previously, we do not learn to render affective preferences. We render such preferences in order to learn by way of framing meaningful organizations, including significant discriminators. Affective assessments of external stimuli can also be reversed, from positive to negative or vice versa, depending on the child's understanding of or participation in the ongoing events of life. For example, having a personal sense of control can be grounds for a positive affection. Thus, a 6-month-old child might become frightened by a mechanical toy that is activated by a parent yet show signs of pleasure when he or she is given the opportunity to activate the toy (Gunnar-vonGnechten, 1978).

There are many indications of affective assessment functioning throughout childhood. Preschool children with a positive affective approach to life are observed helping their peers more often than children with a negative affective outlook (Strayer, 1980). Preschoolers have been shown to imitate only those televised behaviors of a model that they affectively prefer (Slife & Rychlak, 1982). Elementary school children give more detail to pictures they draw of a liked peer than they give to pictures they draw of a disliked peer (Lott & Lott, 1970). They also remember first names that they like more readily than first names they dislike (Rychlak & Saluri, 1973).

A cross-sectional study aimed at testing the developmental influence of affective assessment on recognition studied 169 children across the first six grades of two elementary schools (Rychlak, 1975a). The hypothesis here was that the reliance on affective assessment would be *greater* in the earlier than in the later grade levels—which is precisely the opposite of what a theory claiming that affective assessment is a learned phenomenon would predict. For learnable items we used abstract designs and paintings randomly projected onto a screen. The children then rated them according to the standard like/dislike procedure discussed in chapter 7. The material was then presented a second time in a different randomized order. The task for the children was to recognize those designs and paintings that they had seen earlier. As predicted, children at all grade levels recognized more of their liked material than their disliked material. However, and also as predicted by LLT, a significant statistical interaction between measures of grade level and affective recognition established that first graders had a *larger* preference for liked over disliked materials than did the children in any of the higher grades.

The answer to the question posed for this section is surely in the affirmative. Affective assessment is, in effect, a prememorial capacity enabling children to organize and pattern experience from birth. What is more, it continues to influence learning throughout life.

Language Learning and Development

The Structure and Function of Language

From the LLT perspective, language is the product of a predicating intelligence. Language terms (words, labels, concepts, etc.) are contents of this predicating process that are used instrumentally to convey intentions and expand the realm of what is known. The process relies on generic oppositionality, and language relies on delimiting oppositionality to organize the word meanings (contents) employed by this process. Logical learning theory follows Vygotsky's (1986) discoveries and analysis of a thinking process underlying language. People who have been profoundly deaf from earliest childhood and who have not learned a language can still perform complex thought processes (Furth, 1966). They obviously think without the benefit of previously "input" words, whether this is due to relying on the right brain hemisphere or whatever (see chap. 8).

If we look at the basic structure of extant language systems, we find evidence for the predicational nature of language. Ultan (1969) has examined the basic alignment of the subject (s), verb (v), and object (o) in the known natural language systems of this earth. Of the six possible combinations of s, v, and o, only four have actually been used in natural language systems as the basic linguistic structure (i.e., we are not considering the possibility of rephrasing basic structures in idiosyncratic ways, which is always possible). The percentages of natural languages employing these word orderings in their basic expressions are as follows: sov = 44%, svo = 35%, vso = 19%, vos = 2%, ovs = 0%, and osv = 0%.

Note that in 79% of the cases the sentence begins with the subject (target), and in 98% of the cases the object lies to the right or follows the subject. These findings are highly consistent with LLT. The main evidence for a predicational process would be if the subject takes meaning from the context established by the verb plus the object (i.e., the complete predicate). The object is especially important, because even when the verb is expressed before the subject, a sense of logical order is retained as long as the subject appears before the object. A sentence in this sense is much like any premise, where the consequent (e.g., mortality) predicates the antecedent (humankind), as in "All humans are mortal."

We expect the object to serve as the wider referent, the larger Euler circle, and the subject to serve as the narrower, smaller circle. The fact that no known language system begins its fundamental linguistic formulation with an object is telling evidence against the traditional view of an association of ideas. It seems evident that although ideas might be associated in willy-nilly, chance occurrences, when the person intends to express a meaning in any language, the alignment of words in that idea expression follows what we know about premising qua predication. That is, this alignment is followed in all but 2% of languages.

Linguists have frequently acknowledged the important role that oppositionality plays in linguistic structure and function. Trier (1931) essentially defined delimiting oppositionality when he observed that every antonymic word that is uttered implicitly suggests its opposite meaning to both the speaker and hearer. Lyons (1977) has said that "opposition is one of the most important principles governing the structure of language" (p. 271), and Richards (1967) has singled out opposition as one of the essential principles through which language works (p. 10).

Intention in Early Language Development

Logical learning theory's view of infants as purposive organisms that use language instrumentally to express what they intend to do, learn about, share, and so on, is very compatible with the empirical evidence. Infants who are 3 months old have been found capable of integrating two sounds with different sources and locations to form a coherent speech percept—a patterning that is a required preliminary to predication in verbal communication (Eimas & Miller, 1992). Developmental study of infants suggests that their first communicative gestures begin in pointing efforts ("Look at X" or "Tell me about X") and in reaching efforts with some desire in mind ("Give me X" or "Let me touch X") (Clark & Clark, 1977, p. 313). Harding (1982) reports that 6- to 9-month-olds reflected an intention to communicate. Mediational theorizing would have it that children input words from parents and others in their immediate (i.e., contiguous) environment based on the frequency of such word occurrences, yet Brown (1973) found through tape-recorded comparisons of parents and their preschool children that there was virtually no relationship between the order in which these children acquired 14 morphemes (a, the, be, etc.) and the frequency with which the parents used these morphemes in their everyday speech. McNeill (1968) found similar results in a study of Japanese children's use of linguistic expressions unique to that culture. There is no evidence for linguistic shaping sans intentionality in such findings.

First words are introduced in combination with reaching gestures as an additional instrumentality the child uses to fulfill an intention (Greenfield & Smith, 1976). I noted earlier in this chapter how children of 1 to 2 years prefer thematic over taxonomic categorizations. This suggests that the initial word used by a child would probably not be of the taxonomic variety. The child wants to reach a cup and uses the word *cup* thematically, as an aspect of this motion—reaching with the intention to drink. However, there is evidence that when the child conceives of early words as names for things in experience having other exemplars, this very naming biases the child to begin framing taxonomic categorizations. Thus, Markman and Hutchinson (1984) found that when children were asked to group pictures together, they were more likely to categorize according to taxonomy than to a thematic formulation when the targeted item (comparison stimulus) was first given a name. For example, if a child of 2 or 3 years is presented with the target picture of a poodle and then is shown two other pictures, one of a German shepherd and the other of dog food (e.g., a bone), the child who is asked simply to select which of the latter two pictures is the same as the target will be found to select the shepherd 58% of the time. This percentage does not exceed chance. Dog and bone are categorized thematically by 42% of the children. On the other hand, if the child is told that—in a certain foreign language— the targeted poodle is called a "sud" and is then asked to find a picture that is the same as the target, 83% of the children select the German shepherd. This percentage exceeds chance.

The LLT interpretation of this finding is that the child who is given a word by the experimenter naming the poodle is thereby given a specific predication for the task that is not likely to be of the child's spontaneous preference. The child is interested in what animals do—they eat bones—not what category of the animal kingdom they fall into. Given the name *sud*, however, the child is logically forced to extend meanings from already known characteristics like four-legged, furry things to the targeted word *sud* in precedent-sequacious fashion. Once this affirmation occurs, the targeted word *sud* is known and, according to the additional instructions to find a picture that is the same as a sud, acts as a predicate for the cognition to follow (see Nelson, Rescorla, Gruendel, & Benedict, 1978, who recognize that early words can function as such predicates). Recall that LLT defines learning as the person's use of a former target as a predicate. The task has shifted for the child to one in which using the known word *sud* as a predicate logically demands that the German shepherd be selected, not the dog food (which is not a *sud*). Hence, the child is prevented from framing a thematic categorization by having to meet the taxonomically biasing instructions of the experimenter. Recall from chapter 4 that the *Aufgabe* always influences a subject's *Einstellung* in this fashion.

Expression of intentions is also to be seen in the child's initial two-word sentences, which are predominantly thematic in content. Cross-cultural research has shown that in forming two-word sentences, children in various linguistic environments (including English, Swedish, Hebrew, Samoan, and Finnish) spontaneously pick out a formula to make their intentions known (Braine, 1976). For instance, some children will name the object of interest and its location in that order ("Baby chair," or "Daddy car"), whereas others may take the opposite tack ("Here book," or "Bed Mommy"). The particular order selected reflects what the child is intending to emphasize, either the location or the object being located. In time, of course, cultural expectations come in to align words according to the reigning linguistic climate. Children will also change the order in which they typically express their two-word sentences (Wiemen, 1976), but their intended meaning is still clear when they do this. Findings such as these are highly consistent with the LLT view of an innate capacity to create meaningful expressions within the *Logos* from the very outset of verbal experience.

Research in psycholinguistics has been steadily moving away from the older word-to-word associations to a sentence-based view of cognition in which syntax and context play major roles. Theorizing has progressively become more top-down, viewing comprehension as moving from context to specifically focused linguistic expression, rather than bottom-up, viewing comprehension as moving in sequential stages from lower-level units to integration with a broader context (see Danks & Glucksberg, 1980, p. 410). I interpret this development as an emphasis on formal causation taking over the previous emphasis on efficient causation in the associations of letters in words and words to words. Logical learning theory is right in step with this Kantian development.

I noted above in the discussion of categorization that Kagan (1981) has referred to the child's framing of categorizations in the second year as an un-learned, basic cognitive process (pp. 88, 89). He has also noted that as the child creates categories, he or she is "disposed to invent their complement" (Kagan, 1984, p. 189). Although Kagan is using a Boolean interpretation of delimiting oppositionality here, the examples he gives of word complements are as follows: Soon after learning the meaning of *up*, the child learns the meaning of *down*; after learning the meaning of *high*, the child learns *low*; and *bad* follows *good* in short order as well. Kagan acknowledges that such oppositional learning occurs too early and easily to be the product of parental instruction or modeling, adding that "the idea that a current state of affairs can be reversed in thought or action and a prior state reconstructed seems to be an intrinsic quality of human mental life" (ibid., p. 189).

This opinion is consistent with what LLT has to say about generic oppositionality in the framing of any predication. In terms of our model, there is always an inside and an outside of the predicating Euler circle, which makes possible both judgments of a target as being same or different in terms of some predicate and also the delimitation of additional opposition-ality if the target has the appropriate semantic meaning (e.g., *up* vs. *down* in Kagan's examples). The child learns the predicating meaning of one word (*up*) but then has the innate capacity rapidly to grasp the implied contrast via generic oppositionality (*down*). We speak of this "same-opposite" content as delimiting oppositionality. It follows that the learning of opposite word meanings influences the range of delimiting oppositionality without directly influencing the fundamental generic oppositionality of the underlying process. Although children and even adults may confound "same-different" with "same-opposite," LLT draws a firm distinction here.

The LLT position is supported in the study of words understood by 2-year-olds. By 24 months children are referring appropriately to internal states and personal behaviors that are indicative of an understanding-intentionality that is framed by delimiting oppositionally, such as warm-cold, cry-no cry, good-bad, hungry-full, and happy-sad (Bretherton & Beeghly, 1982; Bretherton, McNew, & Beeghly-Smith, 1981). These children also evaluate and express personal disgust (negative affection) concerning distasteful life events, and they can distinguish reality from the pretense of make-believe. Two-year-old children also reflect a remarkable ability to distinguish between two languages, each with its opposite word meanings, when reared in a bilingual home. They know when it is appropriate to speak in one or the other tongue and can mix the two languages to form a slang combination (Hatch, 1978). All such findings are consistent with an organism that reasons according to a generic oppositionality and enlarges this process through the delimiting oppositionality of certain semantic targets.

The fact that understanding-intentions always precede action-intentions is demonstrated in language learning, where we find that 2- and 3-year-olds can often comprehend and spontaneously produce words signifying actions that they cannot imitate (Slobin & Welsh, 1973). Meaning is central to word and sentence usage, of course. Three-year-old children hearing "The mouse chased the cat" will understand this sentence to mean "The cat chased the mouse" (Nelson, 1974b). The child rearranges the predication to align with his or her biasing understanding-intention. A 4-year-old hearing "John stepped out of the boat and *mibbed* his trousers" will understand this to mean that the trousers were made wet (Wykes & Johnson-Laird, 1977). As the child's experience expands, his or her understanding-intentions will be increasingly influenced by the contexts (schematics, scenarios etc.) within which language is used. Hearing a new word, the child is likely to apply it to what is unfamiliar in experience after it has been preliminarily predicated in some way (Kagan, 1981, p. 124). Recall the experiment by Carey (1978) in which the children assumed that since color was mentioned in a request to fetch a chromium tray, this descriptive word must represent the tray's olive-green color. This is all highly consistent with LLT's principle of meaning-extension.

The importance of words serving as predications in ongoing language learning is best demonstrated in the remarkable growth of language once it gets underway. It has been estimated that children 6 years of age recognize about 13,000 words on average, but a mere two years later they can recognize over twice this number (Templin, 1957). Studies reveal that elementary school children who read a story using words that they already know—hence, words that can be used as predicates—and then read the same story with new, more difficult words are more likely to acquire these latter words than children who have not been given the benefit of framing the story with such already known predicates (Wittrock, Marks, & Doctorow, 1975). Finally, in teaching American high school students French words, Stoddard (1929) found that better learning occurred when the French word was presented first, followed by the English word, rather than in the reverse order—which is the normal alignment for the predication effect in English syntax. All such research supports the LLT view of predication in extending meaning from the known to the knowable. Although it is not the only source of predication in cognition, language is certainly a most important instrumentality in this endeavor.

The Self as Predicating Personal Identity

Because LLT is a teleological formulation, it follows that there should be some recognition of the active agent, or what has usually been called the self, in the description of human behavior (some theorists might call this the ego). It is not uncommon for psychologists to believe that if a theory such as LLT advocates human agency, it has to begin by postulating an already existing identity (sometimes called a homunculus) that supposedly renders decisions, frames purposes, and intends actions. It comes as a surprise to such psychologists to learn that LLT postulates no such initiating identity. What it does postulate, of course, is telosponsivity as a predicational process that is underway from the outset of cognition. Agency is found in this process, in the capacity to negate physical and environmental promptings and thereby carry out alternatives even before there is an established self-image as a content within this process. In this sense, teleology qua process must precede selfhood qua content. Consequently, I will now take a look at the much-debated conception of selfhood, beginning with theoretical matters and then surveying typical researches on the topic.

Theorizing About the Self

There are three essential aspects to the self concept: (1) The word *self* draws on Anglo-Saxon roots suggesting that the behavior of individuals is in some way recognizably the same over time. (2) Since behaviors also differ across individuals, some of whom are aggressive, others passive, and so on, we also have stylistic features to consider in this concept. (3) Finally, people report a sense of personal identity as they continually deal with events in their ongoing behavior. Some variants of the meanings of sameness, style, and identity always wind their way into the concept of selfhood (Rosenthal, 1984, chaps. 1 and 2).

The first two points can be conceptualized entirely through extraspective theoretical formulations. As Jones and Nisbett (1971) found in their research, when we look at people extraspectively, we are biased toward mechanistic formulations such as traits, which are material- and efficient-cause entities supposedly directing the person's recurring behavioral style. In self theory, Cooley's and Mead's extraspectively framed *"looking-glass self"* (Hofstadter, 1955) was furthered both by H. S. Sullivan (1953) and by the Watsonian-Hullian-Skinnerian line of behavioristic theorizing. The thrust of all such formulations is that a person's sense of selfhood is due to reflected appraisals from others, shaped initially in the familial context and then extended to the societal context, where it serves as a mediator of behavior (much like a trait). The mediating self-image has occasionally been described as a "program" or "script" (Vallacher, 1980, pp. 4, 33).

Such mediational theorizing leaves the question of identity unanswered. Indeed, behaviorists have generally dismissed the person's feelings of identity as no more than particular verbalized shapings from the social environment (e.g., Skinner, 1971). Logical learning theory takes identity seriously, however, viewing it as a reflection of human agency. When we look at our subjects' behavior from their point of view, we tend to frame things predicationally, as due to the circumstances facing them (Jones & Nisbett, 1971). It is not difficult at this point to see how people do things for the sake of a purpose that they have affirmed and carry forward in telosponsive fashion. Logical learning theory insists that the agent makes a difference, that the agent can behave in conformance with, in contradiction to, in contrast to, or without regard for stimulating promptings perceived in the biological or environmental spheres. Thanks to the reflexivity of the telosponsive process, the behaving agent can become aware of his or her agency—which translates into identity, characterized in time as the self.

Many psychologists think of the self as a *homunculus*. Logical learning theory does not require a "little person" within the behavioral mechanism to direct things, because there is *no* machine for a homunculus to run in the *Logos*. Machines reside in the *Bios* or *Physikos* formulations of psychology. As such, they are material- and efficient-cause concepts lacking the intentionality afforded by final causation. Since machines cannot direct themselves, they require the homunculus to do the driving. The concept of the homunculus is simply a cover word for telic organism or final causation. Telosponsivity is not mechanical, although it is partially (logically) automatic. That is, once the predication has been framed and the premise has been affirmed, the meaning-extension is automatic (as is true when this meaning is negated). This telosponsive action places the person in the role of the homunculus from the very outset. In LLT the person *is* the homunculus.

The infant is telosponding long before there is any sense of self, and when it can be said that the self has emerged in development, it does not thereby become a little person within the identity doing the telosponding (making the decisions, choosing, etc.). The self is a predicational content rather than a framer of predications (process). Of course, having learned that he or she has identity—is a self—the person can and often does engage in activities to enhance the self, gain advantage in life, and influence others. But there are many situations in which a predication of selfhood does not enter into the meaning-extension. We do not target our selves as we reach for the salt, but when there is an important event coming up in which we play a role, then our selfhood may and usually does become an aspect of the targeted expectancy. The self is a body of self-predications assigned (attributed, construed, etc.) *to* the identity *by* the identity in ongoing telosponsivity (i.e., a self-reflexive predication that I exist, I engage in choices, I can do better and get more, etc.). People are not equally moved by motives of the self or even selfish motives. Some are self-effacing and even self-unaware. It all depends on how they predicate themselves in the ongoing contexts of life. Here is the full definition of *self* as understood in LLT: The self represents predications concerning personal identity as framed telosponsively. The telosponding organism arrives first on the scene in life, but in time it can (1) reflexively target an introspective viewpoint as an I or me, lending this viewpoint meaning based on predications drawn from personal experience, as well as from the opinions and impressions of others ("I am smart"); (2) become increasingly conscious of doing so ("I know myself better now"); and (3) seek to improve on the advantages gained from the use of additional premises in which the "I, me" notion serves as a self-enhancing—or even selfish—predicate ("That is mine") or in which the identity can be said to be promoting self-realization ("I can be even smarter").

Selfhood is learned, usually early in life, and continues to serve as an important predication thereafter (unless dismissed in abnormal states such as psychosis, communal submersions involving "brainwashing," crowd hysteria, and so on). It is important at this point to emphasize that, although the self is a product of learning, this learning is predicational and not mediational. Other theorists propose the concept of self as a learned phenomenon (e.g., Bandura, 1986, p. 39; Harré, 1984, p. 167; Nisbett & Ross, 1980, p. 195), but the way in which this learning takes place is unclear, or if clarified, it comes down to traditional behaviorist-mediational accounts. The problem here stems from the fundamental terminology of traditional learning theory. The LLT advocate believes that there is no way to frame teleological behavior using traditional conceptions of learning (stimulus-response, input-output, etc.), because these conceptions are based on the extraspective theoretical perspective and therefore are rooted completely in efficient causation. We must move on to new foundation conceptions if we are to capture what takes place in the human experience. We require introspective theoretical terms to effect this change.

Empirical Findings Relating to Selfhood

GENERAL DEVELOPMENT

It seems reasonable that selfhood must build on the person's sense of having an existence that is distinctively different from the rest of experience (me vs. that). This suggests identity. Dixon (1957) had infants look at their image in a mirror and believed that they became cognizant of themselves as represented in their reflection at about 12 months. Amsterdam (1968) later presented evidence contradicting this early date of recognition. Some 1-year-old children even moved away from their mirrored images in fright. However, it appeared that children do indeed recognize themselves in the mirror by the time they are 18 months old. Lewis and Brooks (1974) then conducted a more convincing test of identity recognition by placing rouge on the end of children's noses, after which the children looked at themselves in the mirror. None of the 9- and 12-month-olds touched their noses, whereas 25% of the 15- and 18-month-olds and 75% of the 21- and 24-month-olds did so.

The fact that children recognize their image in a mirror is not the only evidence that they have a sense of identity. The many research studies I cited in this chapter indicating willful intentions on the part of children suggest that at least at some point in the first year of life, the child can possibly sense that he or she is an initiating point for action in the immediate circumstances. As I have already noted, children who are permitted to control the motions of an initially frightening toy can be seen to turn this fear to pleasure in the process (Gunnar-vonGnetchen, 1978). Taking turns with an adult in some routine play is another example of such identity (me-you) formation. Children in the second year of life seem to assume that if others perform some action, they should be able to do the same, or that others expect them to do the same thing (Brown & Inouye, 1978). Thus, if a woman other than the mother approaches the 2-year-old, models some brief sequence of play that is difficult for the child to remember or to enact, and returns to her chair, the child will be seen immediately to cry, protest, bury his or her head in mother's bosom, and so on (Kagan, 1984, p. 127). This pattern is seen cross-culturally, and it strikes the LLT advocate as a reflection of implication. It is as if the model is expressing "See what I can do," which implies "Now you do it too"; since the child cannot carry out the act, he or she is upset by the implied demand.

As children mature, their cognizance of self/other differences grows. By their prepubertal age (10 and 11) children are well aware that differences in school performance are due to differences in the effort that the classroom participants expend. Gifted children are especially prone to see differences between themselves and others (Skinner, Schindler, & Tschechne, 1990). The more intelligent the child, the more likely it is that he or she will rate school performance as due to personal control and agency than to circumstances beyond personal control. Adults tend to read self-evaluative significance into most of the things they do (Simon, 1979). Human beings are surely evaluating organisms. In social situations, they will focus on their distinctive looks or performance levels in framing their predications. A person who is short or tall will begin to frame social contact with others in terms of this dimension of height (McGuire & McGuire, 1982). Personal morale is maintained by carefully selecting the standard against which personal judgments might be rendered. Thus, people will try to boost their self-estimation by comparing themselves favorably to superior others, and when they want to make themselves feel good, they will look for an inferior other to act as the standard against which they can render a self-judgment (Gruder, 1977; Taylor, Wood, & Lichtman, 1983). Indeed, people tend to reject information that is inconsistent with their self-image (Swann & Read, 1981).

PERFORMANCE LEVELS

A great deal of work has been done attempting to relate the concept of the self to effective performance levels, both in schoollike tasks and in social adjustments. Early studies of aspiration level established that people usually try to surpass their past performance on a task (Lewin, Dembo, Festinger, & Sears, 1944). The end (telos) is raised based on the previous *that* (performance level) for the sake of which ongoing self-evaluation takes place. Of course, not all people do this with the same confidence. For example, it has been shown that school-age children with a "helpless" self-predication tend to do less of this and in fact will give up too easily in a moderately challenging task, attributing their failure to a lack of personal ability (Dweck & Licht, 1980). More confident individuals can project several possible selves in the future, working toward one or another in the sense meant by the classic view of self-realization (Markus, 1983). Self-incentives are equal to or surpass the effectiveness of incentives arranged by others in the external environment (Martin, 1979).

It is interesting to note that people with low self-confidence in a task tend to target themselves for attentive consideration while performing the task, whereas confident people target the task and forget about themselves (Carver,

Blaney, & Scheier, 1979). In LLT terms, the low-confidence person extends doubts about performance capacity to the (targeted) self as the task is taking place, which also takes the focus off effective completion of the task. This is like a person who has just learned to drive an automobile worrying about his or her performance while driving. Invariably, the raising of such self-reflexive questions leads to an error of some type, adding to the self-doubt and lowering the self-evaluation all the more. Any stage performer or athlete will concur that mistakes happen when you start thinking about yourself doing the task rather than thinking about the task itself. To perform effectively, the agent must target the task, not the identity doing the task. In a sense, the self is akin to the predicate, targeting and doing the task rather than anguishing—as yet another target—over whether it can be done ("Can I do it?").

The studies I reviewed in chapter 7 on the relationship between affection and learning imply that the person has a sense of influence on experience. Affective assessments are rendered by identities who uniquely influence the course of events. In related findings, it has been demonstrated that young adults who feel they are closer in behavior to their ideal self and farther from their undesired self are more satisfied in life than peers who sense the reverse (Ogilvie, 1987). A negative self-evaluation is not easily outgrown. Children who are deeply pessimistic and ill-tempered, reflecting negativity in all that they do, are seen to extend such meanings into their ongoing experience and thereby damage successive social roles as they mature (Caspi, Elder, & Bem, 1987). The depressed person, for example, goes through life focusing on him- or herself, assigning failure to the self, and selectively recalling only negative instances as evidence that the self is inadequate to the tests of life (Beck, 1976, p. 111).

On the other hand, the nondepressed person has a wider focus of attention, taking satisfaction in other people's lives and comparing him- or herself to others in a realistic manner. Evidence over a 14-year period in young adulthood suggests that the self-concept is fairly stable (Mortimer, Finch, & Kumka, 1982). Indeed, as long as there are no catastrophic setbacks, the self-concept becomes more positive from roughly age 60 onward (Nehrke, Hulicka, & Morganti, 1980). Possibly the elderly person predicates her- or himself with more acceptance than during youth. The realities of declining physical performance may have this ironic effect. With declining capacities, standards and expectations may be lowered across the board.

Demonstration Experiment 14: Thematic Analysis of Longitudinal Personal Interview Data Collected in the Management Progress Study

Except for the previously discussed cross-sectional study on affective assessment over the early school years (Rychlak, 1975a), LLT has not been directed to studies of children at different age levels. This neglect probably stems in large measure from the vehicular nature of LLT and must be corrected in due course. Logical learning theory has, however, been applied to one large-scale longitudinal study of adult behavior; that is, to a portion of the data collected by the Management Progress Study (MPS; Bray, Campbell, & Grant, 1974), for which Rychlak and Bray (1967) devised a scoring scheme used in the analysis of personal interviews. Among its other aims, the MPS was concerned with tracing the early adult years (beginning at ages 24 to 29 years) of 311 Caucasian male middle managers who were selected from five operating companies of the American Telephone and Telegraph System.

The section of the MPS that LLT was applied to covered the years 1956–1968, which included an in-depth yearly interview with each subject concerning significant life events (job, family, religion, social relations, self-development, etc.) over an 8-year period (i.e., the period of 13 inclusive years embraced overlapping work with different operating companies, which were introduced to the study in 5 successive years). Assessment centers—modeled after Murray's (1938) diagnostic council approach—were established at both the outset and the end of this 8-year period. Various personality and ability scales were administered to all subjects at the assessment centers, enabling us to study personality stabilities and changes in relation to the developments as gleaned from the interviews (Bray, 1976). The analysis and interpretation of these interview and personality data in terms of our subjects' typical lifestyle is what drew the interest of an LLT analysis. The volume that issued from this analysis was entitled *Personality and Life-Style of Young Male Managers: A Logical Learning Theory Analysis* (Rychlak, 1982).

In essence, I was able to show that we could employ rigorous, empirical measures of personality and yet construe the findings not in terms of "trait" theories—pictured either as inborn (*Bios*) or social (*Socius*) determinants of behavior—but in terms of telosponsivity (*Logos*) (ibid., p. 43). A major finding here was the difference between men who predicated their lives as *enlargers* versus those who predicated their lives as *enfolders* (ibid., chap. 17). Enlargers put more emphasis on their job careers, community service, and self-development (e.g., continuing education) than on their home and family ties. Enfolders, on the other hand, put more emphasis on their immediate and extended families and tied their community service and personal development to church involvements. Enlargers were found to be more successful on the job, but enfolders were generally more satisfied with their lives.

Of course, the challenge for LLT has been to show how these "life premises" (enlarging, enfolding) were anything other than mediators, past inputs shaping present life in efficient-cause fashion. The MPS did not permit this kind of investigation, but the findings on infants discussed earlier in this chapter—not to mention the contents of this entire volume—represent an effort to deal with this question and to show how it is empirically valid to speak of human beings as predicators rather than as mediators. Early experience influences later experience, but this early experience is nevertheless *always* predicated experience.

Concluding Comment

This chapter's review of development, language, and self-image makes a strong case for the validity of LLT. Human organisms are seen to have remarkable organizing capacities quite early in life. There is nothing in the developmental literature to contradict LLT's claim that humans are predicators from the birth of cognition, that is, from whenever the outset of cognition may be said to occur. Telosponsivity captures what takes place in early experience quite well. The principle of meaning-extension plays an important role in early childhood categorization and the concomitant acquisition of language. Children's learning efforts mirror what we know about adult learning—that is, initial organization of a learning task takes precedence over sheer frequency of exposure to that task. I believe that formal causation has replaced efficient causation as the fulcrum concept in psychology, just as it has in the rest of science. As was done in the MPS analysis, if we simply take the person's (introspective) perspective, we can understand a great deal about how life-meanings are framed, understood, and carried over into the creation of overt behavior in agential fashion (reflecting understanding- to action-intentionality). This is the image of humanity that LLT is unalterably committed to investigating.

10

Logical Learning Theory: Summary, Applications, and Objections

This chapter begins with a section summarizing the essentials of LLT in 20 statements. This summary is followed by an analysis of the conceptual relationship that LLT has to other theories in psychology. Next, I draw out the implications that LLT has for typical classroom instruction, particularly at the elementary level. I then discuss the concept of human character, which any theory purporting to deal with human agency should confront. The volume ends with a series of objections to LLT that have been raised over the years.

Summary of Logical Learning Theory

1. The "logical" in LLT signifies that the grounds for explanation are in the (formal-cause) patterns of the *Logos* rather than in the (efficient-cause) energies or (material-cause) structures of the *Bios*.

2. Processes in the *Bios* and *Physikos* make it possible for an organism to participate in the *Logos*, but these organic and physical processes do not produce the *Logos*, which has a process (i.e., predication) and contents all its own. The *Logos* is *not* a content of the *Bios*.

3. The *Logos* is confronted by the person telosponsively. A telosponse is the affirmation regarding a meaningful content (image[s], word[s], judgmental comparison[s], etc.) relating to a referent acting as a purpose for the sake of which behavior is then intended. Affirmation encompasses predication and always involves the taking of a position relative to the circumstances in which the person is contextually situated.

   (a) The position taken by a person in telosponding is termed a premise, which is the initiating meaning affirmed at the outset of thought. The point in logical order at which a premise is affirmed is termed a protopoint. Premises always involve predication.

(b) The purpose is a concept's aim of meaning, or it may be described as the point of the topic under meaningful extension or expression.

(c) Intention refers to the fact that the meaning of the purpose is directed into ongoing understanding or overt behavior. Thus, to intend is to behave for the sake of (final cause) a purposive meaning (formal cause) that has been telosponsively affirmed.

4. Predication is a logical process of affirming, denying, or qualifying precedently broader patterns of meaning in sequacious extension to narrower or targeted patterns of meaning. The target is the point, aim, or end (telos) of the meaning-extension. The process of predication does not rely on the passage of time but is immediate. It relies on a generic oppositionality, which can be modeled by Euler circles. Thus, each time a predication occurs, encircling some target by a wider realm of meaning, the outside of this larger circle immediately frames the target as well.

(a) The breadth of meaning employed in predication is not found exclusively in the words framed as predicates. That is, the same words can be used as either targets or predicates, as in "A person is like a tree" or "A tree is like a person." It is the human reasoner who selects (affirms) what meaning will be employed as a predicating framework, extending it thereby to a target.

(b) Time is a unit of measurement that is itself employed predicationally to array (organize, pattern, plan, etc.) events logically. Time can serve as a standard—a "that"—for the sake of which events are evaluated according to rate of progress, directionality of measured changes, final completion, and so forth.

(c) Generic oppositionality makes judgments of same versus different possible, as well as further oppositional relations delimited by the meanings of the predicating contents under processing. Delimiting oppositionality functions to direct the specific course of predication, away from what is the case to what is not the case but may be possible.

5. The meaning-extension achieved in telosponsivity occurs in precedent-sequacious fashion. The result may be either an understanding-intention, an action-intention, or both. All action-intentions begin as understanding-intentions.

6. Since the telosponder is intrinsically cognizant of the opposite meaning of the premise under affirmation (via generic and delimiting oppositionality), it is always possible to take a contrary approach, frame a contradiction, express a contrast, or negate the grounds on which understanding- or action-intentions are based. In other words, the telosponding person is an agent of her or his behavior. The "shaping" impetus of physical or social forces can always be opposed—even to the detriment of the person involved.

(a) Oppositionality is therefore an intrinsic aspect of the predicational process, for to predicate is to frame a realm of meaning that is then extended to a target. But there is always the nonframed realm to consider in this process of generic oppositionality, which represents an even broader range of meaning under extension to the target. Unlike machines, human reasoners draw implications from predicated meanings that they are specifically *not* affirming in ongoing telosponsivity (termed now a delimiting oppositionality).

7. Meaning-extension in predication is to be thought of as relying on tautology, conceived now introspectively, from the viewpoint of the person who brings affirmed meanings logically forward into ongoing cognizance. As telosponsivity is fundamentally oppositional, there is also the nontautological meaning to consider. This capacity to tautologize identities even as differences are understood (via generic oppositionality) enables the person to reason analogically. Much of learning is based on such analogical (metaphorical, etc.) extensions of meaning.

(a) The first tautological meaning-extensions occur when the infant tautologizes a target (e.g., "nipple") of itself, resulting in the initial sense of identity ("nipple is a nipple"). In this case, the identical pattern (meaning) is both predicate and target. The predicate always frames and extends meaning to the target in a formulation of knowledge.

(b) In a sense, the human learner must already know (i.e., have a framework of understanding-intentionality) to know further.

(c) Such predicating knowledge need not be readily verbalized or even recalled by the learner. Literally all the meanings under extension in ongoing learning are subsumed by even broader ranges of meaning that predicate them in top-down fashion. This is true of language terms as well.

8. Learning may be said to have occurred when the reasoner is confident enough to employ a former target as a predicate. Learning is therefore the product not of already organized inputs but of an (introspectively) organizing affirmation rendered by the predications of telosponsivity. There are always at least two such predications, one in the affirmation of the premise actually extended telosponsively and a second framed pari passu by the opposite meaning of this premise. Both generic and delimiting oppositionality make this duality possible. This duality of predication defines a dimension along which alternative premises might also be organized.

9. Learning follows a principle of meaning-extension that states that the pattern of meaning forming in a predication always extends to the least understood or most poorly known target(s) having relevance to the predicating meaning in question. Thus, all things being equal, a content in the

predicational process that has two potential targets will enrich the lesser-understood target (i.e., the point of the meaning-extension) most directly and immediately. Patterning of meaning tautologically extends to the unpatterned.

10. An important influence on behavior is affection or affective assessment, which is a transcending telosponse—that is, an innate capacity to reflexively evaluate the meanings of one's cognitions (premises, predicates, targets, etc.) as either liked (positive evaluation) or disliked (negative evaluation). Logical learning theory holds that affection is the most basic and abstract cognition carried on by a human being, targeting specific contents with this like/dislike judgment (via delimiting oppositionality). Affective assessments are best studied idiographically, although it is possible to study them nomothetically.

11. Mental representations are contents of the predicational process that take place within telosponsivity.

12. There is always a point at which the person's predications devolving from above are no longer directly or actively involved in the specific predication under affirmation in overt telosponsivity. The knowledge required in such overt telosponses is limited to that which focuses on the relevant target of the moment. More abstract predicating assumptions need not be in the person's cognizance for understanding or action to proceed. There is always more to our knowledge of anything than we need to or can express.

13. People become committed to predications that have cash value—those that have paid off meaningfully even if this payoff is erroneous from the perspective of other people and even if the affective quality is negative. No change in such predication is likely to take place as long as this payoff continues.

14. To reason from premises (containing predications) that are not clearly believed (known) to be true and certain is to draw implications. Implication is closely related to delimiting oppositionality because of the true/false nature of the premises involved. Hence, implications are likely to have an oppositional cast to them. Inference, on the other hand, is extending meanings from premises the person takes to be true or precisely as framed in the predication at issue. Inferences are related more to generic oppositionality, which renders judgments of sameness or difference in a cognitive process. Inferences extend the judgment of sameness framed by the prediction at issue without concern that it may be wrong, contradicted, and so on.

15. Intentions always extend from the predicate to the target. The meaning is focused from the wider predicating realm to the narrower targeted realm. I am not speaking of an interaction here, although it is possible for the target and predicate meanings to exchange logical locations or, as in oppo-

sitionality, to work predicatively in both directions at once. This is not an interaction, however, because there is no modification of one meaning by the other. This is simply one meaning extending as the other is extending. Hence, we can refer to oppositionality proper as "double predication."

16. Human reasoning and memory are always facilitated by having a relevant or suitable (correct, accurate, etc.) pattern extend to some target, even when this occurs by accident or without the person's intention. Understanding-intentions sometimes fall into place like this when the person least expects them to do so.

17. Memory is, in effect, a one-trial affair. Memory depends on the cohesiveness and clarity of a tightly organized initiating predication of the target in question. This initiating framework is termed the prememory. Frequency of practice merely makes it possible for such cohesive organization to take place, but in principle, a memory can be framed in one trial.

18. As the known predications are employed increasingly in ongoing knowledge, some of these meanings take on the prememorial status of an assumption, which is a highly abstract formulation of knowledge (sometimes called an "axiom"). An assumption is not itself subject to targeted examination, for it need not be remembered as thought unfolds. Assumptions are considered self-evident and thus serve as silent frameworks.

19. So-called unconscious behavior is based on a collection of many things, such as the silent assumptions guiding learning, unadmitted (affectively negative) intentions, the opposite meanings of previously affirmed intentions, confounded predications, and so on. Since they occur outside our awareness, which is based on oppositional reasoning, unconscious premises are rigid as well as unrealistic.

20. Logical learning theory places great emphasis on the value judgments rendered by human beings, thanks in large measure to the delimiting oppositionality of affection. Valuations are fundamentally oppositional in nature, in that the person takes a position regarding the direction to follow in ongoing activity.

Logical Learning Theory's Relation to Other Theories

A major aim of LLT is to provide psychologists with a teleological alternative to traditional, extraspective theorizing as reflected in the old learning theories and more recent cognitive theories. Psychology has been so dominated by the efficient-cause conceptions of stimulus-response, input-output, matching, Boolean disjunction (demonstrative reasoning), and so on, that it seems impossible to introduce a new idea into the discipline. Any psychologist who believes that a teleological theory can be framed without immediately being subsumed by some efficiently caused learning or information-processing conception is practicing a monumental self-deception. There is an ongoing conceptual power play taking place in the psychological literature concerning how to construe the human image. Ironically, the power play involves how we psychologists should predicate the human image!

When Dollard and Miller (1950), in their translation of Freud into Hullian theory, set out to bring the benefits of "the rigor of the natural-science laboratory" (p. 3) to psychoanalytical description, they unfortunately undermined all the teleological meanings that Freud was trying to convey—however indirectly (see Rychlak, 1981, pp. 319–321). For example, Freud (1900/1953, p. 593) viewed unconscious thought as highly informed on what was taking place in conscious experience, framing intentions or wishes that could not be expressed openly and cleverly circumventing repressive censorships to make these ends known through parapraxes (intentional "slips" and misactions). Yet Dollard and Miller (1950) describe unconscious behavior as "stupid" (p. 224). That is, unconscious acts are purely instrumental motions in which no mediating cue-producing responses intervene between current inputs and behavioral outputs to make known why a course of behavior is being carried forward.

Freud, as were the other early analysts, was forced by the Newtonian biases of his time to recast his predicational formulations into a quasi-biological explanation, resulting in his unwieldly libido theory—a pale analogy to biological energies that has never sustained itself. Evidence for Freud's predicational model of mind abounds. Consistent with the findings cited in chapter 9, Freud believed that infants could reason before they had language. He called this primary-process thought, which he said was heavily colored by fantasy and therefore "abandons dependence on real objects" (Freud, 1911/1958, p. 222). Indeed, Freud reveals his grasp of Kantian predication when he next observes that "just as Kant warned us not to overlook the fact that our perceptions are subjectively conditioned and must not be regarded as identical with what is perceived though unknowable, so psycho-analysis warns us not to equate perceptions by means of consciousness with the unconscious mental processes which are their object. Like the physical, the psychical is not necessarily in reality what it appears to us to be" (Freud, 1915/1957, p. 171).

And as for oppositionality, Freudian theory is shot through with such formulations. In fact, his very first theoretical effort—which reached print before the *Studies on Hysteria* (Breuer & Freud, 1893/1955)—was founded on a view of cognition in which opposite or antithetical intentions led to symptom formations. A young mother who did not consciously intend to disturb her baby's sleep told herself to be quiet, only to enact precisely the opposite intention by loudly "clacking" her tongue (Freud, 1892/1966). Ideas with opposite meanings are entertained by the same mind quite nicely, and such "illogical" notions as eating one's cake and having it too continually arise in the unconscious, which also readily accepts ideas that are in contradiction to conscious preferences (Freud, 1901/1953b). In his discussion of analytical work, Freud employs a flagrant dialectical switch when he quotes a patient who has said of his dream content, "You [i.e., Freud] ask who this person in the dream can be. It's *not* my mother," only to take from this assertion the opposite implication: "We emend this to: 'So it *is* his mother'" (Freud, 1925/1961, p. 235; emphasis in the original). There are myriad examples of oppositionality in Freudian theory, and it is impossible in principle for a Hullian or an information-processing (e.g., network) theory to capture this side of human nature. But LLT can meet the challenge.

Jung (1929/1961), who once said "I see in all that happens the play of opposites" (p. 337), was just as dependent on this concept as Freud was. The Jungian collective unconscious serves as a broad predication, which targets the individual in ways that he or she has no real grasp of but from which a potential influence is taken nevertheless — or negated altogether (Jung, 1929/1954, p. 69). When Adler (1964) said that *"a person's behavior springs from his ideas"* (p. 19; emphasis in the original), he was not speaking about mediating cue-producing responses or information that had been input, coded, stored, retrieved, and then output. These latter constructs simply fail to capture the active interpretation of cognition on which Adlerian theory is founded. Adlerian prototypes (life plans) are clearly telosponses.

Adler would have agreed with Jung (1916/1961) that "psychologically speaking, we [human beings] are living and working day by day according to the principle of directed aim or purpose" (p. 295). Both these analysts were openly committed to human teleology. They wanted to capture the *that* (life plan, archetypal expression, etc.) in psychic cognition for the sake of which meaning is expressed in thought and action. The same is true of Binswanger's (1963) a priori ontological structure known as the "world design" (p. 31), Rogers' (1951) "phenomenal field" (p. 483), or Kelly's (1955) "personal construct" (p. 76). All these concepts are directly subsumed by telosponsivity, whereas they cannot be subsumed by the efficient-cause conceptions of stimulus-response or input-output theorizing.

If we next turn to the theories in psychology that are usually arrayed against the traditional learning or cognitive theories of our discipline, we find that these views are, in the main, calling for changes to an image of the person that is consistent with LLT. Thus, humanistic psychology which draws on the ideas of theorists like Maslow, Rogers, Goldstein, and Allport, has been called a "third force" (Goble, 1970, p. 14). The articles of organization of the American Association of Humanistic Psychology, framed in 1962, also refer to this movement as a third force departing from the tenets of both behaviorism and psychoanalysis (Shaffer, 1978, p. 1). What does this third force come down to? As detailed by Shaffer (ibid.), humanistic psychology focuses on conscious experience (p. 10), insists on the wholeness and integrity of the person (p. 12), views humans as free and autonomous (p. 13), is antireductionistic (p. 16), and believes that human nature can never be fully defined (p. 17). Although LLT is not limited to consciousness, and it does not pass judgment on whether human nature is ever to be fully defined or not, surely the major thrust of humanistic psychology is consistent with its tenets. "Human" means "teleological."

Another perspective fitting under the telic umbrella is that of the existential-phenomenological theories. Bugental (1989) asserts that a study of phenomenal experience differs from a study of mere behavior in that it views the person as a "subject" and not an "object" (p. x). Blame for thus dehumanizing the person is placed on the "impersonal science" (ibid.) that psychology practices, which of course translates into the material- and efficient-cause bias of extraspective formulations that remove agency from consideration. Existential-phenomenological approaches to psychology claim to study the essence, structure, or form of human experience and to do this through descriptive rather than manipulative efforts (Valle, King, & Halling, 1989). This notion of a descriptive science dates from Brentano (1874/1973), who criticized the early experimental psychologists like Wundt, claiming that they foisted mechanistic preconceptions on analyses of human behavior instead of describing how people spontaneously behaved (pp. 7, 28, 29).

Aided by the limitations that the fallacy of affirming the consequent places on the verification of scientific theories, existential-phenomenological critics of traditional method in psychology hope to introduce alternatives to validating evidence (for some examples, see Giorgi, 1985; Polkinghorne, 1989; Shapiro, 1985). These critics believe that the traditional strategy of manipulating variables to control and predict behavior is what promotes the mechanization of the human image. As I noted in chapter 2, LLT disputes this claim, placing the blame for mechanizing the human image on the theories propounded by traditional researchers, as well as the fact that they have tended to confound their efficient-cause theory (e.g., S-R) with the efficient-cause instrumentalities required to carry out the scientific method (IV-DV). The existential-phenomenologist makes no fundamental claim about personhood that is beyond traditional empirical investigation under the framing and explanatory constructions of LLT, either directly or through a line of theoretical development (Rychlak, 1988, pp. 191, 192, 504).

Another wing in this "liberalizing" school of thought is that of hermeneutics, which is defined as the "study of meaningful human phenomena in a careful and detailed manner as free as possible from prior theoretical assumptions, based instead on practical understanding" (Packer, 1985, pp. 1081, 1082). This is obviously a rephrasing of the existential-phenomenological polemic. There is much talk of the context dependency of behavior among the hermeneuticists, particularly as it relates to social interchanges (ibid., p. 1089; this ties into social constuctionism, of course; see below).

Sounding much like the LLT advocate insisting that all behavior is predicated, the hermeneuticist asserts that interpretations frame the very observations and items that the rigorous scientist takes as his or her data (McCarthy, 1978). Meaning precedes empirical identification. Hermeneutic researchers have shown that personality constructs have no context-independent meaning and hence can be reframed as their opposite meaning by setting them within an appropriate context (Gergen, Hepburn, & Fisher, 1986). This supports rather than challenges the contentions of LLT. In an even more remarkable parallel to LLT, Palmer (1969) has described the so-called hermeneutic circle of textual interpretation, in which precedent understanding is required for there to be a continuing interpretation of the text's meaning. This analysis is readily subsumed by the discussion of tautological meaning-extension in LLT, including the dialectical nature of analogical reasoning.

A further offshoot of the phenomenological tradition that we are now considering is narrative psychology (Sarbin, 1986). The point here is that people cognize their lives in terms of stories that have themes or scenarios based on root metaphors and the like. These concepts are surely predicational in nature, similar to Adlerian life plans. We also have the vast array of social constructionism to consider. If we draw on the writings of Gergen (1989), who asks us to "avoid reducing the social world to the psychological" (p. 427), it is obvious that for him it is the *Socius* that somehow fashions the constructs through interpersonal dynamics of some sort. Gergen is out to "deconstruct local ontologies" (ibid., p. 476) and free the person from the constraints of convention. The development here is not from the individual construing *Logos* to the *Socius*, but vice versa. Logical learning theory would, of course, conceptualize things in the other direction.

On this latter score, we might take heart from the writings of Berger (1963; with Luckmann, 1966), one of the fathers of social constructionism. In line with the oppositionality stressed by LLT, Berger (1963) specifically referred to those "rebellious constructions of the mind" that can "liberate the individual to a considerable extent from the definitory systems of his society" (p. 133). People can "say 'no' to society, and often have done so" (ibid., p. 142). Berger and Luckmann (1966) give the example of how a religious genius might concoct a new mythology that becomes part of the cultural lore (is objectified) and is then used as a grounds for social action (internalized) by succeeding generations (p. 83).

This kind of social constructionism is nicely suited to LLT, which views social norms, communal myths, and so forth, as predications held in common by a people rather than as some kind of supraindividual (efficiently caused) "force in the sky" that patterns or shapes their behavior in a mediational fashion. This is not to deny *Socius* processes. It is merely to assert that LLT is aimed at explaining events in the *Logos*, period. There need be no contradiction between a *Logos* explanation and a *Socius* explanation. Social influences surely do occur. We can show the influence of the group on the individual. Nonetheless, LLT seeks to explain how the individual processes these influences, and I see no contradiction between its tenets and theories of social construction like those of Berger.

Even the traditionally mechanistic formulations can be subsumed by LLT. It is easier to subsume Skinnerian (1938, 1971) than Hullian (1943) theory. Hull's constructs are so closely tied to *Bios* and even *Physikos* groundings that we are hard pressed to show parallels with LLT. Of course, the findings on awareness in classical conditioning discussed in chapters 5 and 6 support LLT more than they do Hullian theory. Skinner's approach is remarkably similar to LLT, except that he tried to retain the extraspective stance of traditional natural-science investigations. However, if we look carefully at the findings on awareness in the light of operant conditioning, it is not difficult to see that Skinner may have actually capitalized on the teleological nature of behavior, including animal behavior. To "operate" on the environment is not well stated as a "response." Operations make better sense as predicating initiators, closer in meaning to proactive stimuli than reactive responses.

I have no compunctions in suggesting that Skinner's theory and empirical findings are readily subsumed by LLT. Skinner assumed the role of an actuarian and relied in large measure on the *Logos* to make his case. The so-called cognitive revolution in psychology can also be seen as a fumbling attempt to deal with a predicating organism in mechanistic ways. I cannot say how long psychologists will persist in framing their task as that of explaining human beings in engineering terms. Maybe this will never change. But if we are willing to step back from all of the unobserved mechanisms that supposedly bring about cognition—the networks, the nodes, the channels, and so on—and in the spirit of existential-phenomenalism try simply to understand what people really do, I think it will soon be apparent that they are engaged in a predicational process.

People do not draw Euler circles in their brains as they reason, of course, but this convenient model nicely conveys the broader-to-narrower meaning-extending and oppositional process that they are observed to manifest. I hope that this volume demonstrates beyond reasonable doubt that the vast majority of empirical findings in human cognition are highly supportive of LLT. All in all, it is reasonable to suggest that LLT has a breadth of applicability that is, if not unequaled in psychology, then surely not surpassed.

Logical Learning Theory in the Classroom

Although LLT was not specifically formulated to influence classroom instruction, it is fair to ask what this approach has to say about efforts in the classroom. Learning theory has frequently been criticized for not offering much to the classroom teacher. This may have been true at one time; however, the findings of recent years belie this criticism. In making recommendations at this point, I rely not only on the specific studies done on LLT but on the vast array of work that I have surveyed in the previous chapters. I admit, however, that a dash of flagrant speculation and opinion must be mixed in here.

As a teleological theory, LLT places considerable responsibility on the activities of the individual learner. Given the realities of many classrooms in the United States today—the anomic atmosphere of inner-city life, the collapse of the family structure at all economic levels, and so forth—it may appear to be academic hubris to make suggestions concerning the roles of student and teacher. Many teachers at the elementary and intermediate school levels have virtually impossible job demands. Another reason for giving pause before commenting on this realm is that just about anything one can suggest has probably been said before, and even attempted before, in the long history of education. Given these provisos, here is what I see being suggested in the research literature as interpreted by LLT.

Organization over Frequency

Logical learning theory holds that learning involves the continual extension of meanings in which a previous target serves as a predicate once it is understood (taken for granted, believed in, etc.). Education should assist the child in facilitating this process of moving from targeted to predicating meaning. Practice or classroom drill is important, not as a rote endeavor, but as a way to encourage the child to use concepts on this wider basis. A learning or practice trial is worthwhile only if the child is intentionally conceptualizing what is under consideration. Rote memories are easily forgotten because the learner never really applies this material as a predication in subsequent behavior. The diffident scholar can be assisted if the subjects to be learned are well organized, of course, but obviously the greatest benefit results when the student adds to the meaningful organization of the material. In the terminology of modern cognitive psychology, LLT might be said to place more emphasis on encoding than on retrieval. From the LLT perspective, examinations and grades should be based more on such preliminary organization of the material to be learned than on the recollection over time of what was organized, however haphazardly and hence fleetingly these memory tests are achieved. A learner will remember what he or she wants (intends) to remember. The trick is to make such memorial contents available in the first place, which is a skill that can be taught.

Thanks to the concern over the future of science in the United States, discussion of educational reform usually produces talk about the study of mathematics. Mathematics' tightly organized content facilitates conceptualization, assuming that the student is affectively drawn to the subject matter in the first place. At the elementary level, however, the student is not ordinarily called on to exert alternative formulations of the mathematical rules. Although mathematics is surely important, considering the potential payoff for the society as a whole, LLT would stress reading in the elementary school years above all other subject matter. Children who are talented in mathematics will emerge spontaneously and should be encouraged individually, but a great number of children in the United States at present seem to have severe deficits in basic reading skills. Not only should children read a great deal, but they should immediately begin to rephrase and comment on what they read, because effective reading is active conceptualization.

Children should be encouraged to anticipate or guess what the next development will be in the unfolding narrative. As they progress, they should begin analyzing the author's intentions. Actually, mathematics can follow similar principles, in that anticipations and alternative formulations of problems can be stressed just as easily in mathematics as in reading. In time, particularly with reading tasks, the child should be encouraged to (positively and negatively) criticize the meanings conveyed. Critical analysis, the stating of affective preferences, and so forth, all facilitate the organization and retention of meanings. Moreover, such analysis teaches the child that there are grounding assumptions in everything that we read about, believe in, or apply to life. Thus, it is not simply a question of critically expressing preferences or empty opinions but rather a matter of clarifying the grounds for the sake of which such evaluations are rendered.

Textbooks should be written with an anticipatory and evaluative emphasis. The young child should grasp as early as possible that reading expresses a point of view and that figuring out the writer's intentions and grounding assumptions is what reading is all about. If the reading content is fiction, the figures in the story can be analyzed in this teleological fashion. Rephrasing passages will also prove beneficial to the maturing child. Words can be taught as targets that have taken their predication from what people wanted to say about things. The child learns that *attic* was coined many years ago when people wanted to describe a part of the house that was not yet named. However, there were houses with structures like this in the region of Attica, with a space beneath the point of a rooftop. Thus, some forgotten writer borrowed the region's name to convey this "Attica-like" idea. Instructions of this sort can be wound into the study of geography and history, which seem to have gone by the boards in our modern era.

To demonstrate that a child actually understands what is conveyed on some topic, he or she should be asked to give an example of the meaning under targeting. This is common practice in teaching circles, but LLT would add the strategy of asking for opposite examples (contrasts, contradictions, etc.) whenever possible. Examples are like word definitions, and if the child can give an analogical example, the meaning under extension will be conveyed successfully. As they are also predications, such examples can be shown to reflect a point of view. Children should come to see that they are always contributing a point of view to what they can know—in the examples they think up to understand something and in their interpretations of what they are reading about. At the higher grade levels they should be cognizant of the fact that alternative viewpoints arise concerning anything to which human intelligence is applied and that it is all right to have conflicting views on issues.

In fact, thanks to the oppositional nature of meaning (hence knowledge), it is impossible to avoid alternatives. What a student should continually strive for, however, is the framing of clear-cut, sound *reasons* for the point of view that he or she favors. In other words, LLT is not advancing a solipsistic view of knowledge. The ultimate goal of education is to fashion reasoned opinions and sound rationales for selecting among such alternatives. Although it is interested in the unsound and invalid form of reasoning, LLT recognizes that it is desirable to promote effectiveness in human cognitive strategies. In addition, sometimes there are equally sound rationales for either side of a controversial issue.

Oppositionality also has relevance to instruction in arithmetic and mathematics, as in showing clearly that addition and subtraction have contrasting roles to play in considering totalities. To grasp the concept of magnitude, the young child must also grasp that this involves both "adding to" and "taking away." The equality sign in arithmetic is nestled between opposites, for positive or negative values change when numbers are reversed. This reversal of sign is brought home with greater impact if the child grasps oppositionality than if not.

Dealing with oppositionality can be made enjoyable for the child. Humorous reversals can be created in the teaching of virtually any subject matter. Humor is underwritten in large measure by oppositionality, the rapid shift in expectations that brings about a silly state of affairs. It is also possible to convey the fact that even with the best of intentions to learn some topic, the opposite result occasionally takes place. Learning means failure at times, but even here there is the oppositionality of turning the negative into a positive because of what can be corrected in the future.

Affective Assessment of Course Content

Attempts to improve educational practice have probably relied more on motivational innovations than on any other means. Since LLT places affective assessment at the very center of learning, it follows that this is of immense importance to any discussion of education. The demonstration experiments at the end of chapter 7 proved that affective assessment influences both the initial encoding and also the retrieval of cognitions. However, consistent with LLT's emphasis on cognitive organization at the outset of learning, we must appreciate that affection plays a dramatic role at this initiating point. This may explain why Apao (1979) found primacy effects for affective assessment but not recency effects. I have often referred to affective assessment as LLT's Kantian a priori category, for this manifestation of delimiting oppositionality (focused on specific contents) is underway at the outset of cognition.

Having said this, I must voice a caution. Education should *not* be seen as exclusively oriented to motivating the learner. This is doubtless a major goal of the teacher, but if the measure of good education is to be the student's level of motivation, translated now into such descriptors as satisfaction with or enjoyment of the educational subject matter, a misplaced emphasis is likely to result. To put it in LLT terms, the target would then have shifted from the subject matter to the student doing the studying. The aim of effective education is to target learnable material and bring it into the learner's predicational capacities as smoothly as possible. If we can count on the learner's positive affection for the material, so much the better, but even if we cannot, it would be unwise to alter the instruction at the expense of the targeted course materials.

Innovations in education should emphasize as their target the material being taught. Questions of student motivation in the sense of pleasure with the activity of learning should be secondary. It is not that we want to return to the rigid classroom of the 19th century, but as recent history has demonstrated, even with all the educational accessories aimed at raising student motivation—visual aides, simplified readers, smaller classrooms, computer instruction, and so on—the level of competence in schoollike tasks has been under steady decline. One possible remedy here is to work on motivations that relate more to the future, the ultimate "telos" of having to make one's way in life, to forge a career, to meet an employer's expectations, and so on. Minimum requirements could be brought home through proper examples, such as classroom guest speakers from a range of occupations, including the most common. I understand John Dewey's (1900, 1929) educational philosophy to express this concern, namely, the applicability of education to the broader ramifications of life in human society. Dewey's so-called progressive education with the open classroom seems to have capitalized on affection.

That is, we have found in LLT research that learners show dramatic non-specific transfer when they move from disliked to liked materials, whereas this facilitation is not seen in the reverse direction (Rychlak & Tobin, 1971; Rychlak, Tuan, & Schneider, 1974). The best strategy for the student is to begin with disliked study topics and then move to liked topics. Learners have a good sense of what they like and do not like to learn, and they accurately predict which study topics they are likely to do well in (see, e.g., Slife & Rychlak, 1981). This metacognitive evaluation might be adapted to the classroom in a more active manner. For example, I once negotiated with a school system to adapt the classroom periods for an experimental group, contrasting it with a (control) group scheduled conventionally. Children in the experimental condition were to be subdivided according to interest in a study topic. The classroom schedule was then to give shorter periods on disliked topics, followed by longer periods on liked topics of instruction. Breaks in the day such as recess and lunch would enable a new affective sequence of this sort to be ordered. The prediction here was that experimental subjects would learn as much as they ordinarily do in spending less time on disliked topics and learn much more in the lengthened periods of liked topics.

As things turned out, parents raised objections before this procedure could get underway. They felt that the school was no place to experiment, so the project fell through. Nevertheless, I think that this affective sequence of learning is probably what takes place in the open classroom, where the child spends a little time on a disliked activity and then indulges in considerable effort on a liked activity—for which he or she is then said to have a talent. In many talks with elementary school children over the years, during affective assessment research, I have found them unable to distinguish between a school subject that they find to be easy and one that they like. Thus, LLT would pursue the contribution that the students' affective preferences make to learning, both within and between topics. Through it all, however, the focus would be on facilitating organization of the targeted subject matter. Much research remains to be done on this topic, including how it is that disliked study topics might be redefined (repredicated) so that they could be reassessed as at least moderately liked (one idea is to tie the short-term disliked topic to a long-term goal that may be liked). Before this emphasis will be generally adopted, we will have to convince psychologists and educators that the learner is an organizer, evaluator, and meaning extender rather than an informational inputter, storer, and retriever who must be continually motivated to perform.

Logical Learning Theory's Relation to Ethics and Morality

As a teleology, LLT is readily drawn into the topics of ethics and morality. I use *morality* here in the sense of ethical concerns underwritten by religious belief (e.g., belief in a deity, in scriptural injunctions, etc.). Both ethics and morality are predicated on the assumption of human agency, of course, and it should now be clear that a theory of agency can be framed rigorously and subjected to empirical test. The contents of this volume attest to this fact. I think I have countered the suggestion advanced by some psychologists that human agency cannot be submitted to theoretical explanation and empirical validation, as other topics in psychology can be, because such teleological claims are axiomatic and hence empirically unassailable (for an argument of this type, see Leahey, 1987). To the contrary, this volume has shown agency as a theoretical assumption to be consistent with many different sources of rigorously collected empirical data.

As viewed by LLT, ethical or moral aspects of human behavior stem from the fact that humans are evaluating organisms. This organism continually takes a position on life, and questions of right and wrong, good and evil, honesty and dishonesty, and so forth, necessarily intrude, thanks to delimiting oppositionality. In addition, the dialectical capacity to take the other's point of view enables the formation of *empathy*. Relative advantage, equity, fair play—all such human manifestations readily follow when we begin thinking of humans as predicating evaluators rather than as mediators. A predicating organism can see that avenues might be taken other than the one chosen, even as this option is being enacted. The chosen alternative would be evaluated on some grounding or assumptive basis, of course, a basis that, in the context of ethical behavior, we call a value.

The LLT advocate cannot see how there could be any weight given to a morality that is simply input and then carried forward into overt behavior by the mechanical impulsions of mediation—by passively input societal injunctions, for example. According to LLT, a *norm* is a predication affirmed in common rather than an impulsion from the group to the individual. Without some personal evaluational effort by the organisms concerned, these orderings would lack the moral suasion that is fundamental to belief and conformity. As I noted above, LLT appreciates the tremendous role that social forces play in human experience, but these forces obtain their influence from the fact that the person affirms their meaning and intends that they be enacted. Of course, the person can negate these forces as well as enact them. The great innovators and heroes of history are frequently individuals who refused to take on the hallowed assumptions of the group and set off on their own to create an alternative that had not previously existed. Others then follow to affirm the beliefs or imitate the actions of such singular persons (this is akin to my previous analysis of the individual's role in social constructionism).

It is no accident that moralistic rules of thumb such as the Golden Rule or the categorical imperative are written quite simply and directly at the level of the individual, for they represent a guide—encompassing the social—by which the person can live. Further, the predicating organism absolutely requires such assumptive guides for the sake of which he or she is to operate. The thought that things could be different (negation by way of generic oppositionality) implies that things could be better (pointing a way via delimiting oppositionality); this sequence ever unfolds in the cognitions of human beings. This capacity for predicational meaning-extension via oppositionality is the source of ethics and morality. To turn such evaluative human practices into mediators is to trivialize them.

It is in the recognition that the person qua individual is a responsible agent that LLT finds much of its uniqueness as a theory of human behavior. The claim is also fraught with the possibility of misunderstanding. LLT defines *responsibility* as a recognition that the person plays a role in the telosponsive affirmation of premises, encompassing the grounds for the sake of which behavior is enacted. This is a purely psychological definition of responsibility, but there is a second definition of this term, one that has to do with the assignment of blame for an action or outcome. The teleologist who holds to the former definition leaves him- or herself open to a charge of wanting to press the latter meaning. As a case in point, I have been accused of being unable to feel sympathy for the disadvantaged because of LLT's claim that people are responsible for their own behavior (see Glassman, 1983).

Charges like this reflect a confounding of a psychological with an ethico-moral formulation of the word *responsible*. Although a person might find support in LLT to hold the disadvantaged person at fault for his or her economic plight, it does not follow that such a judgment stems from the concept of psychological responsibility. In claiming that people are responsible for their behavior based on their predicated (telosponsive) actions, the LLT advocate need not thereby deny that they might have been poorly reared in socially disadvantaged circumstances, misled, denied opportunities, abused, and subjected to all the indignities that social critics usually assign to what "shapes" people into their disadvantaged condition. None of these ascriptions need be denied.

The disadvantaged person need not be blamed for framing certain predications over the course of a generally unsatisfying life. Sometimes what has been framed is all that is possible, given certain realities. A physical limitation intrudes on dreams of the person who would like to do what this limitation precludes. The minority individual may sense that things could be otherwise (different via generic oppositionality) yet have no hope of breaking through the barriers along the way to a more satisfying alternative (delimiting oppositionality). Even within this unfortunate context of disadvantage, however, it is possible to see the influence of personal responsibility taking place—sometimes in heroic proportions. For example, Jenkins (1982) has adopted the tenets of LLT to explain how repressed blacks in America have retained their individual dignity in the face of slavery, economic denial, and continuing racial prejudice. It is entirely up to the theorist how the abstract conceptions of LLT are applied to the targeted topic of interest. Logical learning theory has no political agenda. The entire political spectrum can be subsumed and elaborated by its tenets.

In similar fashion, the entire spectrum of religious ideologies and dogmas can be subsumed by LLT as varying contents in the affirmations of a telosponding organism. The need to believe in something or someone—a power, an identity—greater than the self is commonly found in human beings. Logical learning theory cannot offer proofs for a deity or a life in the hereafter, but the fact that people reason in this teleological fashion, and the form that the resultant belief takes on, is quite amenable to the tenets of LLT. We give the same serious attention to the religious person as we do to the agnostic and the athiest. Cognitively speaking, all such views are framed the same way, and our duty as psychologists is to study this process and not to dictate the contents that it must entertain.

Since LLT emphasizes the affective side to cognition, a side that frequently evaluates questions of right and wrong, it might seem plausible for LLT to take a position on the fundamental nature of human beings, who are often supposed to be creatures oriented to seeking the right and the good, a "higher life." Although it follows that an organism that can evaluate the relative merits of a course of action can indeed seek to raise the level of interpersonal relations, it does not follow that there is some innate propensity to do so. Many people use their evaluative capacities to intend selfish ends in life. People can and do intend to harm others, out of predatory aims, petty vindictiveness, and jealousy—not to mention in retaliation for similar actions directed against themselves or their loved ones. Logical learning theory follows a Jungian balance in suggesting that people are both ethico-moral *and* selfish-predatory creatures. We can hope that the former propensities dominate in interpersonal relations, but we must also face up to explaining and understanding the latter, as they are cut from the same cloth.

Objections Raised Against Logical Learning Theory

Over the years, colleagues have leveled criticisms against LLT, as well as against the approach to science that it represents. I am referring here not to technical questions concerning the fundamentals of the theoretical approach but rather to the wider significance that this view has for the practice of a science of psychology. I will present eight of the more common questions that arise and the answers given to them, before ending the volume with a final observation.

   I. *Psychology has been defined as the science that controls and predicts behavior. In claiming that people are free agents, LLT violates the determinism on which this definition rests. How can we remain scientists and still believe that people are free to behave as they please?*

It is probably a measure of the ease with which psychologists have confounded their theories with their method that so many of them believe their professional role is literally to control and predict behavior. Yet this phrase — control and prediction — is to be understood as a definition of scientific validation and not as a mandate for taking charge of human lives. There is nothing in science that demands that we literally control people's lives. Science is advisory. Because of the limitations placed on it by the fallacy of affirming the consequent, science is also subject to alternative interpretations (predications) of the empirical data array. We can make perfect predictions based on erroneous assumptions, learning after the fact how our good fortune came about. Application is entirely different from the basic investigation of psychological considerations in behavior. My earlier suggestions concerning the classroom are not advanced as behavioral controls. The control involved in generating these suggestions occurred in the experimental design to which we submitted our theoretical hypotheses.

Let's assume that we learn through the control-and-prediction sequence of validation that people are more likely to buy a product in a brightly packaged container than in a dull one and that we put this knowledge to use in the supermarket; precisely how are we controlling those who now reach for the attractive container? Have we somehow flicked the toggle switches of their mind, so that they respond as efficiently caused effects to our manipulative interventions? Or have these telosponding organisms rendered an affective assessment based on discernible aesthetic grounds and made a choice that is best understood in a formal/final-cause sense? I think it is clear that if we have effected a control, this influence is based on the telic evaluation and choice of the person. We can predict this choice because of our previous study of the telosponses of other people. People are pretty much alike. Hence, to quake over the possibility that in formulating the person as a teleological organism we have somehow lost our scientific status is to be needlessly concerned. This concern is misguided because the person is always a contributing factor to the observed lawfulness of his or her behavior.

The same applies to personality and attitude scales. Tests predict the person's behavior because even though there are accidental factors to consider in the error variance, the basic truth is that the person creates the very criterion behavior along which we array her or him in relation to others who have taken the scale. We are not sampling from a genetic pool, reinforcement history, or some container holding long-term memories. It would be much easier to predict behavior if we were sampling such discrete and nonoppositional aspects of behavior. The scale represents a series of predications—framed as the test items—that the person affirms or rejects. Basing our work on a summary calculation of the meanings involved in the test items, we are able to predict to the criterion because of the precedent-sequacious nature of the cognitive process under study (Gruba-McCallister & Rychlak, 1981). The assessed person brings the predications forward behaviorally to create the "dependent variable" under study.

I think it is best to limit the phrase "control and prediction" to the methodological context, where it serves as a definition of validation. The phrase does not make for good theory. Logical learning theory does seek to control and predict behavior, because as a rigorous humanistic psychology it accepts the responsibility of submitting its claims to falsification. There is no contradiction between human agency and predictability. We sometimes forget that the second term in *free-will* refers to an iron-clad and hence predictable determination that certain ends will come about rather than others. Although it is a formal/final-cause determination, the predictability is no less observable and predictable.

> 2. *Logical learning theory tries to be too original, calling for changes that are not necessary. In due time, the mediational models will explain all of those things to which LLT objects. Why change when the evidence that traditional theorizing is wrong is not yet in? Let's allow the facts, not grand theoretical speculations like LLT, to settle things.*

The easiest reply to this objection is that no one intends for LLT to supplant traditional, mediational theorizing in psychology. We are asking for just enough recognition so that when an LLT draft is confronted, a colleague will not dismiss it out of uninformed bias. In this age of concern over minority representation in matters of race, sex, age, and the like, it seems only fair play to give minority theories in psychology a chance for existence as well.

The reactions to LLT are frequently as upsetting to colleagues as discussions of feminism or equal opportunity in racial selections are to parties involved on both sides of these issues. Although one can understand this emotional upheaval as due to the fact that LLT challenges the received view in psychological modeling, it does seem as though a legitimate science should be more self-confident and objective than this. Logical learning theory is not a political movement, although it appears to have inescapable political ramifications for the power structure of psychology.

As my discussion in chapter 1 made clear, the issues raised by LLT cannot be answered by accruing more and more data, results, evidence, and so on. I have surveyed a vast array of empirical findings in this volume. These facts have been generated by many different theories that, in the main, share the Lockean mediational model. Nevertheless, we have seen how an LLT perspective of these data shifts (deconstructs?) their very meaning from a mechanistic to a teleological account of what took place. If the present volume were to be written 20 years from now, would this in any way affect this alternative formulation of these facts? Actually, I believe that the empirical findings in the interim would be closer to LLT than to the mediational models of today, but assuming that the findings would still be framed and understood mechanistically, does the reader for a moment believe that an LLT advocate could not reconceptualize these results in a teleological fashion?

We cannot wait for the facts to clear up the theoretical issue under consideration here. Facts alone do not demolish theories. Better theories demolish poorer theories. If there ever comes a time when LLT begins to intrude on the received view of psychology, it will not occur in the sense of "Wow, look at the empirical findings. They are all supporting LLT and not the spreading network theories of our time." The shift to a predicational model will occur suavely, with an attitude of "Well, we were changing to this predicational form of theorizing in any case, thanks to the development in cognitive science of concepts like schemata, prototypes, plans, and the like." The shift in theorizing will take place as a most natural and inevitable event. No one will be proven wrong and no one will be proven right. The change will just occur. But LLT advocates do not dream of such Kuhnian revolutions smoothly taking place in psychology. We seek only a decent level of recognition and an opportunity to confront mediational theories in fair and open scholarly—not political—competition.

3. *Logical learning theory is historically out of step, a grand theory in the age of functionalism with its miniature theorizing and limited focus. Why oppose this historical trend?*

Although *functionalism* had a meaning quite different at one time (see Boring, 1950, chap. 22), today it seems to refer to conducting research on limited topics and specifically avoiding theoretical accounts having wide applicability. The latter theories are considered "grand" (molar) formulations that are so sweeping as to be meaningless, or at least chronically premature in their expansive claims. Since LLT addresses the broad base of the psychological discipline, many colleagues have considered it to be this sort of theory. Of course, it is difficult to see how LLT could be otherwise than a grand theory. Any formulation that questions the very basis of explanation in psychology has to be of this stripe. To assume that empirical studies of a functional nature do not themselves rest on grand assumptions is to concoct a fantasy.

The problem with limited or so-called miniature theorizing is that it tends to rephrase the experimental design as some kind of theoretical process. This is how the s-r bind in psychology arose in the first place. The efficient-cause manipulations of the independent variable (iv) effecting the dependent variable (dv) was tautologized with the stimulus-response (s-r) formulations of the reigning paradigm. It is comforting to have one's field tied up so neatly into an efficient-cause package. Unfortunately, the loss in objectivity occurring here, where methods dictate the theories to be tested by them, has weakened rather than strengthened psychology. Furthermore, the lack of broader theorizing in psychology has resulted in mounds of research evidence that is not being organized into an instructive, meaningful whole. At least part of the reason that current research efforts are increasingly aimed at ecological questions is the emptiness that has resulted from modern functionalism, where the goal seems to be to find any statistically significant finding, no matter how irrelevant it is to life. Logical learning theory need not apologize for trying to bring psychology closer to the wider reaches of lived experience.

4. *Why is it necessary to introduce so much new jargon into this theory? Can't we find classical terms to achieve the same goal?*

Logical learning theory has suffered under the onus of framing new terminology, and colleagues are understandably put off on first confronting its "strange-sounding" concepts, which seem more like fanciful neologisms than necessary technical concepts. The problem here is that, as I have noted previously in this volume, it is impossible to say one thing and mean another. We cannot take the mechanistic, efficient-cause terminology of psychology and express through its use a teleological, formal/final-cause meaning.

Unfortunately, to appreciate this fact, the person who raises question 4 should already have a grasp of what predication involves. Technical theoretical terms, like all words, borrow from precedent meanings that frame them. Thus, when an efficient-cause meaning predicates the theoretical term in question, we cannot take this term and subsequently use it as a further predication of yet other targets that demand formal/final causation if they are to be represented accurately.

Take the concept of encoding, for example. In Demonstration Experiment 10 I used this term in parenthesis, to draw an informal parallel with cognitive theories. In LLT's terms no encoding takes place; rather, a conceptual affirmation occurs. I find that cognitive theorists rarely define what an encoding involves, but it is nevertheless clear that they conceive of cognition in terms of input and tabula rasa passive reception—at least, the mind is construed as totally passive at the outset of cognition. These initial, externally patterned inputs can serve as mediators of later inputs and thus simulate what LLT calls predication. This concept of encoding takes meaning from efficient (and possibly material) causation. Some psychologists believe that encoding suffices for what we have been calling telosponsive affirmation.

If we were to agree to use their term *encoding* instead of a term like *affirmation* to explain the process taking place, politely ignoring the different precedent meanings involved in these terms, where would that lead to in the end? I think it is a certainty that the mediational theorist would continue thinking of this process as an efficient cause, thereby translating predication to mediation in the blink of an eye. No one would grasp the polemic involved in the LLT alternative. Logical learning theory would end up as just another thematic variation of the received view. I think that it is imperative that a theory claiming to be different *really* be different. Too much "new" theorizing in psychology is simply a variation on the common theme, resulting in many distinctions but no genuine differences in our professional lexicon.

Those colleagues who would call the handful of new terms employed by LLT a jargon must ask themselves whether they have made an honest effort to understand why these terminological innovations have been coined. Without such examination, claims of this sort are probably nothing more than expressions of allegiance to the reigning paradigm. To the teleologist, explanations of human behavior as due to inputs that have been stored, retrieved, output and fed back could be readily characterized as unnecessary jargon when it comes to describing what human beings do in observed behavior. We do not advance psychology by smugly dismissing terminology in this manner, setting up barriers to communication across paradigmatic differences by fiat. We know why the mechanists are mechanists. Let us now try to learn why teleologists are teleologists.

5. Since you admit that any attempt to prove a scientific theory by appealing to empirical data commits the fallacy of affirming the consequent, why do you try to prove LLT empirically? Empirical data are always so much easier to interpret through theories other than LLT that it seems a waste of time to do research. You have to make your case philosophically and not empirically.

Logical learning theory is a rigorous humanism. It embraces empirical validation because it favors science, and even though scientific method does not lead to (logically) necessary truth, there is no more satisfying criterion of truth than being able to arrange circumstances and empirically predicting to a criterion with accuracy (i.e., validation). However, given that we cannot use empirical evidence alone to base our decision on which theory to follow in our psychological science, how do we choose among the alternatives open to us when all the theories concerned stand up to the evidence equally well? In the final analysis, it is a telic consideration that provides the grounds for our selection. What purpose is the theory framed to serve? Knowing our purpose, and intending that we further this end, we will have clear grounds for the selection of a theory that has already met the test of validation. This theory will be the one that will prove most instructive, because it will meet our end.

Additionally, after articulating our purpose, we would then be expected to frame experiments carrying forward the inferences and implications of this theory, working to put our ideas to test even as we recognize the alternative theory that might cast our findings in a contrasting light. We would never, as proper scientists, rest with a theory that has been grounded exclusively in procedural evidence. This means that we conduct experiments to validate our theoretical expectations *for ourselves.* Not every alternative theory will account for the empirical findings equally well. How well are things hanging together for us and for those who follow our line of thought? As the developments in modern science have surely taught us, we are not required to seek, much less conform to, a unified descriptive scheme. Science is a methodological affair, an approach to proof, and not an ideology framed to limit theoretical speculation and understanding.

The reference to philosophical proof in this question is a common detraction of LLT. Because I have found it necessary to base my objections to standard psychological theory on a careful examination of the tenets and history of science, fashioning arguments based on procedural evidence and appeals to authority, the critic has taken this wider (predicating) effort as a kind of philosophical analysis. Although this is true in one sense, what is overlooked here is that LLT advocates have also gathered considerable empirical data in support of their view—over 150 empirical experiments to date, using thousands of subjects. This aspect of the total LLT polemic is conveniently overlooked or dismissed by the critic, who would like to keep such teleological alternatives ensconced within the realm of philosophy (i.e., fanciful speculation, mystery, etc.). It would be a salutary development if more psychologists spent some time stepping back from their frenzied dash to gather data and ask themselves some of the philosophical questions that LLT advocates have reflexively put to themselves.

6. *How can you hope to stay completely in the realm of the* Logos? *Psychological theories must be comprehensive if they are to prove instructive. We must employ all four groundings, including* Physikos, Bios, *and* Socius, *as well as the* Logos. *Isn't this what the "unity of the sciences" is all about?*

I have nothing against unity when it works, but I have come to the regrettable conclusion that this aim for unity in theorizing has been a source of confusion and even disunity in psychology. When we hear the unity of the sciences being lauded, we rarely appreciate that this compatibility was easily achieved because only a few groundings were involved (i.e., the *Physikos-Bios* tandem, each of which drew heavily on efficient- and material-causation). The outcome is quite different when we begin considering all four groundings. As I noted above, when Dollard and Miller (1950) attempted to subsume Freudian teleological terminology by the efficient-cause concepts of Hullian theory, all that resulted was a gross distortion of psychoanalysis. Of course, Freud is guilty of introducing some distortions of his own. As I also noted above, it was in response to the Newtonian pressures of his time that Freud formulated his notoriously confusing and arbitrary libido theory, which can now be seen as an effort to express *Logos* concerns in *Bios* fashion (Freud, 1921/1955, p. 90).

I think it is much better for a psychologist to select just one of the four groundings and then try to stick with it, avoiding the temptation to borrow from other grounds at crucial points, as so often happens. I have recommended this as a *principle of complementarity* for psychology (Rychlak, 1993). There is nothing to stop the psychologist who wishes to back up, shift perspectives, and construe the same target in terms of a different grounding—for example, to shift from *Logos* to *Socius*. Such shifts in groundings would be considered not inconsistencies but simply alternative ways in which to understand the targeted items of interest.

As for our fellow scientists, I think that they are fully cognizant of the importance of the *Logos* and *Socius* as complements to the traditional ground-

ings of the *Physikos* and *Bios*. Physicists today refer to themselves as "participators" (Zukav, 1979, p. 29), which means they appreciate that their framing
grounds influence what they will learn from their observations. These scientists are not going to be upset if some of us in psychology base our explanations exclusively on a *Logos* grounding. The theoretical physicist David Bohm
(1985) has postulated an *implicate order* (p. 14) that functions both in subatomic fields and in generating meanings in human thought (pp. 14, 25, 94).
The theoretical biochemist Rupert Sheldrake (1988) has postulated a related
notion of *morphic fields* (p. 198) that lend uniform behavioral patternings to
entire species of animals "all at once." Such pattern conceptions are readily
understood on the grounds of the *Logos*, construed here in more of an extraspective than an introspective manner. But we can, as psychologists, think of
these order/field concepts as framed by the cognitions of human beings calling themselves scientists. This would represent an introspective use of the
Logos, to which LLT is well suited.

We cannot deny that a compendium of all four groundings may some-
day be worked out to account for human behavior in every detail—or that
one and only one grounding may suffice for everything needing to be explained. Given the history of 20th-century psychology, neither seems likely.
It is more likely that things will remain just as patched together as they are
today. If we were to focus more critically on the grounding assumptions of
our theories, however, and attempt to refine them as we go along in terms
of these grounds, it is my belief that a sharper body of psychological theory
would be the result. It is the slipping and sliding to and fro, from *Physikos* to
Bios to *Logos* to *Socius*, that has hurt the advancement of clarity in psychological theorizing. If theorists continue mixing these grounds, then we should
consider the resultant product in light of what may be the core grounding
actually coming through at crucial points in the theory.

   7. *I can see how an alternative theory like balance or dissonance or reactance
      can account for what LLT is getting at. What makes LLT more
      instructive than such theories?*

Because there are other theories in psychology that rely on oppositional
conceptions, it appears to some colleagues that LLT is not needed to explain
this aspect of human cognition. First of all, I must reiterate that for any fact
pattern there will always be—in principle an infinite number of—alternative
theories accounting for the observed facts. Second, the main answer to this
question is that because of its abstract character, LLT has a greater range of
application than theories like balance, dissonance, reactance, and the like. I
have noted in my demonstration experiments that LLT can address very fundamental issues in human learning, tackling concepts that are familiar to

cognitive science but that are not even considered by the other theories mentioned. Logical learning theory is more abstractly framed than these other theories and can in fact subsume them, whereas the reverse is not possible.

8. *Does the predicational model force me to believe in human agency? Why can't I accept predication and yet also deny agency?*

This final question comes from the colleague who would like to think of people as predicating but who feels thereby that LLT is forcing her or him to believe in agency, with the implication being that this is a marshmallow concept at best and pure spiritualism at worst. This colleague wants to know why this tandem of predication and agency must go together. The answer comes down to an understanding of what predication means. If we recognize that to predicate is to affirm a position that necessarily (logically, automatically, etc.) allows for its opposite meaning to be cognized by way of contrariety, contradiction, contrast, or negation, then we are forced to accept (via logical necessity) that this cognizer has the implicit capacity to extend meanings away from what the circumstance is to what it is not.

This capacity is what is meant by agency. You cannot have the active formulation of predication (inside the Euler circle) without opposition (outside the Euler circle). This oppositionality is generic to the predicational process, and once a content is affirmed, there is a delimitation carrying thought away to possible alternatives (understanding-intentions) as well. The combined result of generic and delimiting oppositionality is nothing short of agency—the capacity to do otherwise, all circumstances remaining the same (a capacity that may itself be negated, of course).

Often, the person raising this question reasons as follows: "Nature is determined [meaning here a material- and efficient-cause determinism], and as I am a product of nature, I must be subjected to these same lawful influences." Harking back to question 6, we can see that this statement mixes *Physikos* and *Bios* groundings into a *Logos* issue. The former two groundings express regularities in terms of laws, and the latter ground captures rule-following regularities. Rules can be framed and reframed, but laws are presumably fixed. Mathematics, which traces physical laws, is a rule-following endeavor (although the terms *law* and *rule* are frequently used interchangeably in this discipline). If we can think of human cognition as a rule-generating and rule-following process, then there is no contradiction in saying that an organism obeying natural laws is capable of understanding and acting through rule-following behavior. Such behavior is agential because the person who can set the predicating (rule-following) grounds for the sake of which he or she is to be understood as a natural product is not behaving like a machine. Computing machines never selectively affirm the grounds that direct them, nor can they negate these grounds. It is for these technical reasons that LLT must insist on agency once predication is accepted. We cannot have one without the other.

Final Concluding Comment

It is the hope of the LLT advocate that more psychologists will begin conceptualizing human beings in terms of telosponsivity rather than in terms of responsivity or inputting and outputting. If we psychologists fail to advance our thinking concerning human behavior, we will fall ever more out of step with the basic assumptions of our very civilization, which include agency, the importance of intention in action, and the capacity to influence circumstances as a unique person seeking valued outcomes. These beliefs are not "folk" psychologies (Stich, 1986), quaintly out of step with the empirical evidence proving that the human organism is a machine. There is no such convincing body of empirical evidence to cite. Indeed, the evidence has been steadily falsifying a mechanistic image of humanity, as this volume has demonstrated.

Glossary

Action-intention: A form of telosponse in which the target is to carry out an observable action sequence that is typically referred to as behavior. All action-intentions begin as understanding-intentions. *See also* Intention, Telosponse, Understanding-intention.

Affective assessment, affection: A transcending telosponse; that is, an innate capacity to reflexively target and thereby evaluate the meanings of one's cognitive contents (premises, concepts, predicates, etc.), characterizing them as either *liked* (positive evaluation) or *disliked* (negative evaluation). Logical learning theory holds that affection is the most basic and abstract cognition carried on by a human being. *See also* Reflexivity, Telosponse.

Affirmation: An aspect of telosponsivity in which a point anywhere along a bipolar dimension of meaning is affirmed as being the grounds for the sake of which understanding or action will be furthered in cognition. Affirmation is the psychic equivalent of drawing the Euler circle of a predication, for it delimits the specific realm of meaning that will be extended to the target. *See also* Euler circle(s), Telosponse.

Affirming the consequent: A logical error growing out of an "If, then" course of reasoning. It takes place when we reason "If A then B" and subsequently affirm "B" to conclude "therefore A." It arises in science when we reason, "If my theory is true then my experimental data will array as predicted" and subsequently affirm, "My experimental data array as predicted" to conclude, "therefore, my theory is [necessarily] true." The latter conclusion is technically incorrect: An alternative theory might *in principle* also be validated by the observed data.

Agency: The capacity that an organism has to behave or believe in conformance with, in contradiction to, in addition to, or without regard for what is perceived to be environmental or biological determinants. *See also* Freedom of the will.

Apposition: The state of being "side by side." In Boolean formulations, apposition replaces opposition. Since the items in apposition do not delimit each other, there is no intrinsic tie between them as there is in an opposition. *See also* Opposition.

Arbitrary cognition/behavior: Cognition and behavior that is under predication but in which the meanings so aligned are readily shifted based on convenience or in the face of some unanticipated advantage that will redound on the telosponder. Although the resultant cognition and behavior may be "unprincipled," they are not without a framing-meaning at the protopoint in question. *See also* Meaning-extension, Predication, Protopoint.

Assumption(s): Highly abstract understanding-intentions that work as a prememory to frame what can then be known. They can be examined via reflexivity but usually are not, because they are taken as unquestionably plausible, self-evident, and so forth. *See also* Ground, Knowledge, Prememory.

Aufgabe: The experimental instructions given to a subject that define the task to be done. *See also Einstellung.*

Awareness: A cognitive state occurring when the person knows that something other than what is now occurring might or could take place. Thus, some subjects who are aware in a conditioning experiment sometimes fail to comply with the instructions (i.e., they behave as agents). They know that it is possible to do otherwise and actually do so. *See also* Agency, Conscious.

Baconian Criticism: The charge that adding telic conceptions into the description of natural processes adds nothing to our understanding of these processes. Bacon did not level this charge against final-cause descriptions of human beings.

Behavior: A global reference to the overt and covert actions or activities of living organisms, including their physiological and biological functions.

Bios: One of the four major grounds used in psychology on which to base explanations. *Bios* grounds draw from the chemical and tissue substances of animate nature to explain events on the basis of such processes as mediation, organic systems, and genetics. *See also Logos, Physikos, Socius.*

Categorization: Another term for the predicational process. This process results in a category, or what is often termed a cognitive representation. *See also* Predication, process of.

Cause(s): Derived from the Greek word *aitiá,* which means the responsible factor in any descriptive understanding of the nature of things, including behaviors, physical bodies, and thoughts. The four causes include the material, efficient, formal, and final. These meanings—singularly or in combination—serve as the predicates of anything in existence. They are highly abstract precedents from which meaning-extension occurs in human thought. *See also* Efficient cause, Final cause, Formal cause, Material cause, Meaning-extension, Precedent.

Choice: In LLT, this refers to a relatively difficult affirmation. The telosponding person continually takes positions in ongoing experience, but this is not perceived as making choices. It is only when ambivalence or complexity arises during premise-affirmation that the person senses the telosponsive process as involving choice. *See also* Affirmation, Taking a position, Telosponse.

Cognition: According to LLT, this is simply an alternative term for telosponsivity. Cognition is essentially evaluative because of the capacity to render affective assessments of the targets under predication. *See also* Affective assessment, Telosponsivity.

Connectionism: Classically, this concept referred to the associationistic theories of learning proposed by theorists like Thorndike and Watson. In more recent cognitive theorizing this refers to an emphasis on connecting links in the nodal network rather than on the nodes per se. This connectionistic network is viewed as a bottom-up system in which the connecting links acquire certain weights that determine the extent and direction of activation relative to the nodes.

Conscious: In addition to its use in describing the *Bios* functions like being awake, alertness, and so forth, this concept refers to the fact that the person is framing understanding- and action-intentions with awareness. Conscious behavior is behavior that the telosponder acknowledges as being internally directed, decided upon, and willful. *See also* Awareness, Unconscious.

Construction: This term has both a Kantian and a Lockean usage. In the Kantian sense, this means to interpret that which is under observation in top-down fashion. In the Lockean sense, this means to heap together, as in building a structure from small units in bottom-up fashion.

Content: An ingredient that is produced, conveyed, or otherwise employed by a process. *See also* Process.

Context: According to LLT, the meaning framed by a context is tantamount to predication. The predication process is what always ensures that there will be contextual meanings at play in human cognizance. *See also* Predication, process of.

Contextualism: One of Pepper's "world hypotheses," based on the view that human action is understandable only when the historical event is taken into consideration. Pepper's theory is actually predicational in nature. *See also* Context, Predication, process of.

Contradiction, law of: Also known as the law of noncontradiction. This is actually a rule holding that A is not non-A. This "law" underwrites both demonstrative reasoning and Boolean (hard) disjunction. *See also* One and many.

Delimiting oppositionality: Bounds a specific meaning that stands in relation to its bipolar counterpart, as when injustice delimits justice and vice versa. Delimiting oppositionality involves the contents of the predicational process, enabling the reasoner to draw implications. Thus, certain opposites lend a direction to thought, as when saying "John is not reliable" implies that he is unreliable. *See also* Generic oppositionality, Implication, Oppositionality.

Demonstrative reasoning: Cognition in which oppositionality is dismissed in favor of the either/or distinctions of the law of contradiction. The region inside the Euler circle is focused on as if it were the only alternative framing reasoning. Aristotle claimed that demonstrative reasoners affirm their major premises based on the fact that these premises are primary and true, hence not open to dispute or negation. *See also* Dialectical reasoning.

Determine, determinism: Refers to the limitation or setting of limits on events, including behavior. Each of the four Aristotelian causes involves a distinctive form of determinism. *See also* Cause.

Dialectic, dialectical: From the Greek word *dialektos*, which refers to discourse, talk, exchanging ideas (*dia* = between; *legein* = talk). Among other uses, this concept was used to describe the exchanges that Socrates had with his students, whereby there was an initial expression of a thesis, a countering antithesis, and a resulting synopsis (the modern term is *synthesis*). The fundamental idea here is that knowledge is tied together through oppositionality ("one and many" thesis). There are many dialectical theories in the history of ideas. Logical learning theory views dialectic as a special case of oppositionality in which the union of bipolar meaning is emphasized. *See also* Dialectical reasoning, Oppositionality.

Dialectical reasoning: Cognition in which oppositionality is employed, so that the region of meaning outside the Euler circle is not dismissed as irrelevant or erroneous. Aristotle claimed that dialectical reasoners affirm the major premise based on opinion (point of view, arbitrary choice, bias, etc.) rather than on a fixed, primary, and true basis. *See also* Demonstrative reasoning, Dialectic, Oppositionality.

Difference: One of the outcomes of generic oppositionality, in which the sameness of a target framed by a predicate is negated. For example, when "John is German" is negated ("John is not German"), removing John from the predicating meaning of *German*, we have a difference expressed. John is different in nationality from German people. *See also* Delimiting oppositionality, Generic oppositionality, Predication, Sameness.

Discriminal theory: A theory that is written to account for differences in behavior per se. This type of theory is written at a somewhat lower level of abstraction than a vehicular theory. Often such theory is based on the *Bios*. *See also* Vehicular theory.

Disjunction: From the Latin, meaning "to disjoin" or "to separate into alternatives." A hard disjunction admits only two alternatives, either x or y but not both. Soft disjunction admits of three alternatives, either x or y or both. Boolean disjunction, which underwrites cognitive psychology and computer science, represents a hard disjunction. Logical learning theory embraces a soft disjunction. *See also* Demonstrative reasoning, Dialectical reasoning.

Efficient cause: A predication used to account for the nature of things (including behavior) based on the impetus in a succession of events over time. Explanations of behavior based on energy pushes, gravity attractions, and the machinelike flow of motion are under predication by efficient causation. *See also* Cause(s).

Einstellung: The set or expectation framed by the subject of an experiment based on his or her understanding of the predicating task instructions. *See also Aufgabe*.

Elaboration: A term used to describe the circumstance in which some targeted item (symbol, word, etc.) is being given additional meaning. In LLT terms, to elaborate a target is to predicate it by several different contexts, thereby enriching it via meaning-extension.

Emotion: According to LLT, this refers to a pattern of physiological feelings in a situation, the sum of which is targeted and thereby organized into meaning by the predications of the person experiencing these feelings and living through the situation. Emotions are not telosponses but are affectively assessed via such transcending telosponses. Emotions are not arbitrarily generated through oppositional cognition but occur in unidirectional fashion, as do all biological and physical promptings in experience. Emotional feelings can be stimulated by certain drugs or by having the person recall an emotion-provoking circumstance. *See also* Affective assessment.

Euler circle(s): A means of representing class or categorical relations through figures that was introduced by the Swiss mathematician Leonhard Euler (1707–1783). Circles of various sizes depict the relations. For example, "All A is B" would be represented by a smaller circle labeled "A" situated within a larger (predicating) circle labeled "B." Logical learning theory employs the Euler circles (or Euler diagrams) as a model to depict the predicational process.

Extraspective perspective of theory: Framing theoretical explanations of things and or events in the third person ("that, it, him, her," etc.), that is, from the perspective of an observer. Extraspection is the natural outlook for validation—where we look at our experimental data unfolding—but it is always possible to test introspective theory through validation if we just keep a clear distinction between method and theory. *See also* Affirming the Consequent, Introspective perspective of theory.

Familiarity: According to LLT, this is a well-organized predication that therefore lends effective meaning to its target(s). Familiarity may be clocked by a person's frequent contact with a "handy" (contiguous) item of knowledge, but such tracking measures fail to explain the precise nature of familiarity.

Final cause: Any concept used to account for the nature of things (including behavior) based on the assumption that there is a reason, end, or goal for the sake of which things exist or events are carried out. Explanations that rely on the person's intentions, aims, or aspirations are final-cause descriptions of behavior. *See also* Cause(s), Teleology.

Forgetting: This phenomenon occurs when the organism is unable to frame a predication in which the target to be recalled is lent relevant meaning—with "relevance" involving the reason why the target is to be brought into current cognizance. *See also* Knowing, Remembering.

Formal cause: Any concept used to account for the nature of things (including behavior) based on their patterned organization, shape, design, or order. Explanations of behavior emphasizing the style or type of behavioral pattern taken on are formal-cause descriptions. Often, these explanations are said to involve the quality or essence of the item in question. *See also* Cause(s).

Freedom of the will: A nontechnical reference to agency. The person who has free will is capable of precedently affirming the ground or assumption for the sake of which she or he will be determined. Before affirmation occurs we can speak of freedom, and after affirmation occurs we can speak of will(-power) in the meaning-extension to follow sequaciously. *See also* Affirmation, Assumption, Final cause, Ground, Sequacious, Telosponse.

Generic oppositionality: A general aspect of the predicational process in which targets fall either under or beyond the meaning being extended by the predicate. In the Euler-circle model, this would involve falling either inside or outside the framing circle. Generic oppositionality is intrinsic to the predicational process and is most clearly reflected in negations of predicate meanings that are not themselves capable of extending a delimiting oppositionality—as in the case of "John is not a German." In this case, although we cannot draw any implication as to John's actual nationality (content), we are nevertheless involved in an oppositional process. *See also* Delimiting oppositionality, Oppositionality.

Ground(s): The basis on which a theory is being framed. There are four major groundings to consider in psychology: *Bios, Logos, Physikos,* and *Socius.* Each of these grounds has its own process and thereby specific contents that are under processing.

Homunculus: The "little person" who supposedly must be concocted to explain how it is that agency can occur in human behavior. The homunculus is needed because of the mechanism that is postulated as an explanation of human behavior. Since the mechanism is without intention, it requires a "driver" or "director." In LLT, the person is the homunculus, because the person is conceptualized as teleological to begin with.

Idiographic: Any approach to the description of things (including behavior) based on what is special or unique rather than on what is generally true (i.e., applying across the board to all such targets). The idiographic (*idios* = one's own) description seeks to capture a particular subject matter and uses measurement devices tailored to the individual. *See also* Nomothetic.

Implication: A line of cognition in which the premises under affirmation are considered by the person to be uncertain—possibly true but possibly false—resulting in conclusions that are not experienced as confidently or certainly the case, really true, and so on. *See also* Affirmation, Inference.

Inference: A line of cognition in which the premises under affirmation are considered to be true, so that any conclusions reached are taken by the person as soundly justified. *See also* Affirmation, Demonstrative reasoning, Implication.

Intention: Behaving for the sake of purposive meanings as encompassed in images, language terms, affections, and so on, all of which are encompassed as premises in the act of predication. When purpose and intention combine, we have telosponsivity. Intentionality is as pure an expression of final causation as possible. Logical learning theory also distinguishes between (1) *understanding-intentions*, in which the meanings under affirmation are restricted to the logical ordering of cognizance, and (2) *action-intentions*, in which the meanings under affirmation are extended into readily observable, overt behavior. *See also* Affirmation, Final cause, Predication, Premise, Purpose, Telosponse.

Introspective perspective of theory: Framing theories of things or events in the first person, from the outlook of an identity acting within them. Introspective theory refers to "I, me" rather than to "that, it." *See also* Extraspective perspective of theory.

Judgment: Another way of referring to the evaluations—including affective assessments—entering into the affirmations of predications. *See also* Affective assessment, Affirmation, Choice, Predication.

Knowing, knowledge: Refers to the abstract predications involving organizations of meanings that lend their significance to other targets in top-down fashion. At the highest level of abstraction, knowledge acts as assumptions or axioms that are not targeted for awareness. In trying to remember a target, knowing places emphasis on the predication involved. It is possible to remember this target without remembering the knowledge required to do so, but if knowing does not occur, remembering cannot occur. *See also* Assumption, Prememory, Remembering.

Law, lawfulness: A law is a presumably inviolate (i.e., nonarbitrary) regularity emanating from the *Physikos* or *Bios*. Lawfulness is a stable and generalizable relationship obtaining between an independent and dependent variable of an experiment. At its base, the law concept borrows from the meaning of formal causation, with the addition of material and efficient causation that stamps laws as necessary patterns. Logical learning theory holds that laws are framed by human beings who observe a stable, reliable relationship among variables in an experimental format and at some point place enough confidence in it to term it a law. *See also* Rule.

Learning: May be said to occur when the learner is confident enough to use a former target as a predicate. *See also* Predicate, Target.

Logic, logical: As used in the present volume, that which is concerned with meaningful patterns in cognition as well as the patterning of these meanings in ongoing experience. Both demonstrative and dialectical logic are involved. The focus is not on accuracy, precision, or correctness but merely on how meanings are patterned into other meanings. Logical explanations stress formal and final causation relying on demonstrative and dialectical rule following.

Logical learning theory: A teleological formulation of cognition and behavior that draws heavily on the concepts of predication and opposition to picture the human being as a telosponding organism, one that is continually taking a position on life as an active agent. *See also* Agency, Logic, Predication, Oppositionality, Telosponse.

Logos: One of the four major grounds used in psychology on which to base explanations. *Logos* grounds draw from the patterned order of events to explain matters according to processes like predication, construing, or mental activity. *See also Bios, Physikos, Socius.*

Material cause: Any concept used to account for the nature of things (including behavior) based on an assumed underlying, unchanging substance. Explanations of behavior based on genetic transmission or chemical elements are examples of material-cause descriptions. *See also* Cause(s).

Meaning: In traditional associationistic theory, the joining of independent units through frequency and contiguity over time. Logical learning theory interprets meaning as the logical relationship organized between an affirmed predicate and its target. Hence, meaning is an organization or pattern that extends its significance to some relevant target. *See also* Meaning-extension.

Meaning-extension: The precedent-sequacious flow of meaning in the conceptualizations of telosponsivity, commonly referred to as the inductive and deductive knowledge of experience. As meaning-extension proceeds, the knowledge framed by the predications of telosponsivity extends its range. *See also* Meaning-extension, principle of.

Meaning-extension, principle of: The idea that, all other considerations being equal, the patterning of meaning forming in a predication extends to the least understood or most poorly known target(s) having relevance to the predicating meaning in question. *See also* Meaning-extension, Predication.

Meaningfulness: As used in research on memory, a measure of the extent (applicability, utility, etc.) of meaning contained within learnable items (words, cvc trigrams), assessed by determining the frequency with which words are used in the standing language structure or what percentage of people find a verbal item linguistically useful. As used in LLT, the extent of personal significance that a particular meaning has for the individual concerned.

Mechanism: An explanation of behavior based predominantly on efficient causation, with occasional use of material causality. In no case is a final-cause concept employed. Hence, mechanism is essentially the opposite of teleology. *See also* Efficient cause, Material cause, Teleology.

Mediation, process of: As used in this volume, a mechanical process in which something that is produced elsewhere and taken in or input comes to play a role in the process that was not initially a part of or intrinsic to it. *See also* Predication.

Memory, as content: A target that has been extended meaning several predications previously and is then reconceptualized once again in the present.

Memory, as process: According to LLT, memory is a concept describing the cohesiveness and clarity of a tightly organized precedent meaning that is extended sequaciously in ongoing experience. The tighter this organization, the better the memory.

Memory cue: A meaningful referent that can act in the predicational location of a statement or broaden the context within which a lone target is situated. The closer a clue can approximate a relevant predication of a target, the better will it serve as a memory prompt for that target.

Metacognition: The knowledge a person possesses concerning his or her cognitive processes, as well as anything relating to them. Metacognitive self-monitoring is having a reflexive understanding-intention that captures or intimates when one is on the right track, going off into error, "getting close" to what is being intended, and so forth.

Method: The means or manner of determining whether a theoretical construct or statement is true or false. There are two broad types of method: (1) cognitive or conceptual method, which makes use of procedural evidence, and (2) research method, which uses validating evidence in addition to procedural. *See also* Procedural evidence, Theory, Validating evidence.

Model: A distinctive conceptual pattern used in the study of some topic as a standard to generate, organize, and communicate knowledge. Models are, in effect, tightly organized predicates.

Motivation: According to LLT, an evaluation of the relative advantage that an affirmed premise, encompassing a predicated target, makes possible in the telosponder's life. This advantage can be leveled by the telosponding individual or by an observer who presumes to know what the intentions enacted comprise and what they will therefore result in relative to the telosponder's total life situation.

Nomothetic: An approach to the description of things (including behavior) based on what is generally the case. The nomothetic approach relies on common laws (*nomos* = law) that describe everything exactly the same way for all time, instead of taking historical or developmental factors into consideration. The traditional assumption of large-scale samplings of items or subjects is that they are being drawn from a general pool or "parameter" that obeys a law that—in its refined state—has universal applicability. Logical learning theory does not endorse this traditional assumption but nevertheless employs nomothetic measurement as an alternative research strategy to idiographic measurement. The former strategy tests across large numbers, and the latter focuses on the individual. *See also* Idiographic, Law.

One and many: The principle holding that all experience is organized meaningfully through opposition, so that "same" delimits the meaning of "different," and vice versa. This principle underwrites dialectical reasoning and soft disjunction and can be opposed to the law of contradiction. *See also* Contradiction, law of.

Opposition, oppositionality: A "double predication" in which one predicate of a duality intrinsically delimits its target as being a contrary, contradiction, contrast, or negation of the meaning under extension, and, pari passu, the target in question—serving now as a reverse predicate—returns the favor. *See also* Apposition, Delimiting oppositionality, Generic oppositionality.

Perception: In LLT, this refers to the predication of sensory input, thereby organizing it into meaning. To perceive is to capture the patterns of sensations that align themselves in the *Logos*. Perception has a logic to it that is employed in a problem-solving effort continually made by the perceiver qua telosponder.

Physikos: One of the four major grounds used in psychology on which to base explanations. *Physikos* grounds are drawn from the material and energic substances of inanimate nature. Examples of the processes of the *Physikos* realm are gravitation, constancy, and conservation. *See also Bios, Logos, Socius.*

Precedent (Pre-cee'-dent): Refers to the ordering of meaning without regard for time's passage; that is, a precedent meaning is one that goes before others in order or arrangement, as the major premise always precedes the minor premise of a syllogism, framing its general meaning so that the minor premise can extend only the meaning contained therein. *See also* Sequacious.

Predicate, predication: Can be understood as either a verb or a noun. As a verb, this refers to a process of affirming or denying; as a noun, it refers to that which is affirmed or denied (i.e., a meaningful content). Logical learning theory holds that cognitive representations such as schemata, plans, scripts, prototypes, and so on, are predicate contents of a predication process. When a predicate is used to frame a target in the process of predication, it is known as the context meaning. *See also* Affirmation, Predication, process of.

Predication, process of: The logical process of affirming, denying, or qualifying precedently broader patterns of meaning in sequacious extension to narrower or targeted patterns of meaning. The target is the point, aim, or end (telos) of the meaning-extension. *See also* Meaning-extension, Precedent, Sequacious.

Prememory: The assumptive framework that gradually forms in the course of learning and is therefore known, although it need not be remembered. Prememory organizes what is to be remembered. Affective assessment can also serve as prememory because it serves as an organizer of cognition from its very inception. The amnesiac patient may be unable to recall the name of an item but can still understand or read a question concerning this item. This capacity to read is a reflection of prememory. Knowing and remembering are not identical. *See also* Affective assessment, Assumption, Knowing.

Premise: A statement of meaning (including assumption, belief, point of view, argument, etc.) that is put forward at the outset of a line of reasoning. Premises always encompass predication and are affirmed at the protopoint. In the traditional syllogistic formula, premises embody precedent major and minor affirmations of meaning that are extended sequaciously to the increasingly focused conclusion. *See also* Affirmation, Predication, Protopoint.

Procedural evidence: A basis for belief in a theory because of its plausibility or consistency with common sense. This is sometimes called face validity or theoretical proof.

Process: A discernible, repeatable course of action on the basis of which some item(s) under description is (are) believed to be sequentially patterned. *See also* Content.

Pro forma: For the sake of a precedent form, organization, or order that is extended sequaciously to the target of interest. In LLT this phrase is used to suggest that human mentation is not a tabula rasa process ordered exclusively by experiential input but instead extends meaning to experience. *See also* Tabula rasa.

Protopoint: The anchoring point of meaning-extension at which affirmations are made. The terms *precedent* and *sequacious* refer to the ordering of meaning-extensions at any point in the course of intentional behavior—for example, over the full course of a deductive or an inductive line of thought. The *initiating* point at which a pro forma intelligence grounds its understanding or intends its purposes is the protopoint. In one sense, this is the first precedent for any one line of intentionality, but all protopoint affirmations are sequaciously extended from ever more abstract meanings. If there are universals in human intelligence, they would represent the ultimate protopoints of reason. *See also* Meaning-extension, Pro forma.

Purpose: The "aim of the meaning" of a concept, which is brought to mental existence by the intentional behavior of a telic organism. Purpose focuses on the formal-cause aspect of telosponsive behavior. When such patterned organizations that have an aim (point, significance, end, etc.) are intended by a conceptualizing organism, we can speak of the combined process as a telosponse. *See also* Intention, Telosponse.

Recognition: The tautologizing of a cognitive content with itself. *See also* Tautology.

Reflectivity, self-reflectivity: The capacity to "look at" the resultant contents of cognitive processing in an extraspective manner. Unlike reflexivity, which is an introspective examination of one's assumptions, biases, and convictions, reflectivity is going over and elaborating what a thought sequence has already accomplished or arrived at. We reflect on what has occurred or is the case in thought. We reflexively examine what otherwise might have been the case in thought. *See also* Extraspection, Introspection, Reflexivity.

Reflexivity, self-reflexivity: The introspective capacity for mentation to turn back on itself by transcending the process taking place and thereby realizing that it is involved in the pro forma framing of experience. Reflexivity always leads to the appreciation that the meanings presently under affirmation could be otherwise. Reflexivity is made possible through oppositionality, in which there is always a sense that the meanings under affirmation could be brought into question, rejected, revised, reaffirmed, and so on. *See also* Affirmation, Oppositionality, Pro forma, Reflectivity, Transcendence.

Rehearsal: An empirical measure of the organism's intentional efforts to organize via predication those meanings that are relevant to some event at hand. This cognitive organization may require many trials to prove effective, or it may occur in a single trial. *See also* Reinforcement.

Reinforcement: In LLT terms, this occurs when understanding- or action-intentionality flows from a premise that successfully (effectively, helpfully) conceptualizes a circumstance for the individual employing it. The meaning-extension thus has cash value, it works for the person concerned as evidently true (although objectively it may be false). Positive reinforcements successfully extend meanings that are rooted in positive predications, and negative reinforcements successfully extend negative premises.

Reinforcement value: The operationalized measure of a subject's affective assessment. In early work on LLT the like-dislike ratings that operationalized affective assessment were given this name, thereby keeping *theory* (affection) separate from *method* (reinforcement value). This concept was dropped from LLT due to the confusion arising over the meaning of *reinforcement*. *See also* Reinforcement.

Remembering: Places emphasis on the target in cognitive efforts to affirm the same predication that was affirmed initially some time ago. To remember a past event or object is to extend meaning from an approximation of the initial predication to the target being remembered. The better the organization of this initial predication, the greater the likelihood that the target will be rememberd. *See also* Knowing, Predication, Prememory.

Representation: Another term for the content of a cognitive process. Representations can be signs or symbols, depending on the process producing them. Predicational modelers consider their representations to be symbols (i.e., meaning-producing organizations). Mediational modelers consider their representations to be signs (i.e., learned cues that act as surrogates for something else).

Responsibility: A recognition that the person plays a role in the telosponsive affirmation of premises, encompassing the grounds for the sake of which thoughts are furthered and behavior is enacted.

Rule(s): Fundamentally arbitrary proscriptions that must be conformed to if they are to retain their integrity. Rules are formal-cause regularities having an internal consistency that dictates a pattern of thought or action. Rules also have a final-cause aspect in that they are subject to change depending on the intentions of those who are to follow them. *See also* Law, Lawfulness.

Sameness: When a target is subsumed by the meaning of a predicate (category, attribute, etc.). In the case of "John is German," the target ("John") is the same as all other members of the category ("German"), so far as this specific meaning is concerned. *See also* Difference.

Self: In LLT, this refers to the predications concerning personal identity as framed telosponsively. The telosponding organism arrives first on the scene in life, but in time can (1) reflexively target an introspective viewpoint as an "I, me," lending it meaning based on predications drawn from personal experience, as well as the opinions and impressions of others ("I am smart"); (2) become increasingly conscious of doing so ("I know myself better now"); and (3) seek to improve on the advantages gained from the use of further premises in which the "I, me" serves as a self-enhancing predicate ("That is mine") or in which the identity is targeted for enhancement ("I can be even smarter").

Semantic(s): Having to do with meaning. *See also* Syntax.

Sequacious (See-qway'-shus): Refers to the ordering of meaning without regard for time considerations. A sequacious meaning is one that follows or flows logically from the meanings of precedents, extending these as understanding- or action-intentions in a necessary fashion once they have been affirmed. Sequacious meaning-extensions can be entirely or partially tautological of their precedents. Partial sequacious extensions of a precedent meaning include analogies, metaphors, and so on. *See also* Meaning-extension, Precedent, Tautology.

Sign(s), Signal(s): Surrogate designations for that to which they are related— as when the number "7" stands for a specific number of single markers. Nontelic theories rely on signs as associated stand-ins for environmental influencers. Based on the frequency and contiguity of past experience, such environmentally produced surrogates are bonded together and input cognitively, totally without intention. *See also* Symbol.

Socius: One of the four major grounds used in psychology on which to base explanations. The *Socius* ground draws from the supra-individual organizations that influence through such processes as socialization, historicism, and political collectivism. *See also Bios, Logos, Physikos.*

Symbol(s): Vehicles for the creation of meaning that act like predications because they are pregnant with meanings, not all of which are clearly delimited in any one target. In linguistic theory, a symbol employs words instrumentally to convey the meaning symbolized. *See also* Sign.

Syntax: Having to do with the grammatical structure of word usage in a language. *See also* Semantic.

Tabula rasa: The view that mind is like a "smoothed table" at birth and that all it subsequently manifests in mentation is input or etched on it by external determinants. *See also* Pro forma.

Taking a position: Affirming a meaning for the sake of which behavior is intended, given that there is always an alternative meaning that could be the grounds for understanding or action. This is merely a recognition that any meaning under affirmation in telosponsivity can be transcended and hence reflexively put to question, rejected, and so forth. *See also* Affirmation, Reflexivity, Transcendence.

Target: Essentially the telos or aim (goal, etc.) of meaning-extension. The target is an integral aspect of predication. Meanings framed in predication are extended to targets. *See also* Predication, process of.

Tautology: A relation of identity in meaning, considered either extraspectively as redundant, analytically true statements or introspectively as the premised meaning being extended from what is known to what can be known.

Teleology, telic: The view that events are predicated according to plan, design, or assumption—that is, based on purposive meanings or reasons—and therefore directed to some intended end. Teleologies can be natural, deity, or human in formulation. Telic accounts rely on final causation and thus are the opposite of mechanistic accounts. *See also* Mechanism.

Telos: Greek word for end, goal, or grounding reason for the sake of which things exist or an event (behavior) is taking place. *See also* Final cause, Teleology, Telosponse.

Telosponse: The affirmation or taking of a position regarding a meaningful content (image, word, judgmental comparison, etc.) relating to a referent acting as a purpose for the sake of which behavior is then intended. Affirmation encompasses predication. *See also* Affirmation, Intention, Predication, Purpose.

Theory: A series of two or more schematic labels (words, visual images that we name, etc.) that have been hypothesized, presumed, or even factually demonstrated to bear a meaningful relationship, one with the other(s). *See also* Method.

Thought: Essentially synonyous with predication; the taking of a position relating to a target given the grounding context of a framework, as well as the continuing meaning-extension to follow. *See also* Meaning-extension, Predication.

Tightness of organization: Refers to the internal consistency and clarity of the meaning (content) under extension in predication. When a predicate content is tightly organized, the likelihood of retention in memory is increased. *See also* Predicate, Content.

Time: A unit of measurement employed to array (organize, pattern, plan, etc.) events logically. Time can thus serve as a standard—a that—for the sake of which life events are evaluated according to rate of progress, completion, and so forth.

Transcendence: According to LLT, the capacity that all humans have to rise above their ongoing predicational process even as it is taking place. Since human cognition involves affirmation and the taking of a position within oppositional possibilities, there is always this capacity to extend meanings away from the given to a realm of awareness that goes beyond what is under processing. Transcendence is closely tied to reflexivity. *See also* Affirmation, Reflexivity, Taking a position.

Unconscious: Logical learning theory would prefer that the term *unadmitted* be used for this concept. Thus, it is possible for a telosponder to know but not admit that an understanding- or action-intention is being carried forward. Such unconscious intentions are frequently the mirror-image of intentions that were carried out consciously. That is, negated intentions in consciousness can show up subsequently as unconscious intentions, symbolized in dreams and the like. As they lack awareness, unconscious intentions are demonstrative in nature, which means that they are often exceptionally rigid and poorly adapted to changing circumstances. *See also* Awareness, Conscious.

Understanding-intention: A telosponse in which the meaning affirmed frames understanding but is not necessarily manifested in overt action. Understanding-intentions can be fleeting impressions as well as deep-seated convictions. *See also* Action-intention, Intention.

Validating evidence: Believing in something only after it has been put to test in a prearranged course of events designed specifically to show what it relates to meaningfully. This is how scientists prove things, relying on the control of events and the prediction of an observable outcome. *See also* Procedural evidence.

Value: The relative worth of an object or action, in comparison to possible alternatives. The judgment rendered here places great emphasis on affective assessment, since values are essentially positive predications that can be wound into a social group's mores or norms. *See also* Affective assessment.

Vehicular theory: A theory that aims at capturing a process that will explain events regardless of the specific differences obtaining in the contents being conveyed by this process. Differences are understood as due to the different meanings of the contents being formulated by the vehicular process. *See also* Discriminal theory.

Will: A term capturing the determinism of sequacious meaning-extension that follows the affirmation of a premise. This concept encompasses a psychic (final-cause) determinism. *See also* Determine, Freedom of the will, Sequacious.

References

Abramson, Y., Tasto, D. L., & Rychlak, J. F. (1969). Nomothetic vs. idiographic influences of association value and reinforcement value on learning. *Journal of Experimental Research in Personality, 4,* 65–71.

Ackerman, B. P. (1992). The sources of children's errors in judging causal inferences. *Journal of Experimental Child Psychology, 54,* 90–119.

Adams, G. R., & Hamm, N. H. (1973). A partial test of the "contiguity" and "generalized imitation" theories of the social modeling process. *The Journal of Genetic Psychology, 123,* 145–154.

Adams, J. S. (1965). Inequity in social exchange. In L. Berkowitz (Ed.), *Advances in experimental social psychology* (Vol. 2, pp. 267–299). New York: Academic Press.

Adler, A. (1964). *Social interest, A challenge to mankind.* New York: Capricorn.

Aitken, S. (1977). *Gender preference in infancy.* Unpublished master's thesis, University of Edinburgh, Edinburgh, Scotland.

Alegria, J., & Noirot, E. (1978). Neonate orientation behaviour towards human voice. *International Journal of Behavioral Development, 1,* 291–312.

Alloy, L. B., & Abramson, L. Y. (1979). Judgment of contingency in depressed and non-depressed students: Sadder but wiser? *Journal of Experimental Psychology: General, 108,* 441–485.

Alloy, L. B., Abramson, L. Y., & Viscusi, D. (1981). Induced mood and the illusion of control. *Journal of Personality and Social Psychology, 41,* 1129–1140.

Allport, G. W. (1962). The general and the unique in psychological science. *Journal of Personality, 30,* 405–422.

Amsel, A. (1989). *Behaviorism, neobehaviorism, and cognitivism in learning theory: Historical and contemporary perspectives.* Hillsdale, NJ: Erlbaum.

Amsterdam, B. K. (1968). *Mirror behavior in children under two years of age.* Unpublished doctoral dissertation, University of North Carolina, Chapel Hill.

Anchor, K. N., Beck, S. E., Sieveking, N., & Adkins, J. (1982). A history of clinical biofeedback. *American Journal of Clinical Biofeedback, 5,* 3–16.

Anderson, J. R. (1985). *Cognitive psychology and its implications* (2nd ed.). New York: Freeman.

Anderson, N. H. (1968). Likeableness ratings of 555 personality-trait words. *Journal of Personality and Social Psychology, 9,* 272–279.

Anderson, R. C., & Ortony, A. (1975). On putting apples into bottles—a problem of polysemy. *Cognitive Psychology, 7,* 167–180.

Apao, W. K. (1979). *Affect and memory: Tests of the serial position effects.* Unpublished doctoral dissertation, Purdue University, West Lafayette, IN.

Apter, M. J. (1982). *The experience of motivation: The theory of psychological reversals.* New York: Academic Press.

Apter, M. J. (1989). *Reversal theory: Motivation, emotion, and personality.* New York: Routledge.

Archer, E. J. (1960). A re-evaluation of the meaningfulness of all possible CVC trigrams. *Psychological Monographs, 74*, No. 10 (Whole No. 497).

Aristotle. (1952a). *Topics*. In R. M. Hutchins (Ed.), *Great books of the western world* (Vol. 8, pp. 139–223). Chicago: Encyclopedia Britannica.

Aristotle. (1952b). *Physics*. In R. M. Hutchins (Ed.), *Great books of the western world* (Vol. 8, pp. 257–355). Chicago: Encyclopedia Britannica.

Aristotle. (1952c). *Metaphysics*. In R. M. Hutchins (Ed.), *Great books of the western world* (Vol. 8, pp. 495–626). Chicago: Encyclopedia Britannica.

Aristotle. (1952d). On memory and reminiscence. In R. M. Hutchins (Ed.), *Great books of the western world* (Vol. 8, pp. 690–695). Chicago: Encyclopedia Britannica.

Aristotle. (1952e). On the parts of animals. In R. M. Hutchins (Ed.), *Great books of the western world* (Vol. 9, pp. 159–229). Chicago: Encyclopedia Britannica.

Arkin, R., & Duval, S. (1975). Focus of attention and causal attributions of actors and observers. *Journal of Experimental Social Psychology, 11*, 427–438.

Armstrong, S. L., Gleitman, L. R., & Gleitman, H. (1983). On what some concepts might not be. *Cognition, 13*, 263–308.

Arnold, M. B. (Ed.). (1970). *Feelings and emotions: The Loyola symposium*. New York: Academic Press.

Asch, S. (1946). Forming impressions of personality. *Journal of Abnormal and Social Psychology, 41*, 258–290.

Ashworth, P. D., Giorgi, A., & de Konig, A. J. J. (Eds). (1986). *Qualitative research in psychology*. Pittsburgh: Duquesne University Press.

Atkinson, R. C., & Shiffrin, R. M. (1968). Human memory: A proposed system and its control processes. In K. W. Spence & J. T. Spence (Eds.), *The psychology of learning and motivation: Advances in research and theory*. (Vol. 2, pp. 90–197). New York: Academic Press.

August, G. J., & Rychlak, J. F. (1978). Role of intelligence and task difficulty in the affective learning styles of children with high and low self-concepts. *Journal of Educational Psychology, 70*, 406–413.

August, G. J., Rychlak, J. F., & Felker, D. W. (1975). Affective assessment, self-concept, and the verbal learning styles of fifth-grade children. *Journal of Educational Psychology, 67*, 801–806.

Bacon, F. (1605/1952). *Advancement of learning*. In R. M. Hutchins (Ed.), *Great books of the western world* (Vol. 30, pp. 1–101). Chicago: Encyclopedia Britannica.

Baddeley, A. D. (1981). The concept of working memory: A view of its current state and probable future development. *Cognition, 10*, 17–23.

Baddeley, A. D. (1986). *Working memory*. New York: Oxford University Press.

Baddeley, A. D., & Hitch, G. J. (1977). Recency re-examined. In S. Dornic (Ed.), *Attention and performance: VI* (pp. 647–667). Hillsdale, NJ: Erlbaum.

Bahrick, H. P., & Phelps, E. (1987). Retention of Spanish vocabulary over eight years. *Journal of Experimental Psychology: Learning, Memory and Cognition, 13*, 344–349.

Bahrick, L. E., Walker, A. S., & Neisser, U. (1981). Selective looking by infants. *Cognitive Psychology, 13*, 377–390.

Baker, L., & Santa, J. L. (1977). Context, integration, and retrieval. *Memory & Cognition, 5*, 308–314.

Baker-Ward, L., Ornstein, P. A., & Holden, D. J. (1984). The expression of memorization in early childhood. *Journal of Experimental Child Psychology, 37*, 555–575.

Balota, D. A., & Neely, J. H. (1980). Test-expectancy and word-frequency effects in recall and recognition. *Journal of Experimental Psychology: Human Learning and Memory, 6,* 576–587.

Bandura, A. (1979). Self-referent mechanisms in social learning theory. *American Psychologist, 34,* 439–442.

Bandura, A. (1986). *The social foundations of thought and action: A social cognitive theory.* Englewood Cliffs, NJ: Prentice-Hall.

Bandura, A., Ross, D., & Ross, S. (1963a). Imitation of film-mediated aggressive models. *Journal of Abnormal and Social Psychology, 66,* 3–11.

Bandura, A., Ross, D., & Ross, S. (1963b). Vicarious reinforcement and imitative learning. *Journal of Abnormal and Social Psychology, 67,* 601–607.

Banks, M. S., & Salapatek, P. (1983). Infant visual perception. In P. H. Mussen (Ed.), *Handbook of child psychology* (Vol. 2, 4th ed., pp. 435–571). New York: Wiley.

Barclay, J. R. (1973). The role of comprehension in remembering sentences. *Cognitive Psychology, 4,* 229–254.

Bargh, J. A. (1989). Conditional automaticity: Varieties of automatic influence in social perception and cognition. In J. S. Uleman & J. A. Bargh (Eds.), *Unintended thought* (pp. 3–51). New York: Guilford Press.

Barnard, S. (1989). *Negation and opposition in drawing implications.* Unpublished master's thesis, Loyola University of Chicago, Chicago.

Barsalou, L. W. (1983). Ad hoc categories. *Memory & Cognition, 11,* 211–227.

Bartlett, F. C. (1932). *Remembering: A study in experimental and social psychology.* Cambridge: Cambridge University Press.

Bastian, J. (1961). Associative factors in verbal transfer. *Journal of Experimental Psychology, 62,* 70–79.

Bateson, P. P. G. (1964). Changes in chick's responses to novel moving objects over the sensitive period for imprinting. *Animal Behavior, 12,* 479–489.

Bateson, P. P. G., & Chantrey, D. F. (1972). Retardation of discrimination learning in monkeys and chicks previously exposed to both stimuli. *Nature, 237,* 173–174.

Baum, W. M. (1973). The correlation-based law of effect. *Journal of the Experimental Analysis of Behavior, 20,* 137–153.

Bazerman, C. (1985). Physicists reading physics: Schema-laden purposes and purpose-laden schema. *Written Communication, 2,* 3–23.

Beck, A. T. (1976). *Cognitive therapy and the emotional disorders.* New York: International Universities Press.

Bellezza, F. S. (1984). Reliability of retrieval from semantic memory: Noun meanings. *Bulletin of the Psychonomic Society, 22,* 377–380.

Benelli, B., D'Odorico, L., Levorato, C., & Simion, F. (1977). Formation and extension of the concept in a prelinguistic child. *Italian Journal of Psychology, 3,* 429–448.

Berg, I. A. (1957). Deviant responses and deviant people: The formulation of the deviation hypothesis. *Journal of Counseling Psychology, 4,* 154–161.

Berger, P. L. (1963). *Invitation to sociology: A humanistic perspective.* New York: Doubleday/Anchor.

Berger, P. L., & Luckmann, T. (1966). *The social construction of reality: A treatise in the sociology of knowledge.* New York: Doubleday/Anchor.

Berlin, B., & Kay, P. (1969). *Basic color terms: Their universality and evolution.* Berkeley and Los Angeles: University of California Press.

Berlyne, D. E. (1960). *Conflict, arousal, and curiosity.* New York: McGraw-Hill.

Berlyne, D. E. (1966). Curiosity and exploration. *Science, 153,* 25–33.

Bever, T. G. (1975). Psychologically real grammar emerges because of its role in language acquisition. In D. Dato (Ed.), *Developmental psycholinguistics: Theory and applications* (pp. 63–75). Washington, DC: Georgetown University Round Table on Languages and Linguistics.

Binswanger, L. (1963). *Being-in-the-world* (J. Needleman, Trans.). New York: Basic.

Black, J. B., & Bower, G. H. (1980). Story understanding as problem-solving. *Poetics, 9,* 223–250.

Blaney, P. H. (1986). Affect and memory: A review. *Psychological Bulletin, 99,* 229–246.

Blaxton, T. A. (1989). Investigating dissociations among memory measures: Support for a transfer-appropriate processing framework. *Journal of Experimental Psychology: Learning, Memory, and Cognition, 15,* 657–668.

Bobrow, S. A., & Bower, G. H. (1969). Comprehension and recall of sentences. *Journal of Experimental Psychology, 80,* 455–461.

Bogdan, R. J. (1986). The importance of belief. In R. J. Bogdan (Ed.), *Belief: Form, content, and function* (pp. 1–16). Oxford: Clarendon.

Bohm, D. (1985). *Unfolding meaning: A weekend of dialogue with David Bohm.* New York: Ark.

Bolger, N., DeLongis, A., Kessler, R. C., & Schilling, E. A. (1989). Effects of daily stress on negative mood. *Journal of Personality and Social Psychology, 57,* 808–818.

Bond, M. H. (1972). Effects of an impression set on subsequent behavior. *Journal of Personality and Social Psychology, 24,* 301–305.

Boneau, C. A. (1974). Paradigm regained? Cognitive behaviorism restated. *American Psychologist, 29,* 297–309.

Boole, G. (1854/1958). *The laws of thought.* New York: Dover.

Boring, E. G. (1950). *A history of experimental psychology* (2nd ed.). New York: Appleton-Century-Crofts.

Bousfield, W. A. (1953). The occurrence of clustering in the recall of randomly arranged associates. *Journal of General Psychology, 49,* 229–240.

Bousfield, W. A., Cohen, B. H., & Whitmarsh, G. A. (1958). *Verbal generalization: A theoretical rationale and an experimental technique.* [Technical Report No. 23, Contract NONR 631(00)]. Washington, DC: U.S. Government Printing Office.

Bousfield, W. A., & Sedgewick, C. H. W. (1944). An analysis of sequences of restricted associative responses. *Journal of General Psychology, 30,* 149–165.

Bower, G. H. (1972). Stimulus-sampling theory of encoding variablity. In A. W. Melton & E. Martin (Eds.), *Coding processes in human memory* (pp. 85–123). Washington, DC: Winston.

Bower, G. H. (1981). Mood and memory. *American Psychologist, 36,* 129–148.

Bower, G. H. (1983). Affect and cognition. *Philosophical Transactions of the Royal Society of London* (Series B), *302,* 387–402.

Bower, T. G. R. (1974). *Development in infancy.* San Francisco: Freeman.

Bower, T. G. R. (1989). *The rational infant: Learning in infancy.* New York: Freeman.

Bower, T. G. R., Broughton, J., & Moore, M. K. (1970). Demonstration of intention in the reaching behavior of neonate humans. *Science, 228,* 679–680.

Bower, T. G. R., Broughton, J., & Moore, M. K. (1971). Development of the object concept as manifested in changes in the tracking behavior of infants between 7 and 20 weeks of age. *Journal of Experimental Child Psychology, 11,* 182–193.

Bowers, K. S. (1984). On being unconsciously influenced and informed. In K. S. Bowers & D. Meichenbaum (Eds.), *The unconscious reconsidered* (pp. 23–42). New York: Wiley.

Bowlby, J. (1969). *Attachment and loss: Vol. 1: Attachment.* London: Hogarth.

Braine, M. D. S. (1976). Children's first word combinations. *Monograph of the Society for Research in Child Development,* 41 (serial no. 164).

Brainerd, C. J., & Reyna, V. F. (1993). Memory independence and memory inference in cognitive development. *Psychological Review, 100,* 42–67.

Bransford, J. D. (1979). *Human cognition: Learning, understanding, and remembering.* Belmont, CA: Wadsworth.

Bransford, J. D., Barclay, J. R., & Franks, J. J. (1972). Sentence memory: A constructive versus interpretive approach. *Cognitive Psychology, 3,* 193–209.

Bransford, J. D., & Franks, J. J. (1971). The abstraction of linguistic ideas. *Cognitive Psychology, 2,* 331–350.

Bransford, J. D., & Johnson, M. K. (1972). Contextual prerequisites for understanding: Some investigations of comprehension and recall. *Journal of Verbal Learning and Verbal Behavior, 11,* 717–726.

Bray, D. W. (1976). The assessment center method. In R. L. Craig (Ed.), *Training and development handbook: A guide to human resource development* (2nd ed.). New York: McGraw-Hill.

Bray, D. W., Campbell, R. J., & Grant, D. L. (1974). *Formative years in business: A long-term AT&T study of management lives.* New York: Wiley-Interscience.

Brehm, J. W. (1966). *A theory of psychological reactance.* New York: Academic Press.

Brentano, F. C. (1874/1973). *Psychology from an empirical standpoint.* New York: Humanities.

Bretherton, I., & Beeghly, M. (1982). Talking about internal states: The acquisition of an explicit theory of mind. *Developmental Psychology, 18,* 906–921.

Bretherton, I., McNew, S., & Beeghly-Smith, M. (1981). Early person knowledge as expressed in gestural and verbal communication: When do infants acquire a "theory of mind"? In M. E. Lamb & L. R. Sherrod (Eds.), *Infant social cognition* (pp. 333–373). Hillsdale, NJ: Erlbaum.

Breuer, J., & Freud, S. (1893/1955). Studies on hysteria. In J. Strachey (Ed.), *The standard edition of the complete psychological works of Sigmund Freud* (Vol. 2). London: Hogarth.

Brewer, W. F. (1974). There is no convincing evidence for operant or classical conditioning in adult humans. In W. B. Weimer & D. S. Palermo (Eds.), *Cognition and the symbolic processes* (pp. 1–42). Hillsdale, NJ: Erlbaum.

Brewer, W. F., & Lichtenstein, E. H. (1975). Recall of logical and pragmatic implications in sentences with dichotomous and continuous antonyms. *Memory & Cognition, 3,* 315–318.

Brickman, P., Redfield, J., Harrison, A. A., & Crandall, R. (1972). Drive and predisposition as factors in the attitudinal effects of mere exposure. *Journal of Experimental Social Psychology, 8,* 31–44.

Brown, A. L. (1978). Knowing when, where, and how to remember: A problem of metacognition. In R. Glaser (Ed.), *Advances in instructional psychology* (Vol. 1, pp. 77–165). Hillsdale, NJ: Erlbaum.

Brown, A. L., & DeLoache, J. S. (1978). Skills, plans, and self-regulation. In R. S. Siegler (Ed.), *Children's thinking: What develops?* (pp. 3–35). Hillsdale, NJ: Erlbaum.

Brown, A. S. (1991). A review of the tip-of-the-tongue experience. *Psychological Bulletin, 109,* 204–223.

Brown, I., Jr., & Inouye, D. K. (1978). Learned helplessness through modeling: The role of perceived similarity in competence. *Journal of Personality and Social Psychology, 36,* 900–908.

Brown, J. (1958). Some tests of the decay theory of immediate memory. *Quarterly Journal of Experimental Psychology, 10,* 12–21.

Brown, J. D., & McGill, K. L. (1989). The cost of good fortune: When positive life events produce negative health consequences. *Journal of Personality and Social Psychology, 57,* 1103–1110.

Brown, J. D., & Siegel, J. M. (1988). Attributions for negative life events and depression: The role of perceived control. *Journal of Personality and Social Psychology, 54,* 316–322.

Brown, P. L., & Jenkins, H. M. (1968). Autoshaping of the pigeon's key-peck. *Journal of the Experimental Analysis of Behavior, 11,* 1–8.

Brown, R. (1973). *A first language: The early stages.* Cambridge, MA: Harvard University Press.

Brown, R., & McNeill, D. (1966). The "tip of the tongue" phenomenon. *Journal of Verbal Learning and Verbal Behavior, 5,* 325–337.

Browne, M. P. (1976). The role of primary reinforcement and overt movements in autoshaping in the pigeon. *Animal Learning and Behavior, 4,* 287–292.

Bruner, J. S. (1973). Organization of early skilled action. *Child Development, 44,* 1–11.

Buchwald, A. M. (1960). Supplementary report: Alteration in the reinforcement value of a positive reinforcer. *Journal of Experimental Psychology, 60,* 416–417.

Buchwald, A. M. (1977). Depressive mood and estimates of reinforcement frequency. *Journal of Abnormal Psychology, 86,* 443–446.

Buck, R. (1991). Motivation, emotion and cognition: A developmental-interactionist view. In K. T. Strongman (Ed.), *International Review of Studies on Emotion.* Chichester: Wiley.

Bugaj, A. M. (1984). *Affect and the cognitive organization of social information.* Unpublished doctoral dissertation, Purdue University, West Lafayette, IN.

Bugental, J. F. T. (1989). Foreword. In R. S. Valle & S. Halling (Eds.), *Existential-phenomenological perspectives in psychology: Exploring the breadth of human experience* (pp. ix–xi). New York: Plenum.

Bullock, M., Gelman, R., & Baillargeon, R. (1982). The development of causal reasoning. In W. J. Friedman (Ed.), *The development of psychology of time.* New York: Academic Press.

Bulman, R. J., & Wortman, C. B. (1977). Attributions of blame and coping in the "real world": Severe accident victims react to their lot. *Journal of Personality and Social Psychology, 35,* 351–363.

Bunch, M. E., & Wientge, K. (1933). The relative susceptibility of pleasant, unpleasant, and indifferent material to retroactive inhibition. *Journal of General Psychology, 9,* 157–178.

Bunge, M. (1980). *The mind-body problem: A psychobiological approach.* New York: Pergamon.

Buss, A. R. (1978). Causes and reasons in attribution theory: A conceptual critique. *Journal of Personality and Social Psychology, 36,* 1311–1321.

Butterworth, G. (1978). Review of "A primer of infant development." *Perception, 7,* 363–364.

Butterworth, G. & Hopkins, B. (1988). Hand-mouth coordination in the new-born baby. *British Journal of Developmental Psychology, 6,* 303–314.

Cameron, N., & Rychlak, J. F. (1985). *Personality development and psychopathology: A dynamic approach* (2nd ed.). Boston: Houghton Mifflin.

Campbell, D. T. (1974). "Downward causation" in hierarchically organized biological systems. In F. J. Ayala & T. Dobshansky (Eds.), *Studies in the philosophy of biology* (pp. 179–186). London: Macmillan.

Campbell, K. A. (1983). *Affective assessment and awareness in the operant conditioning of verbal response*. Unpublished doctoral dissertation, Purdue University, West Lafayette, IN.

Cannon, W. B. (1927). The James-Lange theory of emotions: A critical examination and an alternative theory. *American Journal of Psychology, 39*, 106–124.

Cantor, N. (1990). From thought to behavior: "Having" and "doing" in the study of personality and cognition. *American Psychologist, 45*, 735–750.

Carey, S. (1978). The child as word learner. In M. Halle, J. Bresnan, & G. A. Miller (Eds.), *Linguistic theory and psychological reality* (pp. 264–293). Cambridge, MA: MIT Press.

Carey, S. (1985). *Conceptual change in childhood*. Cambridge, MA: MIT Press.

Carlson, J. G., & Wielkiewicz, R. M. (1976). Mediators of the effects of magnitude of reinforcement. *Learning and Motivation, 7*, 184–196.

Carmichael, L., Hogan, H. P., & Walter, A. A. (1932). An experimental study of the effect of language on the reproduction of visually perceived form. *Journal of Experimental Psychology, 15*, 73–86.

Carter, H. D. (1935). Effects of emotional factors upon recall. *Journal of Psychology, 1*, 49–59.

Carter, H. D. (1937). Emotional factors in verbal learning: IV. Evidence from reaction time. *Journal of Educational Psychology, 28*, 101–108.

Carter, H. D., & Jones, H. E. (1937). A further study of affective factors in learning. *Journal of Genetic Psychology, 50*, 157–163.

Carver, C. S., Blaney, P. H., & Scheier, M. F. (1979). Focus of attention, chronic expectancy, and responses to a feared stimulus. *Journal of Personality and Social Psychology, 37*, 1186–1195.

Caspi, A., Elder, G. H., Jr., & Bem, D. J. (1987). Moving against the world: Life-course patterns of explosive children. *Developmental Psychology, 23*, 308–313.

Cassirer, E. (1950). *The problem of knowledge: Philosophy, science, and history since Hegel*. New Haven, CT: Yale University Press.

Cerella, J. (1979). Visual classes and natural categories in the pigeon. *Journal of Experimental Psychology: Human Perceptual Performance, 5*, 68–77.

Cermak, L. S. (1976). *Improving your memory*. New York: McGraw-Hill.

Chandler, M. J., Fritz, A. S., & Hala, S. (1989). Small-scale deceit: Deception as a marker of two-, three-, and four-year-olds' early theories of mind. *Child Development, 60*, 1263–1277.

Chaplin, J. P. (1985). *Dictionary of psychology*. New York: Laurel/Dell.

Chase, W. G., & Simon, H. A. (1973). Perception in chess. *Cognitive Psychology, 4*, 55–81.

Chatterjee, B. B., & Eriksen, C. W. (1962). Cognitive factors in heart rate conditioning. *Journal of Experimental Psychology, 64*, 272–279.

Cheney, D. L., & Seyfarth, R. M. (1985). Social and non-social knowledge in vervet monkeys. *Philosophical Transactions of the Royal Society, London, Series B, 308*, 187–201.

Chi, M. T. H. (1978). Knowledge structures and memory development. In R. S. Siegler (Ed.), *Children's thinking: What develops?* (pp. 73–96). Hillsdale, NJ: Erlbaum.

Cieutat, V. J., Stockwell, F. E., & Noble, C. E. (1958). The interaction of ability and amount of practice with stimulus and response meaningfulness (m, m') in paired-associate learning. *Journal of Experimental Psychology, 56*, 193–202.

Clark, H. H., & Clark, E. V. (1977). *Psychology and language: An introduction to psycholinguistics*. New York: Harcourt Brace Jovanovich.

Coates, D., Wortman, C. B., & Abbey, A. (1979). Reaction to victims. In I. H. Frieze, D. Bar-Tal, & J. S. Carroll (Eds.), *New approaches to social problems: Applications of attribution theory* (pp. 76–94). San Francisco: Jossey-Bass.

Cohen, L. B., & Caputo, N. F. (1975). *Instructing infants to respond to perceptual categories.* Paper presented at the Midwestern Psychological Association Convention, Chicago.

Cohen, L. B., DeLoache, J. S., & Strauss, M. S. (1979). Infant visual perception. In J. D. Osofsky (Ed.), *Handbook of infant development* (pp. 393–438). New York: Wiley.

Cohen, L. B., & Gelber, E. R. (1975). Infant visual memory. In L. B. Cohen & P. Salapatek (Eds.), *Infant perception: From sensation to cognition: Basic visual processes* (Vol. 1, pp. 347–403). New York: Academic Press.

Cohen, L. B., & Salapatek, P. H. (Eds). (1975). *Infant perception: From sensation to cognition* (2 vols.). New York: Academic Press.

Cohen, L. B., & Strauss, M. S. (1979). Concept acquisition in the human infant. *Child Development, 50,* 419–424.

Cohen, L. B., & Younger, B. A. (1983). Perceptual categorization in the infant. In E. K. Scholwick (Ed.), *New trends in conceptual representation: Challenges to Piaget's theory* (pp. 197–220). Hillsdale, NJ: Erlbaum.

Collins, A. (1977). Processes in acquiring knowledge. In R. C. Anderson, R. J. Spiro, & W. E. Montague (Eds.), *Schooling and the acquisition of knowledge* (pp. 339–363). Hillsdale, NJ: Erlbaum.

Corbin, C. B. (1972). Mental practice. In W. P. Morgan (Ed.), *Ergogenic aids and muscular performance* (pp. 93–118). New York: Academic Press.

Cordua, G. D., McGraw, K. O., & Drabman, R. S. (1979). Doctor or nurse: Children's perception of sex typed occupations. *Child Development, 50,* 590–593.

Coyne, J. C. (1976). Depression and the response of others. *Journal of Abnormal Psychology, 85,* 186–193.

Craik, F. I. M., & Jacoby, L. L. (1979). Elaboration and distinctiveness in episodic memory. In L-G Nilsson (Ed.), *Perspectives on memory research: Essays in honor of Uppsala University's 500th Anniversary* (pp. 145–166). Hillsdale, NJ: Erlbaum.

Craik, F. I. M., & Lockhart, R. S. (1972). Levels of processing: A framework for memory research. *Journal of Verbal Learning and Verbal Behavior, 11,* 671–684.

Craik, F. I. M., & Tulving, E. (1975). Depth of processing and the retention of words in episodic memory. *Journal of Experimental Psychology: General, 104,* 268–294.

Cranston, M. (1957). *John Locke: A biography.* New York: Macmillan Co.

Cromwell, R. L. (1956). Factors in the serial recall of names of acquaintances. *Journal of Abnormal and Social Psychology, 53,* 63–67.

Crutcher, R. J., & Healy, A. F. (1989). Cognitive operations and the generation effect. *Journal of Experimental Psychology: Learning, Memory, and Cognition, 15,* 669–679.

Danks, J. H., & Glucksberg, S. (1980). Experimental psycholinguistics. *Annual Review of Psychology, 31,* 391–417.

Danner, F. W. (1976). Children's understanding of intersentence organization in the recall of short descriptive passages. *Journal of Educational Psychology, 68,* 174–183.

David, K. L. (1977). *The relationship of replacement condition and an affective dimension of meaningfulness to rate of learning.* Unpublished master's thesis, Purdue University, West Lafayette, IN.

Davis, P. (1964). Discrimination without awareness in a psychophysical task. *Perceptual and Motor Skills, 18,* 87–90.

Dawson, M. E. (1973). Can classical conditioning occur without contingency learning? A review and evaluation of the evidence. *Psychophysiology, 10,* 82–86.

Dawson, M. E., & Furedy, J. J. (1976). The role of awareness in human differential autonomic classical conditioning: The necessary-gate hypothesis. *Psychophysiology, 13,* 50–53.

DeCasper, A. J., & Carstens, A. A. (1981). Contingencies of stimulation: Effects on learning and emotion in neonates. *Infant Behavior and Development, 4,* 19–35.

DeCasper, A. J., & Fifer, W. P. (1980). Of human bonding: Newborns prefer their mothers' voices. *Science, 208,* 1174–1176.

Deese, J. (1962). On the structure of associative meaning. *Psychological Review, 69,* 161–175.

de Groot, A. M. B. (1989). Representational aspects of word imageability and word frequency as assessed through word association. *Journal of Experimental Psychology: Learning, Memory, and Cognition, 15,* 824–845.

DeLoache, J. S., Cassidy, D. J., & Brown, A. L. (1985). Precursors of mnemonic strategies in very young children's memory. *Child Development, 56,* 125–137.

DeNike, L. D. (1964). The temporal relationship between awareness and performance in verbal conditioning. *Journal of Experimental Psychology, 68,* 521–529.

Dennett, D. C. (1984). *Elbow room: The varieties of free will worth wanting.* Cambridge, MA: Bradford/MIT Press.

Derrida, J. (1985). Des tours de babel [The towers of Babel]. In J. F. Graham (Ed.), *Difference in Translation* (pp. 12–68). Ithaca, NY: Cornell University Press.

de Waal, F. B. M. (1982). *Chimpanzee politics: Power and sex among apes.* New York: Harper & Row.

de Waal, F. B. M. (1986). Deception in the natural communication of chimpanzees. In R. W. Mitchell & N. S. Thompson (Eds.), *Deception, perspectives on human and nonhuman deceit* (pp. 37–65). Albany: State University of New York Press.

Dewey, J. (1900). *The school and society.* Chicago: University of Chicago Press.

Dewey, J. (1929). *The sources of a science of education.* New York: Liveright.

Diener, E., Dineen, J., Endresen, K., Beaman, A. L., & Fraser, S. C. (1975). Effects of altered responsibility, cognitive set, and modeling on physical aggression and deindividuation. *Journal of Personality and Social Psychology, 31,* 328–337.

Dimond, S., & Beaumont, G. (1974). Hemisphere function and paired-associate learning. *British Journal of Psychology, 65,* 275–278.

Dinsmoor, J. A. (1983). Observing and conditioned reinforcement. *Behavioral and Brain Sciences, 6,* 693–728.

Dixon, J. C. (1957). Development of self recognition. *Journal of Genetic Psychology, 91,* 251–256.

Dixon, N. F. (1971). *Subliminal perception: The nature of a controversy.* London: McGraw-Hill.

Dollard, J., & Miller, N. E. (1950). *Personality and psychotherapy: An analysis in terms of learning, thinking and culture.* New York: McGraw-Hill.

Dong, T. (1972). Cued partial recall of categorized words. *Journal of Experimental Psychology, 93,* 123–129.

Dooling, D. J., & Christiaansen, R. E. (1977). Episodic and semantic aspects of memory for prose. *Journal of Experimental Psychology: Human Learning and Memory, 3,* 428–436.

Dreyfus, H. L. (1979). *What computers can't do: The limits of artificial intelligence* (rev. ed.). New York: Harper & Row.

Duffy, E. (1962). *Activation and behavior.* New York: John Wiley & Sons.

Dulany, D. E. (1961). Hypotheses and habits in verbal "operant conditioning." *Journal of Abnormal and Social Psychology, 63,* 251–263.

Dulany, D. E. (1968). Awareness, rules, and propositional control: A confrontation with S-R behavior theory. In T. R. Dixon & D. L. Horton (Eds.), *Verbal behavior and general behavior theory* (pp. 340–387). Englewood Cliffs, NJ: Prentice-Hall.

Dweck, C. S., & Licht, B. G. (1980). Learned helplessness and intellectual achievement. In J. Garber & M. E. P. Seligman (Eds.), *Human helplessness: Theory and applications* (pp. 197–221). New York: Academic Press.

Eagle, M., & Leiter, E. (1964). Recall and recognition in intentional and incidental learning. *Journal of Experimental Psychology, 68,* 58–63.

Ebbinghaus, H. (1885/1964). *Memory: A contribution to experimental psychology* (H. A. Ruger & C. E. Bussenius, Trans.). New York: Dover.

Eccles, J. C. (1977). Part II. In K. R. Popper & J. C. Eccles. *The self and its brain* (pp. 225–421). London: Springer International.

Ehrlichman, H., & Halpern, J. N. (1988). Affect and memory: Effects of pleasant and unpleasant odors on retrieval of happy and unhappy memories. *Journal of Personality and Social Psychology, 55,* 769–779.

Eimas, P. D., & Miller, J. L. (1992). Organization in the perception of speech by young infants. *Psychological Science, 3,* 340–345.

Einstein, A. (1934). *Essays in science.* New York: Philosophical Library.

Einstein, G. O., & Hunt, R. R. (1980). Levels of processing and organization: Additive effects of individual-item and relational processing. *Journal of Experimental Psychology: Human Learning and Memory, 6,* 588–598.

Ekman, P. (1992). Are there basic emotions? *Psychological Review, 99,* 550–553.

Ekman, P., Friesen, W. V., & Ellsworth, P. (1972). *Emotion in the human face.* Elmsford, NY: Pergamon.

English, H. B., & English, A. C. (1958). *A comprehensive dictionary of psychological and psychoanalytical terms.* New York: Longmans, Green.

Erdelyi, M. H. (1974). A new look at the new look: Perceptual defense and vigilance. *Psychological Review, 81,* 1–25.

Erickson, J. R., & Jones, M. R. (1978). Thinking. *Annual Review of Psychology, 29,* 61–90.

Evans, R. I. (1968). *B. F. Skinner: The man and his ideas.* New York: Dutton.

Eysenck, H. J. (1947). *Dimensions of personality.* London: Routledge & Kegan Paul.

Eysenck, M. W., & Keane, M. T. (1990). *Cognitive psychology: A student's handbook.* Hillsdale, NJ: Erlbaum.

Fantz, R. L., & Yeh, J. (1979). Configurational selectivities: Critical for development of visual perception and attention. *Canadian Journal of Psychology, 33,* 277–287.

Farrington, B. (1949). *Francis Bacon: Philosopher of industrial science.* New York: Henry Schuman.

Feingold, A. (1992). Good-looking people are not what we think. *Psychological Bulletin, 111,* 304–341.

Feldman, S. E. (1963). Probabilistic hierarchies to ambiguous concept classes. *Journal of Experimental Psychology, 65,* 240–247.

Festinger, L. A. (1957). *A theory of cognitive dissonance.* Evanston, IL: Row, Peterson.

Filbey, R. A., & Gazzaniga, M. S. (1969). Splitting the normal brain with reaction time. *Psychonomic Science, 17,* 335–336.

Fisher, R. P., & Craik, F. I. M. (1977). Interaction between encoding and retrieval operations in cued recall. *Journal of Experimental Psychology: Human Learning and Memory, 3,* 701–711.

Flavell, J. H. (1977). *Cognitive development.* Englewood Cliffs, NJ: Prentice-Hall.

Foa, U. G., & Foa, E. B. (1974). *Societal structures of the mind.* Springfield, IL: Charles C. Thomas.

Fodor, J. A., & Pylyshyn, Z. W. (1981). How direct is visual perception?: Some reflections on Gibson's "Ecological Approach." *Cognition, 9,* 139–196.

Fodor, J. A., & Pylyshyn, Z. W. (1988). Connectionism and cognitive architecture: A critical analysis. In S. Pinker & J. Mehler (Eds.), *Connections and symbols* (pp. 3–71). Cambridge, MA: Bradford/MIT Press.

Forgas, J. P., & Bower, G. H. (1987). Mood effects on person-perception judgments. *Journal of Personality and Social Psychology, 53,* 53–60.

Fouts, R. S. (1972). Use of guidance in teaching sign language to a chimpanzee (*Pan troglodytes*). *Journal of Comparative and Physiological Psychology, 80,* 515–522.

Fowler, C. A., Wolford, G., Slade, R., & Tassinary, L. (1981). Lexical access with and without awareness. *Journal of Experimental Psychology: General, 110,* 341–362.

Frankenhaeuser, M. (1975). Experimental approaches to the study of catelcholamines and emotion. In L. Levi (Ed.), *Emotions: Their parameters and measurement* (pp. 209–234). New York: Raven.

Fraser, J. T. (1987). *Time: The familiar stranger.* Amherst: The University of Massachusetts Press.

Freud, S. (1900/1953a). *The interpretation of dreams (second part).* In J. Strachey (Ed.), *The standard edition of the complete psychological works of Sigmund Freud* (Vol. 5, pp. 339–621). London: Hogarth.

Freud, S. (1901/1953b). Fragment of an analysis of a case of hysteria. In J. Strachey (Ed.), *The standard edition of the complete psychological works of Sigmund Freud* (Vol. 7, pp. 7–122). London: Hogarth.

Freud, S. (1921/1955). Suggestion and libido. In J. Strachey (Ed.), *The standard edition of the complete psychological works of Sigmund Freud* (Vol. 18, pp. 88–92). London: Hogarth.

Freud, S. (1915/1957). The unconscious. In J. Strachey (Ed.), *The standard edition of the complete psychological works of Sigmund Freud* (Vol. 14, pp. 166–171). London: Hogarth.

Freud, S. (1911/1958). Formulations on the two principles of mental functioning. In J. Strachey (Ed.), *The standard edition of the complete psychological works of Sigmund Freud* (Vol. 12, pp. 215–226). London: Hogarth.

Freud, S. (1913/1958). The theme of the three caskets. In J. Strachey (Ed.), *The standard edition of the complete psychological works of Sigmund Freud* (Vol. 12, pp. 291–301). London: Hogarth.

Freud, S. (1925/1961). Negation. In J. Strachey (Ed.), *The standard edition of the complete psychological works of Sigmund Freud* (Vol. 19, pp. 235–239). London: Hogarth.

Freud, S. (1892/1966). A case of successful treatment by hypnotism. In J. Strachey (Ed.), *The standard edition of the complete psychological works of Sigmund Freud* (Vol. 1, pp. 117–128). London: Hogarth.

Friedman, W. J. (1993). Memory for the time of past events. *Psychological Bulletin, 113,* 44–66.

Frijda, N. H. (1986). *The emotions.* Cambridge: Cambridge University Press.

Frye, D., & Moore, C. (1991). *Children's theories of mind: Mental states and social understanding.* Hillsdale, NJ: Erlbaum.

Funder, D. C. (1982). On the accuracy of dispositional vs. situational attributions. *Social Cognition, 1,* 205–222.

Furth, H. G. (1966). *Thinking without language.* New York: Free Press.

Gage, D. F., & Safer, M. A. (1985). Hemisphere differences in the mood state-dependent effect for recognition of emotional faces. *Journal of Experimental Psychology: Learning, Memory, and Cognition, 11,* 752–763.

Galbraith, R. C., Olsen, S. F., Duerden, D. S., & Harris, W. L. (1982). The differentiation hypothesis: Distinguishing between perceiving and memorizing. *American Journal of Psychology, 95,* 655–667.

Gamzu, E. R., & Williams, D. R. (1973). Associative factors underlying the pigeon's key pecking in auto-shaping procedures. *Journal of the Experimental Analysis of Behavior, 19,* 225–232.

Garcia, J., & Koelling, R. A. (1966). Relation of cue to consequence in avoidance learning. *Psychonomic Science, 4,* 123–124.

Garcia, J., & Rusniak, K. W. (1980). What the nose learns from the mouth. In D. Muller-Schwartze & R. M. Silverstein (Eds.), *Chemical signals* (pp. 141–156). New York: Plenum.

Gardiner, J. M., Gregg, V. H., & Hampton, J. A. (1988). Word frequency and generation effects. *Journal of Experimental Psychology: Learning, Memory, and Cognition, 14,* 687–693.

Gardner, H. (1985). *The mind's new science: A history of the cognitive revolution.* New York: Basic.

Gardner, R. A., & Gardner, B. T. (1969). Teaching sign language to a chimpanzee. *Science, 165,* 664–672.

Garza, R. T. (1975). *Affective and associative meaningfulness in the learning styles of Chicano and Anglo college students.* Unpublished doctoral dissertation, Purdue University, West Lafayette, IN.

Gazzaniga, M. S. (1970). *The bisected brain.* New York: Appleton-Century-Crofts.

Gazzaniga, M. S. (1985). *The social brain: Discovering the networks of the mind.* New York: Basic.

Gazzaniga, M. S., & LeDoux, J. E. (1978). *The integrated mind.* New York: Plenum.

Geffen, G., Bradshaw, J. L., & Wallace, G. (1971). Interhemispheric effects on reaction time to verbal and nonverbal visual stimuli. *Journal of Experimental Psychology, 87,* 415–422.

Gehring, R. E., Toglia, M. P., & Kimble, G. A. (1976). Recognition memory for words and pictures at short and long retention intervals. *Memory and Cognition, 4,* 256–260.

Gelman, R. (1978). Cognitive development. *Annual Review of Psychology, 29,* 297–332.

Gentner, D., & Stevens, A. L. (1983). *Mental models.* Hillsdale, NJ: Erlbaum.

Gergen, K. J. (1982). *Toward transformation in social knowledge.* New York: Springer-Verlag.

Gergen, K. J. (1989). Social psychology and the wrong revolution. *European Journal of Social Psychology, 19,* 463–484.

Gergen, K. J., Hepburn, A., & Fisher, D. C. (1986). Hermeneutics of personality description. *Journal of Personality and Social Psychology, 50,* 1261–1270.

Gibbs, R. W., Jr. (1986). On the psycholinguistics of sarcasm. *Journal of Experimental Psychology: General, 115,* 3–15.

Gibson, J. J. (1966). *The senses considered as perceptual systems.* Boston: Houghton Mifflin.

Gibson, J. J. (1979). *The ecological approach to visual perception.* Boston: Houghton Mifflin.

Gigerenzer, G. (1991). From tools to theories: A heuristic of discovery in cognitive psychology. *Psychological Review, 98,* 254–267.

Gilbert, D. T. (1991). How mental systems believe. *American Psychologist, 46,* 107–119.

Gilgen, A. R. (1987). The psychological level of organization in nature and interdependencies among major psychological concepts. In A. W. Staats & L. P. Mos (Eds.), *Annals of theoretical psychology* (Vol. 5, pp. 179–209). New York: Plenum.

Giorgi, A. (1985). Sketch of a psychological phenomenological method. In A. Giorgi (Ed.), *Phenomenology and psychological research* (pp. 8–22). Pittsburgh: Duquesne University Press.

Glass, A. L., Holyoak, K. J., & Kiger, J. I. (1979). Role of antonymy relations in semantic judgments. *Journal of Experimental Psychology: Human Learning and Memory, 5*, 598–606.

Glassman, R. B. (1983). Free will has a neural substrate: Critique of Joseph F. Rychlak's "Discovering free will and personal responsibility." *Zygon, 18*, 67–82.

Goble, F. G. (1970). *The third force: The psychology of Abraham Maslow.* New York: Grossman.

Godden, D. R., & Baddeley, A. D. (1975). Context-dependent memory in two natural environments: On land and underwater. *British Journal of Psychology, 66*, 325–331.

Goss, A. E., & Nodine, C. F. (1965). *Paired-associates learning.* New York: Academic Press.

Gough, P. B., Odom, P. B., & Jenkins, J. J. (1967). Intralist association in paired-associate learning. *Journal of Verbal Learning and Verbal Behavior, 6*, 11–16.

Graesser, A. C., Robertson, S. P., Lovelace, E. R., & Swinehart, D. M. (1980). Answers to why-questions expose the organization of story plot and predict recall of actions. *Journal of Verbal Learning and Verbal Behavior, 19*, 110–119.

Granit, R. (1977). *The purposive brain.* Cambridge, MA: MIT Press.

Gratch, G. (1979). The development of thought and language in infancy. In J. D. Osofsky (Ed.), *Handbook of infant development* (pp. 439–461). New York: Wiley.

Greene, R. L. (1984). Incidental learning of event frequency. *Memory & Cognition, 12*, 90–95.

Greene, R. L. (1986). Effects of intentionality and strategy on memory for frequency. *Journal of Experimental Psychology: Learning, Memory, and Cognition, 12*, 489–495.

Greenfield, P. M., & Smith, J. H. (1976). *The structure of communication in early language development.* New York: Academic Press.

Griffin, D. R. (1981). *The question of animal awareness: Evolutionary continuity of mental experience.* New York: Rockefeller University Press.

Gross, D., Fischer, U., & Miller, G. A. (1989). The organization of adjectival meanings. *Journal of Memory and Language, 28*, 92–106.

Grossman, L., & Eagle, M. (1970). Synonymity, antonymity, and association in false recognition responses. *Journal of Experimental Psychology, 83*, 244–248.

Gruba-McCallister, F. P., & Rychlak, J. F. (1981). A logical learning theory explanation of why personality scales predict behavior. *Journal of Personality Assessment, 45*, 494–504.

Gruder, C. L. (1977). Choice of comparison persons in evaluating oneself. In J. M. Suls & R. L. Miller (Eds.), *Social comparison processes* (pp. 21–41). Washington, DC: Hemisphere.

Gunnar-vonGnechten, M. R. (1978). Changing a frightening toy into a pleasant toy by allowing the infant to control its actions. *Developmental Psychology, 14*, 157–162.

Haber, R. N. (1983). Stimulus information and processing mechanisms in visual space perception. In J. Beck, B. Hope, & A. Rosenfeld (Eds.), *Human and machine vision* (pp. 157–235). New York: Academic Press.

Haith, M. M. (1980). *Rules that babies look by: The organization of newborn visual acuity.* Hillsdale, NJ: Erlbaum.

Haith, M. M., Bergman, T., & Moore, M. J. (1977). Eye contact and face scanning in early infancy. *Science, 198*, 853–855.

Hall, G. S. (1906). *Youth.* New York: Appleton.

Hamilton, V. L. (1980). Intuitive psychologist or intuitive lawyer? Alternative models of the attribution process. *Journal of Personality and Social Psychology, 39*, 767–772.

Hampton, J. A., & Taylor, P. J. (1985). Effects of semantic relatedness on same-different decisions in a good-bad categorization task. *Journal of Experimental Psychology: Learning, Memory, and Cognition, 11*, 85–93.

Harding, C. G. (1982). Development of the intention to communicate. *Human Development,* *25,* 140–151.

Harré, R. (1984). *Personal being: A theory for individual psychology.* Cambridge, MA: Harvard University Press.

Harris, P. L., Cassel, T. Z., & Bamborough, P. (1974). Tracking by young infants. *British Journal of Psychology, 65,* 345–349.

Harris, R. J. (1974). Memory and comprehension of implications and inferences of complex sentences. *Journal of Verbal Learning and Verbal Behavior, 13,* 626–637.

Hart, J. T. (1965). Memory and the feeling of knowing experience. *Journal of Educational Psychology, 56,* 208–216.

Hart, J. T. (1967). Memory and the memory-monitoring-process. *Journal of Verbal Learning and Verbal Behavior, 6,* 685–691.

Harvey, J. H., Town, J. P., & Yarkin, K. L. (1981). How fundamental is "The fundamental attribution error"? *Journal of Personality and Social Psychology, 40,* 346–349.

Hastie, R. (1984). Causes and effects of causal attribution. *Journal of Personality and Social Psychology, 46,* 44–56.

Hastie, R., & Kumar, P. A. (1979). Person memory: Personality traits as organizing principles in memory for behaviors. *Journal of Personality and Social Psychology, 37,* 25–38.

Hastie, R., & Park, B. (1986). The relationship between memory and judgment depends on whether the judgment task is memory-based or on-line. *Psychological Review, 93,* 258–268.

Hastorf, A. H., & Cantril, H. (1954). They saw a game: A case study. *Journal of Abnormal and Social Psychology, 49,* 129–134.

Hatch, E. M. (Ed.). (1978). *Second language acquisition.* Rowley, MA: Newbury House.

Hawking, S. W. (1988). *A brief history of time: From the big bang to black holes.* New York: Bantam.

Hayes, D. S., & Birnbaum, D. W. (1980). Preschoolers' retention of televised events: Is a picture worth a thousand words? *Developmental Psychology, 16,* 410–416.

Hebb, D. O. (1949/1961). *The organization of behavior.* New York: Wiley.

Hebb, D. O. (1974). What psychology is about. *American Psychologist, 29,* 71–79.

Heck, V. L. (1920). Ueber die Bildung einer Assoziation beim Regenwurm auf Grund von Dressurversuchen. *Lotos, 8,* 168–189.

Heidbreder, E. (1947). The attainment of concepts: III. The process. *The Journal of Psychology, 24,* 93–138.

Heil, J. (1983). *Perception and cognition.* Berkeley: University of California Press.

Herbert, M. J., & Harsh, C. M. (1944). Observational learning by cats. *Journal of Comparative Psychology, 37,* 81–95.

Herrmann, D. J., Chaffin, R. J. S., Conti, G., Peters, D., & Robbins, P. H. (1979). Comprehension of antonymy and the generality of categorization models. *Journal of Experimental Psychology: Human Learning and Memory, 5,* 585–597.

Herrmann, D. J., Papperman, T. J., & Armstrong, A. D. (1978). Synonym comprehension and the generality of categorization models. *Memory & Cognition, 6,* 150–155.

Herrnstein, R. J., Loveland, D. H., & Cable, C. (1976). Natural concepts in pigeons. *Journal of Experimental Psychology: Animal Behavior Processes, 2,* 285–302.

Higuchi, H. (1987). Cast master. *Natural History, 96,* 40–43.

Hilliard, R. D. (1973). Hemispheric laterality effects on a facial recognition task in normal subjects. *Cortex, 9,* 246–258.

Hofstadter, D. R. (1980). *Gödel, Escher, Bach: An eternal golden braid.* New York: Vintage.

Hofstadter, R. (1955). *Social Darwinism in American thought.* Boston: Beacon.

Holland, M. K., & Tarlow, G. (1975). Blinking and thinking. *Perceptual Motor Skills, 41,* 403–406.

Holton, G. (1972). Mach, Einstein and the search for reality. In G. Holton (Ed.), *The twentieth-century sciences: Studies in the biography of ideas* (pp. 354–386). New York: Norton.

Holton, G. (1973). *Thematic origins of scientific thought: Kepler to Einstein.* Cambridge, MA: Harvard University Press.

Holyoak, K. J., & Spellman, B. A. (1993). Thinking. *Annual Review of Psychology, 44,* 265–315.

Homa, D., & Vosburgh, R. (1976). Category breadth and the abstraction of prototypical information. *Journal of Experimental Psychology: Human Learning and Memory, 2,* 322–330.

Horton, D. L., & Bergfeld Mills, C. (1984). Human learning and memory. *Annual Review of Psychology, 35,* 361–394.

Hovland, C. I., Janis, I. L., & Kelley, H. H. (1953). *Communication and persuasion.* New Haven, CT: Yale University Press.

Howard, D. V. (1983). *Cognitive psychology.* New York: Macmillan.

Howard, G. S., & Conway, C. G. (1986). Can there be an empirical science of volitional action? *American Psychologist, 41,* 1241–1251.

Howard, G. S., Youngs, W. H., & Siatcynski, A. (1985). *Reforming methodology in psychological research.* Unpublished manuscript, University of Notre Dame, Notre Dame, IN.

Hughes, D. G. (1993). *Affective predication and the retrieval of personality-trait words.* Unpublished master's thesis, Loyola University of Chicago, Chicago.

Hull, C. L. (1937). Mind, mechanism, and adaptive behavior. *Psychological Review, 44,* 1–32.

Hull, C. L. (1943). *Principles of behavior.* New York: Appleton-Century-Crofts.

Hummert, M. L., Crockett, W. H., & Kemper, S. (1990). Processing mechanisms underlying use of the balance schema. *Journal of Personality and Social Psychology, 58,* 5–21.

Hunt, E. (1989). Cognitive science: Definition, status, and questions. *Annual Review of Psychology, 40,* 603–629.

Hyde, T. S., & Jenkins, J. J. (1969). Differential effects of incidental tasks on the organization of recall of a list of highly associated words. *Journal of Experimental Psychology, 82,* 472–481.

Immergluck, L. (1964). Determinism-freedom in contemporary psychology: An ancient problem revisited. *American Psychologist, 19,* 270–281.

Isen, A. M., & Levin, P. F. (1972). The effect of feeling good on helping: Cookies and kindness. *Journal of Personality and Social Psychology, 21,* 384–388.

Isen, A. M., Shalker, T. E., Clark, M., & Karp, L. (1978). Affect, accessibility of material in memory, and behavior: A cognitive loop? *Journal of Personality and Social Psychology, 36,* 1–12.

Isen, A. M., & Simonds, S. F. (1978). The effect of feeling good on a helping task that is incompatible with good mood. *Social Psychology, 41,* 346–349.

Itoh, H., & Fujita, K. (1982). An analysis of eye movements during observational concept learning: Characterization of individual scanning pattern successes and failures. In R. Groner & P. Fraisse (Eds.), *Cognition and eye movements* (pp. 84–99). Amsterdam: North-Holland.

Izard, C. E. (1978). On the ontogenesis of emotions and emotion-cognition relationships in infancy. In M. Lewis & L. A. Rosenblum (Eds.), *The development of affect* (pp. 112–138). New York: Plenum.

Jackson, R. L., Alexander, J. H., & Maier, S. F. (1980). Learned helplessness, inactivity, and associative deficits: Effects of inescapable shock on response choice escape learning. *Journal of Experimental Psychology: Animal Behavioral Processes, 6,* 1–20.

Jacoby, L. L. (1973). Test appropriate strategies in retention of categorized lists. *Journal of Verbal Learning and Verbal Behavior, 12,* 675–682.

James, C. T., & Hillinger, M. L. (1977). The role of confusion in the semantic integration paradigm. *Journal of Verbal Learning and Verbal Behavior, 16,* 711–721.

James, W. (1884). What is an emotion? *Mind, 9,* 188–205.

James, W. (1890/1952). *The principles of psychology.* In R. M. Hutchins (Ed.), *Great books of the western world* (Vol. 53). Chicago: Encyclopedia Britannica.

James, W. (1907/1943). *Pragmatism, and four essays from the meaning of truth.* New York: Longmans, Green.

Janet, P. (1920). *The major symptoms of hysteria* (2nd ed.). New York: Macmillan.

Jenkins, A. H. (1982). *The psychology of the Afro-American: A humanistic approach.* Elmsford, NY: Pergamon.

Jenkins, H. M., & Sainsbury, R. S. (1970). Discrimination learning with the distinctive feature on positive or negative trials. In D. I. Mostofsky (Ed.), *Attention: Contemporary theory and analysis* (pp. 239–273). New York: Appleton-Century-Crofts.

Jenkins, J. J. (1974). Remember that old theory of memory? Well, forget it! *American Psychologist, 29,* 785–795.

Jenkins, J. J., & Russell, W. A. (1952). Associative clustering during recall. *Journal of Abnormal and Social Psychology, 47,* 818–821.

Jenkins, P. M., & Cofer, C. N. (1957). An exploratory study of discrete free association to compound verbal stimuli. *Psychological Reports, 3,* 599–602.

Johansson, G. (1973). Visual perception of biological motion and a model for its analysis. *Perception and Psychophysics, 14,* 201–211.

Johnson, M. K., Bransford, J. D., & Solomon, S. K. (1973). Memory for tacit implications of sentences. *Journal of Experimental Psychology, 98,* 203–205.

Johnson, M. K., Doll, T. J., Bransford, J. D., & Lapinski, R. H. (1974). Context effects in sentence memory. *Journal of Experimental Psychology, 103,* 358–360.

Johnson, M. K., & Hasher, L. (1987). Human learning and memory. *Annual Review of Psychology, 38,* 631–668.

Johnson, R. C., Frincke, G., & Martin, L. (1961). Meaningfulness, frequency, and affective character of words as related to visual duration threshold. *Canadian Journal of Psychology, 15,* 199–204.

Johnson, R. C., Thomson, C. W., & Frincke, G. (1960). Word values, word frequency, and visual duration thresholds. *Psychological Review, 67,* 332–342.

Johnson, W. E. (1922). *Logic (Part II): Demonstrative inference: Deductive and inductive.* New York: Dover.

Johnson-Laird, P. N., Gibbs, G., & de Mowbray, J. (1978). Meaning, amount of processing, and memory for words. *Memory and Cognition, 6,* 372–375.

Johnston, W. A., & Dark, V. J. (1986). Selective attention. *Annual Review of Psychology, 37,* 43–75.

Jones, E. E., & Davis, K. E. (1965). From acts to dispositions: The attribution process in person perception. In L. Berkowitz (Ed.), *Advances in Experimental Social Psychology* (Vol. 2, pp. 219–266). New York: Academic Press.

Jones, E. E., Kanouse, D. E., Kelley, H. H., Nisbett, R. E., Valins, S., & Weiner, B. (Eds.). (1972). *Attribution: Perceiving the causes of behavior.* Morristown, NJ: General Learning.

Jones, E. E., & Nisbett, R. E. (1971). *The actor and the observer: Divergent perceptions of the causes of behavior.* Morristown, NJ: General Learning.

Jones, H. E. (1929). Emotional factors in learning. *Journal of General Psychology, 2,* 263–272.

Jung, C. G. (1929/1954). Problems of modern psychotherapy. In H. Read, M. Fordham, & G. Adler (Eds.), *The collected works of C. G. Jung* (Vol. 16, pp. 53–75). *Bollingen Series.* New York: Pantheon Books; London: Routledge & Kegan Paul.

Jung, C. G. (1929/1961). Freud and Jung: Contrasts. In H. Read, M. Fordham, & G. Adler (Eds.), *The collected works of C. G. Jung* (Vol. 4, pp. 333–340). *Bollingen Series.* New York: Pantheon Books; London: Routledge & Kegan Paul.

Jung, C. G. (1916/1961). Prefaces to "Collected papers on analytical psychology." In H. Read, M. Fordham, & G. Adler (Eds.), *The collected works of C. G. Jung* (Vol. 4, pp. 290–297). *Bollingen Series.* New York: Pantheon Books; London: Routledge & Kegan Paul.

Jussim, L. (1986). Self-fulfilling prophecies: A theoretical and integrative review. *Psychological Review, 93,* 429–445.

Justice, E. M. (1985). Categorization as a preferred memory strategy: Developmental changes during elementary school. *Developmental Psychology, 21,* 1105–1110.

Kagan, J. (1981). *The second year: The emergence of self-awareness.* Cambridge: Harvard University Press.

Kagan, J. (1984). *The nature of the child.* New York: Basic.

Kahneman, D., Slovic, P., & Tversky, A. (Eds.). (1982). *Judgment under uncertainty: Heuristics and biases.* Cambridge: Cambridge University Press.

Kahneman, D., & Tversky, A. (1972). Subjective probability: A judgment of representativeness. *Cognitive Psychology, 3,* 430–454.

Kahneman, D., & Tversky, A. (1973). On the psychology of prediction. *Psychological Review, 80,* 237–251.

Kail, R. V. (1990). *Memory development in children* (3rd. ed.). New York: Freeman.

Kalnins, I. V., & Bruner, J. S. (1973). The coordination of visual observation and instrumental behavior in early infancy. *Perception, 2,* 307–314.

Kanfer, R., & Zeiss, A. M. (1983). Depression, interpersonal standard setting, and judgments of self-efficacy. *Journal of Abnormal Psychology, 92,* 319–329.

Kant, I. (1781/1952). *The critique of pure reason.* In R. M. Hutchins (Ed.), *Great books of the western world* (Vol. 42, pp. 1–250). Chicago: Encyclopedia Britannica.

Karwoski, T. F., & Schachter, J. (1948). Psychological studies in semantics: III. Reaction times for similarity and difference. *Journal of Social Psychology, 28,* 103–120.

Katz, A. N. (1982). Metaphoric relationships: The role of feature saliency. *Journal of Psycholinguistic Research, 11,* 283–296.

Kaye, K., & Marcus, J. (1981). Infant imitation. The sensory-motor agenda. *Developmental Psychology, 17,* 258–265.

Keeney, T. J., Cannizzo, S. R., & Flavell, J. H. (1967). Spontaneous and induced verbal rehearsal in a recall task. *Child Development, 38,* 953–966.

Kelley, H. H. (1972). Causal schemata and the attribution process. In E. E. Jones, et al. (Eds.), *Attribution: Perceiving the causes of behavior* (pp. 151–174). Morristown, NJ: General Learning.

Kelley, H. H. (1973). The processes of causal attribution. *American Psychologist, 28,* 107–128.

Kelley, H. H., & Stahelski, A. J. (1970). Social interaction basis of cooperators' and competitors' beliefs about others. *Journal of Personality and Social Psychology, 16,* 66–91.

Kellogg, R. T., Robbins, D. W., & Bourne, L. E., Jr. (1978). Memory for intertrial events in feature identification. *Journal of Experimental Psychology: Human Learning and Memory, 4,* 256–265.

Kelly, G. A. (1955). *The psychology of personal constructs (Vol. 1). A theory of personality.* New York: Norton.

Kieras, D. E., & Greeno, J. G. (1975). Effect of meaningfulness on judgments of computability. *Memory and Cognition, 3,* 349–355.

Kintsch, W. (1968). Recognition and free recall of organized lists. *Journal of Experimental Psychology, 78,* 481–487.

Kjeldergaard, P. M. (1962). Commonality scores under instructions to give opposites. *Psychological Reports, 11,* 219–220.

Klatsky, R. L., Martin, G. L., & Kane, R. A. (1982). Semantic interpretation effects on memory for faces. *Memory & Cognition, 10,* 195–206.

Kleck, R. (1967). The effects of interpersonal affect on errors made when reconstructing a stimulus display. *Psychonomic Science, 9,* 449–450.

Klein, D., Moscovitch, M., & Vigna, C. (1976). Attentional mechanisms and perceptual asymmetries in tachistoscopic recognition of words and faces. *Neuropsychologia, 14,* 55–66.

Klein, J. G. (1991). Negativity effects in impression formation: A test in the political arena. *Personality and Social Psychology Bulletin, 17,* 412–418.

Koen, F. (1962). Polarization, *m* and emotionality in words. *Journal of Verbal Learning and Verbal Behavior, 1,* 183–187.

Koffka, K. (1935). *Principles of gestalt psychology.* New York: Harcourt, Brace.

Kolers, P. A., & Palef, S. R. (1976). Knowing not. *Memory & Cognition, 4,* 553–558.

Kondo, H. (1969). *Albert Einstein and the theory of relativity.* New York: Franklin Watts.

Kornhuber, H. H., & Deecke, L. (1965). Hirnpotential-änderungen bei willkurbewegungen und passiven bewegungendes menschen: Bereitschaftspotential und reafferente potentiale. *Pflugers Archive fur die gesamte Physiologie des Menschen und der Tiere, 284,* 1–17.

Kosslyn, S. M. (1975). Information representation in visual imagery? *Cognitive Psychology, 7,* 341–370.

Kothurkar, V. K. (1963). Effect of stimulus-response meaningfulness on paired-associate learning and retention. *Journal of Experimental Psychology, 65,* 305–308.

Kreutzer, M. A., Leonard, C., & Flavell, J. H. (1975). An interview study of children's knowledge about memory. *Monographs of the Society for Research in Child Development, 40,* (1, Serial No. 159), 1–60.

Krumhansl, C. L., & Jusczyk, P. W. (1990). Infants' perception of phrase structure in music. *Psychological Science, 1,* 70–73.

Kuhn, T. S. (1970). *The structure of scientific revolutions* (2nd ed.). Chicago: University of Chicago Press.

Kukla, A. (1972). Foundations of an attributional theory of performance. *Psychological Review, 79,* 454–470.

Kunst-Wilson, W. R., & Zajonc, R. B. (1980). Affective discrimination of stimuli that cannot be recognized. *Science, 207,* 557–558.

Lachter, J., & Bever, T. G. (1988). The relation between linguistic structure and associative theories of language learning: A constructive critique of some connectionist learning models. In S. Pinker & J. Mehler (Eds.), *Connections and symbols* (pp. 195–247). Cambridge, MA: Bradford/MIT Press.

Lakoff, G. (1972). Hedges: A study in meaning criteria and the logic of fuzzy concepts. *Papers from the Eighth Regional Meeting, Chicago Linguistic Society* (pp. 183–228). Chicago: Chicago Linguistic Society.

Lakoff, G. (1987). *Women, fire, and dangerous things: What categories reveal about the mind.* Chicago: University of Chicago Press.

Lakoff, G., & Johnson, M. (1980). *Metaphors we live by.* Chicago: University of Chicago Press.

Lamiell, J. T. (1987). *The psychology of personality: An epistemological inquiry.* New York: Columbia University Press.

Lamiell, J. (1992). *What did Windelband mean by nomothetic?* Paper presented at the 100th Annual Convention of the American Psychological Association, Washington, DC.

Lamiell, J. T., Foss, M. A., Larsen, R. J., & Hempel, A. M. (1983). Studies in intuitive personology from an idiothetic point of view: Implications for personality theory. *Journal of Personality, 51,* 438–467.

Lamiell, J. T., Foss, M. A., Trierweiler, S. J., & Leffel, G. M. (1983). Toward a further understanding of the intuitive personologist: Some preliminary evidence for the dialectical quality of subjective personality impressions. *Journal of Personality, 51,* 213–235.

Landau, B. (1982). Will the real grandmother please stand up? The psychological reality of dual meaning representations. *Journal of Psycholinguistic Research, 11,* 47–62.

Landauer, T. K., & Freedman, J. L. (1968). Information retrieval from long-term memory: Category size and recognition time. *Journal of Verbal Learning and Verbal Behavior, 7,* 291–295.

Lane, D. M. (1979). Developmental changes in attention-deployment skills. *Journal of Experimental Child Psychology, 28,* 16–29.

Langer, S. K. (1948). *Philosophy in a new key.* New York: Penguin Books.

Lashley, K. S. (1929). Learning: I. Nervous mechanisms in learning. In C. Murchison (Ed.), *The foundations of experimental psychology* (pp. 524–563). Worcester, MA: Clark University Press.

Lau, R. R., & Russell, D. (1980). Attributions in the sports pages. *Journal of Personality and Social Psychology, 39,* 29–38.

Lazarus, R. S. (1982). Thoughts on the relations between emotion and cognition. *American Psychologist, 37,* 1019–1024.

Lazarus, R. S. (1984). On the primacy of cognition. *American Psychologist, 39,* 124–129.

Lazarus, R. S. (1991a). Cognition and motivation in emotion. *American Psychologist, 46,* 352–367.

Lazarus, R. S. (1991b). Progress on a cognitive-motivational-relational theory of emotion. *American Psychologist, 46,* 819–834.

Leahey, T. H. (1987). On having purpose and explaining it, too. *The Journal of Mind and Behavior, 8,* 255–260.

Leary, T. (1957). *Interpersonal diagnosis of personality.* New York: Ronald.

Lefcourt, H. M. (1973). The function of the illusions of control and freedom. *American Psychologist, 28,* 417–425.

Leslie, A. M. (1982). The perception of causality in infants. *Perception, 11,* 173–186.

Leslie, A. M. (1984). Spatiotemporal continuity and the perception of causality in infants. *Perception, 13,* 287–305.

Leslie, A. M., & Keeble, S. (1987). Do six-month-old infants perceive causality? *Cognition, 25*, 265–288.

Levi, L. (1972). Stress and distress in response to psychosocial stimuli. *Acta Medica Scandinavica, 191*, Supplementum No. 528: 1–166.

Levin, S. M. (1961). The effects of awareness on verbal conditioning. *Journal of Experimental Psychology, 61*, 67–75.

Levine, S. C., & Carey, S. (1982). Up front: The acquisition of a concept and a word. *Journal of Child Language, 9*, 645–657.

Lewin, K., Dembo, T., Festinger, L, & Sears, P. S. (1944). Level of aspiration. In J. McV. Hunt (Ed.), *Personality and the behavior disorders* (Vol. 1, pp. 333–378). New York: Ronald.

Lewinsohn, P. M., Mischel, W., Chaplin, W., & Barton, R. (1980). Social competence and depression: The role of illusory self-perceptions. *Journal of Abnormal Psychology, 89*, 203–212.

Lewis, M., & Brooks, J. (1974). Self, other, and fear: Infants' reactions to people. In M. Lewis & L. Rosenblum (Eds.), *Fear: The origins of behavior* (Vol II, pp. 54–73). New York: Wiley.

Lewis, M., & Brooks, J. (1975). Infants' social perception: A constructivist view. In L. B. Cohen & P. Salapatek (Eds.), *Infant perception: From sensation to cognition* (Vol. 2, pp. 23–41). New York: Academic Press.

Lewis, M., Sullivan, M. W., & Brooks-Gunn, J. (1985). Emotional behaviour during the learning of a contingency in early infancy. *British Journal of Developmental Psychology, 3*, 307–316.

Lewis, V. E., & Williams, R. N. (1989). Mood-congruent vs. mood-state-dependent learning: Implications for a view of emotion. *Journal of Social Behavior and Personality, 4*, 157–171.

Libet, B. (1973). Electrical stimulation of cortex in human subjects, and conscious sensory aspects. In A. Iggo (Ed.), *Handbook of Sensory Physiology* (Vol. 2, pp. 743–790). New York: Springer-Verlag.

Libet, B. (1985). Unconscious cerebral initiative and the role of conscious will in voluntary action. *Behavioral and Brain Sciences, 8*, 529–566.

Libet, B., Gleason, C. A., Wright, E. W., & Pearl, D. K. (1983). Time of conscious intention to act in relation to onset of cerebral activity (readiness-potential); the unconscious initiation of a freely voluntary act. *Brain, 106*, 623–642.

Lindsay, D. S. (1990). Misleading suggestions can impair eyewitnesses' ability to remember event details. *Journal of Experimental Psychology: Learning, Memory, and Cognition, 16*, 1077–1083.

Lippmann, W. (1946). *Public opinion*. New York: Penguin.

Locke, J. (1690/1952). *An essay concerning human understanding*. In R. M. Hutchins (Ed.), *Great books of the western world* (Vol. 35, pp. 85–395). Chicago: Encyclopedia Britannica.

Loftus, E. F., & Palmer, J. C. (1974). Reconstruction of automobile destruction: An example of the interaction between language and memory. *Journal of Verbal Learning and Verbal Behavior, 13*, 585–589.

Loftus, G. R. (1972). Eye fixations and recognition memory for pictures. *Cognitive Psychology, 3*, 525–551.

Lord, C. G., Lepper, M. R., & Preston, E. (1984). Considering the opposite: A corrective strategy for social judgment. *Journal of Personality and Social Psychology, 47*, 1231–1243.

Lott, A. J., & Lott, B. E. (1970). Some indirect measures of interpersonal attraction among children. *Journal of Educational Psychology, 61*, 124–135.

Lovelace, E. A. (1984). Metamemory: Monitoring future recallability during study. *Journal of Experimental Psychology: Learning, Memory, & Cognition, 10,* 756–766.

Lucas, J. R. (1961). Minds, machines, and Gödel. *Philosophy, 36,* 112–127.

Lupker, S. J., Harbluk, J. L., & Patrick, A. S. (1991). Memory for things forgotten. *Journal of Experimental Psychology: Learning, Memory, and Cognition, 17,* 897–907.

Lynch, C. A. (1932). The memory values of certain alleged emotionally toned words. *Journal of Experimental Psychology, 15,* 298–315.

Lyons, J. (1977). *Semantics* (Vol. 1). Cambridge: Cambridge University Press.

Maccoby, E. E., & Martin, J. A. (1983). Socialization in the context of the family: Parent-child interaction. In E. M. Hetherington (Vol. Ed.) and P. H. Mussen (Gen. Ed.), *Handbook of child psychology: Socialization, personality, and social development* (Vol. 4, pp. 1–101). New York: Wiley.

MacDonald, M. C., & Just, M. A. (1989). Changes in activation levels with negation. *Journal of Experimental Psychology: Learning, Memory, and Cognition, 15,* 633–642.

Mackintosh, N. J. (1983). *Conditioning and associative learning.* New York: Oxford University Press.

Macnamara, J. (1972). Cognitive basis of language learning in infants. *Psychological Review, 79,* 1–13.

Maier, N. R. F. (1931). Reasoning in humans: II. The solution of a problem and its appearance in consciousness. *Journal of Comparative Psychology, 12,* 181–194.

Mandler, G. (1967). Organization and memory. In K. W. Spence & J. T. Spence (Eds.), *The psychology of learning and motivation: Advances in research and theory* (pp. 327–372). New York: Academic Press.

Mandler, G. (1985). *Cognitive psychology: An essay in cognitive science.* Hillsdale, NJ: Erlbaum.

Mandler, G., & Pearlstone, Z. (1966). Free and constrained concept learning and subsequent recall. *Journal of Verbal Learning and Verbal Behavior, 5,* 126–131.

Mandler, J. M. (1982). Recent research on story grammars. In J.-F. Le Ny & W. Kintsch (Eds.), *Language and comprehension* (pp. 207–218). Amsterdam: Alphen.

Marañon, G. (1924). Contribution a l'étude de l'action émotive de l'adrénaline [Contribution to the study of the emotive action of adrenaline]. *Revue Francaise d'Endocrinologie, 2,* 301–325.

Marcel, A. J. (1983). Conscious and unconscious perception: An approach to the relations between phenomenal experience and perceptual processes. *Cognitive Psychology, 15,* 238–300.

Markman, E. M. (1989). *Categorization and naming in children: Problems of induction.* Cambridge, MA: Bradford/MIT Press.

Markman, E. M., & Hutchinson, J. E. (1984). Children's sensitivity to constraints on word meaning: Taxonomic versus thematic relations. *Cognitive Psychology, 16,* 1–27.

Markus, H. (1983). Self-knowledge: An expanded view. *Journal of Personality, 51,* 543–565.

Martin, J. (1979). Laboratory studies of self-reinforcement (SR) phenomena. *The Journal of General Psychology, 101,* 103–149.

Mast, V. K., Fagen, J. W., Rovee-Collier, C. K., & Sullivan, M. W. (1980). Immediate and long-term memory for reinforcement context: The development of learned expectancies in early infancy. *Child Development, 51,* 700–707.

Matlin, M. W., & Stang, D. (1979). *The pollyanna principle: Selectivity in language, memory, and thought.* Cambridge, MA: Shenkman.

May, R. (1977). Freedom, determinism, and the future. *Psychology* (April, Trial issue), 3–8.

McCabe, A. (1982). Conceptual similarity and the quality of metaphor in isolated sentences versus extended contexts. *Journal of Psycholinguistic Research, 12*, 41–68.

McCarthy, T. A. (1978). *The critical theory of Jurgen Habermas.* Cambridge, MA: MIT Press.

McClelland, D. C., Atkinson, J. W., Clark, R. A., & Lowell, E. L. (1953). *The achievement motive.* New York: Appleton-Century-Crofts.

McCloskey, M. E., & Glucksberg, S. (1978). Natural categories. Well defined or fuzzy sets? *Memory and Cognition, 6*, 462–472.

McCloskey, M. E., & Zaragoza, M. (1985). Misleading postevent information and memory for events: Arguments and evidence against memory impairment hypotheses. *Journal of Experimental Psychology: General, 114*, 1–16.

McCullers, J. C. (1965). Type of associative interference as a factor in verbal paired-associate learning. *Journal of Verbal Learning and Verbal Behavior, 4*, 12–16.

McCulloch, W., & Pitts, W. (1943). A logical calculus of the ideas immanent in nervous activity. *Bulletin of Mathematical Biophysics, 5*, 115–133.

McDaniel, M. A., Waddill, P. J., & Einstein, G. O. (1988). A contextual account of the generation effect: A three-factor theory. *Journal of Memory and Language, 27*, 521–536.

McGuire, W. J., & McGuire, C. V. (1982). Significant others in self-space: Sex differences and developmental trends in the social self. In J. Suls (Ed.), *Psychological perspectives on the self* (Vol. 1, pp. 71–96). Hillsdale, NJ: Erlbaum.

McKeever, W. F., & Huling, M. D. (1971). Bilateral tachistoscopic word recognition as a function of hemisphere stimulated and interhemispheric transfer time. *Neuropsychologia, 9*, 281–288.

McKoon, G., & Ratcliff, R. (1980). The comprehension processes and memory structures involved in anaphoric reference. *Journal of Verbal Learning and Verbal Behavior, 19*, 668–682.

McNeill, D. (1968). On theories of language acquisition. In T. R. Dixon & D. L. Horton (Eds.), *Verbal behavior and general behavior theory* (pp. 406–420). Englewood Cliffs, NJ: Prentice-Hall.

Mead, G. H. (1934). *Mind, self, and society.* Chicago: University of Chicago Press.

Medin, D. L. (1989). Concepts and conceptual structure. *American Psychologist, 44*, 1469–1481.

Medin, D. L., & Shoben, E. J. (1988). Context and structure in conceptual combination. *Cognitive Psychology, 20*, 158–190.

Mehler, J. (1963). Some effects of grammatical transformations on the recall of English sentences. *Journal of Verbal Learning and Verbal Behavior, 2*, 346–351.

Mehler, J., Bertoncini, J., Barriere, M., & Jassik-Gerschenfeld, D. (1978). Infant recognition of mother's voice. *Perception, 7*, 491–497.

Meichenbaum, D., & Gilmore, J. B. (1984). The nature of unconscious processes: A cognitive-behavioral perspective. In K. S. Bowers & D. Meichenbaum (Eds.), *The unconscious reconsidered* (pp. 273–298). New York: Wiley.

Melkman, R., & Deutsch, C. (1977). Memory functioning as related to developmental changes in bases of organization. *Journal of Experimental Child Psychology, 23*, 84–97.

Meltzoff, A. N., & Moore, M. K. (1977). Imitation of facial and manual gestures by human neonates. *Science, 198*, 75–78.

Menzel, E. W., & Halperin, S. (1975). Purposive behavior as a basis for objective communication between chimpanzees. *Science, 189*, 652–654.

Merleau-Ponty, M. (1964). The child's relations with others. In J. M. Edie (Ed.), *The primacy of perception and other essays on phenomenological psychology: The philosophy of art, history, and politics* (pp. 96–158). Evanston, IL: Northwestern University Press.

Mervis, C. B. (1985). On the existence of prelinguistic categories: A case study. *Infant Behavior and Development, 8,* 293–300.

Michotte, A. (1963). *The perception of causality.* London: Methuen.

Mill, J. S. (1872/1974). *A system of logic ratiocinative and inductive.* Toronto: University of Toronto Press.

Miller, D. T., & Turnbull, W. (1986). Expectancies and interpersonal processes. *Annual Review of Psychology, 37,* 233–256.

Miller, G. A. (1956). The magical number seven, plus or minus two: Some limits on our capacity for processing information. *Psychological Review, 63,* 81–97.

Miller, G. A., Galanter, E., & Pribram, K. H. (1960). *Plans and the structure of behavior.* New York: Holt, Rinehart & Winston.

Millis, K. K., & Neimeyer, R. A. (1990). A test of the dichotomy corollary: Propositions versus constructs as basic cognitive units. *International Journal of Personal Construct Psychology, 3,* 167–181.

Mink, W. D. (1963). Semantic generalization as related to word association. *Psychological Reports, 12,* 59–67.

Minsky, M. (1986). *The society of mind.* New York: Simon and Schuster.

Mirels, H. L. (1980). The avowal of responsibility for good and bad outcomes: The effects of generalized self-serving biases. *Personality and Social Psychology Bulletin, 6,* 299–306.

Mischel, W. (1968). *Personality and assessment.* New York: Wiley.

Mischel, W., Ebbesen, E. B., & Zeiss, A. M. (1973). Selective attention to the self: Situational and dispositional determinants. *Journal of Personality and Social Psychology, 27,* 129-142.

Mischel, W., Ebbesen, E. B., & Zeiss, A. M. (1976). Determinants of selective memory about the self. *Journal of Counseling and Clinical Psychology, 44,* 92-103.

Mitroff, I. I. (1974). Norms and counter-norms in a select group of the Apollo moon scientists: A case study of the ambivalence of scientists. *American Sociological Review, 39,* 579–595.

Miyake, N., & Norman, D. A. (1979). To ask a question, one must know enough to know what is not known. *Journal of Verbal Learning and Verbal Behavior, 18,* 357–364.

Moely, B. E., Olson, F. A., Halwes, T. G., & Flavell, J. H. (1969). Production deficiency in young children's clustered recall. *Developmental Psychology, 1,* 26–34.

Morrison, F. J., & Lord, C. (1982). Age differences in recall of categorized material: Organization or retrieval? *Journal of Genetic Psychology, 141,* 233–241.

Mortimer, J. T., Finch, M. D., & Kumka, D. (1982). Persistence and change in development: The multidimensional self-concept. In P. B. Baltes & O. G. Brim, Jr. (Eds.), *Life-span development and behavior* (Vol. 4, pp. 263–313). New York: Academic Press.

Mosbacher, B. J. (1984). *Depression and alcohol ingestion: A teleological perspective.* Unpublished doctoral dissertation, Purdue University, West Lafayette, IN.

Mosbacher, B. J., Gruen, G. E., & Rychlak, J. F. (1985). Incentive value: The overlooked dimension in childhood sharing. *Journal of Genetic Psychology, 146,* 197–204.

Mountcastle, V. B. (1975). Modality and topographic properties of single neurones of cat's somatic sensory cortex. *Journal of Neurophysiology, 20,* 408–434.

Moynahan, E. D. (1973). The development of knowledge concerning the effect of categorization upon free recall. *Child Development, 44,* 238–246.

Moynahan, E. D. (1976). The development of the ability to assess recall performance. *Journal of Experimental Child Psychology, 21,* 94–97.

Muller, J. B., & Rychlak, J. F. (1979). Reinforcement as positive or negative meaning-extension: An empirical demonstration. *Motivation and Emotion, 3,* 287–297.

Munn, C. A. (1986). The deceptive use of alarm calls by sentinel species in mixed-species flocks of neotropical birds. In R. W. Mitchell & N. S. Thompson (Eds.), *Deception: Perspectives on human and nonhuman deceit* (pp. 169–175). Albany: State University of New York Press.

Murphy, G. L., & Medin, D. L. (1985). The role of theories in conceptual coherence. *Psychological Review, 92,* 289–316.

Murray, H. A. (1938). *Explorations in personality.* New York: Oxford University Press.

Myers, R. E., & Sperry, R. W. (1953). Interocular transfer of a visual form discrimination habit in cats after section of the optic chiasma and corpus callosum. *Anatomical Record, 115,* 351–352.

Nagel, E., & Newman, J. R. (1958). *Gödel's proof.* New York: New York University Press.

Nairne, J. S., Pusen, C., & Widner, R. L., Jr. (1985). Representation in the mental lexicon: Implications for theories of the generation effect. *Memory & Cognition, 13,* 183–191.

Nasby, W., & Yando, R. (1982). Selective encoding and retrieval of affectively valent information: Two cognitive consequences of children's mood states. *Journal of Personality and Social Psychology, 43,* 1244–1253.

Nehrke, M. F., Hulicka, I. M., & Morganti, J. B. (1980). Age differences in life satisfaction, locus of control, and self-concept. *International Journal of Aging and Human Development, 11,* 25–33.

Neisser, U. (1991a). Direct perception and other forms of knowing. In R. R. Hoffman & D. S. Palermo (Eds.), *Cognition and the symbolic processes: Applied and ecological perspectives* (pp. 17–30). Hillsdale, NJ: Erlbaum.

Neisser, U. (1991b). *Without perception, there is no knowledge: Implications for artificial intelligence.* Emory Cognition Project Report (No. 18). Atlanta: Emory University.

Nelson, K. (1974a). Variations in children's concepts by age and category. *Child Development, 45,* 577–584.

Nelson, K. (1974b). Concept, word, and sentence: Interrelations in acquisition and development. *Psychological Review, 81,* 267–285.

Nelson, K., Rescorla, L., Gruendel, J., & Benedict, H. (1978). Early lexicons: What do they mean? *Child Development, 49,* 960–968.

Newell, A., Shaw, J. C., & Simon, H. A. (1958). Elements of a theory of human problem solving. *Psychological Review, 65,* 151–166.

Newtson, D. (1976). Foundations of attribution: The perception of ongoing behavior. In J. H. Harvey, W. J. Ickes, & R. F. Kidd (Eds.), *New directions in attribution research* (Vol. 1, pp. 223–247). Hillsdale, NJ: Erlbaum.

Nguyen, M. L. (1975). *Clustering in terms of categorization and reinforcement value in randomly arranged associates.* Unpublished master's thesis, Purdue University, West Lafayette, IN.

Nickerson, R. S. (1978). On the time it takes to tell things apart. In J. Requin (Ed.), *Attention and performance VII* (pp. 77–88). Hillsdale, NJ: Erlbaum.

Nisbett, R. E., & Ross, L. (1980). *Human inference: Strategies and shortcomings of social judgment.* Englewood Cliffs, NJ: Prentice-Hall.

Nisbett, R. E., & Wilson, T. D. (1977a). The halo effect: Evidence for unconscious alteration of judgments. *Journal of Personality and Social Psychology, 35,* 250–256.

Nisbett, R. E., & Wilson, T. D. (1977b). Telling more than we can know: Verbal reports on mental processes. *Psychological Review, 84,* 231–259.

Nissen, M. J., & Bullemer, P. (1987). Attentional requirements of learning: Evidence from performance measures. *Cognitive Psychology, 19*, 1–32.

Norris, K. S. (1992). Dolphins in crisis. *National Geographic, 182*, 2–35.

Oatley, K., & Jenkins, J. M. (1992). Human emotions: Function and dysfunction. *Annual Review of Psychology, 43*, 55–85.

Oatley, K., & Johnson-Laird, P. N. (1987). Towards a cognitive theory of emotion. *Cognition and Emotion, 1*, 29–50.

O'Brien, E. J., Duffy, S. A., & Myers, J. L. (1986). Anaphoric inference during reading. *Journal of Experimental Psychology: Learning, Memory, and Cognition, 12*, 346–352.

O'Connor, D. J. (1971). *Free will*. Garden City, NY: Doubleday.

O'Connor, K. P. (1981). The intentional paradigm and cognitive psychophysiology. *Psychophysiology, 18*, 121–128.

Ogden, C. K. (1967). *Opposition: A linguistic and psychological analysis*. Bloomington: Indiana University Press.

Ogilvie, D. M. (1987). The undesired self: A neglected variable in personality research. *Journal of Personality and Social Psychology, 52*, 379–385.

O'Leary, L. R. (1969). *The effect of idiographic meaningfulness on the learning of subjects from different racial backgrounds, social classes, and ability levels*. Unpublished doctoral dissertation, St. Louis University, St. Louis, MO.

Orne, M. T. (1959). The nature of hypnosis: Artifact and essence. *Journal of Abnormal and Social Psychology, 58*, 277–299.

Orne, M. T. (1962). On the social psychology of the psychological experiment: With particular reference to demand characteristics and their implications. *American Psychologist, 17*, 776–783.

Ornstein, P. A., Naus, M. J., & Liberty, C. (1975). Rehearsal and organizational processes in children's memory. *Child Development, 46*, 818–830.

Osgood, C. E. (1949). The similarity paradox in human learning: A resolution. *Psychological Review, 56*, 132–143.

Osgood, C. E. (1952). The nature and measurement of meaning. *Psychological Bulletin, 49*, 197–237.

Osgood, C. E. (1962). *An alternative to war or surrender*. Urbana: University of Illinois Press.

Osgood, C. E., Suci, G. J., & Tannenbaum, P. H. (1957). *The measurement of meaning*. Urbana: University of Illinois Press.

Ozier, M. (1978). Access to the memory trace through orthographic and categoric information. *Journal of Experimental Psychology: Human Learning and Memory, 4*, 469–485.

Packer, M. J. (1985). Hermeneutic inquiry in the study of human conduct. *American Psychologist, 40*, 1081–1093.

Page, M. M. (1969). Social psychology of a classical conditioning of attitudes experiment. *Journal of Personality and Social Psychology, 11*, 177–186.

Page, M. M. (1972). Demand characteristics and the verbal operant conditioning experiment. *Journal of Personality and Social Psychology, 23*, 372–378.

Paivio, A. (1971). *Imagery and verbal processes*. New York: Holt, Rinehart, & Winston.

Palermo, D. S., & Jenkins, J. J. (1964). *Word association norms: Grade school through college*. Minneapolis: University of Minnesota Press.

Palmer, R. E. (1969). *Hermeneutics: Interpretation theory in Schleiermacher, Dilthey, Heidegger and Gadamer*. Evanston, IL: Northwestern University Press.

Palter, R. (1956). Philosophic principles and scientific theory. *Philosophy of Science, 23*, 111–135.

Papoušek, H. (1967). Conditioning during early postnatal development. In Y. Brackbill & G. G. Thompson (Eds.), *Behavior in infancy and early childhood* (pp. 11–41). New York: Free Press.

Papoušek, H. (1969). Individual variability in learned responses in human infants. In R. J. Robinson (Ed.), *Brain and early behaviour* (pp. 251–266). New York: Academic Press.

Park, B. (1986). A method for studying the development of impressions of real people. *Journal of Personality and Social Psychology, 51*, 907–917.

Parrott, W. G., & Sabini, J. (1990). Mood and memory under natural conditions: Evidence for mood incongruent recall. *Journal of Personality and Social Psychology, 59*, 321–336.

Pátkai, P. (1971). Catecholamine excretion in pleasant and unpleasant situations. *Acta Psychologica, 35*, 352–363.

Patterson, F. C. (1978a). The gestures of a gorilla: Language acquisition in another pongid. *Brain and Language, 5*, 72–97.

Patterson, F. C. (1978b). Conversations with a gorilla. *National Geographic, 154*, 438–465.

Penfield, W. (1975). *The mystery of the mind: A critical study of consciousness and the human brain.* Princeton, NJ: Princeton University Press.

Pepper, S. C. (1970). *World hypotheses: A study in evidence.* Berkeley: University of California Press.

Pepperberg, I. M. (1987). Acquisition of the same/different concept by an African Grey parrot (*Psittacus erithacus*): Learning with respect to categories of color, shape, and material. *Animal Learning and Behavior, 15*, 423–432.

Perlmutter, M. (1984). Continuities and discontinuities in early human memory paradigms, processes, and performance. In R. Kail & N. E. Spear (Eds.), *Comparative perspectives on the development of memory* (pp. 253–284). Hillsdale, NJ: Erlbaum.

Perlmutter, M., & Myers, N. A. (1979). Development of recall in 2- to 4-year-old children. *Developmental Psychology, 15*, 73–83.

Peterson, L. R., & Peterson, M. J. (1959). Short-term retention of individual verbal items. *Journal of Experimental Psychology, 58*, 193–198.

Petty, R. E., Schumann, D. W., Richman, S. A., & Strathman, A. J. (1993). Positive mood and persuasion: Different roles for affect under high- and low-elaboration conditions. *Journal of Personality and Social Psychology, 64*, 5–20.

Pezdek, K., Whetstone, T., Reynolds, K., Askari, N., & Dougherty, T. (1989). Memory for real-world scenes: The role of consistency with schema expectation. *Journal of Experimental Psychology: Learning, Memory, and Cognition, 15*, 587–595.

Piaget, J. (1929). *The child's conception of the world* (Trans. J. Tomlinson and A. Tomlinson). New York: Harcourt, Brace, & World.

Piaget, J. (1952). *The origins of intelligence in children.* New York: International Universities Press.

Piaget, J. (1971). *Psychology and epistemology: Towards a theory of knowledge.* New York: Viking.

Piaget, J. (1978). *Behavior and evolution.* New York: Pantheon.

Pichert, J. W., & Anderson, R. C. (1977). Taking different perspectives on a story. *Journal of Educational Psychology, 69*, 309–315.

Pinker, S., & Prince, A. (1988). On language and connectionism: Analysis of a parallel distributed processing model of language acquisition. In S. Pinker & J. Mehler (Eds.), *Connections and symbols* (pp. 73–193). Cambridge, MA: Bradford/ MIT Press.

Poincaré, H. (1929). *The foundations of science.* New York: Science House.

Polkinghorne, D. E. (1989). Phenomenological research methods. In R. S. Valle & S. Halling

(Eds.), *Existential-phenomenological perspectives in psychology: Exploring the breadth of human experience* (pp. 41–60). New York: Plenum.

Popper, K. R. (1959). *The logic of scientific discovery.* New York: Basic.

Postman, L. (1964). Short-term memory and incidental learning. In A. W. Melton (Ed.), *Categories of human learning* (pp. 26–53). New York: Academic Press.

Potter, M. C. (1975). Meaning in visual search. *Science, 187,* 965–966.

Potter, M. C., Moryadas, A., Abrams, I., & Noel, A. (1993). Word perception and misperception in context. *Journal of Experimental Psychology: Learning, Memory, and Cognition, 19,* 3–22.

Premack, D. (1965). Reinforcement theory. In D. Levine (Ed.), *Nebraska Symposium on Motivation* (Vol. 13, pp. 123–180). Lincoln: University of Nebraska Press.

Premack, D. (1971). Catching up with common sense or two sides of a generalization: Reinforcement and punishment. In R. Glaser (Ed.), *The nature of reinforcement* (pp. 121–150). New York: Academic Press.

Premack, D. (1976). *Intelligence in ape and man.* Hillsdale, NJ: Erlbaum.

Pressley, M., Borkowski, J. G., & Schneider, W. (1987). Cognitive strategies: Good strategy users coordinate metacognition and knowledge. In R. Vasta (Ed.), *Annals of Child Development* (Vol. 4, pp. 89–129). Greenwich, CT: JAI.

Pribram, K. H. (1991). *Brain and perception: Holonomy and structure in figural processing.* Hillsdale, NJ: Erlbaum.

Prigogine, I., & Stengers, I. (1984). *Order out of chaos: Man's new dialogue with nature.* New York: Bantam.

Proctor, R. W. (1981). A unified theory for matching-task phenomena. *Psychological Review, 88,* 291–326.

Pyszczynski, T. A., & Greenberg, J. (1981). Role of disconfirmed expectancies in the instigation of attributional processing. *Journal of Personality and Social Psychology, 40,* 31–38.

Quillian, M. R. (1967). *Semantic memory.* Unpublished doctoral dissertation, Carnegie-Mellon University, Pittsburgh.

Rahman, M. M. (1987). *The psychological quest: From Socrates to Freud.* North York, Ontario: University Press of Canada.

Ramsey, W., Stich, S., & Garon, J. (1993). Connectionism, eliminativism, and the future of folk psychology. In S. C. Christensen & D. R. Turner (Eds.), *Folk psychology and the philosophy of mind* (pp. 315–339). Hillsdale, NJ: Erlbaum.

Rausch, H. L. (1965). Interaction sequences. *Journal of Personality and Social Psychology, 2,* 487–499.

Reber, A. S. (1989). Implicit learning and tacit knowledge. *Journal of Experimental Psychology, 118,* 219–235.

Reed, E. S., & Jones, R. K. (1978). Gibson's theory of perception: A case of hasty epistemologizing. *Philosophy of Science, 45,* 519–530.

Reese, W. L. (1980). *Dictionary of philosophy and religion: Eastern and western thought.* Atlantic Highlands, NJ: Humanities.

Reschly, D. J., & Mittman, A. (1973). The relationship of self-esteem status and task ambiguity to the self-reinforcement behavior of children. *Developmental Psychology, 9,* 16–19.

Rescorla, R. A. (1967). Pavlovian conditioning and its proper control procedures. *Psychological Review, 74,* 71–80.

Rescorla, R. A. (1972). Informational variables in Pavlovian conditioning. In G. H. Bower

(Ed.), *The psychology of learning and motivation: Advances in research and theory* (Vol. 6, pp. 1–46). New York: Academic Press.

Rescorla, R. A. (1978). Some implications of a cognitive perspective on Pavlovian conditioning. In S. H. Hulse, H. Fowler, & W. K. Honig (Eds.), *Cognitive processes in animal behavior* (pp. 15–50). Hillsdale, NJ: Erlbaum.

Rheingold, H. L., & Eckerman, C. O. (1969). The infant's free entry into a new environment. *Journal of Experimental Child Psychology, 8,* 271–283.

Ricciuti, H. N. (1965). Object grouping and selective ordering behavior in infants 12 to 24 months old. *Merrill-Palmer Quarterly, 11,* 129–148.

Richards, I. A. (1967). Introduction. In C. K. Ogden, *Opposition: A linguistic and psychological analysis* (pp. 7–13). Bloomington: Indiana University Press.

Rock, I. (1957). The role of repetition in associative learning. *American Journal of Psychology, 70,* 186–193.

Rock, I. (1983). *The logic of perception.* Cambridge, MA: MIT Press.

Roediger, H. L., III. (1990). Implicit memory: retention without remembering. *American Psychologist, 45,* 1043–1056.

Rogers, C. R. (1951). *Client-centered therapy.* Boston: Houghton Mifflin.

Rogers, T. B., Kuiper, N. A., & Kirker, W. S. (1977). Self-reference and the encoding of personal information. *Journal of Personality & Social Psychology, 35,* 677–688.

Roitblat, H. L., & Von Fersen, L. (1992). Comparative cognition: Representations and processes in learning and memory. *Annual Review of Psychology, 43,* 671–710.

Romanes, G. J. (1883). *Animal intelligence.* New York: Appleton.

Rosch, E. H. (1973a). Natural categories. *Cognitive Psychology, 4,* 328–350.

Rosch, E. H. (1973b). On the internal structure of perceptual and semantic categories. In T. E. Moore (Ed.), *Cognitive development and the acquisition of language* (pp. 111–141). New York: Academic Press.

Rosch, E. H. (1975). Cognitive reference points. *Cognitive Psychology, 7,* 532–547.

Rosch, E. H. (1978). Principles of categorization. In E. Rosch & B. B. Lloyd (Eds.), *Cognition and categorization* (pp. 27–48). Hillsdale, NJ: Erlbaum.

Rosch, E. H., Mervis, C. B., Gray, W. D., Johnson, D. M., & Boyes-Braem, P. (1976). Basic objects in natural categories. *Cognitive Psychology, 8,* 382–439.

Rosenberg, S. (1969). The recall of verbal material accompanying semantically well-integrated and semantically poorly-integrated sentences. *Journal of Verbal Learning and Verbal Behavior, 8,* 732–736.

Rosenblueth, A., Wiener, N., & Bigelow, J. (1943). Behavior, purpose and teleology. *Philosophy of Science, 10,* 18–24.

Rosenhan, D. L., Salovey, P., Karylowski, J., & Hargis, K. (1981). Emotion and altruism. In J. P. Rushton & R. M. Sorrentino (Eds.), *Altruism and helping behavior: Social, personality, and developmental perspectives* (pp. 233–248). Hillsdale, NJ: Erlbaum.

Rosenthal, P. (1984). *Words and values: Some leading words and where they lead us.* New York: Oxford University Press.

Rosenthal, R., & Jacobson, L. (1968). *Pygmalion in the classroom.* New York: Holt, Rinehart & Winston.

Rosenthal, R., & Rubin, D. B. (1978). Interpersonal expectancy effects: The first 345 studies. *Behavior and Brain Sciences, 1,* 377–415.

Ross, H. S., & Kay, D. A. (1980). The origins of social games. In K. Rubin (Ed.), *Children's Play* (pp. 17–32). San Francisco: Jossey-Bass.

Ross, L. (1978). Some afterthoughts on the intuitive psychologist. In L. Berkowitz (Ed.), *Cognitive theories in social psychology*. New York: Academic Press.

Ross, L., Lepper, M. R., Areack, F., & Steinmetz, J. (1977). Social explanation and social expectation: Effects of real and hypothetical explanations on subjective likelihood. *Journal of Personality and Social Psychology, 35*, 817–829.

Ross, M. (1989). Relation of implicit theories to the construction of personal histories. *Psychological Review, 96*, 341–357.

Ross, M., McFarland, C., Conway, M., & Zanna, M. P. (1983). Reciprocal relation between attitudes and behavior recall: Committing people to newly formed attitudes. *Journal of Personality and Social Psychology, 45*, 257–267.

Roth, E. M., & Shoben, E. J. (1983). The effect of context on the structure of categories. *Cognitive Psychology, 15*, 346–378.

Rothbart, M., Evans, M., & Fulero, S. (1979). Recall for confirming events: Memory processes and the maintenance of social stereotypes. *Journal of Experimental Social Psychology, 15*, 343–355.

Rothbart, M., & Lewis, S. (1988). Inferring category attributes from exemplar attributes: Geometric shapes and social categories. *Journal of Personality and Social Psychology, 55*, 861–872.

Rothenberg, A. (1973a). Word association and creativity. *Psychological Reports, 33*, 3–12.

Rothenberg, A. (1973b). Opposite responding as a measure of creativity. *Psychological Reports, 33*, 15–18.

Rotter, J. B. (1954). *Social learning and clinical psychology*. Englewood Cliffs, NJ: Prentice-Hall.

Rubin, E. (1921). *Visuell wahrgenomenne figuren*. Copenhagen: Gyldendalske.

Ruble, D. N., & Stangor, C. (1986). Stalking the elusive schema: Insights from developmental and social-psychological analyses of gender schemas. *Social Cognition, 4*, 227–261.

Rumbaugh, D. M. (Ed.). (1977). *Language learning by a chimpanzee: The LANA project*. New York: Academic Press.

Rumelhart, D. E. (1977). Toward an interactive model of reading. In S. Dornic (Ed.), *Attention and performance VI* (pp. 573–603). Hillsdale, NJ: Erlbaum.

Rumelhart, D. E., & McClelland, J. L. (Eds.). (1986a). *Parallel distributed processing: Explorations in the microstructure of cognition (Vol. 1): Foundations*. Cambridge MA: MIT Press.

Rumelhart, D. E., & McClelland, J. L. (1986b). On learning the past tenses of English verbs. In J. L. McClelland & D. E. Rumelhart (Eds.), *Parallel distributed processing: Explorations in the microstructure of cognition. (Vol. 2): Psychological and biological models* (pp. 216–271). Cambridge, MA: MIT Press.

Rumelhart, D. E., & Norman, D. A. (1981). Analogical processes in learning. In J. R. Anderson (Ed.), *Cognitive skills and their acquisition* (pp. 335–359). Hillsdale, NJ: Erlbaum.

Rundus, D. (1971). Analysis of rehearsal processes in free recall. *Journal of Experimental Psychology, 89*, 63–77.

Runes, D. D. (1960). *Dictionary of philosophy*. New York: Philosophical Library.

Russell, B. (1959). *Wisdom of the west*. Garden City, NY: Doubleday.

Ryan, J. J. (1960). Comparison of verbal response transfer mediated by meaningfully similar and associated stimuli. *Journal of Experimental Psychology, 60*, 408–415.

Rychlak, J. F. (1966). Reinforcement value: A suggested idiographic, intensity dimension of meaningfulness for the personality theorist. *Journal of Personality, 34*, 311–335.

Rychlak, J. F. (1975a). Affective assessment in the recognition of designs and paintings by elementary school children. *Child Development, 46*, 62–70.

Rychlak, J. F. (1975b). Affective assessment, intelligence, social class, and racial learning style. *Journal of Personality and Social Psychology, 32,* 989–995.

Rychlak, J. F. (1979). *Discovering free will and personal responsibility.* New York: Oxford University Press.

Rychlak, J. F. (1980). The false promise of falsification. *The Journal of Mind and Behavior, 1,* 183–195.

Rychlak, J. F. (1981). *A philosophy of science for personality theory* (2nd ed.). Malabar, FL: Krieger.

Rychlak, J. F. (1982). *Personality and life-style of young male managers: A logical learning theory analysis.* New York: Academic Press.

Rychlak, J. F. (1984). *Drawing inferences and implications in person perception.* Unpublished manuscript, Loyola University of Chicago, Chicago.

Rychlak, J. F. (1987). The concept of telosponsivity: Answering an unmet need in psychology. In W. J. Baker, M. E. Hyland, H. Van Rappard, & A. W. Staats (Eds.), *Current issues in theoretical psychology.* Amsterdam: North-Holland.

Rychlak, J. F. (1988). *The psychology of rigorous humanism* (2nd ed.). New York: New York University Press.

Rychlak, J. F. (1991). *Artificial intelligence and human reason: A teleological critique.* New York: Columbia University Press.

Rychlak, J. F. (1993). A suggested principle of complementarity for psychology: In theory, not method. *American Psychologist, 48,* 344–364.

Rychlak, J. F., Barnard, S., Williams, R. N., & Wollman, N. (1989). The recognition and cognitive utilization of oppositionality. *Journal of Psycholinguistic Research, 18,* 181–199.

Rychlak, J. F., & Bray, D. W. (1967). A life-theme method for scoring of interviews in the longitudinal study of young business managers. *Psychological Reports Monograph Supplement, 21,* 277–326.

Rychlak, J. F., Carlsen, N. L., & Dunning, L. P. (1974). Personal adjustment and the free recall of material with affectively positive or negative meaningfulness. *Journal of Abnormal Psychology, 83,* 480–487.

Rychlak, J. F., Flynn, E. J., & Burger, G. (1979). Affection and evaluation as logical processes of meaningfulness independent of associative frequency. *Journal of General Psychology, 100,* 143–157.

Rychlak, J. F., Galster, J., & McFarland, K. K. (1972). The role of affective assessment in associative learning: From designs and cvc trigrams to faces and names. *Journal of Experimental Research in Personality, 6,* 186–194.

Rychlak, J. F., Hewitt, C. W., & Hewitt, J. (1973). Affective evaluation, word quality, and the verbal learning styles of black versus white junior college females. *Journal of Personality and Social Psychology, 27,* 248–255.

Rychlak, J. F., & Marceil, J. C. (1986). Task predication and affective learning style. *Journal of Social Behavior and Personality, 1,* 557–564.

Rychlak, J. F., & Marceil, J. C. (1992). Affective task and self predication in the learning of affectively connotative materials. *Journal of Social Behavior and Personality, 7,* 201–210.

Rychlak, J. F., McKee, D. B., Schneider, W. E., & Abramson, Y. (1971). Affective evaluation in the verbal learning styles of normals and abnormals. *Journal of Abnormal Psychology, 77,* 247–257.

Rychlak, J. F., & Nguyen, T. D. (1979). The role of frequency and affective assessment in associative enrichment. *Journal of General Psychology, 100,* 295–311.

Rychlak, J. F., & Rychlak, L. S. (1984). *Subject versus object recall in memory for sentences.* Unpublished manuscript, Loyola University of Chicago, Chicago.

Rychlak, J. F., & Rychlak, L. S. (1985). *Cueing subjects and predicates of unrecalled sentences.* Unpublished manuscript, Loyola University of Chicago, Chicago.

Rychlak, J. F., & Rychlak, L. S. (1986). *Further data on the cueing of subjects and predicates in unrecalled sentences.* Unpublished manuscript, Loyola University of Chicago, Chicago.

Rychlak, J. F., & Rychlak, L. S. (1991). Evidence for a predication effect in deciding on the personal significance of abstract word meanings. *Journal of Psycholinguistic Research, 20,* 403–418.

Rychlak, J. F., & Saluri, R. E. (1973). Affective assessment in the learning of names by fifth- and sixth-grade children. *Journal of Genetic Psychology, 123,* 251–261.

Rychlak, J. F., & Slife, B. D. (1984). Affection as a cognitive judgment process: A theoretical assumption put to test through brain-lateralization methodology. *Journal of Mind and Behavior, 5,* 131–150.

Rychlak, J. F., Stilson, S. R., & Rychlak, L. S. (1993). Testing a predicational model of cognition: Cueing predicate meanings in sentences and word triplets. *Journal of Psycholinguistic Research, 22,* 479–503.

Rychlak, J. F., Tasto, D. L., Andrews, J. E., & Ellis, H. C. (1973). The application of an affective dimension of meaningfulness to personality-related verbal learning. *Journal of Personality, 41,* 341–360.

Rychlak, J. F., & Tobin, T. J. (1971). Order effects in the affective learning styles of over-achievers and underachievers. *Journal of Educational Psychology, 62,* 141–147.

Rychlak, J. F., Tuan, N. D., & Schneider, W. E. (1974). Formal discipline revisited: Affective assessment and nonspecific transfer. *Journal of Educational Psychology, 66,* 139–151.

Rychlak, J. F., & Ulasevich, A. (1987). *Cueing of subjects and predicates in unrecalled metaphors.* Unpublished manuscript, Loyola University of Chicago, Chicago.

Rychlak, J. F., & Ulasevich, A. (1991). *The relationship between ratings of meaning and organization of dot patterns.* Unpublished manuscript, Loyola University of Chicago, Chicago.

Rychlak, J. F., Williams, R. N., & Bugaj, A. M. (1986). The heuristic properties of dialectical oppositionality in predication. *Journal of General Psychology, 113,* 359–368.

Sadler, D. D., & Shoben, E. J. (1993). Context effects on semantic domains as seen in analogy solution. *Journal of Experimental Psychology: Learning, Memory, and Cognition, 19,* 128–147.

Salovey, P., & Birnbaum, D. (1989). Influence of mood on health-relevant cognitions. *Journal of Personality and Social Psychology, 57,* 539–551.

Sameroff, A. J., & Cavanagh, P. J. (1979). Learning in infancy: A developmental perspective. In J. D. Osofsky (Ed.), *Handbook of infant development.* New York: Wiley.

Sarbin, T. R. (Ed.). (1986). *Narrative psychology: The storied nature of human conduct.* New York: Praeger.

Sarbin, T. R., & Quenk, A. (1964). The rationality of nonsense: Intensity of meaning of nonreferential verbal units. *Psychological Record, 14,* 401–409.

Savage-Rumbaugh, E. S. (1986). *Ape language: From conditioned response to symbol.* New York: Columbia University Press.

Savin, H. B., & Bever, T. G. (1970). The nonperceptual reality of the phoneme. *Journal of Verbal Learning and Verbal Behavior, 9,* 295–302.

Schab, F. R. (1990). Odors and the remembrance of things past. *Journal of Experimental Psychology: Learning, Memory, and Cognition, 16,* 648–655.

Schachter, S. (1964). The interaction of cognitive and physiological determinants of emotional state. In L. Berkowitz (Ed.), *Advances in Experimental Social Psychology* (pp. 49–80). New York: Academic Press.

Schachter, S., & Singer, J. (1962). Cognitive, social, and physiological determinants of emotional state. *Psychological Review, 69*, 379–399.

Schank, R. C., & Abelson, R. P. (1977). *Scripts, plans, goals, and understanding: An inquiry into human knowledge structures.* Hillsdale, NJ: Erlbaum.

Schmucker, K. J. (1984). *Fuzzy sets, natural language, computations, and risk analysis.* Rockville, MD: Computer Science Press.

Schneider, D. J. (1991). Social cognition. *Annual Review of Psychology, 42*, 527–561.

Schneider, W. (1986). The role of conceptual knowledge and metamemory in the development of organizational processes in memory. *Journal of Experimental Child Psychology, 42*, 218–236.

Schneider, W., & Pressley, M. (1989). *Memory and development between 2 and 20.* New York: Springer-Verlag.

Schvaneveldt, R. W., Durso, F. T., & Mukherji, B. R. (1982). Semantic distance effects in categorization tasks. *Journal of Experimental Psychology: Learning, Memory, and Cognition, 8*, 1–15.

Schwartz, B. (1982). Reinforcement-induced behavioral stereotypy: How not to teach people to discover rules. *Journal of Experimental Psychology: General, 111*, 23–59.

Schwartz, G. E., Weinberger, D. A., & Singer, J. A. (1981). Cardiovascular differentiation of happiness, sadness, anger, and fear following imagery and exercise. *Psychosomatic Medicine, 43*, 343–364.

Schwarz, N., Clore, G. L. (1983). Mood, misattribution, and judgments of well-being: Informative and directive functions of affective states. *Journal of Personality and Social Psychology, 45*, 513–523.

Secord, P. F. (1990). Explaining social behavior. *Theoretical and Philosophical Psychology, 10*, 25–38.

Sedikides, C., Olsen, N., & Reis, H. T. (1993). Relationships as natural categories. *Journal of Personality and Social Psychology, 64*, 71–82.

Seidenberg, M. S. & Petitto, L. A. (1979). Signing behavior in apes: A critical review. *Cognition, 7*, 177–215.

Seligman, M. E. P. (1970). On the generality of the laws of learning. *Psychological Review, 77*, 406–418.

Shaffer, J. B. P. (1978). *Humanistic psychology.* Englewood Cliffs, NJ: Prentice-Hall.

Shannon, C. E. (1938). *A symbolic analysis of relay and switching circuits.* Unpublished master's thesis, Massachussets Institute of Technology, Cambridge.

Shannon, C. E., & Weaver, W. (Eds.). (1962). *The mathematical theory of communication.* Urbana: University of Illinois Press.

Shapiro, K. J. (1985). *Bodily reflective modes: A phenomenological method for psychology.* Durham, NC: Duke University Press.

Shedler, J., & Manis, M. (1986). Can the availability heuristic explain vividness effects? *Journal of Personality and Social Psychology, 51*, 26–36.

Sheffield, F. D. (1946). *The role of meaningfulness of stimulus and response in verbal learning.* Unpublished doctoral dissertation, Yale University, New Haven, CT.

Sheldrake, A. R. (1988). *The presence of the past: Morphic resonance and the habits of nature.* New York: Viking.

Shepard, R. N. (1967). Recognition memory for words, sentences, and pictures. *Journal of Verbal Learning & Verbal Behavior, 6*, 156–163.

Shepard, R. N. (1975). Form, formation and transformation of internal representations. In R. L. Solso (Ed.), *Theories in cognitive psychology: The Loyola Symposium* (pp. 87–122). Hillsdale, NJ: Erlbaum.

Sherman, S. J. (1980). On the self-erasing nature of errors of prediction. *Journal of Personality and Social Psychology, 39*, 211–221.

Sherman, T. (1985). Categorization skills in infants. *Child Development, 56*, 1561–1573.

Sherrington, C. S. (1906). *The integrative action of the nervous system.* New Haven, CT: Yale University Press.

Shultz, T. R. (1982). *Rules of causal attribution.* Monographs of the Society for Research in Child Development, 47 (1, Serial No. 194). Chicago: University of Chicago Press.

Signorella, M. L., & Liben, L. S. (1984). Recall and reconstruction of gender-related pictures: Effects of attitudes, task difficulty, and age. *Child Development, 55*, 393–405.

Siipola, E., Walker, W. N., & Kolb, D. (1955). Task attitudes in word association, projective and nonprojective. *Journal of Personality, 23*, 441–459.

Silverman, A., & Cason, H. (1934). Incidental memory for pleasant, unpleasant, and indifferent words. *American Journal of Psychology, 46*, 315–320.

Simon, K. M. (1979). Self-evaluative reactions: The role of personal valuation of the activity. *Cognitive Therapy and Research, 3*, 111–116.

Siqueland, E. R., & DeLucia, C. A. (1969). Visual reinforcement of nonnutritive sucking in human infants. *Science, 165*, 1144–1146.

Skinner, B. F. (1938). *The behavior of organisms: An experimental analysis.* New York: Appleton-Century.

Skinner, B. F. (1948). *Walden two.* New York: Macmillan.

Skinner, B. F. (1950). Are theories of learning necessary? *Psychological Review, 57*, 193–216.

Skinner, B. F. (1953). *Science and human behavior.* New York: Macmillan.

Skinner, B. F. (1961). The design of cultures. *Daedalus, 90*, 534–546.

Skinner, B. F. (1971). *Beyond freedom and dignity.* New York: Knopf.

Skinner, E. A., Schindler, A., & Tschechne, M. (1990). Self-other differences in children's perceptions about the causes of important events. *Journal of Personality and Social Psychology, 58*, 144–155.

Slamecka, N. J., & Graf, P. (1978). The generation effect: Delineation of a phenomenon. *Journal of Experimental Psychology: Human Learning and Memory, 4*, 592–604.

Slife, B. D. (1993). *Time and psychological explanation.* New York: SUNY Press.

Slife, B. D., Miura, S., Thompson, L. W., Shapiro, J. L., & Gallagher, D. (1984). Differential recall as a function of mood disorder in clinically depressed patients: Between- and within-subject differences. *Journal of Abnormal Psychology, 93*, 391–400.

Slife, B. D., & Rychlak, J. F. (1981). Affection as a separate dimension of meaningfulness. *Contemporary Educational Psychology, 6*, 140–150.

Slife, B. D., & Rychlak, J. F. (1982). Role of affective assessment in modeling aggressive behavior. *Journal of Personality and Social Psychology, 43*, 861–868.

Slobin, D. I. (1978). A case study of early language awareness. In A. Sinclair, R. J. Jarvella, & W. J. M. Levelt (Eds.), *The child's conception of language* (pp. 45–54). New York: Springer-Verlag.

Slobin, D. I., & Welsh, C. A. (1973). Elicited imitation as a research tool in developmental psycholinguistics. In C. A. Ferguson, & D. I. Slobin (Eds.), *Studies of child language development* (pp. 485–497). New York: Holt, Rinehart & Winston.

Smiley, S. S., & Brown, A. L. (1979). Conceptual preference for thematic or taxonomic relations: A nonmonotonic age trend from preschool to old age. *Journal of Experimental Child Psychology, 28,* 249–257.

Smith, E. E. (1977). Theories of semantic memory. In W. K. Estes (Ed.), *Handbook of learning and cognitive processes* (Vol. 5, pp. 146–162). Hillsdale, NJ: Erlbaum.

Smith, E. E., Shoben, E. J., & Rips, L. J. (1974). Structure and process in semantic memory: A featural model for semantic decisions. *Psychological Review, 81,* 214–241.

Smith, S. M., Glenberg, A., & Bjork, R. A. (1978). Environmental context and human memory. *Memory & Cognition, 6,* 342–353.

Smith, W. W. (1921). Experiments on memory and affective tone. *British Journal of Psychology, 11,* 236–250.

Snyder, M., Tanke, E. D., & Berscheid, E. (1977). Social perception and interpersonal behavior: On the self-fulfilling nature of social stereotypes. *Journal of Personality and Social Psychology, 35,* 656–666.

Sodian, B., Schneider, W., & Perlmutter, M. (1986). Recall, clustering, and metamemory in young children. *Journal of Experimental Child Psychology, 41,* 395–410.

Sperry, R. W. (1961). Cerebral organization and behavior. *Science, 133,* 1749–1757.

Sperry, R. W. (1985). *Science & Moral Priority: Merging mind, brain, and human values.* New York: Praeger.

Spielberger, C. D., & Levin, S. M. (1962). What is learned in verbal conditioning? *Journal of Verbal Learning and Verbal Behavior, 1,* 125–132.

Spiro, R. J. (1980). Accommodative reconstruction in prose recall. *Journal of Verbal Learning and Verbal Behavior, 19,* 84–95.

Sporer, S. L. (1991). Deep—deeper—deepest? Encoding strategies and the recognition of human faces. *Journal of Experimental Psychology: Learning, Memory, and Cognition, 17,* 323–333.

Squire, L. R., Knowlton, B., & Musen, G. (1993). The structure and organization of memory. *Annual Review of Psychology, 44,* 453–495.

Srull, T. K., & Wyer, R. S., Jr. (1989). Person memory and judgment. *Psychological Review, 96,* 58–83.

Staats, A. W. (1959). *Meaning and word associations: Separate processes.* Technical Report No. 12. Contract Nonr. 2794 (02), Arizona State University.

Stagner, R. (1933). Factors influencing the memory value of words in a series. *Journal of Experimental Psychology, 16,* 129–137.

Stagner, R. (1948). *Psychology of personality.* New York: McGraw-Hill.

Standing, L. (1973). Learning 10,000 pictures. *Quarterly Journal of Experimental Psychology, 25,* 207–222.

Standing, L., Conezio, J., & Haber, R. N. (1970). Perception and memory for pictures: Single-trial learning of 2500 visual stimuli. *Psychonomic Science, 19,* 73–74.

Stangor, C., Lynch, L., Duan, C., & Glass, B. (1992). Categorization of individuals on the basis of multiple social features. *Journal of Personality and Social Psychology, 62,* 207–218.

Stangor, C., & Ruble, D. N. (1989). Strength of expectancies and memory for social information: What we remember depends on how much we know. *Journal of Experimental Social Psychology, 25,* 18–35.

Stein, B. (1977). The effects of cue-target uniqueness on cued recall performance. *Memory and Cognition, 5,* 319–322.

Stein, B. S., & Bransford, J. D. (1979). Constraints on effective elaboration: Effects of precision and subject generation. *Journal of Verbal Learning and Verbal Behavior, 18,* 769–777.

Stillings, N. A., Feinstein, M. H., Garfield, J. L., Rissland, E. L., Rosenbaum, D. A., Weisler, S. E., & Baker-Ward, L. (1987). *Cognitive science: An introduction.* Cambridge, MA: Bradford/MIT Press.

Stilson, S. R. (1988). *Cueing predication in memory for word triplets.* Unpublished manuscript, Loyola University of Chicago, Chicago.

Stich, S. P. (1986). *From folk psychology to cognitive science: The case against belief.* Cambridge, MA: MIT Press.

Stoddard, G. D. (1929). An experiment in verbal learning. *Journal of Educational Psychology, 20,* 452–457.

Storms, M. D. (1973). Videotape and the attribution process: Reversing actors' and observers' points of view. *Journal of Personality and Social Psychology, 27,* 165–175.

Strauss, M. S. (1979). Abstraction of prototypical information by adults and 10-month-old infants. *Journal of Experimental Psychology: Human Learning and Memory, 5,* 618–632.

Strayer, J. (1980). A naturalistic study of empathic behaviors and their relation to affective states and perspective-taking skills in preschool children. *Child Development, 51,* 815–822.

Stroop, J. R. (1935). Studies of interference in serial verbal reactions. *Journal of Experimental Psychology, 18,* 643–662.

Sugarman, S. (1983). Why talk? Comments on Savage-Rumbaugh et al. *Journal of Experimental Psychology: General, 112,* 493–497.

Sullivan, H. S. (1953). *The interpersonal theory of psychiatry.* (Ed. H. S. Perry & M. L. Gawell). New York: Norton.

Super, C. M. (1972). *Long-term memory in early infancy.* Unpublished doctoral dissertation, Harvard University, Cambridge, MA.

Swann, W. B., Jr., & Read, S. J. (1981). Acquiring self-knowledge: The search for feedback that fits. *Journal of Personality and Social Psychology, 41,* 1119–1128.

Sweller, J., & Gee, W. (1978). *Einstellung,* the sequence effect, and hypothesis theory. *Journal of Experimental Psychology: Human Learning and Memory, 4,* 513–526.

Swets, J. A. (1964). *Signal detection and recognition by human observers.* New York: Wiley.

Tait, W. D. (1913). The effect of psycho-physical attitudes on memory. *Journal of Abnormal Psychology, 8,* 10–37.

Tannenbaum, P. H., & Zillmann, D. (1975). Emotional arousal in the facilitation of aggression through communication. In L. Berkowitz (Ed.), *Advances in experimental social psychology* (Vol. 8, pp. 149–192). New York: Academic Press.

Taylor, S. E., Wood, J. V., & Lichtman, R. R. (1983). It could be worse: Selective evaluation as a response to victimization. *Journal of Social Issues, 39,* 19–40.

Teasdale, J. D., & Russell, M. L. (1983). Differential effects of induced mood on the recall of positive, negative and neutral words. *British Journal of Clinical Psychology, 22,* 163–171.

Templin, M. C. (1957). *Certain language skills in children: Their development and interrelationships.* Minneapolis: University of Minnesota Press.

Tenbrunsel, T. W., Nishball, E. R., & Rychlak, J. F. (1968). The idiographic relationship between association value and reinforcement value, and the nature of meaning. *Journal of Personality, 36,* 126–137.

Tenney, Y. J. (1975). The child's conception of organization and recall. *Journal of Experimental Child Psychology, 19,* 100–114.

Terrace, H. S. (1979). *NIM.* New York: Knopf.

Terrace, H. S. (1984). Animal cognition. In H. L. Roitblat, T. G. Bever, & H. S. Terrace (Eds.). *Animal cognition* (pp. 7–28). Hillsdale, NJ: Erlbaum.

Tesser, A., & Shaffer, D. R. (1990). Attitudes and attitude change. *Annual Review of Psychology, 41,* 479–523.

Thomson, D. M., & Tulving, E. (1970). Associative encoding and retrieval: Weak and strong cues. *Journal of Experimental Psychology, 86,* 255–262.

Thomson, R. H. (1930). An experimental study of memory as influenced by feeling tone. *Journal of Experimental Psychology, 13,* 462–468.

Thorndike, E. L., & Lorge, I. (1944). *The teacher's word book of 30,000 words.* New York: Bureau of Publications, Teachers College, Columbia University.

Thornhill, R. (1979). Adaptive female-mimicking behavior in a scorpionfly. *Science, 205,* 412–414.

Tinklepaugh, O. L. (1928). An experimental study of representative factors in monkeys. *Journal of Comparative Psychology, 8,* 197–236.

Titchener, E. B. (1909). *A text-book in psychology.* New York: Macmillan.

Tolman, E. C. (1917). Retroactive inhibition as affected by conditions of learning. *Psychological Monographs, 25* (No. 107, 1–50).

Tolman, E. C. (1932/1967). *Purposive behavior in animals and men.* New York: Appleton-Century-Crofts.

Trapold, M. A. (1970). Are expectancies based upon different positive reinforcing events discriminably different? *Learning and Motivation, 1,* 129–140.

Trevarthen, C., & Hubley, P. (1978). Secondary intersubjectivity: Confidence, confiding and acts of meaning in the first year. In A. Lock (Ed.), *Action, gesture and symbol: The emergence of language* (pp. 183–229). New York: Academic Press.

Triandis, H. C. (1977). Cross-cultural social and personality psychology. *Personality and Social Psychology Bulletin, 3,* 143–158.

Trier, J. (1931). *Der deutsche wortschatz im sinnbezirk des verstandes.* Heidelberg: Winter.

Tulving, E. (1962). Subjective organization in free recall of "unrelated" words. *Psychological Review, 69,* 344–354.

Tulving, E. (1966). Subjective organization and effects of repetition in multi-trial free-recall learning. *Journal of Verbal Learning and Verbal Behavior, 5,* 193–197.

Tulving, E. (1983). *Elements of episodic memory.* New York: Oxford University Press.

Tulving, E., & Madigan, S. A. (1970). Memory and verbal learning. *Annual Review of Psychology, 21,* 437–484.

Tulving, E., & Osler, S. (1968). Effectiveness of retrieval cues in memory for words. *Journal of Experimental Psychology, 77,* 593–601.

Tulving, E., & Pearlstone, Z. (1966). Availability versus accessibility of information in memory for words. *Journal of Verbal Learning and Verbal Behavior, 5,* 381–391.

Tulving, E., & Thomson, D. M. (1973). Encoding specificity and retrieval processes in episodic memory. *Psychological Review, 80,* 352–373.

Tversky, A. (1977). Features of similarity. *Psychological Review, 84,* 327–352.

Tversky, A., & Kahneman, D. (1983). Extensional versus intuitive reasoning: The conjunction fallacy in probability judgment. *Psychological Review, 90,* 293–315.

Tweney, R. D., Doherty, M. E., & Mynatt, C. R. (Eds.), (1981). *On scientific thinking*. New York: Columbia University Press.

Ulasevich, A. (1991). *Affective predication in memory for sentences: Anticipating meaningfulness before meaning*. Unpublished master's thesis, Loyola University of Chicago, Chicago.

Ullman, S. (1980). Against direct perception. *Behavioral and Brain Sciences, 3*, 373–415.

Ultan, R. (1969). Some general characterisics of interrogative systems. *Working Papers in Language Universals* (Stanford University), *1*, 41–63.

Umemoto, T. (1959). Japanese studies in verbal learning and memory. *Psychologia, 2*, 1–19.

Umiker-Sebeok, J., & Sebeok, T. A. (1981). Clever Hans and smart simians: The self-fulfilling prophecy and kindred methodological pitfalls. *Anthropos, 76*, 89–165.

Vallacher, R. R. (1980). An introduction to self theory. In D. M. Wegner & R. R. Vallacher (Eds.), *The self in social psychology* (pp. 3–30). New York: Oxford University Press.

Valle, R. S., & Halling, S. (1989). *Existential-phenomenological perspectives in psychology: Exploring the breadth of human experience*. New York: Plenum.

Valle, R. S., King, M., & Halling, S. (1989). An introduction to existential-phenomenological thought in psychology. In R. S. Valle & S. Halling (Eds.), *Existential-phenomenological perspectives in psychology: Exploring the breadth of human experience* (pp. 3–16). New York: Plenum.

Velten, E., Jr. (1968). A laboratory task for induction of mood states. *Behavior Research and Therapy, 6*, 473–482.

Vygotsky, L. (1986). *Thought and language*. (A. Kozulin, Trans.). Cambridge, MA: MIT Press.

Wagner, A. R. (1978). Expectancies and the priming of STM. In S. H. Hulse, H. Fowler, & W. Honig (Eds.), *Cognitive processes in animal behavior* (pp. 177–209). Hillsdale, NJ: Erlbaum.

Wagner, D. A. (1978). Memories of Morocco: The influence of age, schooling, and environment on memory. *Cognitive Psychology, 10*, 1–28.

Walker, S. F. (1983). *Animal thought*. London: Routledge & Kegan Paul.

Walther, G. H., & O'Neill, H. F., Jr. (1974). On-line user-computer interface, the effects of interface flexibility, terminal type, and experience on performance. *Proceedings of the National Computer Conference, 13*, 286–310.

Warren, R. M., & Warren, R. P. (1970). Auditory illusions and confusions. *Scientific American, 223*, 30–36.

Warrington, E. K., & Weiskrantz, L. (1970). Amnesic syndrome: Consolidation or retrieval? *Nature, 228*, 628–630.

Wason, P. C. (1960). On the failure to eliminate hypotheses in a conceptual task. *Quarterly Journal of Experimental Psychology, 12*, 129–140.

Wason, P. C., & Johnson-Laird, P. N. (1972). *Psychology of reasoning: Structure and content*. Cambridge, MA: Harvard University Press.

Watkins, M. J., & Tulving, E. (1975). Episodic memory: When recognition fails. *Journal of Experimental Psychology: General, 104*, 5–29.

Watson, D., & Clark, L. A. (1984). Negative affectivity: The disposition to experience aversive emotional states. *Psychological Bulletin, 96*, 465–490.

Watson, J. B. (1913). Psychology as the behaviorist views it. *Psychological Review, 20*, 158–177.

Watson, J. B. (1924). *Behaviorism*. New York: Norton.

Watson, R. I. (1978). *The great psychologists* (4th ed.). Philadelphia: Lippincott.

Wegner, D. M., Schneider, D. J., Carter, S. R., III, & White, T. L. (1987). Paradoxical effects of thought suppression. *Journal of Personality and Social Psychology, 53*, 5–13.

Weiner, B., Russell, D., & Lerman, D. (1978). Affective consequences of causal ascriptions. In J. H. Harvey, W. Ickes, & R. F. Kidd (Eds.), *New directions in attribution research* (Vol. 2, pp. 59–90). New York: Erlbaum.

Weinstein, N. D. (1980). Unrealistic optimism about future life events. *Journal of Personality and Social Psychology, 39*, 806–820.

Weinstein, N. D., & Lachendro, E. (1982). Egocentrism as a source of unrealistic optimism. *Personality and Social Psychology Bulletin, 8*, 195–200.

Weisberg, R. W. (1969). Sentence processing assessed through intrasentence word associations. *Journal of Experimental Psychology, 82*, 332–338.

Weiss-Shed, E. (1973). Synonyms, antonyms and retroactive inhibition with meaningful material. *Psychological Reports, 33*, 459–465.

Wellman, H. M., Ritter, K., & Flavell, J. H. (1975). Deliberate memory behavior in the delayed reactions of very young children. *Developmental Psychology, 11*, 780–787.

Wells, F. L. (1925). Reactions to visual stimuli in affective settings. *Journal of Experimental Psychology, 8*, 64–76.

Wells, G. L., & Gavanski, I. (1989). Mental simulation of causality. *Journal of Personality and Social Psychology, 56*, 161–169.

Westcott, M. R. (1981). Direct and dialectical semantics of human freedom. *Et Cetera: A review of general semantics, 38*, 64–75.

Westcott, M. (1982). Quantitative and qualitative aspects of experienced freedom. *Journal of Mind and Behavior, 3*, 99–126.

White, B. L., Kaban, B., Shapiro, B., & Attanucci, J. (1977). Competence and experience. In I. C. Užgiris & F. Weizmann (Eds.), *The structuring of experience* (pp. 115–152). New York: Plenum.

White, M. J. (1968). Laterality differences in perception: A review. *Psychological Bulletin, 72*, 387–405.

White, M. M. (1936). Some factors influencing recall of pleasant and unpleasant words. *American Journal of Psychology, 48*, 134–139.

White, M. M., & Powell, M. (1936). The differential reaction-time for pleasant and unpleasant words. *American Journal of Psychology, 48*, 126–133.

White, M. M., & Ratliff, M. M. (1934). The relation of affective tone to the learning and recall of words. *American Journal of Psychology, 46*, 92–98.

White, R. W. (1959). Motivation reconsidered: The concept of competence. *Psychological Review, 66*, 297–333.

Whitehead, A. N., & Russell, B. A. W. (1963). *Principia mathematica* (3 vols.; 2nd ed.). Cambridge: Cambridge University Press.

Whiten, A., & Byrne, R. W. (1988a). Tactical deception in primates. *Behavioral and Brain Sciences, 11*, 233–273.

Whiten, A., & Byrne, R. W. (1988b). The manipulation of attention in primate tactical deception. In R. W. Byrne & A. Whiten (Eds.), *Machiavellian intelligence* (pp. 211–223). Oxford: Oxford University Press.

Wickens, D. D., & Cermak, L. S. (1967). Transfer effects of synonyms and antonyms in mixed and unmixed lists. *Journal of Verbal Learning and Verbal Behavior, 6*, 832–839.

Wieman, L. A. (1976). Stress patterns of early child language. *Journal of Child Language, 3*, 283–386.

Wiener, N. (1954). *The human use of human beings*. New York: Doubleday/Anchor.

Wightman, W. P. D. (1951). *The growth of scientific ideas*. New Haven, CT: Yale University Press.

Windelband, W. (1894/1904). *Geschichte und Naturwissenschaft* [History and natural science]. Strassburg: Heiz.

Wine, J. (1971). Test anxiety and direction of attention. *Psychological Bulletin, 76*, 92–104.

Wittgenstein, L. (1968). *Philosophical investigations* (3rd ed., G. E. M. Anscomb, Trans.). New York: Macmillan.

Wittrock, M. C., Marks, C. B., & Doctorow, M. J. (1975). Reading as a generative process. *Journal of Educational Psychology, 67*, 484–489.

Wong, P. T. P., & Weiner, B. (1981). When people ask "why" questions, and the heuristics of attributional search. *Journal of Personality and Social Psychology, 40*, 650–663.

Wyer, R. S., Jr., & Budesheim, T. L. (1987). Person memory and judgments: The impact of information that one is told to disregard. *Journal of Personality and Social Psychology, 53*, 14–29.

Wyer, R. S., Jr., & Carlston, D. E. (1979). *Social cognition, inference, and attribution*. Hillsdale, NJ: Erlbaum.

Wyer, R. S., Jr., & Gordon, S. E. (1982). The recall of information about persons and groups. *Journal of Experimental Social Psychology, 18*, 128–164.

Wykes, T., & Johnson-Laird, P. N. (1977). How do children learn the meanings of verbs? *Nature, 268*, 326–327.

Yekovich, F. R., & Thorndyke, P. W. (1981). An evaluation of alternative functional models of narrative schemata. *Journal of Verbal Learning and Verbal Behavior, 20*, 454–469.

Yerkes, R. M. (1912). The intelligence of earthworms. *Journal of Animal Behavior, 2*, 332–352.

Zajonc, R. B. (1968). Attitudinal effects of mere exposure. *Journal of Personality and Social Psychology Monograph Supplement, 9* (2, Part 2), 1–27.

Zajonc, R. B. (1980). Feeling and thinking: Preferences need no inferences. *American Psychologist, 35*, 151–175.

Zajonc, R. B. (1984). On the primacy of affect. *American Psychologist, 39*, 117–123.

Zener, K. (1937). The significance of behavior accompanying conditioned salivary secretion for theories of the conditioned response. *American Journal of Psychology, 50*, 384–403.

Zillmann, D. (1978). Attribution and misattribution of excitatory reactions. In J. H. Harvey, W. Ickes, & R. F. Kidd (Eds.), *New directions in attribution research* (Vol. 2, pp. 335–368). Hillsdale, NJ: Erlbaum.

Zukav, G. (1979). *The dancing wu li masters: An overview of the new physics*. New York: Bantam.

Name Index

Subject Index

abstraction: in all affirmed meanings, 106; greater and lesser, 26; and omitting details, 26; in predicating predications, 142; in predication, 41

action-intention: and understanding-intention, 40, 105, 272; in infancy, 257; observable, 105; omitted or avoided, 40; in reinforcement, 196

affective assessment/affection: in ambivalence, 191; vs. association value, 194; as basic cognition, 191; and being liked over disliked, 193, 204; and being disliked over liked, 206–208; of classroom courses, 294–296; as complaint factor, 210; as central in all motivation, 195; in choice, 196; as cognitive evaluation, 192; defined, 53–54; delimiting oppositionality in, 266; demonstration experiment of, 212; early research in, 203–204; in elementary school children, 267; vs. emotion, 57, 191–192; as first prememory, 223; idiographic measure of, 54–55, 193–194; in intellectual feeling, 198–199; as Kantian a priori concept, 191, 294; LLT research in, 204–208; measure of reinforcement value of, 192; in modeling, 212, 261; as negative affectivity, 210; nomothetic measure of, 54–55; nonspecific transfer in, 211; in operant conditioning, 211; operationalizing, 192–193; at outset of life, 266; rarely avoided, 57, 58; in research on CVC trigrams, 193; role of context in, 192; role of in moving from understanding to action, 197; self-reflexivity in, 195; and strength of association, 194; and transcending telosponsivity, 53, 190, 284; unlearned capacity to evaluate, 265–267

affirmation: as akin to a Euler circle, 36; in choice and affection, 196; can "hang fire," 62; intentional, as practice, 263; at the protopoint, 47; in suggesting a bias, 102; as taking a position, 38

affirming the consequent: and alternative explanations of data, 86; fallacy of, 3; influence on psychology of, 130

agency: defined, 1, 307; via oppositionality, 58, 282, 307; rigorous study of, 296; in self theory, 273

analogy: vs. generalization of response and stimulus, 50; in infant learning, 264–265; as partial tautology, 50

anthropomorphization: in animal study, 125–127; children's preference for, 260

arbitrariness: in cognition, 41, 44; vs. life's necessities, 58

artificial intelligence, 67

aspiration, levels of, 189

association/associationism: British, 120, 138; in connectionism, 98; laws of, 138; limitations of in animal study, 127; and oppositionality in word, 157, 159, 165; patterns of as learning, 121; as predication, 138; preparedness in, 127; and S-R in animal study, 125; in short- vs. long-term memory, 123; strength of as meaning, 143; use of mnemonics in, 144

association value: vs. affection, 194; measures of, 194; idiographic measure of, 194

assumption(s): initial meaning of in abstract, 131, 285; as knowledge, 137

attitude(s): defined, 197; as related to affection, 197

attribution theory: as based on meaning of "to bestow," 78–79; and consistency with LLT, 77; and fundamental attribution error, 79; and telosponsivity, 78–79

Aufgabe: in conditioning experiments, 171; as logical not mechanical, 94; in recall vs. recognition, 140; and task instruction, 80, 99, 108, 270

auto-shaping: counters operant theory, 128; and oppositionality in cats, 162

availability heuristic, 100